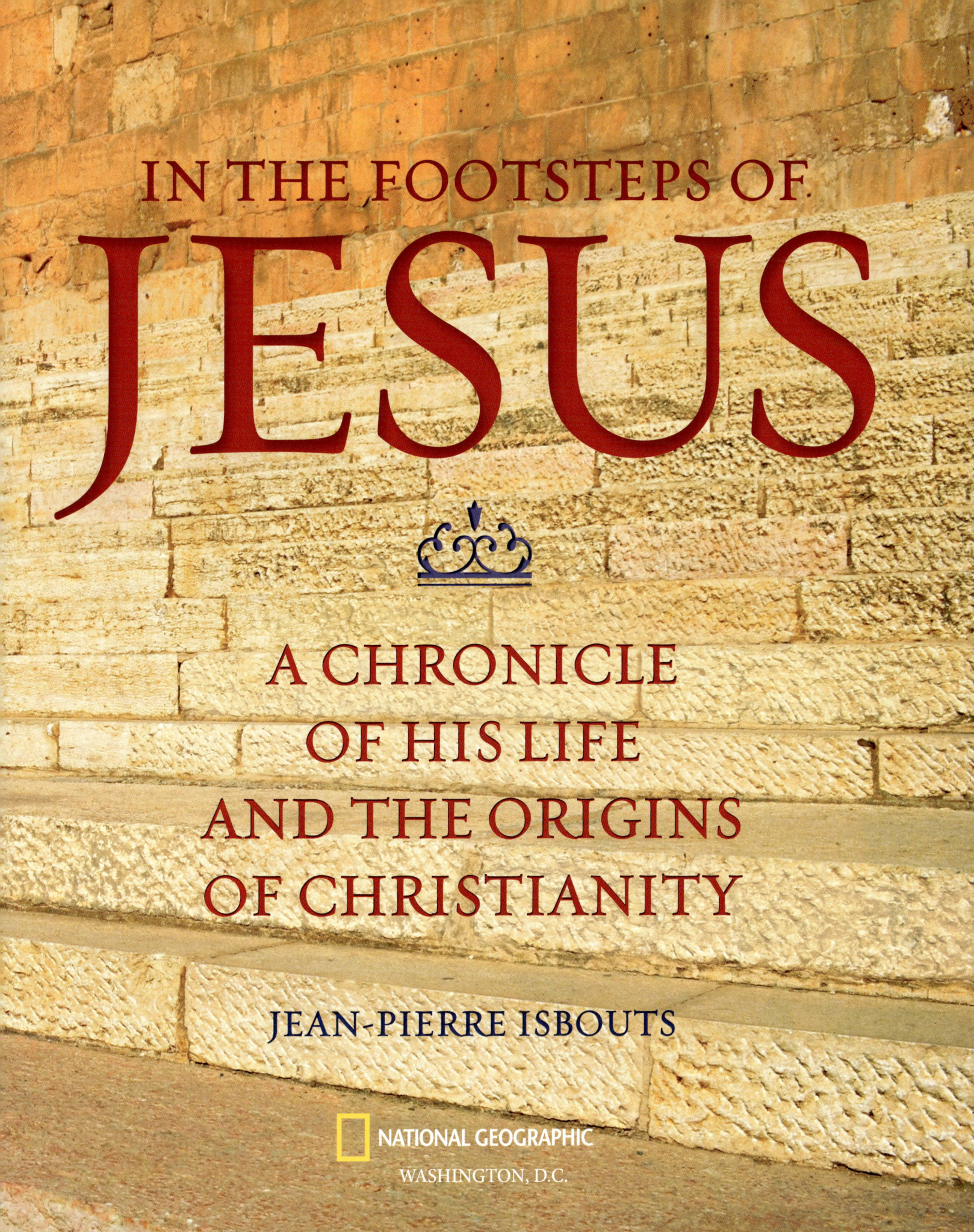
IN THE FOOTSTEPS OF JESUS

A CHRONICLE OF HIS LIFE AND THE ORIGINS OF CHRISTIANITY

JEAN-PIERRE ISBOUTS

NATIONAL GEOGRAPHIC
WASHINGTON, D.C.

CONTENTS

INTRODUCTION
RECONSTRUCTING THE
PATH OF JESUS 6

PART I
THE WORLD OF JESUS 16

CHAPTER 1
THE ROMAN WORLD 18

CHAPTER 2
THE KINGDOM
OF HEROD THE GREAT 40

CHAPTER 3
LIFE IN LOWER GALILEE 62

PART II
THE LIFE OF JESUS 80

CHAPTER 4
MARY AND JOSEPH 82

CHAPTER 5
THE EARLY YEARS OF JESUS 102

CHAPTER 6
JOHN THE BAPTIST
IN THE JORDAN 124

CHAPTER 7
JESUS' MINISTRY BEGINS 146

CHAPTER 8
THE GALILEAN CAMPAIGN 168

CHAPTER 9
JOURNEYS BEYOND GALILEE 190

CHAPTER 10
THE ROAD TO JERUSALEM 208

CHAPTER 11
THE PASSOVER EVENTS
IN JERUSALEM 228

CHAPTER 12
THE TRIAL AND CRUCIFIXION 246

PART III
THE LEGACY OF JESUS 268

CHAPTER 13
THE FIRST CHRISTIANS 270

CHAPTER 14
THE GROWTH OF THE CHURCH 298

CHAPTER 15
THE CHRISTIAN TRIUMPH 322

EPILOGUE
PILGRIMAGE AFTER THE
ISLAMIC CONQUEST 348

APPENDIX 354

FURTHER READING 356

ABOUT THE AUTHOR
AND BOARD OF ADVISERS 358

ACKNOWLEDGMENTS 358

ILLUSTRATIONS CREDITS 359

INDEX 360

PRECEDING PAGES: *Many scholars agree that Jesus would have used these steps, now restored, to ascend Temple Mount from the Kidron Valley, which separated Jerusalem from the Mount of Olives.* OPPOSITE PAGE: *Originating in Upper Galilee, located close to Mount Hermon, this stream will ultimately join the River Jordan on its way down to Judea, to the place of Jesus' baptism by John the Baptist.*

INTRODUCTION
Reconstructing the Path of Jesus

The purpose of this book is to reconstruct the unique historical, social, and cultural conditions of Jesus' time, and thus help us to visualize the Gospel stories in their proper context. To imagine the unique world of Jesus' ministry, and the particular conditions in which the evangelists wrote their story, is perhaps the greatest challenge to our understanding of the Gospels.

That is why this book aims to transport the reader back to first-century Palestine in order to reconstruct the path that Jesus took—not only in narrative form, but also with scores of maps, ancient artifacts, artwork, and location photography.

In doing so, we will avail ourselves of a wide range of sources and methods that modern scholars have at their disposal. This naturally includes a number of exciting new archaeological discoveries, but also modern topographical research, forensic analysis, anthropology, cartography, as well as fascinating insights into the social and political conditions of first-century Palestine, based on Roman as well as Jewish literary sources.

Part of the reason why it is so difficult for us to visualize the world of Jesus is that we are so saturated with media information—through television, the Internet, smart phones, billboards, and print media—that it takes a superhuman effort to imagine what it was like to live in Jesus' world. In rural Galilee, information was communicated almost exclusively through the spoken word. The vast majority of men and women were illiterate or barely literate, did not have a proper education, and did not know any language other than that spoken by their parents. They married within their greater family or clan, and they made a living from tilling the land that had been in their family's possession for generations.

What's more, in Jesus' time none of the institutions existed that we in our modern world take for granted. Schools were virtually nonexistent. Roads, other than the main trade routes, were the responsibility of the villages that relied on them to

In this moving fifth-century funerary monument from Athens, a mother who has died takes her leave from her grieving daughter.

INTRODUCTION

bring their produce to market. Food, housing, clean water, and security were likewise the responsibility of the family or the village community in which one lived. None of these services was forthcoming from the state, even though most states in Antiquity, including Roman Palestine, taxed their population mercilessly.

Life in Ancient Palestine

At the same time, life in the Greco-Roman world, including ancient Palestine, revolved around institutions that by contrast would be utterly alien to us. One such institution is slavery, for us a repugnant concept, and yet one without which the Roman Empire would not have been able to function. *Telones* or *architelones*, a term that frequently appears in the Gospels, was not only a tax collector but also the official to whom farmers turned for personal loans when they were unable to pay their taxes, using their land as collateral. It was usually the same tax collector who then foreclosed on a farmer's land when, inevitably, the loan was not repaid, which is why these officials were so heartily despised by Jesus' contemporaries.

What's more, the Gospels use no less than three different terms to describe an owner of a large agricultural estate, a crucial character in many of Jesus' parables.

This is quite remarkable, given that until the Herodian era, agriculture in Galilee was largely the domain of small subsistence farmers who owned little more than their own ancestral plots of land.

Lastly, the world of ancient Palestine was a class society, with a clear and distinct hierarchy of social ranks. At the top stood the ruler, who in the time of Jesus was really a vassal lord who served at the pleasure of Rome. Jesus scathingly refers to Palestine's puppet regimes and their allegiance to Rome in the Gospel of Mark: "You know that among the Gentiles those whom they recognize as their rulers lord it over them, and their great ones are tyrants over them." (Mark 10:42)

Below the ruler came a thin layer of aristocracy, which in Jesus' lifetime included both Hasmonean noblemen, as well as "new men" who owed their wealth and status to the patronage of Herod and his sons. Another form of aristocracy was presented by the caste of chief priests attached to the Temple.

Under the aristocracy came another thin layer of the professional class, men who were literate, educated, and trained to hold any number of positions in the local administration; many of these laymen were Pharisees. Others were in private practice as a notary or scribe, to whom one turned for marriage certificates or the transfer of land deeds. Since the prevailing law in Palestine was a religious law, the Torah, these scribes were of necessity also schooled in religious matters. This is why the Gospels often depict Jesus in debate with both Pharisees and scribes on any number of religious topics.

Beneath the small professional class came a vast majority of illiterate peasants and day workers, who made up the bulk of Galilee's population—by some estimates, as much as 90 percent. This also included the great mass of the poor, the unemployed, and the disabled.

The New Testament

To help us imagine the stories of the Gospels in their proper context, we will cite extensively from the canonical Gospels of Matthew, Mark, Luke, and John that, since the fourth century C.E., have formed the core of the New Testament canon. The first three books are often referred to as the *Synoptic Gospels* (from the Greek word *synoptikos,* meaning "seen together") given their obvious similarities, in contrast to the Gospel of John.

Other works of the New Testament described in this book are (1) the Book of Acts of the Apostles, which covers the early development of the Christian Church; (2) the Letters or Epistles attributed to Paul that offer a broad range of guidelines for early Christian communities under his stewardship; (3) additional apostolic letters; and (4) the apocalyptic Book of Revelation. The New Testament is so called because Christians believe that Jesus Christ is the fulfillment of the promise of the Old Testament, which we will refer to as the Hebrew Scriptures.

The seventh-century Dome of the Rock on the Temple Mount in Jerusalem, built by the Umayyad caliph Abd el-Malik (685–705 C.E.), is considered one of the greatest achievements of early Islamic art.

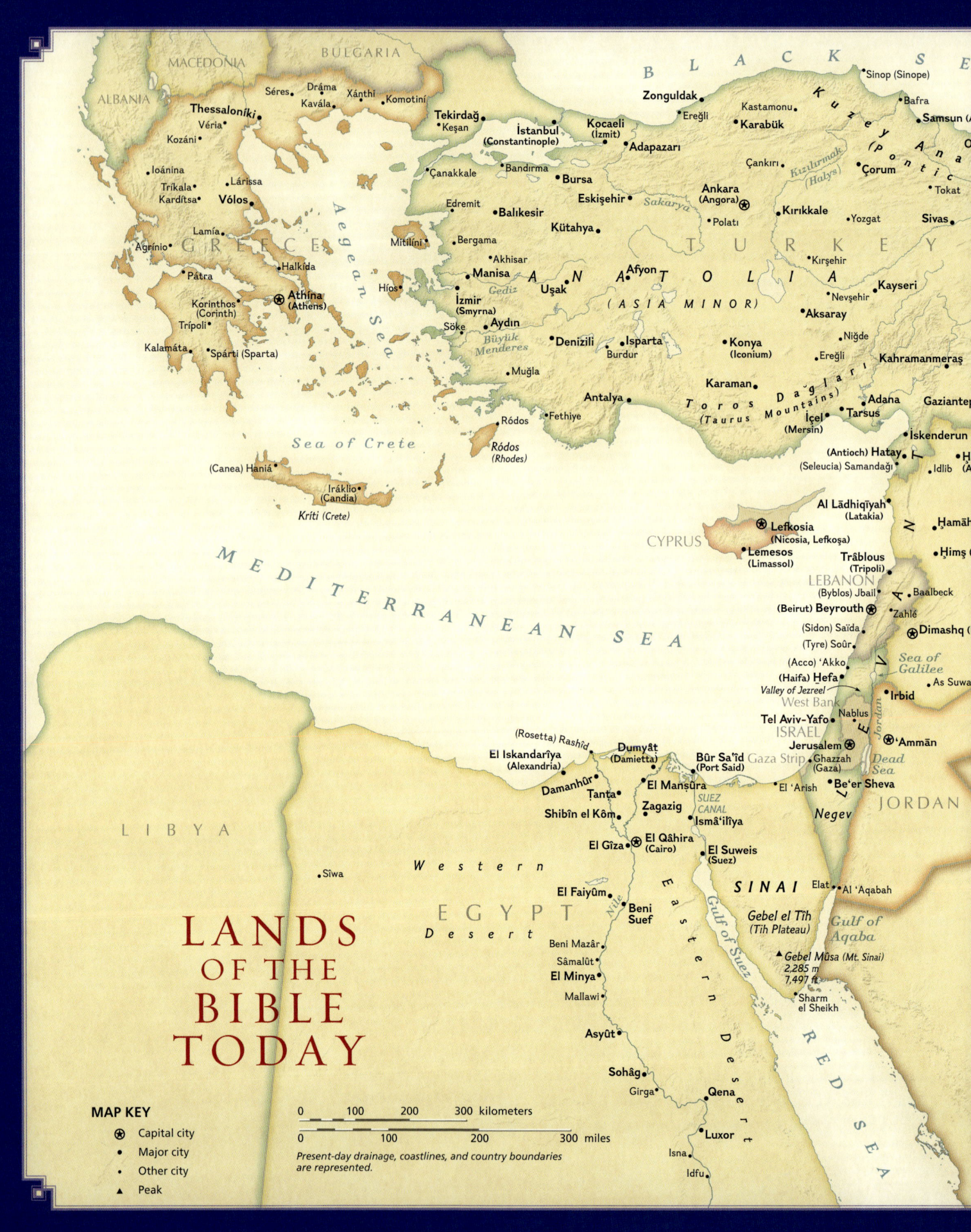

INTRODUCTION

The last decade has seen a number of exciting archaeological discoveries that shed new light on the New Testament, as in this dig in Jerusalem during the summer of 2006.

This bronze vessel supported by oxen (opposite), found in Susa and dated to around 1500 B.C.E., is similar to the Molten Sea vessel as described in the Book of I Kings, which once stood in front of Solomon's Temple in Jerusalem.

THE HEBREW SCRIPTURES

The Hebrew Bible, which both Jesus and the evangelists cite extensively, is traditionally organized into three divisions:

(1) The *Torah* or Law, also known as the Laws of Moses, that consist of Genesis, Exodus, Leviticus, Numbers, and Deuteronomy;

(2) The *Nevi'im* or Prophets, including the *former* prophets (Joshua, Judges, Samuel, and Kings) and the *latter* prophets (including Isaiah, Jeremiah, Ezekiel, and the Twelve Minor Prophets); and

(3) The *Ketuvim* or Writings, which include the Psalms, Proverbs, the Book of Job, the Book of Daniel, the Book of Chronicles, and others.

In Jesus' lifetime, only the first two divisions were collectively recognized as Scripture. That is why Jesus often refers to the Bible as "the Law and the Prophets." (Luke 16:16) Nevertheless, although the third division, that of the Writings, was still being formed in the first century C.E., Jesus was most likely familiar with some of these books, specifically the Psalms. Throughout this book we will often refer to the Torah or Law as the guiding legislative and liturgical source of Judaism in the time of Jesus.

While the Hebrew Scriptures were mostly written in Hebrew, the Gospels

were written in Greek, using a common patois known as *koinè*. The biblical citations in this book use the English translation from the 1989 New Revised Standard Version translation (NRSV) of the Old and New Testament.

We will also use a source document known as "Q" (for *Quelle* or "source" in German), which scholars believe contained a number of Jesus' sayings used by Matthew and Luke, and other Christian documents not included in the New Testament canon, such as the so-called Gnostic Gospels. Another important source is the Jewish Mishnah. Edited around 200 C.E., the book is a record of rabbinical discussions over the application of the Jewish Law in everyday life. Since it is believed that some of these discussions reflect situations and practices from before the destruction of the Temple in 70 C.E., the Mishnah may help to shed further light on Galilee and Judea in the time of Jesus.

THE BIBLE CODE

In reading the Gospels, it is important to remember that the evangelists did not have any form of illumination at their disposal, other than the power of their words. Their texts could not use pictures, graphs, photographs, or any other device that modern authors use to enhance the meaning of their narrative. Consequently, they did what most authors of Antiquity did—they availed themselves of another form of illumination, namely, the language of symbolism. By leavening his text with symbolic imagery, the author could provide his narrative with the didactic depth and meaning that his audience would expect. Ancient authors, for example, often harkened back to the symbolic imagery of Greek and Roman mythology. The evangelists, by contrast, used a symbolic vocabulary with which many in their audience were already familiar, namely, the Hebrew Scriptures.

For example, Mark tells us that Jesus prayed in the desert for 40 days before beginning his ministry. Mark's audience would not have failed to see the symbolic link to the 40 years the Israelites spent in the desert, before their entry into the Promised Land. Hence, Jesus' 40 days in the desert is really a hallowed period of extensive preparation, before the beginning of Jesus' ministry.

In this context, it is important to emphasize that the Gospels were not conceived as documents of history, but of faith. The evangelists weren't interested in creating a historical chronicle of Jesus' life, but in educating and inspiring their audience about Jesus as the Messiah, foretold in the Scriptures. Nonetheless, the Gospel narratives are clearly placed in a specific place and time—first-century Galilee and Judea before the destruction of the Second Temple—so that it is possible for us to identify areas where biblical narrative and scientific discovery overlap. This, then, will make it possible for us to reconstruct the path that Jesus walked.

INTRODUCTION

These archers of molded enameled brick from King Darius's palace at Susa, dated around 510 B.C.E., may have been members of the Persian Guard of the Immortals.

THE ORGANIZATION OF THIS BOOK

This book is divided into the following principal segments:

• Part 1 offers an overview of the Roman Empire before the birth of Jesus, before zooming in to sketch the traumatic changes wrought by Herod the Great in Palestine, followed by an intimate re-creation of everyday life in a small Galilean village such as Nazareth.

• Part 2 follows closely in Jesus' footsteps by re-creating the journeys of his ministry as reported by the Gospels. Beginning with his ministry within the immediate vicinity of Capernaum, the book traces his travels throughout Galilee, culminating in the journeys to Tyre, Sidon, the Decapolis, and finally Jerusalem. Here, the narrative offers a detailed, hour-by-hour reconstruction of the Passion events, based on the latest scholarly and archaeological findings.

• Part 3 traces the gradual emergence of Christian communities in the decades after the Easter events, both in Palestine as well as Syria, Asia Minor, and Greece, in addition to many other Christian chapels seeded by the rapidly modernizing land and sea routes in the Early Roman Empire.

• Lastly, the book traces the growing popularity of pilgrimage routes to the Holy Land, which has enabled thousands of pilgrims from the fourth century to today to walk in the footsteps of Jesus.

In the Footsteps of Jesus is deliberately written from a nondenominational perspective. As has become common practice, the book uses the temporal indicators of B.C.E. (Before the Common Era) instead of the traditional B.C. (Before Christ), and likewise C.E. (Common Era) rather than A.D. (*Anno Domini* or Year of the Lord) to identify key dates in history.

This book will also follow the practice of many modern scholars and, for lack of a better word, refer to the former kingdom of Herod the Great—the territory of Judea, Samaria, and Galilee in which Jesus lived and moved—as Roman "Palestine," even though strictly speaking, these lands were not called as such until after the suppression of the Second Jewish Revolt in 135 C.E.

In tracing the path that Jesus walked, this book is deeply respectful of Christian tradition. At the same time, it will address some of the intriguing questions and hypotheses raised by biblical scholarship in recent years. It is by virtue of this historical approach that I hope this book will not only resonate with Christians, but also with those readers who are intrigued by the historical figure of Jesus, or by Christianity as the continuing ethical framework of our modern civilization.

Jean-Pierre Isbouts
Santa Monica, California

PART I

CIRCA 64 B.C.E. TO 4 B.C.E.

Octavian, later known as Augustus, emerges triumphant from the Roman Civil War and initiates Rome's Imperial Period. Herod the Great wrests control of Judea from the Hasmonean House and for the next thirty-three years, transforms the nation with magnificent construction projects. Both developments have a lasting impact on the people of Lower Galilee, including a man named Joseph and his betrothed, Mary.

THE WORLD OF JESUS

[CHAPTER] I

The ROMAN WORLD

AUGUSTUS FOUND
A STATE EXHAUSTED
BY INTERNAL DISSENSIONS,
AND ESTABLISHED OVER IT
A PERSONAL REGIME KNOWN AS
THE PRINCIPATE.

TACITUS, *THE ANNALS OF IMPERIAL ROME*
Circa 116 C.E.

This temple, dedicated to Zeus and dating from the second century C.E., was built in Euromos, also known as Herakleia, located close to Lake Bafa in today's Turkey.

PART I | THE WORLD OF JESUS

The life of Jesus coincided with one of the most seminal periods in the history of Antiquity: the rise of the Roman Empire under Augustus, when much of Europe, Western Asia, and Northern Africa fell under the sway of a Roman *imperator,* or emperor. The unfolding of Rome's new imperial power would have a profound influence on Jesus, his ministry, and, ultimately, the growth of Early Christianity.

The Empire's rapid expansion is fairly astonishing when we imagine that as late as the fourth century B.C.E., few people had even heard of Rome. At the time, the city was little more than a group of settlements, scattered across seven hills rising along the river Tiber. According to Rome's founding myth, the city was originally established by two brothers, Romulus and Remus, who were raised by a she-wolf, though archaeologists believe that Rome's origins are more prosaic, with origins going back to the tenth century B.C.E. Nevertheless, we have no reason to doubt the claim of Roman historians such as Livy that around 509 B.C.E., the citizens of Rome were fed up with their kings and decided to establish a republic.

This "republic" (a term rooted in the Latin words *res publica*, or public matter) was—like its precedent in Athens—unquestionably more inclusive than the monarchies of its time, but it was hardly a democracy. Most of Rome's political power remained in the hands of a landed aristocracy. They controlled the Senate, which soon became the principal executive and legislative body. During the next five centuries, which historians call Rome's Republican Period, the city slowly but steadily expanded its commercial and territorial influence, aided by the fact that in the east, Greece and Persia were too busy fighting each other to take any notice. This prolonged clash between the Greek and Persian superpowers—between East and West—was brought to a close when a prince of Macedon, Alexander the Great, dealt the Persian king Darius III a crushing defeat in 333 B.C.E.

Alexander then pushed his conquest deep into the Persian realm, capturing Tyre, Syria, and Egypt, as well as a small Persian province known as Yehud, or Judah. Judah, the former Southern Kingdom of the Israelites, had originally been conquered by the Neo-Babylonian king Nebuchadnezzar in 587 B.C.E., but 50 years later, Babylon itself was captured by the Persian king Cyrus II, also known as Cyrus the Great. Judah had thus been a Persian satrapy for two centuries when Alexander and his forces flooded the Levant. But Alexander's reign was brief. In 323 B.C.E., he died in Nebuchadnezzar's palace in Babylon at age 32, and a power struggle ensued among his generals regarding

control of the new Macedonian Empire. In the end they decided to carve up the territory. Ptolemy, one of Alexander's ablest generals, crowned himself King Ptolemy I of Egypt and Palestine, thus founding the Ptolemaic dynasty. Another general, Seleucus, took Syria and the better part of Persia and founded the Seleucid dynasty.

As a new world order emerged in the East, no one paid much attention to the small republic called Rome as it steadily took control of the Italian peninsula following the defeat of its last main enemy, the Samnites of southern Italy, in 290 B.C.E. On Rome went, pushing from the southern tip of Italy to Sicily. The western part of that island was a prized possession of Carthage, located in today's Tunisia, and the leading power in the Western Mediterranean. Rome and Carthage fought fiercely in a series of "Punic" Wars (based on the Latin word *Punici*, or Phoenicians). By the beginning of the second century, Rome emerged triumphant and found that much of the East lay ready for conquest as well.

An overview of the Roman Forum shows the House of the Vestals in front, the Basilica of Constantine and Maxentius in the top left, and the Arch of Titus in the top right.

The Growth of the Roman Empire

The reason was the growing hostility between the Ptolemaic and Seleucid empires, which reached a flash point in 200 B.C.E. when the Seleucid king Antiochus III decided to invade Ptolemaic Palestine, including Judah and the northern region known as Galilee. The Egyptian king Ptolemy V was defeated, after which Galilee and Judah were absorbed in the *eparchy*, or prefecture, of Samaria, which in turn formed part of the Seleucid province of Coele-Syria.

Confident in the power of his army, Antiochus III then embarked on an ill-fated invasion of Greece. This put him on a collision course with a far more powerful opponent, for the Roman Republic considered Greece part of its sphere of influence. When the king of Pergamum (located in the northwest of today's Turkey) asked Rome for military intervention, the Roman Senate was more than happy to oblige. Antiochus suffered a decisive defeat, whereupon Rome imposed such crippling war indemnities that Antiochus's successor, Antiochus IV, was forced to start looting temples throughout his realm—including the Temple in Jerusalem—in order to come up with the payments. Worse, an altar dedicated to the Greek god Zeus was placed inside the Temple, while Jewish Temple services were suspended. In response, the Jews, under the leadership of the Maccabees and the *Hasidim* (the pious ones), rose in revolt; their success led to a century of Jewish independence.

A polychrome depiction of Alexander the Great on his horse, routing the Persians, forms part of the so-called "Alexander Sarcophagus," which dates from the late fourth century B.C.E.

The outcome of these years of turmoil was that Rome gradually became the dominant power in the Mediterranean. In 133 B.C.E., for example, the king of Pergamum simply bequeathed his entire kingdom to the Roman Republic, knowing that Roman hegemony was inevitable and that any resistance would only jeopardize Asia Minor's growing commercial activity. Rome's aristocracy, which had traditionally drawn its riches from extensive land holdings, now became fabulously wealthy. Senators eagerly sought appointments to the provinces overseas, where they could make a fortune through the sale of local trade monopolies, kickbacks, and other lucrative concessions.

This further widened the gap between Rome's ruling élites and Italy's vast majority of peasants, most of whom tilled the land as little more than serfs. Worse, as Rome's expansion required the levy of more and more legions, drafting thousands of able-bodied young men, landowners were forced to import slaves by the thousands to work as field hands. This further distanced the nobility from the people, or "plebs," and lay the foundation for large-scale unemployment in the years to come. In response, the people clamored for the

The Roman World

redistribution of public lands, but no real action was taken until the rise of a man named Julius Caesar.

Intervention in the Near East

Though a nobleman himself, who traced his lineage to the goddess Venus, Caesar had early on aligned himself with the populist cause. In 59 B.C.E., following a period of great political upheaval, Caesar had deftly created a triumvirate, or "reign of three men," which represented Rome's principal factions: the aristocracy, represented by Crassus, the city's wealthiest nobleman; the military, represented by the famous general Pompeius Magnus, or Pompey the Great; and the people, represented by Caesar himself. Pompey's fame was well deserved: In 67 B.C.E., he had effectively cleared the Mediterranean of pirates, who previously had preyed on Roman naval traffic and trade.

Pompey's legions next intervened in the Third Mithridatic War, thus putting an end to the territorial ambitions of Mithradates VI, the king of Pontus (the northern coastal region of modern Turkey). This brought the Roman general tantalizingly close to Syria, still ruled by the Seleucid dynasty, and Palestine,

This statue of Aphrodite, the Greek goddess of love, is a second-century C.E. Roman copy of a Greek original.

ROMAN GODS

At the time of Jesus' birth, the world outside Palestine was still overwhelmingly polytheistic. Rome's original gods were its divine ancestors, but as Roman civilization became increasingly Hellenized, it adopted a number of Greek deities. Aphrodite, the goddess of love whom the Romans called Venus, can be traced back to the fertility goddess Ishtar in Mesopotamia, who was subsequently introduced to the Mediterranean basin by the Phoenicians as Astarte. The Greek god of the heavens, Zeus, became Jupiter; Ares became Mars; and Athena became Minerva. Only Apollo, the god of light, music, and prophecy, was revered by his original Greek name. Roman intellectuals like Cicero questioned Roman religion, but readily acknowledged its role in maintaining law and order. In the Imperial Period, Roman religion lost much of its moral credibility when an obsequious Senate began to declare every emperor a god upon his death. When lying on his deathbed, Vespasian dryly remarked, "I think I'm becoming a god." Augustus tried to rejuvenate religious ceremony and Roman piety to help reunify Roman society after the civil war. But overseas, the imperial cult became a political extension of Roman rule since each subject was required to sacrifice to statues of the Roman emperor. Remarkably, Augustus exempted the Jews of Palestine from such sacrifice, declaring that "the Jews shall use their own customs in accordance with their ancestral law." Moreover, Augustus authorized the collection of Temple tithes throughout the Diaspora, and decreed "that their sacred offerings shall be inviolable," exempt from Roman taxation.

PART I | THE WORLD OF JESUS

The so-called "Tomb of Absalom" in the Kidron Valley in Jerusalem is a rock-cut burial monument in the Hellenistic style, probably from the early first century C.E.

> **POMPEY CAME UPON THEM BY SURPRISE, DEPRIVED THEM OF THEIR POWER, AND DESTROYED THEIR FORTRESSES, FIRST TAKING JERUSALEM ITSELF BY STORM.**
>
> STRABO, *THE GEOGRAPHY*
> *Circa 24 C.E.*

which was now an independent Jewish kingdom ruled by the Hasmonean House. Rome and Syria were not at war, but the Seleucid Empire was located at a critical juncture of Rome's new trade routes to the East. While he had his legions still at his disposal, Pompey decided to invade Syria, march on its capital of Antioch, and depose the ruling king, Antiochus XIII Asiaticus. Some scholars believe that this was the intent of the Roman Senate all along—that Pompey was to use the pretext of the Mithridatic War to expand Roman control of the Near East. The purpose of this strategy was to create a buffer state between Rome's principal source of grain, Egypt, and the empire of the Parthians, heirs to the ancient Persian Empire.

Pompey may also have been pleased to hear of a quarrel that had broken out in the Hasmonean Kingdom. Upon the death of Queen Salome Alexandra in 67 B.C.E., her two sons Hyrcanus II and Aristobulus II both vied for the throne. Hyrcanus II, the heir apparent who was already serving as high priest, was defeated by his younger brother, but the governor of the southern province of Idumea, named Antipater, rallied to his cause. Antipater, father of the future Herod the Great, also solicited the help of King Aretas III, ruler of Nabatea, a region roughly analogous to today's Jordan. Aretas agreed to come to Hyrcanus's aid and invaded Judea with his forces, thus plunging the nation into civil war.

As soon as the news spread that Pompey had arrived in Judea, three separate Jewish delegations set out to lobby for Roman support of their claims. One faction pressed the cause of Aristobulus, while another tried hard to convince Pompey of the righteousness of Hyrcanus's claim—both backed by generous bribes.

Instead, Pompey decided to conquer the Hasmonean Kingdom for Rome and install Hyrcanus as a vassal prince. In 63 B.C.E, he led his legions down south to Jerusalem. The Roman geographer Strabo reports that at the time, Jerusalem "was a stronghold situated on a rock, well-fortified and well-supplied with water." Behind its walls sat Aristobulus, who refused to surrender the city. Pompey, however, had been appraised of a Jewish custom known as the Sabbath, "on which day," Strabo says, "the Jews were in the habit of abstaining from all work"—including military action. Pompey cunningly ordered his soldiers to wait until the Sabbath, and then, knowing that the Jewish population would refuse to interfere, he built large earthen walls for siege engines. Once these engines were in place, the Jewish historian Josephus writes, "the battering-engine was brought near, and one of the largest towers was targeted and destroyed, thus creating a gap in the fortifications." The Romans poured through and captured the city; Aristobulus fled. Hyrcanus was installed as a vassal ruler with the title of *ethnarch*

PART I | THE WORLD OF JESUS

The Roman World

(Greek for "ruler of the people"). The brief flame of Jewish independence under the Hasmoneans had been extinguished and would not be rekindled again, save for a brief period during the Second Jewish Revolt of C.E. 132, until the 20th century.

THE ROMAN CIVIL WAR

The Triumvirate of Caesar, Crassus, and Pompey lasted for six years, by Roman standards an extraordinarily long time, in part because the three men forced the Senate to adopt a long-delayed plan for the redistribution of public lands to the poor. The Triumvirate then divided the empire among themselves. Caesar took control of Northern Italy, southeastern Europe, and Transalpine Gaul (the south of France). With four legions under his command, he then left Rome to pacify the tribes of France and to cross into German territory and Britain. Despite tenacious resistance, by 52 B.C.E Caesar had conquered all of Gaul. But upon Crassus's death, Pompey broke their alliance and accused Caesar of exceeding his authority. Enraged, Caesar crossed into Rome's home territory with his 13th legion at the Rubicon River, something every Roman commander was expressly forbidden to do. The result was civil war. Pompey fled to Greece, where he hoped to raise new armies; but Caesar gave chase and defeated him at the Battle of Pharsalus in 48 B.C.E.

A grateful Senate voted to give Caesar the title of dictator—a magistrate with extraordinary powers. Caesar accepted, and promptly set sail for Egypt, where Pompey had reportedly fled in search of asylum. Before Caesar could catch up with his former ally, however, the boy-king of Egypt, Ptolemy XIII, had Pompey killed, hoping to curry favor with the new Roman dictator. Caesar never forgave the king, since no foreign ruler had the right to harm a Roman consul. In response, he threw his support behind Ptolemy's sister, Cleopatra, who had been banished from Alexandria. At 21, and 30 years younger than Caesar, Cleopatra became his lover; shortly thereafter, Ptolemy XIII was ousted by Roman forces and drowned in the Nile.

Caesar's return to Rome was greeted with great enthusiasm and celebrated with triumphal processions and spectacular games at the Circus Maximus. Seizing the moment, Caesar forced a series of highly popular reforms through the Senate, including the reduction of private debt, the redistribution of land to some 15,000 veterans, and the establishment of a new calendar that closely matches our modern one. The Senate responded by naming him

Archaeologists discovered this sculpture of a sphinx, possibly a portrait of Ptolemy II Philadelphus (309–246 B.C.E.), submerged in the ancient harbor of Alexandria.

British artist John William Waterhouse (1849–1917) painted this canvas of a brooding Queen Cleopatra (opposite) in 1887.

PART I | THE WORLD OF JESUS

The King's Highway, the ancient trade route linking Egypt with Mesopotamia, ran through these barren hills in today's Jordan.

This portrait of Emperor Augustus (opposite) wearing the civic crown, known as "Augustus Bevilacqua," was probably completed after his death in 14 C.E.

Pater Patriae, Father of the Fatherland. The seventh month in the new calendar, called *Quintilis,* was renamed *Julius,* or July, in his honor—a name that endures to this day.

The old aristocracy, however, was now implacably allied against Caesar. A conspiracy began to form, led by Caesar's former legate, Gaius Cassius, and Caesar's old friend Marcus Brutus. As one Roman historian and a close friend of Herod the Great, Nicolaus of Damascus, tells us, "the reputation which had long been attached to the Brutus family was very influential in causing the uprising, for Brutus' ancestors had overthrown the kings who ruled from the time of Romulus." On March 15, 44 B.C.E, the Ides of March, the conspirators struck just as Caesar entered the Senate. The dictator was reportedly stabbed more than 20 times and died on the marble pavement.

The Roman World

Julius Caesar's assassination sent shock waves through the Empire and precipitated the Second Roman Civil War, which would last more than a decade. Caesar's most able general, Mark Antony, allied himself with the dictator's designated heir, his 18-year-old grandnephew Gaius Octavian, to crush all Senate opposition. They then pursued the assassins, principally Cassius and Brutus, who had fled to Egypt and later Syria. While in Syria, Cassius desperately sought financial support in order to raise new legions. One of those who came to his aid was the governor of Galilee, a young Idumean nobleman named Herod. Partly with Herod's help, Brutus and Cassius were able to levy 14 legions against the 17 legions raised by Octavian and Mark Antony. There followed a series of epic clashes near Philippi in Macedonia in 43 B.C.E., which left Mark Antony and Octavian in command of the field. Brutus committed suicide, while Cassius ordered his aide-de-camp to kill him.

But the civil war was still not at an end. A long-simmering rivalry between Octavian and Mark Antony erupted into open enmity. "The alliance between him and Antony, which had always been precarious and often interrupted," says the early second century Roman historian Suetonius, "was at last entirely dissolved." When Mark Antony established himself in Egypt as Cleopatra's lover and co-regent, even though he was married to Octavian's sister Octavia, Octavian declared war. This was Egypt's last grasp at glory and a desperate attempt to regain its former status as a regional superpower. The showdown came in 31 B.C.E., when Octavian's and Mark Antony's forces clashed during a sea battle off the coast of Actium. Egypt's warriors were never mariners, and the Egyptian ships were no match for the Roman navy. Mark Antony and Cleopatra fled to their palace in Alexandria, where they both committed suicide.

Octavian was now the sole ruler of the Roman Empire.

The *Pax Romana*

During the next four decades, a long reign by any measure, Octavian succeeded in re-creating the Roman Empire as a thoroughly integrated body politic led by a single individual, an emperor. At the same time, he established the Julio-Claudian family as a dynasty that was to rule for much of the first century. Ironically, by killing Julius Caesar the aristocrats had precipitated the very thing they had hoped to avoid: the end of the Roman Republic. But the concentration of power into a hereditary monarchical system had practical benefits. The Roman Empire had become too vast to be managed by the quarrelsome and ever-shifting factions of the Roman Senate. For this empire to survive, it needed a strong hand, wielded by a single emperor, free from the cycle

> MEN GAVE HIM THIS NAME IN VIEW OF [AUGUSTUS'S] CLAIM TO HONOR; AND, SCATTERED OVER ISLANDS AND CONTINENTS, THROUGH CITY AND TRIBE, THEY REVERE HIM BY BUILDING TEMPLES.
>
> NICOLAUS OF DAMASCUS,
> *THE LIFE OF AUGUSTUS*
> *Circa 14 C.E.*

PART I | THE WORLD OF JESUS

The Ara Pacis Augustae or "Altar of Augustan Peace" was commissioned by the Roman Senate and completed in 9 B.C.E. to celebrate the peace established by Emperor Augustus.

This detail of a Roman road near Aleppo (opposite) in today's Syria reveals the meticulous care with which Roman engineers built the highways of the Roman Empire.

of internecine strife that had bedeviled the Roman Republic during its previous 100 years.

Octavian, on whom the Senate bestowed the reverential title Augustus or "August One" in 27 B.C.E., had precisely that strong hand. Content to accept the role of *princeps,* "first citizen," Augustus maintained the powers that had been granted to his great-uncle Caesar, though he never acknowledged such in public. Using these powers, he stabilized the Senate and other government institutions that had been substantially damaged by the civil war; brought an end to the seething tensions between the plebs and the aristocracy; and established a system of international administration that essentially functioned unchanged until the days of Emperor Diocletian (r. 284–305 C.E.). Stretched across the empire, this imperial bureaucracy collected taxes, administered justice, paid local salaries from the lowest legionnaire to the highest ranking Roman official, and provided public assistance. At the same time, Augustus extended and solidified Rome's territorial gains, until in Lionel Casson's phrase "any person could make his way from the burning sun of Mesopotamia to the mists of Scotland without ever crossing a national frontier." The

The Roman World

result was a *Pax Romana,* a "Roman Peace" whereby the subject peoples of the realm were finally free from the cycles of war. By the second century, most inhabitants in the empire could not imagine living in a world other than the Roman commonwealth. Even though their political independence was forfeit, they had grown accustomed to the stability and economic benefits of a single market, a single currency, and a single security system that stretched from the Atlantic coast to the Arabian Gulf.

To support this new status quo, Augustus took several astute political steps. First, he broke with Rome's precedent of raising armies only in times of war and established a full-time standing army of territorial and overseas legions to maintain the Augustan Peace. These legions were stationed in provinces that not only had strategic value, but that also could defray the cost of a large military presence from local taxes and other proceeds. Rome was sensitive to this issue: The famous orator Cicero had created a stir by claiming that some of Rome's provinces could not justify the money it cost to defend them. Consequently, legions were usually stationed in big cities that could support a garrison with taxes paid in coin, rather than in agricultural products.

In the early first century C.E., for example, the Roman 10th Legion, *Fretensis,* was based in Antioch, the headquarters of the Roman governor in charge of Syria and Palestine. Judea, by contrast, was poor, so its tax yield did not justify the cost of maintaining a full Roman legion. At best, the Roman Prefect of Judea had only a few cohorts at his disposal, each numbering around 500 men, and those were made up of locally recruited auxiliaries rather than fully trained legionnaires. The principal Roman garrison in Judea and Samaria was located in Caesarea Maritima on the Mediterranean coast, while a smaller garrison was based in the Antonia Fortress overlooking the Temple in Jerusalem.

In order to move these legions across the empire at speed, Augustus initiated a vast effort to build a comprehensive road network. Traditionally, roads were the responsibility of cities and townships that relied on them—including villages that needed a road to the nearest town to bring their produce to market. Main roads, to the extent that these existed, were limited to the principal caravan routes; these often dated back hundreds of years, such as the Way of the Philistines along the Mediterranean coast, or the King's Highway from Damascus through Judea and to the Egyptian border. The Romans were the first to conceive of a systematic road network that would link all principal cities within the Empire. At its peak, this road system covered some 250,000 miles, of which some 50,000 miles were paved—an astonishing achievement by the standards of Antiquity. Under Trajan (r. c.e. 98–117), no fewer than 29 major highways connected the city of Rome in all directions of the compass. Some of the roads built in the Augustan age continue to be used to this day.

Roman roads enabled the population of the empire to leave their hometowns on an unprecedented scale. International trade grew exponentially, but so did other forms of travel, such as religious tourism. People in the Greco-Roman Empire were not only deeply religious, they devoutly believed in the miraculous properties of shrines and oracles, and they visited them whenever they could—including places such as the Greek healing shrine of Epidaurus, the Oracle in Delphi, the sacred island of Delos, the Temple of Artemis in Ephesus, or the great medicinal center of Hippocrates in Pergamum. In between were countless lesser pilgrimage destinations, as well as the popular *thermae,* or spa resorts in Gaul, where Rome's elite went to relax and restore themselves. Those interested in ancient monuments set sail for Athens, Halicarnassus (today's Bodrum, Turkey), or the great pyramids of Giza; graffiti from Roman tourists can still be read on the stones of the Great Pyramid and other Egyptian monuments.

Soon, Rome's thriving markets forged paths to lands outside the empire, including the world's other great civilization of the time, the Chinese Empire. The Spice Route through Persia, for example, carried Chinese bolts of silk and finished silk garments, as well as elephant tusks, amber, pearls, and spices from India; most of these goods were carried on donkeys. The Incense Route through Arabia, by contrast, used camels to ferry such luxuries as aloes, myrrh, and other perfume agents from Yemen, or frankincense from Oman, to burn as incense in Rome's temples. A camel's splayed hooves enabled it to trod over sand, while its humps could store up to 25 gallons of water, good for two to three weeks of travel. A typical caravan of the Roman Imperial Period would be composed of some 100 camels, each laden with about 500 pounds of cargo and capable of traveling 20 to 30 miles a day. The main terminus for this desert highway was the Nabatean city of Petra, today located in southern Jordan, which soon became one of the wealthiest cities on the Arabian peninsula. Other cities along the Arabian trade routes, including Palmyra on the rim between Syria and Arabia, or Gerasa in northern Jordan, competed with one another in showcasing their urban splendor.

The Cultural Unification of the Empire

A major factor that fostered a sense of Empire-wide unity and loyalty was Augustus's generous policy of conferring Roman citizenship on colonials

> THE CITY, WHICH WAS NOT BUILT IN A MANNER SUITABLE TO THE GRANDEUR OF THE EMPIRE . . . WAS SO MUCH IMPROVED UNDER HIS ADMINISTRATION, THAT HE BOASTED . . . THAT HE FOUND IT OF BRICK, BUT LEFT IT OF MARBLE.
>
> Suetonius, "Augustus"
> from *The Twelve Caesars*
> *Circa 119 c.e.*

worthy of the honor. The Roman Republic had, on occasion, awarded deserving individuals and even communities with citizenship, but Augustus raised the practice to new heights, shrewdly calculating that Roman citizenship, and the right to wear a toga, would soon become the goal of many ambitious men, regardless of their ethnicity. Not only did citizenship confer prestige and social status, it also qualified the individual for employment in Rome's bureaucracy and thus a political career. Enlisting in a Roman legion would likewise lead to citizenship upon honorable discharge, as would faithful service in Rome's local administration.

Another salient example of the power of citizenship is provided by the city of Tarsus, capital of Cilicia in Asia Minor. Ever since its conquest by Pompey's forces in 64 B.C.E., the city had been so fastidious in its tribute to Rome—which included the provision of mercenary soldiers—that either Julius Caesar or Augustus (the record is not clear) granted the entire community the exceptional status of a free Roman city. As a result, one of Tarsus's natives, a man named Paul, would proudly state upon his arrest in Jerusalem that as a Roman citizen he was entitled to being tried by a magistrate in Rome, rather than by a local provincial court. By

Exotic spices such as these from the souk of Cairo, Egypt, were carried by camel on caravan routes across the Arabian Peninsula.

FLAVIUS JOSEPHUS

A 12th-century Flemish artist created this impression of Flavius Josephus from an illuminated copy of his book *Antiquities of the Jews*.

Our understanding of the Roman world during the time of Jesus is based in part on the writings of a Jewish historian named Josephus. Born in Jerusalem to a noble family that traced its lineage from the high priest Jonathan Maccabee, youngest of the Maccabean brothers, Josephus received a formal education, possibly under the aegis of Temple tutors. In his biography, Josephus relates how in his early twenties he was sent to the court of Emperor Nero to negotiate the release of several Jewish priests, which suggests that he was born in the late 20s or early 30s of the first century C.E., possibly around the time of Jesus' ministry. In C.E. 66, when war broke out between Judea and Rome, Josephus reluctantly accepted a commission in the Jewish militia and was put in charge of a regiment in Galilee. Following his capture, he was interrogated by the Roman general Vespasian and saved from a death sentence after he prophesied that Vespasian would one day become emperor. Indeed, in C.E. 69, Vespasian's own legions pronounced him emperor and Josephus was released. He eventually joined the imperial household in Rome, where he wrote a book about the Jewish War. He later published another book on Jewish history, entitled *Antiquities of the Jews*, as well as an autobiographical work. Since *Antiquities* features a short (though highly controversial) paragraph about Jesus, as well as a less contested section about John the Baptist, Josephus's works were copied by monks throughout the Middle Ages and preserved until modern times.

PART I | THE WORLD OF JESUS

ROMAN TRADE

The *Pax Romana* fostered the growth of a global economy that was unprecedented in Western civilization. Greece was a leading exporter of white linen, olive oil, honey, and some of the best wine in the empire, as well as paintings and statuary; Syria was prized for popular snacks such as dates, figs, and sugared plums. Liquid commodities such as wine, olive oil, and *garum*, a fish sauce condiment that was as popular in ancient Rome as ketchup is today, were typically transported in *amphorae*, many of which have been found almost intact from shipwrecks off the coast of Asia Minor—today's Turkey. Egypt was the empire's principal breadbasket, with grain ships leaving for Rome on an almost daily basis, but the country was also famous for its glass, jewelry, alabaster, porphyry, and granite, as well as the fine quality of its papyrus. Spain yielded silver, while the timber from Gaul (France) was considered second only to the cedar from Lebanon. Other regions provided products such as almonds, walnuts, coconuts, apricots, and peaches. Most of these commodities poured into Rome as tribute. It has been estimated that during the reign of Emperor Vespasian in the middle of the first century C.E., Roman treasury receipts from overseas tribute totaled 1.5 billion *sesterces*, roughly the equivalent of $6 billion today. This did not include import duties, which were levied whenever a shipment crossed from one Roman province into another. Much of this wealth was used, in turn, for imports from outside the empire, because the Romans had by this time developed an appetite for luxury goods from the East.

This rare pre-Islamic (ca third century C.E.) relief depicts Arab traders on camels.

the beginning of the second century, the enfranchisement of subject peoples had become so widespread that two of the empire's most capable emperors, Trajan (r. 98-117 C.E.) and Hadrian (r. 117–138 C.E.), were of Spanish extraction.

But the most important method by which Augustus sought to fuse the empire into one nation was his attempt to impose a uniform aesthetic on all principal urban centers using the Greek model of an ideal city, or polis. The inspiration to do so may have come from Alexander the Great, who likewise founded countless poleis in the areas he conquered, complete with Greek-style temples, theaters, gymnasia, and agorae or marketplaces. Before Alexander, cities in Asia Minor were strikingly different from those in Phoenicia, Syria, or Egypt—a reflection of their indigenous cultures. But after Alexander, much of that diversity was lost as cities from Pergamum to Ptolemaic Egypt, from Antioch to Petra tried to outdo one another in the imitation of ancient Athens. Augustus revived this ideal, since much of Roman art and architecture was a near-archaeological re-creation of Classical Greece anyway; to this the Romans applied their superior knowledge of construction technology. Whereas the Greeks primarily used the traditional post and beam structure to build their monuments, the Romans developed arches and vaults as the principal support system. They also added some quintessentially

Roman buildings to the repertoire, such as public baths, a central forum, and sometimes even an aqueduct that could carry fresh water from faraway mountains to fountains in the city center.

While existing cities were upgraded in this Roman manner, new cities were planned, using a gridlike pattern originally developed by Hippodamus (498–408 B.C.E.) in Miletus (located near the southeastern coast of today's Turkey). In this scheme, all streets were anchored on a main boulevard, the *Cardo Maximus,* which was then bisected by a secondary avenue, the *Decumanus.* The Cardo inevitably led to the forum, where visitors would find the temple dedicated to the city's patron god, the business center, and the regional administration. Along the way, their eyes would be drawn to beautiful frescoes, brightly colored mosaics, as well as sparkling fountains and sculpted ornamentations, all executed in the magnificent realism established by Greek artists some 300 years before.

As part of this urbanization, the Romans introduced new standards of hygiene. Communal latrines used running water to funnel human waste into a subterranean sewage system, thus boosting the city's defenses against disease. Frequent visits to the public baths, a previously unknown luxury for many of the empire's residents, became an ingrained feature of urban life. At the same time, theaters spread the Roman taste for public entertainment in the form of gladiatorial battles, the gorier the better, rather than the Greek tragedies of the past.

Augustus himself raised the bar of civic splendor by turning Rome, a town largely built of brick, into a city made of marble. Previously, Romans had cared little for the exterior of their structures and preferred to spend their money on the lavish appointments of its interior. But Augustus envisioned a city cast in the pristine white of veined marble, glittering in the glow of the Italianate sun. The result was a massive boom in the excavation and trading of marble; by the beginning of the first century, every major city was engaged in fierce competition to build the most magnificent marble structures. This influence was even reflected in some of Herod's building projects, including the city of Sebaste.

The Jewish Response to Hellenization

The Jewish reaction to this new Hellenistic impetus differed by territory. Throughout the Diaspora outside of Palestine, many Jews had absorbed the Greek language, Greek literature, and Greek customs, even if they remained faithful to the practices of the Law and their worship of one God. Over time, these Jews had become inured to the sight of sculptures of human beings, even those

These delicate Roman glass flasks, found in Palestine and dating from the first century C.E., were used for perfumed oils.

PART I | THE WORLD OF JESUS

depicting gods in the nude, though Judaism abhorred such graven images. By the same token, Greco-Roman religion, being polytheistic in nature, was inherently tolerant of other faiths and deities; Judaism itself was an officially recognized religion. In Alexandria, for example, the Jewish community was able to create a Greek translation of the Hebrew Scriptures, known as the Septuagint. One legend even suggests that the translation was paid for by none other than King Ptolemy II, an avowed bibliophile who wanted to equip the Library of Alexandria with the scriptures of every people in the empire. By that time, few Jews in Egypt could speak either Hebrew or Aramaic, the lingua franca of the Near East, let alone read their Scripture in the original Hebrew language.

But in Palestine proper, the response of observant Jews to the renewed encroachment of a polytheistic faith, this time at the behest of the Romans, was very different. As the Books of the Prophets attest, ancient Israel had always fought an ongoing struggle against the worship of foreign gods. Indeed, the Maccabean Revolt against Antiochus IV was fueled in part by the king's insistence that Judah conform to Greek practice in every manner and form—including pagan sacrifice to the Greek gods.

Now a new conqueror had come to Judea. Not only did the Roman conquest spell the end of Jewish independence, but it also led to a renewed introduction of Greco-Roman polytheism and lifestyle. Little wonder, then, that many Jews in Palestine harbored a deep resentment toward the Romans. Not everyone felt this way; after all, the Hasmonean nobility had themselves shown a predilection for Greek ways. In time, many of Judea's elites became quite attracted to the luxury of Roman civilization. And this revealed the problematic side of the Augustan revolution: It mostly favored the upper social strata of the territories it absorbed. Vassal kings and their court, the landed gentry, and enterprising merchants who eagerly collaborated with the occupying power reaped the rewards of being integrated in the new Roman economy.

The impact on the vast majority of peasants was exactly the reverse. Whereas before they had been left alone to a quiet life of subsistence farming, with only modest yields beyond the immediate needs of their families, the empire's developing markets now put pressure on agricultural areas to create export-quality surplus. Most farmers in the empire, and Palestine in particular, were not equipped to cultivate in that way. Their land was typically parsed into small plots that each yielded a measure of grain, legumes, and fruit, so as to provide their families with a balanced diet. But the Augustan economy dictated otherwise. Its booming cities were hungry and needed to be fed. Throughout the empire, local authorities began to confiscate and convert peasant plots into large, single-purpose estates for export, to feed the markets of cities at home and abroad rather than the local peasant population. This had a devastating impact on farming communities such as Galilee, to which we shall turn shortly.

This bust of a Ptolemaic king is believed to be the portrait of Ptolemy II Philadelphus (309–246 B.C.E.) or Ptolemy III Euergetes (246–222 B.C.E.).

The sacred island of Delos (opposite), revered as the birthplace of Apollo, was a major pilgrimage destination well into the second century C.E.

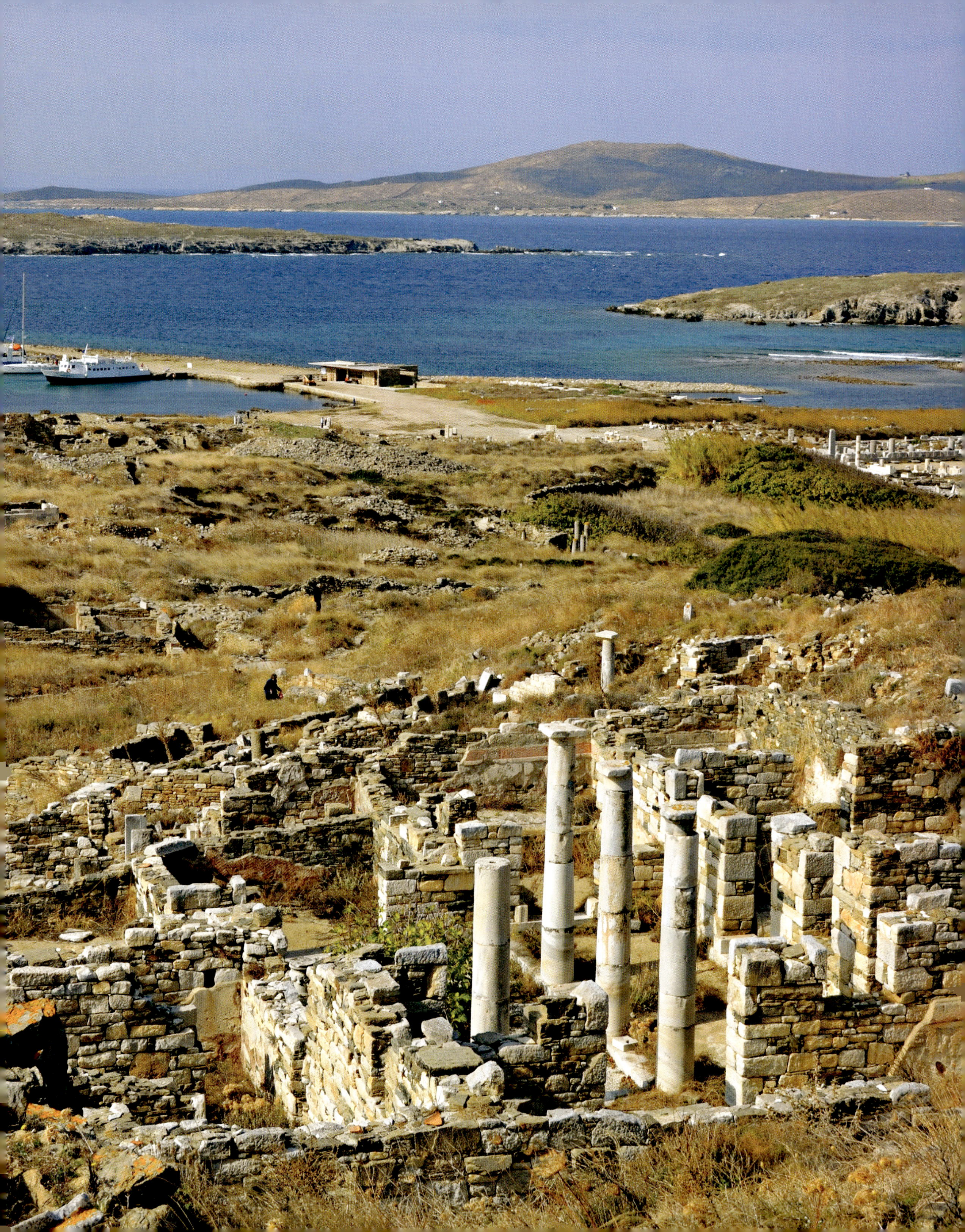

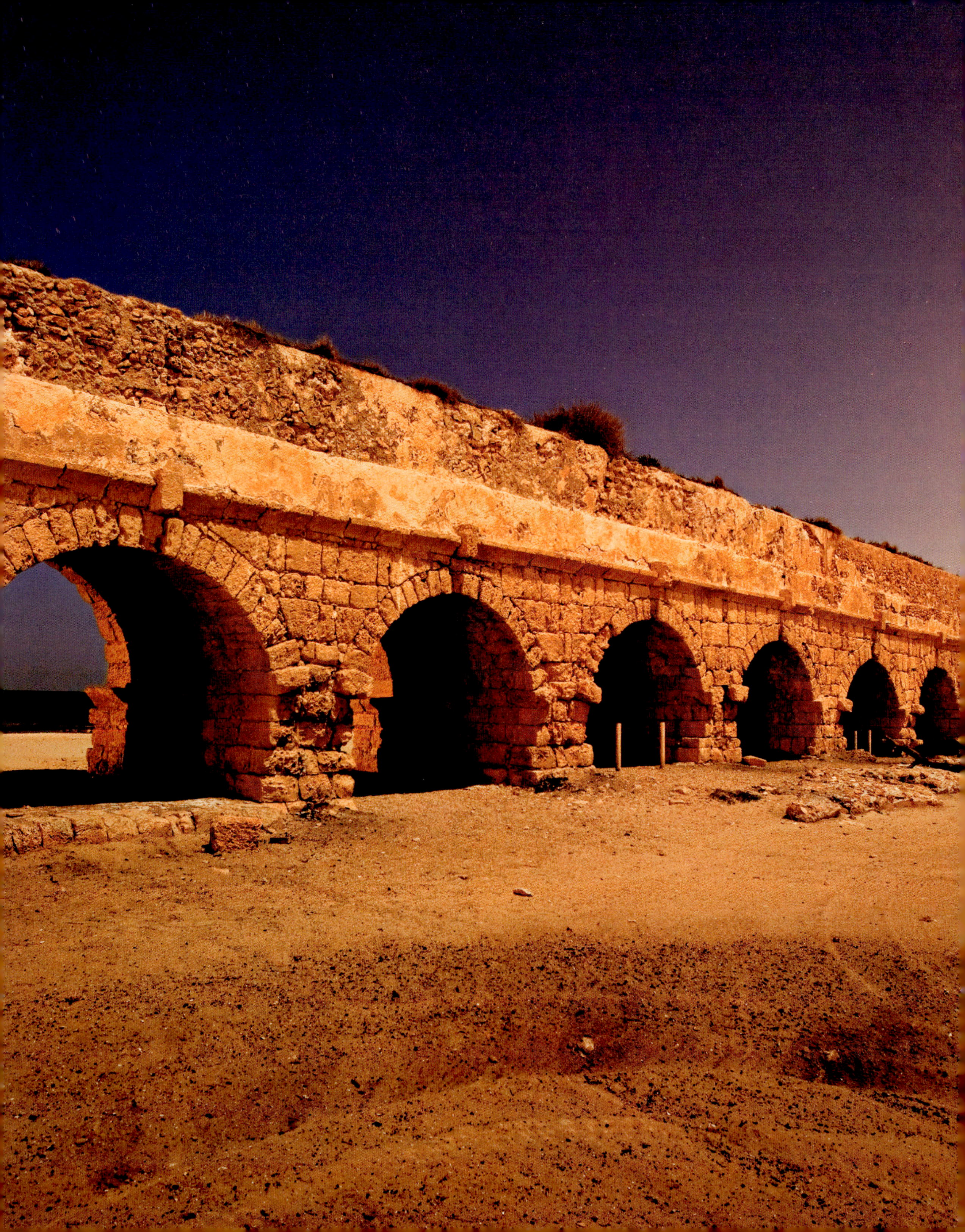

| CHAPTER |
2

The KINGDOM of HEROD THE GREAT

AN INSOLENT KING
SHALL SUCCEED THEM,
WHO WILL NOT BE
OF THE RACE OF THE PRIESTS,
A MAN BOLD AND SHAMELESS,
AND HE SHALL JUDGE THEM
AS THEY SHALL DESERVE.

TESTAMENT OF MOSES 6
Early first century C.E.

This impressive aqueduct, built on orders of Herod the Great, carried water from a spring some four miles away to his new port city of Caesarea.

PART I | **THE WORLD OF JESUS**

The Gospels only refer to King Herod in the context of the events surrounding Jesus' birth. But even after the death of the king, his reign would throw a long shadow over the region of Galilee, with significant consequences for Jesus and his ministry. Ironically, though Herod was appointed by the Romans to be "King of the Jews," he himself was not of Jewish origin.

His family hailed from Idumea, a territory referred to as "Edom" in the Hebrew Scriptures. It is roughly equivalent to today's Negev desert and southern Jordan. It was still ruled by the Seleucid Empire when in 125 B.C.E. the Hasmonean king John Hyrcanus conquered the territory and annexed it to the Jewish kingdom. Idumea, however, was largely pagan; its religion was probably an amalgamation of local deities and Greek gods introduced by the Seleucids.

John Hyrcanus decided to change that. He made the unprecedented decision to convert the Idumean population to Judaism. This is how Herod's family became outwardly Jewish, though their ethnicity was Idumean and their family cult was most likely pagan. Herod himself would later show little interest in Jewish cultic practice or the Jewish Law, and instead preferred to surround himself with the trappings of Greek paganism.

As we saw, Herod's father, an Idumean nobleman named Antipater, was serving in the Hasmonean administration when the death of Queen Alexandra plunged the nation into civil war, forcing Antipater to look for new allies. Though he supported the claim of Hyrcanus II to the throne, Antipater recognized that the arrival of Pompey was a key opportunity to advance his family's fortunes. He sought an audience with the Roman general and pledged his full support for Rome's ambitions. Pompey, surprised and pleased by this demonstration of allegiance, invited Antipater into his influential circle and introduced him to Julius Caesar. Several years later, when Caesar was pursuing the fugitive Pompey to Egypt, Antipater showed his loyalty by coming to the aid of Caesar's forces in Alexandria.

Antipater's efforts paid off. Caesar granted him Roman citizenship and appointed him as *epitropos,* a position comparable to that of prime minister, under the new vassal ruler, Hyrcanus II. Hyrcanus, however, was growing increasingly feeble, so Antipater ruled the former Hasmonean kingdom in all but name. He immediately solidified his family's position by appointing his two sons, Phasael and Herod, as provincial governors. Phasael, the elder, received the heartland of Judea and Perea, while Herod was put in charge of the northern province of Galilee.

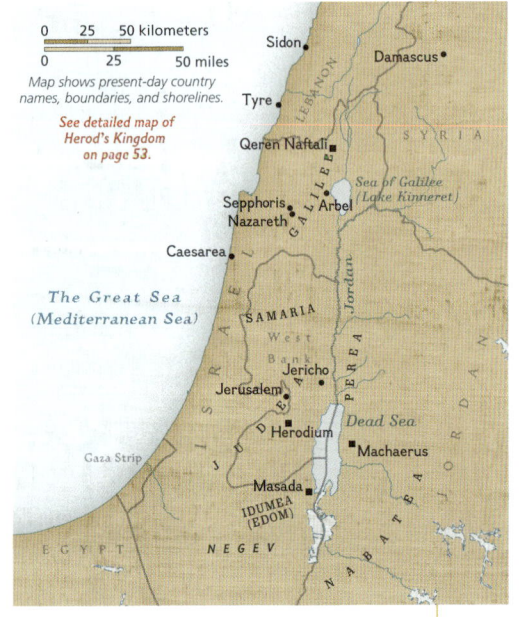

Herod and the Roman Civil War

The reign of Antipater's patron Julius Caesar was cut short by his assassination in 44 B.C.E., which precipitated the Roman Civil War. His death was a major setback for Jews throughout the realm. Caesar had granted the Jewish nation a range of exemptions, including the need to provide troops, as other vassal nations were expected to do. Many thousands of Roman Jews mourned at his bier as his body was surrendered to the flames. Antipater and his sons were now forced to choose sides between the warring factions in Rome: the aristocratic faction, led by the assassins Brutus and Cassius; or the popular party represented by Octavian and Mark Antony. Antipater and Herod chose to side with the former—perhaps because Cassius was in closer proximity to Judea, having established himself in Syria in order to raise new legions to defeat Mark Antony.

To do so, Cassius needed cash—lots of it. Josephus claims that Cassius charged Antipater with raising the exorbitant sum of 700 silver talents. The talent, which

Today, the remains of the great breakwater that once sheltered ships at Caesarea's magnificent Sebastos harbor are just visible below the waterline.

PART I | THE WORLD OF JESUS

This aerial view of the Masada stronghold shows the three levels of Herod's spectacular Suspended Palace, which included a reception hall, a peristyle court, and a bath complex.

Even today, Galilee's legendary fecundity can be glimpsed in countless fields (opposite) filled with wildflowers, sustained by rainfall in winter and underground aquifers in summer.

in Matthew's Gospel appears in Jesus' parable of the three servants (Matthew 25:14-30), was roughly worth around $9,000 in modern currency. In other words, Antipater was expected to raise some $6.3 million—a near-impossible task in a country as poor as Palestine. To make sure that all local governors understood what was at stake, Cassius threatened to sell into slavery any official who failed to pay his share.

Herod needed no such incentive; no less an opportunist than his father, he sought to impress Cassius with a huge contribution so as to further ingratiate himself with Rome. However, his province of Galilee was an agricultural region with no appreciable assets such as mines or timber, nor any significant urban centers where concentrations of wealth could be found. What Galilee did have, as Herod had found out, were farmers. These were for the most part subsistence farmers who cultivated just enough to feed their families and pay their taxes. This did not concern Herod; the purpose of governance, in Roman times, was to extract the highest possible tribute while keeping the subjects docile. Herod understood this very well and decided to increase the tax burden so mercilessly that, as Josephus tells us, he was indeed "the first to bring in his share from Galilee."

The Kingdom of Herod the Great

This forceful fund-raising campaign did not endear Herod to the Galilean people. Josephus suggests that his tax regime prompted a revolt among the Galilean peasantry, led by a man named Hezekiah, who operated close to the Syrian border in northern Galilee. Josephus, who wrote on the behest of the Flavian Imperial House, invariably refers to such resistance movements as "bandits." It is possible, however, that Hezekiah was not an outlaw but a local nobleman, a member of the rural landed gentry who owed their wealth, title, and lands to the Hasmonean dynasty. Many of these noblemen remained loyal to the Aristobulus faction and opposed to the regime of Hyrcanus and Antipater, who openly collaborated with the Roman occupation.

Using his militia, Herod was able to track down Hezekiah and his followers. Bloody clashes erupted at Sepphoris, Arbel, and a fortress in northern Galilee, possibly Qeren Naftali. Hezekiah was arrested, brought before a sham tribunal, and summarily put to death. This act lit the fuse of the simmering resentment against Antipater's family, and an outcry followed. The mothers of the men whom Herod had put to death began to stage daily demonstrations in the Temple, demanding that Herod be held to account. Indeed, under the prevailing laws every Jew accused of a capital crime, even as grave as rebellion, was entitled to a trial before the Council of the Sanhedrin in Jerusalem. The protest grew so vocal that even the weak Hyrcanus could not ignore it, and he ordered Herod to Jerusalem to stand trial. Herod, however, had by now so thoroughly ingratiated himself with Rome that the Roman governor of Syria, whose jurisdiction included Judea, made it known that Herod should be acquitted. Herod was indeed freed—but not before one of his accusers prophesied, "This man whom you now release will one day punish both you and the king."

Herod did not return to Galilee, where local resentment against his rule was intense. Instead, he fled to Damascus, where he enjoyed the protection of the Roman governor. Nevertheless, Herod's brief rule in Galilee—including the levy of exorbitant taxes and the killing of Hezekiah and his men—left a deep-seated enmity between the Herodians and the Galilean population that would last well into the ministry of Jesus.

PART I | **THE WORLD OF JESUS**

The Parthians Invade

The Roman Civil War did not produce the outcome that Antipater's family had anticipated. Mark Antony and Octavian defeated Cassius at the Battle of Philippi in 42 B.C.E., and Herod realized he had supported the wrong side. He promptly began to shower Antony with bribes, which was a wise move, given that several Jewish delegations were besieging Antony to do away with the Antipater clan in Judea altogether. In the end, it was neither the Romans nor the Jews who brought about Antipater's fall—it was the Parthians.

Antigonus, the son of the Hasmonean prince Aristobulus, had persuaded the Parthians to back his claim for the throne. In 40 B.C.E., the Parthians invaded Judea, besieged Jerusalem, and successfully captured the old king Hyrcanus as well as Herod's brother, Phasael. Herod and his family—including one of his ten wives, the Hasmonean princess Mariamne, and their children—escaped Jerusalem and made their way to a Hasmonean fortress on a mountain near the Dead Sea, known as Masada. Herod left them there and immediately set sail for Rome, where he pleaded his case before Mark Antony. Invited to address the Roman Senate, a rare honor, Herod was able to convince the senators that the Parthian invasion was a direct challenge to Roman sovereignty in southwest Asia. His oratory and genteel manners impressed the Romans. Moreover, his timing was impeccable. Rome, weary from years of civil war, craved stability in the Eastern provinces. The invasion of Judea had brought the Parthians, Rome's most implacable archenemy, uncomfortably close to the empire's principal grain supply in Egypt. Herod and his family had proven their loyalty to Rome; there was little doubt that Herod would be a loyal client king, who could keep his nation in check and who would provide a buffer against Parthian interests.

That most of the Jews in Palestine loathed Herod was not a matter that troubled the Roman Senate. The Romans did not practice democracy, nor did they expect their vassal kings to do so. Thus, with Octavian and Antony's blessing, the Senate not only voted Herod "King of the Jews" and heir to the Hasmonean Kingdom, but they also granted him a Roman army to drive the Parthians out and to secure his throne in Jerusalem.

Herod and his Roman overlords faced a number of obstacles, however. The usurper-king Antigonus, the heir to the Hasmonean throne, still controlled much of Galilee, Samaria, and Judea, with the support of Parthian forces. Further, Herod's brother Phasael had been murdered, and Herod's family was still at Masada, which by this time had come under siege by the Parthians.

> AS SOON AS HEROD HAD CAPTURED JERUSALEM, HE CARRIED OFF ALL THE ROYAL ORNAMENTS AND STOLE FROM WEALTHY MEN WHATEVER HE COULD; AND ALL THIS SILVER AND GOLD HE GAVE TO ANTONY AND HIS FRIENDS.
>
> JOSEPHUS, *ANTIQUITIES OF THE JEWS*
> *Circa 95 C.E.*

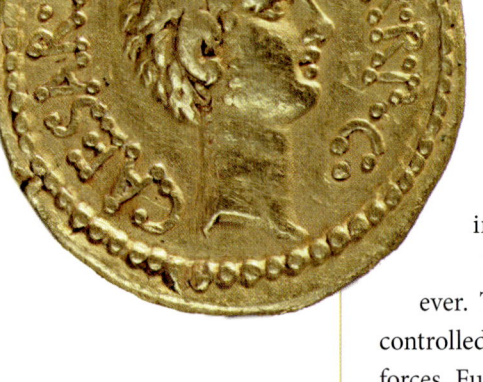

The Kingdom of Herod the Great

It would take Herod nearly three years of hard fighting before he could make his way to Jerusalem and attack the city. Along the way, he was bitterly opposed in Galilee, not only by the forces of Antigonus but also by "bands of bandits"—Josephus' favorite epithet denoting popular resistance—who tried to prevent his return. Many of these guerilla forces were hiding with their families in caves carved in the soft limestone rock of the Arbel Heights, close to the Sea of Galilee. To flush them out, Herod lowered cages filled with his soldiers from the top of the mountain, and as soon as these came abreast of the cave opening, the soldiers attacked with javelins, grappling hooks, and fire. Whoever was found in the cave—man, woman, or child—was massacred. Thus, Herod gave notice that he had returned to Galilee; this time, he was determined to stay.

By 37 B.C.E., Herod's control of Roman Judea was complete. For the next 33 years, he would rule with an iron fist, enjoying greater autonomy and latitude than any other Roman vassal king in the region. He was, however, sensitive to the fact that to many Jews he was a foreigner. During the siege of Jerusalem, Antigonus had loudly denounced Herod "as a pseudo-Jewish Idumean unworthy of the crown." This touched a nerve; the Book of Deuteronomy expressly stated only "one from among you brethren shall you set as king over you; you may not put a foreigner over you." (Deuteronomy 17:15)

The new king tried to overcome these handicaps by highlighting his marriage

Around 37 B.C.E., Herod's troops scoured these caves in the Arbel Heights to flush out resistance fighters loyal to Antigonus, heir to the Hasmonean throne.

This aureus (opposite), a gold coin that served as Rome's most valuable currency unit, was struck in 43 B.C.E. to commemorate the Triumvirate of Octavian (shown), Antony, and Lepidus.

PART I | THE WORLD OF JESUS

to the Hasmonean princess Mariamne, granddaughter of Aristobulus II. The marriage had the additional benefit of sidelining Mariamne's brother, Aristobulus III, who was the next heir in line for the Hasmonean throne. Herod was also keenly aware of the Jewish aversion of Roman coins, given the biblical prohibition of "graven images." All of the coins struck during his reign for use in Jewish areas avoid the usual portrait of the Roman emperor, or any other representation of living beings.

Yet Herod also wholeheartedly confessed himself a loyal servant of Rome, and he eagerly followed Augustus's lead in "Hellenizing" Palestine through vast urban construction projects in the Greco-Roman mold. For Herod, Hellenization and Judaism were compatible rather than antithetical.

Herod's Fortresses

First, Herod created a defensive bulwark around his kingdom, anchored by a number of fortresses. Several of these fortifications were built on top of prominent hills or cliffs, such as Masada—where Phasael, Mariamne, and her children had found refuge—or the Herodion, which likewise was perched on a high hill. Both of these fortresses were expanded to include a lavish palace complex so they

The Herodion, about seven miles south of Jerusalem, was built by Herod the Great between 24 and 15 B.C.E. to serve as his palace and mausoleum.

This diagram (opposite) shows how the Herodion, built on top of a volcano-like mound, included a fortress anchored by towers, a mausoleum, and a luxurious palace complex that was accessible via a monumental stairway.

The Kingdom of Herod the Great

A fragment from a monumental frieze from Caesarea reveals the sheer artistry of Herod's builders and sculptors, steeped in the art of Rome's Early Imperial Period.

could serve not only as Herod's holiday residences but also as a place of refuge in times of trouble.

The Masada complex was expanded with large cisterns to catch rainwater—both to serve as drinking water and to fill the elaborate Roman-style bathing complex Herod built on the site. On the north side, Herod created a "suspended palace" on three levels precariously perched on stepped cliffs, offering the king and his guests breathtaking views of the Judean Hills and the Dead Sea.

The equally spectacular Herodion, some eight miles south of Jerusalem, also exploited the natural contours of its location, in this case a 197-foot-high, volcano-like hill. During construction, workers filled in the hillsides with earth and rock to create the peculiar cone-shaped, truncated form that still exists today. "At the base of the hill," Josephus wrote, "there are pleasure grounds of truly astonishing dimensions, in part because of the way in which water, which is lacking in that place, is brought in from a great distance and at great expense." Another palatial fortress was built on the other side of the Dead Sea, in today's Jordan, on top of the remains of the Hasmonean fortress of Machaerus. This region was called Perea in New Testament times, and the Machaerus stronghold would soon become an important location in the story of John the Baptist.

Herod's Urban Projects

With his kingdom thus secured by a ring of defensive palaces, Herod could turn to beautifying his realm. During his remaining 30 years on the throne, he initiated building projects on a scale that had never been seen before in the Levant. The first of these was the creation of a vast, state-of-the-art harbor along the Mediterranean coast. On the surface, the project made sense;

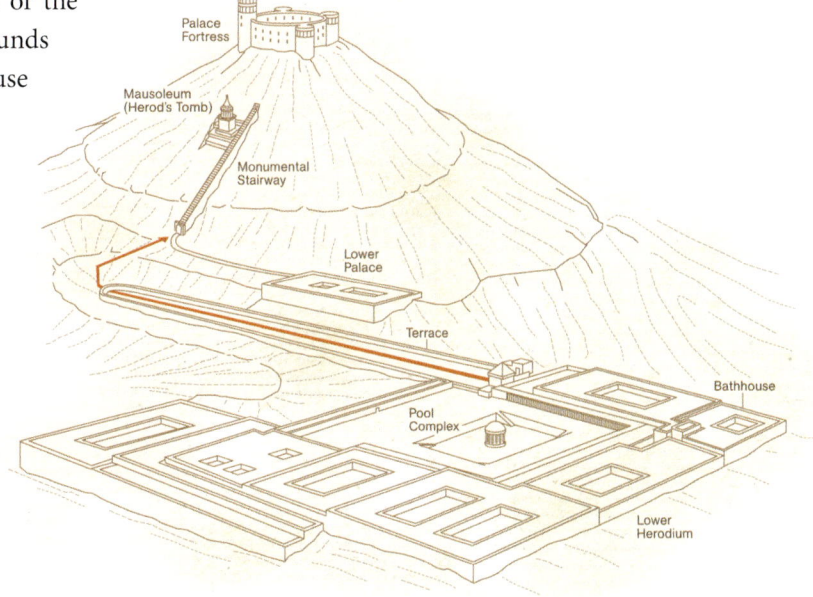

THE CITY AND PORT OF CAESAREA

In building the port of Caesarea, Herod relied on the most talented Roman designers and engineers. Since there was no existing dock, his architects built two vast breakwaters equipped with sluice gates, which extended some 1,600 feet into the Mediterranean and were long enough to accommodate multiple cargo ships. Recent underwater excavations have shown that the architects accomplished this feat through the use of hydraulic concrete (mortar mixed with volcanic sand, pumice, and lime), which was poured *in situ* in large, pre-positioned wooden crates placed on the sea bottom—a procedure not unlike our modern use of concrete. Equally impressive was the city of Caesarea itself, which was laid out in the familiar Roman grid pattern and equipped with a sewage system, a theater, a forum, a hippodrome for chariot races, and the inevitable Roman bath complex. Following Augustus's renovation of Rome, most of these structures were encased in white marble and surrounded by elegant colonnades—"a city in white stone," as Josephus put it. To supply this new city with water, Herod ordered the construction of a vast aqueduct complex; this engineering marvel brought sparkling mountain water from Mount Carmel, some ten miles away. Herod also built a large temple dedicated to Augustus Caesar and Rome, as was expected of a loyal vassal. This did not raise the ire of the local population since during Herod's rule, Caesarea was substantially a pagan rather than a Jewish city. In the decades to come, however, that would change. As Josephus attests, on the eve of the Jewish War in 66 C.E., Roman soldiers massacred many thousands of Jews in the city.

The breakwater complex of Sebastos harbor, a major feat of engineering, once ended in a magnificent lighthouse.

The Kingdom of Herod the Great

This reconstruction of the port of Sebastos in Caesarea shows both the lighthouse and the long quays, at which multiple ships could be loaded and offloaded simultaneously.

the regions of Judea, Samaria, and Galilee had never had a major, industrial-size harbor, which is why most of their trade—such as it was—was funneled through foreign ports including Tyre and Sidon. Then again, Palestine never had a reason for a large port, for it had never produced much agricultural surplus. Under Herod, that was going to change.

The new harbor consisted of a newly designed city, built on the location of an older anchorage known as Strabo's Tower. Herod named the city Caesarea (in honor of Octavian Caesar and his adoptive father, Julius), and called the port complex Sebastos, likewise dedicated to the Roman Emperor ("Sebastos" is the Greek version of Augustus). The Gospels do not record Jesus ever visiting Caesarea, but his disciples Peter, Philip, and Paul did, as described in the Book of Acts of the Apostles.

In Jericho, known for its mild climate even during the winter, Herod built a pleasure palace equipped with every luxury known at his time. Spring water from the nearby Wadi Qelt was channeled to provide water for lavish gardens, forests of palm trees, Roman-style baths, and even a large swimming pool. Many of these facilities were decorated with intricate mosaic floors. Nor was Herod's fondness for pagan luxury limited to Caesarea, Jericho, or any of the other cities

PART I | THE WORLD OF JESUS

he either built or renovated in the Hellenistic style. Right in the heart of Jerusalem, the king built a theater, a hippodrome, and an amphitheater, designed for "contests of various kinds, including those featuring men fighting wild animals," as Josephus tells us, "which greatly offended the Jews." Herod also erected for himself a magnificent palace decorated in gold and precious stones, in the Upper City of Jerusalem. Though very few remains have been found, scholars speculate that it contained two opposite buildings, each equipped with banquet halls, baths, and bedrooms for Herod's vast entourage.

For some Jews, the blatant idolatry and ostentatious paganism of Herod's conceits were too much to bear. A conspiracy was hatched to kill Herod during one of the public performances in his newly built theater. The plot was exposed, and the conspirators—including the informer—were literally cut to pieces and thrown to the dogs.

> IN THE 18TH YEAR OF HIS REIGN, HEROD STARTED TO ENLARGE AND RECONSTRUCT THE TEMPLE AT HIS OWN EXPENSE, WHICH HE KNEW WOULD BE HIS GREATEST ENTERPRISE.
>
> JOSEPHUS, *ANTIQUITIES OF THE JEWS*
> *Circa 95 C.E.*

THE SECOND TEMPLE

Herod may have felt that with so much of the nation's treasure spent on pagan monuments, a conciliatory gesture to his Jewish subjects was in order. If this is true, then the gesture was a grand one, indeed: His focus was the Jerusalem Temple. The first Temple was built in the time of Solomon, but it had been demolished by the Neo-Babylonian king Nebuchadnezzar in 586 B.C.E. Seventy years later, it was rebuilt, as the books of Haggai and Zechariah in the Hebrew Scriptures attest, with support of the Persian king Cyrus the Great. This is why historians refer to the period between 515 B.C.E. and 70 C.E. as the Second Temple Period.

During the last two centuries before the birth of Jesus, the Temple had become the center of Jewish worship. The priestly community, including the chief priests described in the Gospels, had been in command of the sacrificial cult since the second century B.C.E. This did not mean that the Temple staff consisted solely of priests, since daily operations were managed by hundreds of officials, including laymen. But in the time of Jesus, overall control of the Temple cult was certainly in the hands of the Sadducees, an aristocratic élite that occupied the finest mansions in the Upper City. Much of their wealth derived from the fact that the Temple treasury, or *korban*—into which flowed the tithes from Jewish communities all through the empire—also served as a quasi central bank. Now that the collection of the Temple tax was protected and facilitated by the Romans, massive amounts of money poured into the coffers of the Temple, bolstering the power of the Sadducees—which may explain some of the animus toward the Sadducees in the Gospels.

Herod, too, had allowed the Sadducees to retain control of Temple operations, but he soon began to import priestly families from Babylonia from which

KINGDOM OF HEROD THE GREAT

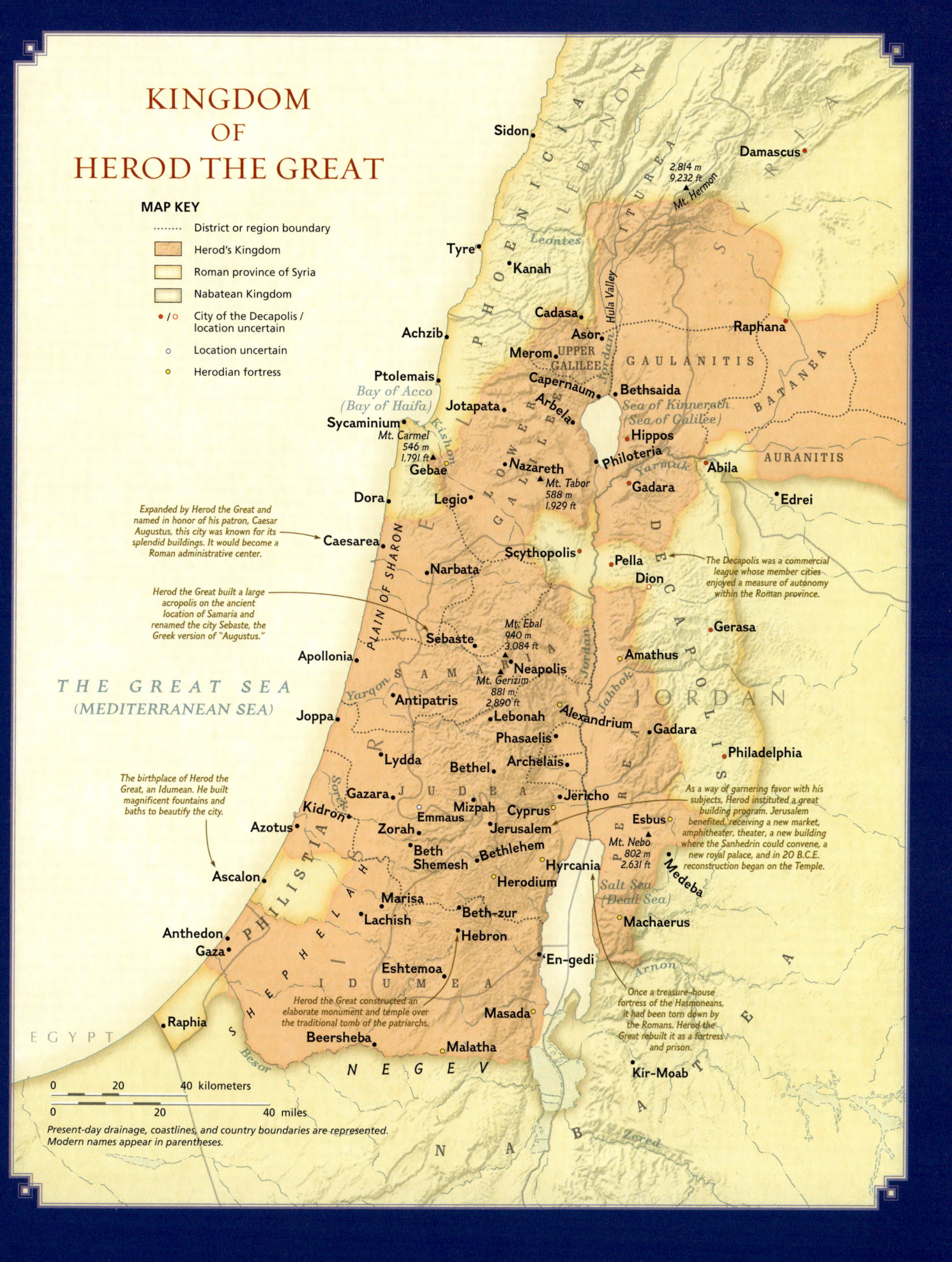

MAP KEY

- ········· District or region boundary
- ▨ Herod's Kingdom
- ▨ Roman province of Syria
- ▨ Nabatean Kingdom
- ● / ○ City of the Decapolis / location uncertain
- ○ Location uncertain
- ● Herodian fortress

Expanded by Herod the Great and named in honor of his patron, Caesar Augustus, this city was known for its splendid buildings. It would become a Roman administrative center.

Herod the Great built a large acropolis on the ancient location of Samaria and renamed the city Sebaste, the Greek version of "Augustus."

The birthplace of Herod the Great, an Idumean. He built magnificent fountains and baths to beautify the city.

The Decapolis was a commercial league whose member cities enjoyed a measure of autonomy within the Roman province.

As a way of garnering favor with his subjects, Herod instituted a great building program. Jerusalem benefited, receiving a new market, amphitheater, theater, a new building where the Sanhedrin could convene, a new royal palace, and in 20 B.C.E. reconstruction began on the Temple.

Herod the Great constructed an elaborate monument and temple over the traditional tomb of the patriarchs.

Once a treasure-house fortress of the Hasmoneans, it had been torn down by the Romans. Herod the Great rebuilt it as a fortress and prison.

THE GREAT SEA (MEDITERRANEAN SEA)

Scale: 0–40 kilometers / 0–40 miles

Present-day drainage, coastlines, and country boundaries are represented. Modern names appear in parentheses.

PART I | THE WORLD OF JESUS

This sixth-century C.E. mosaic depicts the parable of the Pharisee and the Publican in the St. Apollinare Nuovo in Ravenna.

SADDUCEES AND PHARISEES

Virtually all that we know about the Sadducees (or *Tsaddiqim* in Hebrew) is derived from the Gospels, Josephus, and later Pharisaic texts, which all view this party with a certain negative bias. The root of the word "Sadducee" is possibly derived from the name Zadok, Solomon's high priest. Many scholars assume that in the time of Jesus, the Sadducees (including, presumably, the high priests and chief priests) were in control of Temple operations. They were a conservative faction, which did not accept any Scripture beyond the Torah or Law—including the Book of the Prophets—and rejected any idea of an afterlife or the immortality of the soul. The Pharisees (derived from the Hebrew *perushim,* or separated ones) were a group composed of both priests and pious laymen who were passionately devoted to the application of the Jewish Law in everyday life, rather than just within the Temple precinct. Whereas the Sadducees (naturally) emphasized the sacrificial cult as the principal redemptive activity, the Pharisees felt that Jews should please God in everything they did. The Pharisaic concern for purity, so often maligned in the Gospels, was actually an attempt to transfer the priestly rules governing purity from the Temple to the home. Whereas the Sadducees considered the written texts of the Hebrew Scriptures a closed book, the Pharisees continued to debate and interpret the application of Scripture to everyday life—a corpus of wisdom and exegesis that became known as the Oral Law. The Pharisees also accepted the idea of the immortality of the soul, as well as the belief in the resurrection after Judgment Day—two concepts that would return in the teachings of Jesus.

he could appoint high officials—including the high priest—whose loyalty to their benefactor would be unquestioned. By so doing, Herod deliberately weakened the position of the existing Jewish élite, including many who owed their wealth or influence to the old Hasmonean dynasty. One such priestly family, the house of the high priest Ananas, was particularly favored by Herod. His son-in-law, a man named Caiaphas, would soon sit in judgment of Jesus.

The Expansion of the Temple Complex

Having thus brought the Temple operations under his control, Herod decided to expand the modest Second Temple into one of the largest sanctuaries built in Antiquity, second only to the temple complex at Karnak in Egypt. The Roman Empire had many elaborate religious centers, most of which were Greek in origin, such as the magnificent Artemisium in Ephesus, the Acropolis in Athens, and the equally elaborate Apollo complex in Didyma (today's Didim, Turkey). Most of these shrines featured a massive temple supported by a tall peristyle, or colonnade, and crowned by a plethora of sculptures and bas-reliefs. Herod could not follow this Greek paradigm because the Second Temple itself was a rather modest structure of the Syrian-Phoenician *megaron* type. Consequently, Herod turned the Hellenistic model of a major temple inside out; the large peristyle, surmounted by Corinthian columns and moldings, was now used to create a vast outdoor enclosure, an esplanade large enough to hold thousands of worshippers with the Temple at its center. Around this enclosure rose scores of subsidiary buildings, including special chambers for a variety of functions and a large covered gallery known as the Royal Stoa. This basilica-type structure served as the seat of the Sanhedrin, while its open arcades offered shelter for a range of administrative and civic activities, in imitation of other such *stoae* in the Roman Empire.

There was only one problem: The Temple did not stand on level ground but on top of a hill (either Mount Moriah or Mount Zion; the precise identification is disputed). To create the large forecourt that Herod had in mind, his architects had to turn the hill into a floating platform, supported by massive arches and retaining walls towering high above the Lower City of Jerusalem. One of these retaining walls still exists: the so-called Western Wall, which today is the holiest place in Judaism. Covering no less than one-sixth the area of the city, this vast esplanade was accessible through two floating staircases on the west, each

This model of the Second Temple of Jerusalem reveals the ornate facade, adorned with gold, as described by the Jewish historian Josephus.

PART I | THE WORLD OF JESUS

supported by arches. A small portion of one of these arches, known as Robinson's Arch, is still visible today, as are the monumental stairs that led to the Double Gate on the south.

Construction on the Temple expansion was begun in 22 B.C.E. and was still ongoing when Jesus visited the Temple prior to his Passion. So ambitious was Herod's design that the Temple complex was only finished in 62 C.E., as corroborated by coins found recently underneath the old Herodian walls. It then stood for a mere eight years—until its destruction at the hands of the Roman general Titus near the end of the Jewish War.

Herod's Source of Wealth

If indeed Herod had hoped that the expansion of the Temple would endear him to his Jewish subjects, he was soon disappointed. Outside of his immediate entourage and the urban élites who profited by his reign, the king was heartily despised by the vast majority of the Jewish population. Part of the reason was the manner in which Herod obtained the large funds to finance his zeal for building. As noted before, Palestine possessed no natural or mineral wealth. As Josephus regretfully noted, "We neither inhabit a maritime country, nor do we delight in merchandise . . . having a fruitful country for our habitation, we take pains in cultivating that only." Herod did receive revenues from several monopolies he had leased from Queen Cleopatra of Egypt, such as the extraction of asphalt from the Dead Sea for use in shipbuilding, and various plantations near Jericho. The king also profited from copper mines on Cyprus, which he leased from Rome. But none of these could possibly yield the funds that Herod needed for his ambitious building projects.

The only resource that Herod's kingdom had in abundance was its fertile valleys, particularly the agricultural regions in Galilee. As we have seen, while serving as Galilee's governor under Hyrcanus, Herod had imposed a heavy tax on the region's peasant farmers to help equip Cassius's armies. When it came time for Mark Antony to face Octavian's legions, he too turned to Herod for assistance in raising sufficient forces for the fateful Battle of Actium. Herod, says Josephus, was in a position to do so because "the countryside had been yielding him rich crops." Now that he was king, Herod resolved to pursue this policy to the full. Galilee was to be exploited in order to fund improvements in all other parts in the kingdom.

Traditionally, a Galilean farmer was expected to pay taxes (usually in kind) to two constituencies: the Temple and the secular authority governing the land. According to Scripture, the land of Israel was God's land; the

HEROD'S TOMB

Josephus tells us that Herod was buried in his palatial fortress of Herodion. The fortress proper was excavated between 1963 and 1967 by Virgilio Corbo, but in the years that followed, excavators searched in vain for Herod's tomb. In May 2007, a team of Israeli archaeologists led by Ehud Netzer announced that they had located a tomb halfway up the peculiar, conelike shape of the hill. They uncovered "a palatial resort, a sort of country club in modern terms," which featured a large pool for both swimming and small-boat sailing. They also discovered a monumental stairway, which led to an elaborate mausoleum—a circular structure surrounded by 18 columns, not unlike the so-called Tomb of Absalom in Jerusalem's Kidron Valley. Nearby, three sarcophagi were found; one of these, carved from pink Jerusalem limestone, may have contained Herod's body. Ehud Netzer returned to the Herodion in 2010 for further excavations, but he injured his neck in a fall. He died two days later.

The Kingdom of Herod the Great

Israelites were merely tenant farmers, tilling the land at the Lord's pleasure. Therefore, it was only proper that a share of the harvest should be returned to the rightful owner, in this case the Lord's representatives on Earth—the priesthood and their priestly servants, the Levites. The Book of Numbers states that a tenth of the harvest was to be given to the Levites, including "the grain of the threshing floor and the fullness of the wine press." (Numbers 18:27) Only once every seven years, during the so-called Sabbatical year, were farmers exempt from paying the tithe, since the land was supposed to lie fallow and enjoy "a sabbath of complete rest." (Leviticus 25:4) In addition, farmers were expected to pay an annual Temple tax of one half-shekel. This temple tax was collected from every male Jew, including from Jewish communities throughout the empire.

But a third and most onerous tax was claimed by the secular authorities—whoever happened to rule Judea, Samaria, and Galilee at any given time. During the Assyrian occupation, for example, Galilean farmers owed their taxes to the Assyrian province of Megiddo. The Persians extracted taxes from Galilee through the subprovince of the fifth Persian satrapy known as Abar nahara (Beyond the [Euphrates] River), whereas the Ptolemies in Alexandria subjected Galilee to a

In May 2007, a team of archaeologists uncovered this mausoleum complex on the slopes of the Herodion, including a pink sarcophagus that may have contained the body of Herod the Great.

This inscription (opposite) on a stone jar found near the west corner of the Temple walls refers to a sacrifice, probably involving two doves as depicted below the text.

PART I | **THE WORLD OF JESUS**

Even today, farmers use the time-honored technique of tossing the harvested stalks in the air to allow the breeze to separate the heavier grain from the chaff.

The parable of the "Vineyard and Tenants" is illustrated in this 15th-century illuminated manuscript of Flemish origin (opposite).

hyparchy named Galila. After the Seleucid king Antiochus III defeated Ptolemy V, the Seleucid Empire absorbed Galilee in yet another administrative unit, known as the eparchy of Samaria.

When Galilee was conquered by the Hasmonean kings and annexed to the Jewish nation, the identity of the tax agent changed yet again—this time, to the Hasmonean House in Jerusalem. In every instance, the Galilean farmer dutifully paid taxes, regardless of whether the king of the land resided in Persepolis, Alexandria, Damascus, or Jerusalem.

Matters changed drastically under King Herod. Although Herod surrounded himself with the trappings of an autonomous monarch, he was still very much a vassal king expected to pay a hefty tribute to Rome. As a consequence, he doubled the secular tax layer on his subjects: Instead of paying taxes to *either* a foreign ruler *or* a Jewish king, Galileans now saw themselves compelled to support *both*. According to Richard Horsley, the peasants of Galilee were now faced with "*three* layers of payments due: taxes to Herod, tribute to Rome, as well as

The Kingdom of Herod the Great

the tithes and offerings to Temple and Priesthood." Were this not enough, Herod also developed other ways to squeeze the Galilean peasantry: a salt tax, fishing polls, custom duties for the shipment of produce from one region to the other, and taxes on other sources of "manufacturing," notably the production of salted fish. Scholars such as E. P. Sanders have estimated that as much as 28 to 33 percent of a farmer's harvest was used for meeting the combined demands of tithing and taxes; Horsley believes it may have been as high as 40 percent. This stands in sharp contrast to tax rates elsewhere in the Roman Empire, such as Egypt, were peasants paid taxes of approximately 9 to 12 percent of the harvest.

The Economic Impact on Galilee's Farmers

Given the meager yields of a family plot and the frequency of droughts and other natural disasters, the new tax burden in Galilee was quite unsustainable. This, of course, was precisely what Herod had anticipated, because to stave off the inevitable—foreclosure of land to the tax collector—peasants began to borrow, and borrow heavily. They essentially mortgaged their harvests so as to feed their families. The impact of these policies would reverberate for decades and permeate Jesus' teachings. In the Gospel of Luke, we learn of debtors who owed their creditors the staggering amount of "fifty measures of oil" or "fourscore measures of wheat," suggesting interest rates ranging between 25 and 50 percent (Luke 16:7). Such extortionate terms were all but designed to bring the peasant to impoverishment, shortening the time it took for the landlord to foreclose on the poor man's land.

Once these small, ancestral plots were confiscated, they were either sold or gifted to the local landed gentry, or to priests and other high officials in Herod's inner circle, with one specific goal in mind: to create large, single-purpose estates that could yield produce of sufficient quantity and quality for export. The steward who typically managed such an estate (referred to as a *phronimos* or *oikonomos* in the Gospels, for example Luke 12:42, 16:1, and 16:8) had, unlike the Galilean peasant, a keen appreciation of marketplace forces in the Roman Empire. That was the reason Herod had created the port of Caesarea: Without surplus goods to trade within the Roman global economy, there was no point in building a large harbor.

The rapidly escalating tax burden had a devastating impact on the social fabric of Galilee, and it explains one of the main themes of the Gospels: the widening divide between rich and poor, and the masses of dispossessed peasantry that came to cleave to Jesus' teachings. His parables are filled with "landlords," as well as the "stewards" who manage large estates on their behalf. One parable in the Gospel of

PART I | THE WORLD OF JESUS

The British Pre-Raphaelite artist John William Waterhouse (1849–1917) painted this portrait of Mariamne after being condemned to death by her husband, King Herod the Great, for infidelity.

> PEOPLE ACCUSED THEIR ENEMIES OF PLOTS, SO THAT THE KING WOULD KILL THEM; THERE WAS A GENERAL CLIMATE OF TERROR.
>
> JOSEPHUS, *ANTIQUITIES OF THE JEWS*
> *Circa 95 C.E.*

Luke tells the story of "the land of a rich man," which had "produced abundantly." "What should I do, for I have no place to store my crops?" the rich man wondered. He decided to pull down all his barns so as to build larger ones. With all that wealth, he would be able to "relax, eat, drink, be merry." But God said to him, "You fool! This very night your life is being demanded of you. And the things you have prepared, whose will they be?" (Luke 12:16-20)

The story of the wicked tenants in Mark and Matthew indicates that Jesus was familiar with the way in which the payment of taxes or interest was enforced. Landlords would sometimes send slaves as inspectors at the beginning of the harvest season, lest any crops escape their surveillance. In Jesus' parable, the unfortunate inspectors are beaten by the tenant farmers "and sent away empty-handed," which reveals the deep resentment these farmers felt toward the owners of their land (Luke 20:10). Likewise, it is not difficult to understand the loathing with which publicans or tax collectors are received in the Gospels. Galilee, in short, was squeezed and exploited like any other colonial possession.

THE END OF HEROD'S REIGN

Herod responded to the growing resentment of his subjects by creating a police state. Officials and citizens were ordered to swear an oath of allegiance to Herod; large public gatherings were outlawed. Everyone arousing even the slightest suspicion was closely watched by Herod's secret police. Citizens were encouraged to inform on one another; "even in the cities and on the open roads, there were men who spied on those who met together," says Josephus. Dissidents were arrested and sent to Herod's fortresses, where they were executed without trial. The constant threat of plots even penetrated Herod's family; Antipater, the son of his first wife, openly sought to murder the children of Herod's second wife Mariamne, so as to eliminate them as rivals to the throne. Herod's distrust even turned on his beloved Mariamne, the mother of five of his children. Herod erroneously suspected her of plotting against him and put her on trial, where her own mother appeared as a witness for the prosecution. Mariamne was executed, as was her mother shortly thereafter. Long after his wife's death, Herod would "wander around the palace," says Josephus, "calling for his wife and ordering the servants to bring her to him."

As he grew older, Herod's paranoia increased. He ordered all the "leading men" of Judea to be rounded up and imprisoned in the stadium he'd built in Jerusalem. He then instructed his officers that as soon as his death was announced, the hostages were to be executed. When Herod finally died in March or April in 4 B.C.E, his sister Salome ordered the prisoners in the stadium released.

Around the same time, a young child in Nazareth was just beginning to walk.

The Kingdom of Herod the Great

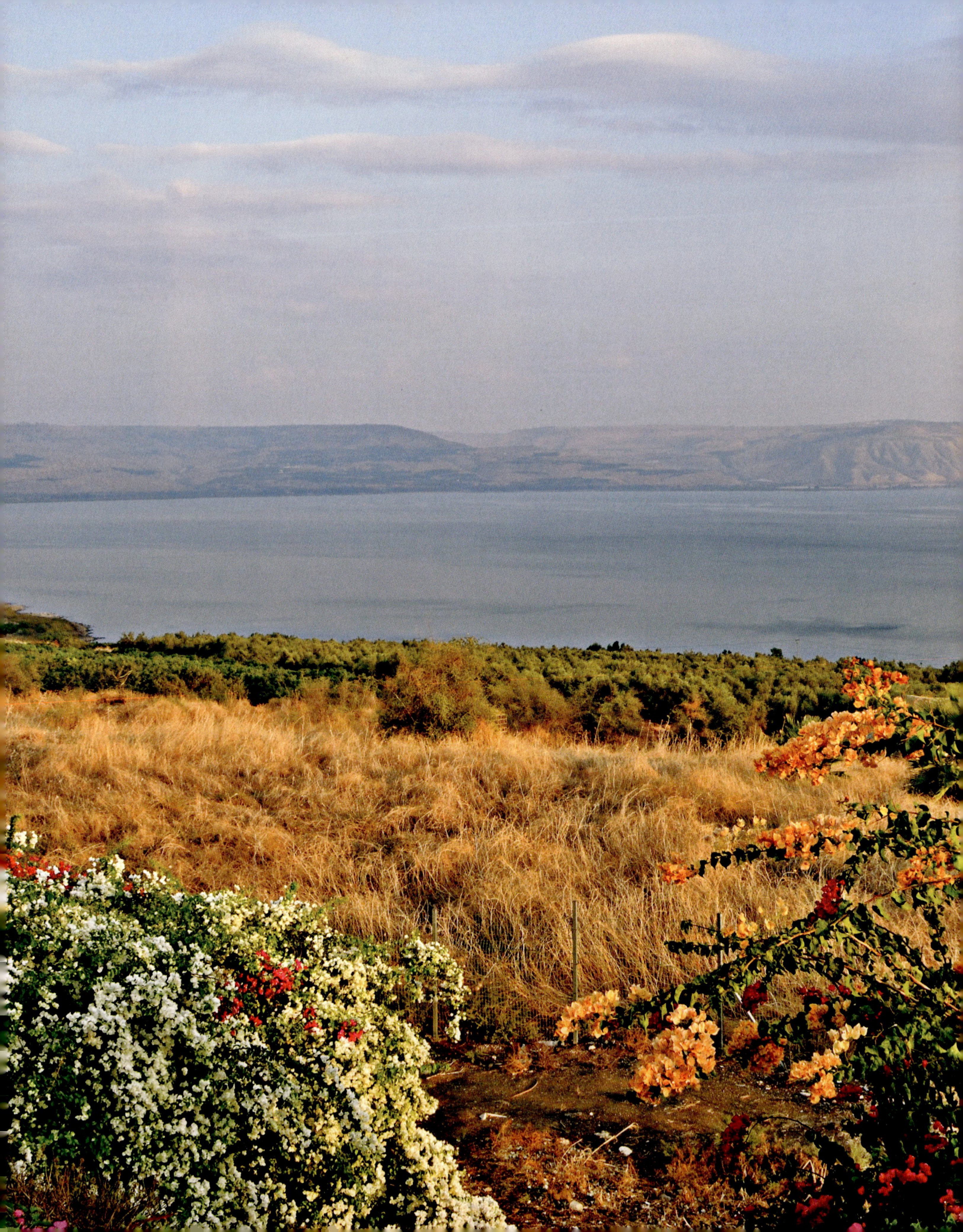

CHAPTER 3

LIFE *in* LOWER GALILEE

LAND OF ZEBULUN,
LAND OF NAPHTALI,
ON THE ROAD
BY THE SEA,
ACROSS THE JORDAN,
GALILEE OF THE GENTILES

Isaiah 9:1

Circa late eighth century B.C.E.

During late March and early April, the hills around the Sea of Galilee are filled with a profusion of spring colors.

PART I | THE WORLD OF JESUS

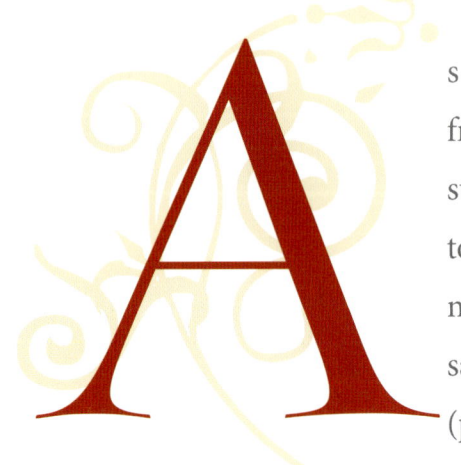

As a social and cultural entity, Galilee had always been different from the heartland of Judea. Its very geography was different, surrounded by mountain ranges on nearly all sides. According to Josephus, Galilee was divided into two sections: Upper (or northern) Galilee and Lower (or southern) Galilee. Upper Galilee, said Josephus, ran from the Litani River in Lebanon to "Bersaba" (possibly Abu Sheba), and from "Meroth" in the west to the Jordan.

It was, and still is, far more rugged than Lower Galilee, with some of its limestone peaks rising as high as 3,000 feet, carved by countless streams and spectacular waterfalls. With an annual rainfall of up to 44 inches per year, the mountains served as the region's principal source of water—which explains Galilee's abundant fecundity.

Below the natural boundary of the HaKerem Valley was Lower Galilee, which according to Josephus ran from the Plain of Ptolemais (or Acco) in the east to Mount Tabor and Beth She'an (or Scythopolis) in the south, and the Sea of Galilee in the west. The Sea of Galilee, shaped in the form of a harp (*kinor* in Hebrew) was known in Scripture as Lake Kinneret (Numbers 34:11). East of this region rose highlands made of basalt, a forbidding element for natural growth, so that most of these hills could stretch for miles without any cultivation other than low-level brush and grass.

In Jesus' time, some terebinth trees and evergreen oak could be glimpsed on the ridges, while the hillsides often teemed with carob brush and mastic trees, or in drier areas, dense clusters of styrax trees. In the northern region, juniper and Lebanese cedar would grow in groves around Mount Meron. Olive trees, a native species, could be found in far greater quantity, specifically in family-tended orchards, where their silvery leaves offered welcome shade to people and animals alike. Olive trees are hardy and could live for a long time, sometimes hundreds of years; Pliny the Elder once referred to a sacred olive tree that was believed to be 1,600 years old. But olive wood is often gnarly and ill suited for fine carpentry.

The geographical contours of Galilee had defined its cultural identity since the earliest days of the Israelite kingdom. Even then, as a northern outpost, it was always surrounded by foreign territory. To the northwest was the Phoenician region of Sidon and Tyre, which in the centuries to come would serve as the main conduit of Hellenistic influence. To the north was the land of Aram-Damascus, later Syria, while to the east lay the territory of Ammon and Moab (later known as Nabatea, today's Jordan). Galilee was thus an enclave

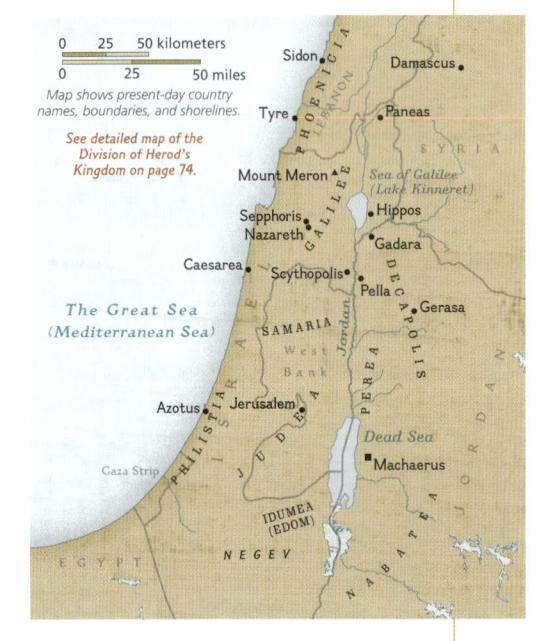

Map shows present-day country names, boundaries, and shorelines.

See detailed map of the Division of Herod's Kingdom on page 74.

of sorts, though it was blessed with access to the Sea of Galilee. This idea of an almost perfect circle of land surrounded by foreign lands may have inspired the root of the word Galilee *(ha-galil)*, a shortening of the Hebrew *galil ha-goyim*, meaning "circle of the peoples."

Galilee in Biblical Times

Galilee was a very attractive area to the tribes of Israel who, according to the Bible, followed Joshua during the entry into the Promised Land. Eventually, the Book of Joshua tells us, four tribes settled in this land. The tribe of Asher was assigned to the area of western Galilee, while the tribe of Zebulun was located in central Galilee, roughly between Carmel and Nazareth, and the tribe of Naphtali settled in eastern Galilee (Joshua 19:24-31). The tribe of Issachar, meanwhile, received the coveted Plain of Esdraelon, also known as the Jezreel Valley; it was by far the most fertile land in Israel, if not the Near East altogether (Joshua 19:17-23).

These remnants of a residential dwelling in Sepphoris, located close to the modern city of Zippori, probably date to the early second century C.E.

PART I | THE WORLD OF JESUS

After the split of Solomon's empire into the Northern Kingdom of Israel and the Southern Kingdom of Judah, the agricultural development of Galilee grew rapidly, actively abetted by the new central government located in Samaria. Even when the Northern Kingdom fell to Assyrian invaders, Galilean farmers were permitted to plow their fields in peace, provided they paid their tribute on time. This situation changed when the new Assyrian king Tiglath-pileser III (r. 745–727 B.C.E.) moved down to annex all of Assyria's vassal lands. The Book of II Kings tells us that the king captured "Kedesh, Hazor, Gilead, and Galilee, [and] all the land of Naphtali," after which the Assyrian host "carried the people captive to Assyria" (II Kings 15:29). So thorough were these deportations that, as recent excavations have shown, Galilee experienced a dramatic drop in population, putting its large swaths of cultivated land at risk. Assyria responded by repopulating the region with Assyrian veterans as well as displaced farmers from other parts of its empire. Thus, says Isaiah, "[The Lord] brought into contempt the land of Zebulun and the land of Naphtali." (Isaiah 9:7)

In this gripping relief from Nimrud, ca 860 B.C.E., Assyrian soldiers impale captured prisoners on stakes.

This eighth-century B.C.E. weight (below) in the form of a lion, excavated at Nimrud, was equal to twice the value of a mina, weighing two pounds, four ounces.

The forced resettlement drastically changed Galilee's demographic character. What had previously been a homogenous nation now became a patchwork of different cultures and languages. Populated by so many foreigners it had truly become, as Matthew wrote, a "Galilee of the Peoples" (Matthew 4:15)—or as Isaiah had put it, *galil goyim*, "Galilee of the Nations" (Isaiah 9:1). During the reign of King Josiah (640–609 B.C.E.), when Israelite control of Galilee was restored, efforts were made to cleanse the nation of all pagan influences, but this respite was brief. Soon, the new Babylonian king Nebuchadnezzar (r. 605–562 B.C.E.) was on the march to capture and destroy Jerusalem; along the way, Galilee was once again annexed, followed by the inevitable deportations and resettlement.

The Babylonian Empire then fell to the Persian king Cyrus II (r. 559–530 B.C.E.). Two Jewish officials from the Persian court, Nehemiah and Ezra, were dispatched with the task of restoring the Jewish character of society, but their efforts were strictly focused on Judah, or *Yehud* as it was now called; Galilee was omitted. When the northern regions, including Samaria, petitioned to be included in the Jewish renaissance and offered to help rebuild the Temple, they were rebuffed (Ezra 4:1-2). Persia's intent was clear: While Judah would be permitted a measure of religious autonomy, Galilee would not.

Galilee's Cultural Transformation

This is when the growing estrangement between Galilee and Judea began—an estrangement that would extend well into the time of Jesus and imbue Judeans with a certain prejudice against Galileans. The idea that Galilee was "different" was further strengthened in the wake of the conquest by Alexander

Life in Lower Galilee

The fields of Lower Galilee, close to the location of ancient Magdala (the putative city of Mary Magdalene), are still a major source of agriculture today.

A FARMER'S CROPS

Galilean peasants usually prepared their soil for seeding in the month of Tishri (September–October) or Marchesvan (October–November). After the first rains of the season had softened the sun-baked topsoil, the ground would be cleared of rocks and plowing could begin. Most farmers used a curved, hardwood plow fitted with an iron plowshare and pulled by one or two oxen. A pair of oxen (a "yoke") was a treasured possession, often owned by larger estates but lent out to individual farmers, with a share of the future harvest as payment. Farmers would then take a sack of seeds culled from the previous harvest and walk in straight lines across their land, throwing the seed with the full sweep of their arms. As a young boy, Jesus may have observed farmers seeding their land in this manner. Years later, the experience would inspire Jesus' parable of the sower: "Some [seed] fell on the path, and the birds came and ate them up. Other seeds fell on rocky ground." (Matthew 13:4-5) The most important grain types were wheat and barley, planted in late November. Wheat was used for bread, the most important staple of a farmer's diet, whereas barley usually served as fodder for farm animals. In times of drought or hardship, barley would be used for bread as well, though it contained far less of the vitamins needed for a healthy diet. The parable of the servants who were beaten when they came to "collect the produce" on their master's behalf suggests that in Jesus' time, many of these orchards were harvested by tenant labor on behalf of estate owners (Mark 12:1; Matthew 21:33; Luke 20:9).

PART I | THE WORLD OF JESUS

the Great, when Galilee became disproportionately inculcated by Hellenistic influences, largely because of its proximity to Phoenicia and Seleucid Syria. Even though the new rulers in the region, the Ptolemies in Egypt, helped to restore Galilee's great agricultural output, such efforts inevitably invited a new layer of foreigners, in the form of Greek officials tasked with managing the region's cultivation. One such official was Zenon, a private secretary to the finance minister of Ptolemy II and III, who traveled up and down the Ptolemaic Empire and spent some time in Galilee in 259 B.C.E. His record of Galilean agricultural output is preserved in a series of documents known as the *Zenon Papyri*.

The Seleucid conquest of Ptolemaic Palestine united Galilee and Judea once again into one political entity, the Seleucid province of Coele-Syria and Phoenicia, but the cultural differences between the two continued. After the Maccabean Revolt liberated Judea and made it an independent kingdom in 142 B.C.E., Galilee remained firmly under Seleucid control.

By that time, Galilee had undergone some profound changes. Many Syrian, Phoenician, and Greek settlers from throughout the Seleucid Empire had settled in Lower Galilee, attracted by the region's legendary fertility. Whether, in due course, these foreign immigrants actually outnumbered the native Jewish population is a matter of scholarly debate. The Book of I Maccabees, for example, depicts a strong antagonism between Gentiles and Jews in Galilee. "The people of Ptolemais and Tyre and Sidon, and all Galilee of the Gentiles had gathered together against them," messengers from Galilee reported to Judas Maccabeus, "in order to annihilate us." In response, Judas sent his brother Simon "with 3,000 men" to liberate the besieged Jews, but Simon was unable to defeat the Gentile forces. The expedition became a rescue party of sorts; Jewish farmers "with their wives and children" were repatriated to Judea, leaving the Gentiles to take control of their land (I Maccabees 5:17-23). Some scholars question the historicity of this account, believing it exaggerates the actual threat posed by the Gentile population, but few question that there was indeed some tension between Jew and Gentile in Galilee.

The struggle for control of the region would continue for another 40 years, until Galilee was finally conquered and annexed to the Hasmonean Kingdom by the Hasmonean king Aristobulus I around 103 B.C.E. Josephus tells us that the Hasmoneans tried to "cleanse" the Galilean population of foreign influences, just as Idumea had been converted to Judaism by force. It is unclear to what degree these efforts were successful, but it could explain the suspicion that many Judeans harbored toward Galilean Jews less than 90 years later.

Jewish and Gentile Influences

The question of whether Galilee in Jesus' time was, in a cultural sense, predominantly Jewish or Gentile continues to be a subject of considerable scholarly debate. The question is important because without knowing the cultural and religious

Life in Lower Galilee

makeup of Galilee in the first century C.E., it is difficult to understand how Jesus' ministry would have resonated with his Galilean audience. Mark Chancey, in *Myth of a Gentile Galilee*, argues for a largely rural Jewish culture, with Greco-Roman influences concentrated in the region's urban centers. Many of these towns, says Chancey, were "no less Hellenized than anywhere else in the Roman world." Jonathan Reed also depicts a Jewish population that was as simple as it was devout, and that "did not import foreign wine amphorae, used little or no glass, and befitting Jewish Law, avoided images of humans or animals." His argument is based on the fact that archaeologists have found scores of limestone vessels throughout the Galilean countryside. Limestone jars and cups are a lot less manageable and affordable than clay pottery, but they carried a special significance for Jewish families, for stone vessels were believed to be impervious to impurity. Hence, liquids such as water or oil stored in such vessels remained pure, which for observant Jews, and particularly the Pharisees, was a particular concern.

Excavators such as Zvi Gal and Eric Meyers, on the other hand, have found many coins and pottery fragments of Greek or Hellenistic origin throughout the region, not just in the cities, which suggest that in many places a certain Hellenistic influence did persist.

This fragment of the Zenon Papyri refers to the loan of 34 drachmae by Dionysios, a native of Gaza, to a man named Isidorus, to be repaid after the harvest in three months' time.

WOMEN AND THE HARVEST

During harvest time, a married woman was expected to help her husband in the fields or orchards. Sometime in February, during the Jewish month of Adar, the first sprouts of barley would appear, and by April (Nisan/Iyyar) these ears would be ready for harvesting. The wheat harvest followed a month later. The reaping was done with a scythe, after which the sheaves were stacked in the fields, or near the farmer's house, to await their turn at the threshing floor. The Mishnah warns that "if a man stacked his sheaves in his fellow's field without permission and the cattle of his neighbor consumed them, the owner of the field is not culpable." Nevertheless, every observant farmer left the stalks at the corners of his field intact, so that they could be reaped by the poor. The farmer's family would also tend to their orchards; Mishnaic case laws indicate that most subsistence farmers cultivated grain, olive, as well as grape for their own needs. The women in the family would also be called upon to help with binding and propping the saplings while pruning the branches of dead wood, in preparation for the growth of grapes, figs, and olives. By early summer, during the month of Tammuz, the vineyards would be ready to be harvested. Jesus would often use the metaphor of the vineyard or orchard for his parables.

A delicate Roman fresco from the first century C.E. shows two women in intimate conversation.

PART I | THE WORLD OF JESUS

Perhaps the answer, then, is that while Greek influences were strongest in major townships and cities that depended on trade and coin, the Jewish character of the region was most profound among the largely rural peasant population. It is not by accident, for example, that the Talmud literature contrasts the hamlet or village (*kfr* or *kefar*) on the one hand, with the town (*'yr*) or city (*kerakh*, equivalent to the Greek *polis*) on the other, knowing that, as Jacob Neusner has argued, the differences between town and city were slight.

According to Josephus, there were some 204 towns and villages in Galilee, based on which archaeologists have extrapolated that the total population must have ranged from 150,000 to 250,000. This includes larger villages such as Japha, Simonias, and Besara, and townships such as Capernaum and Sepphoris. "Cities" in the Greco-Roman mold were found farther to the east and south, particularly in the grouping known as the Decapolis (League of Ten Cities), which included such predominantly Hellenistic towns as Scythopolis west of the Jordan, and Gadara, Hippos, and Pella on the eastern side. It seems plausible to think, therefore, that in small rural enclaves such as Nazareth, the indigenous Jewish culture of Galilee was preserved and exposure to Hellenistic influences was limited. Further, Herod's love for building lavish Greco-Roman monuments was focused on Judea; he never undertook any improvements in Galilee.

All this may explain why throughout his ministry, Jesus would eschew the larger cities and townships of Galilee. "Go nowhere among the Gentiles," Jesus tells his followers in the Gospel of Matthew. Instead, the efforts of his disciples should be solely focused on Jewish communities, "the lost sheep of the house of Israel." (Matthew 10:5-6)

Herod's Succession

The death of King Herod left the urgent question of who would be his successor. His will specified that there shouldn't be one, at least not a single ruler. After spending most of his reign to expand, defend, and embellish his kingdom, Herod now saw fit to break it up after his death. One reason may be that Herod had fathered nine sons (in addition to at least five daughters) by various wives; he had executed three of his sons for various offenses real and imagined, but six were still very much alive. Perhaps Herod feared a civil war if he were to entrust his kingdom to only one of his children; or perhaps he believed that not one of them had the ability to govern so large a nation. Whatever the reason, Herod decreed that the kingdom should be broken up into three parts—signaling a return to the traditional separation of Israel's southern heartland, Judea, from the north, including

> HEROD HAD CHANGED HIS MIND AND ALTERED HIS TESTAMENT; FOR HE APPOINTED ANTIPAS, TO WHOM HE HAD BEFORE LEFT THE KINGDOM, TO BE TETRARCH OF GALILEE AND PEREA, AND GRANTED THE KINGDOM TO ARCHELAUS.
>
> Josephus, *Antiquities of the Jews*
> Circa 95 c.e.

Life in Lower Galilee

Galilee. Archelaus, one of his sons by his Samaritan wife Malthace, was to rule over the largest territory, that of Judea, Idumea, and Samaria.

The second portion, that of Galilee, was curiously combined with Perea (the Transjordan), though these regions were not contiguous, and separated by the Syrian region of the Decapolis. Perea, while small and located to the east of the Jordan River, contained some prosperous trading towns such as Gadara (near today's Umm Qays), as well as the Herodian fortress of Machaerus. This second territory, then, was given to Herod's son Antipas, the younger brother of Archelaus, also a son of Malthace.

The third segment consisted of large areas to the northeast of the Sea of Galilee, including the Gaulanitis (today's Golan region), Batanea, Panias, Auranitis, Iturea, and Trachonitis. Much of the area to the east of the Golan was sparsely populated, but it likewise contained important trading posts such as Bostra, as well as the lovely resortlike springs and waterfalls of Panias, later developed into the capital city of Caesarea-Philippi. This area was allotted to Herod's son Philip, whose mother was referred to as "Cleopatra of Jerusalem," perhaps to distinguish her from the more famous Cleopatra VII of Egypt. The vast majority of Philip's allotted territory was Gentile, not Jewish. By all accounts he turned out to be a just and competent ruler who married Salome, the daughter of Herodias, of whom we shall hear more in a future chapter.

Another Salome, Herod's sister, received what was left of Herod's kingdom, which wasn't much: just the coastal enclave around Azotus, today's Ashdod, and the region around Phaesalis, the town that Herod founded in honor of his older brother.

Archelaus Assumes Power

Such were the terms of Herod's will, but only Rome had the authority to carry them out. While a delegation prepared to submit Herod's will to Rome and solicit imperial approval, Archelaus began a campaign to win the hearts and minds of the Judean people. He first treated Jerusalem to a great feast and thanked all those who had gathered for their allegiance and trust. He also declared that he would not assume the title of king—*basileus* in Greek—until the Emperor decided it was just for him to do so, but assured the people that he would be a kinder and gentler ruler than his father had been.

The assembled crowd decided to put this kindness to the test by airing their comments, petitions, and grievances. Some Jews loudly clamored for Archelaus to release the hundreds of political prisoners who were still in Herod's jails. Others pleaded with him to "ease some of the annual payments"—that is, the heavy

This red burnished jug, used for water or wine, was excavated in southern Palestine and probably dates to the late first century C.E.

This lovely cup (opposite) with blue and white marbling from the first century C.E. reveals the sheer artistry of Roman glassmaking, in sharp contrast to the simple earthenware shown above.

PART I | THE WORLD OF JESUS

A street in Herculaneum, which was covered by volcanic flow during the Vesuvius eruption of 79 C.E., provides an excellent impression of a midsize Roman city in the late first century C.E.

The River Jordan (opposite) winds its way through the Judean desert and into the Dead Sea in this dramatic photo taken from high altitude.

yoke of the Herodian taxes that were still in force. Others again were so bold as to demand that certain members of the former regime should be brought to justice for their crimes against the Jewish people.

Another group also decided to have their voices heard. These were pious men who insisted that Archelaus immediately dismiss the high priest, who had been appointed by Herod and was regarded as one of his cronies. They yearned for a true high priest, a man chosen for his piety and pedigree, who would dispense justice in accordance with the Law and wholly adhere to Scripture. Thus, Archelaus's experiment with openness provoked a groundswell of suppressed anger, for which he was utterly unprepared. Backed into a corner, he brought in a handful of soldiers to try to calm the crowd, but these were greeted with jeers and stones.

Archelaus's timing was poor. It was the season of Passover, when tens of thousands of Jews streamed into the city in preparation for the festival. As the protests began to spread, Archelaus believed he had a rebellion on his hands. If word of these mass demonstrations reached Augustus, his chances of becoming king of Judea would be in jeopardy. Archelaus therefore did what most leaders of autocratic regimes do: He called in the army. Herod's infantry and cavalry were not yet disbanded, and they

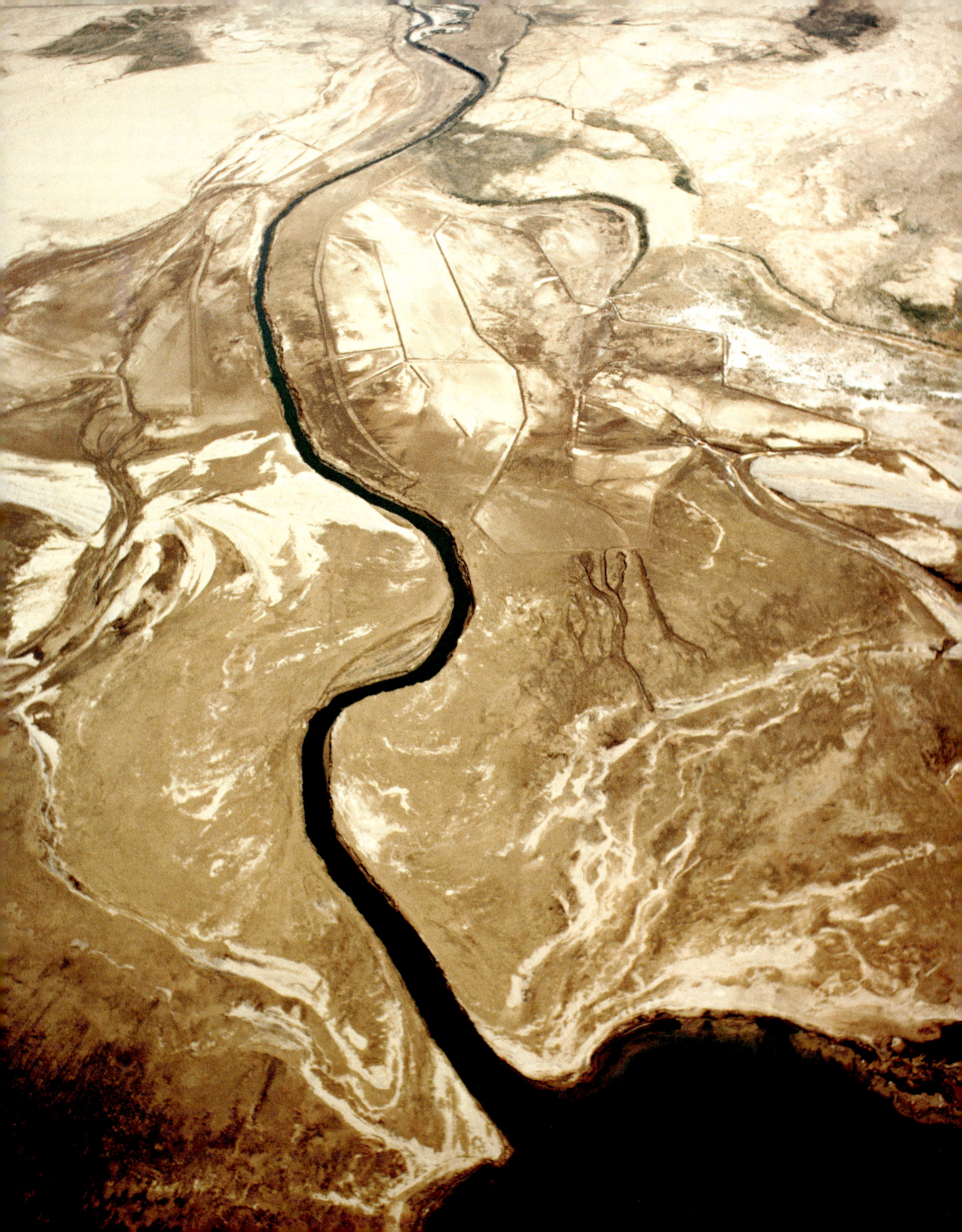

Division of the Kingdom of Herod the Great

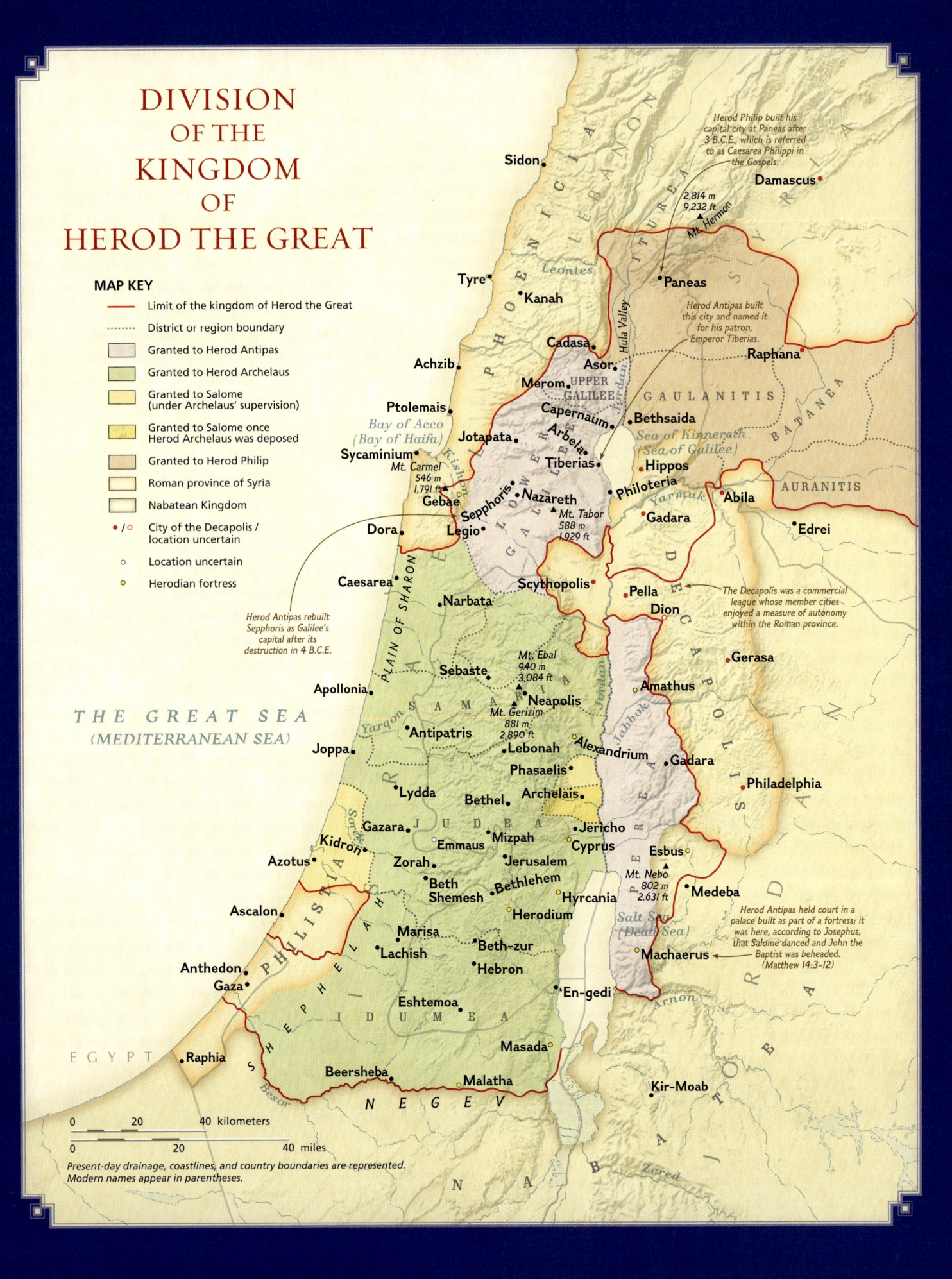

Life in Lower Galilee

were still loyal to his son and heir. These soldiers quickly fought their way into the Temple forecourt while cavalry thundered down the narrow streets of the Lower City. The result was a bloodbath. "In all, they killed some 3,000 of the demonstrators," says Josephus, while the survivors ran to the nearby hills. The Passover festivities were canceled. Clearly, Herod's son was no better than his tyrannical father.

So far, the violence had been largely limited to Jerusalem, but this was about to change. As Archelaus prepared to leave for Rome in the fervent hope that Augustus would confirm Herod's will, the news of the massacre had come to the attention of the highest Roman official in the Near East, the governor of Syria-Palestine. Quinctilius Varus, who was married to Augustus's grandniece, enjoyed a close relationship with the Imperial family. Together with Augustus's stepson Tiberius, Varus had previously served as junior consul in Rome, and had just completed a tour as governor of Africa. Since it was difficult to gauge the extent of the disturbances in Jerusalem, Varus charged a Roman legate named Sabinus to investigate. Sabinus duly left for Judea and intercepted Archelaus just as he was about to board his ship in Caesarea.

But instead of investigating the events that led to the Passover massacre, Sabinus began to compile a complete accounting of all of Herod's possessions and state income. This gave him a fairly accurate summary of what the province of

The main cardo or boulevard of the Hellenistic city of Gerasa (today's Jerash, Jordan) led to the main forum, where the religious, civic, and commercial facilities of the city could be found.

PART I | THE WORLD OF JESUS

Judea, including its surrounding regions, was worth. In effect, Sabinus was laying the groundwork for Rome's complete takeover of Judea.

A NEW REBELLION ERUPTS

Meanwhile, Archelaus arrived in Rome and found that he was not the only one to petition the Emperor. Rather than presenting a harmonious case for implementing their father's will, his sister Salome and his brother Antipas had been lobbying hard to confer Herod's crown to Antipas instead. Shocked by the machinations of Herod's dysfunctional family, Augustus refused to declare himself either way. This is when the news reached Rome that the situation in Judea was moving toward rebellion.

Fifty days after Passover was the feast of Shavuot, "Weeks" in English or "Pentecost" in Greek, when once again Jerusalem was filled with tens of thousands of worshippers. The Roman legate Sabinus was still in the city, and soon rumor spread that he was planning to rob the treasury and use the money to take control of the country. An angry mob formed in the courtyard of the Temple and lay siege to Sabinus and his guards, who were ensconced in one of the Temple buildings. The protestors "mounted the roofs of the porticoes surrounding the courts of the Temple," says Josephus, "and from there began to hurl stones at their enemies." In response, the Romans set fire to the porticoes, some of which were still under construction. Fed by the fresh pitch and timber, the flames quickly spread and soon engulfed the protestors as well as innocent worshippers who had come to sacrifice at the Temple. Another massacre ensued; all those standing near the gates were "either burned alive or slaughtered by the enemy when they attempted to retreat," says Josephus. Sabinus then broke into the Temple treasury, just as the Jewish population had feared, and calmly helped himself to "400 talents"—the equivalent of about $3.6 million in modern currency. Furious, all of Jerusalem rose up and besieged the local Roman garrison. This time, Sabinus realized he was outnumbered. He dispatched urgent messages to governor Varus for reinforcements that, he knew, would take time—a month, if not more.

In the meantime, all semblance of authority in Herod's former orderly kingdom broke down. Two thousand troops of Herod's army formed an armed band and began to terrorize the Judean countryside. Other movements sprang up, seizing the moment to either engage in banditry or try to reestablish self-rule. One of these groups operated in Galilee and was led by the son of Hezekiah, the man who 40 years earlier had led a revolt against then-governor Herod for his attempt to squeeze the Galilean peasantry for cash on Cassius's behalf. Hezekiah's son was named Judas, who knew that a large store of weapons could be had from the arsenal of Sepphoris, the provincial capital of Galilee, located close to a hamlet called Nazareth. His men succeeded in breaking into the building and made off with a large cache of arms with which, Josephus claims, "he was able to equip every single man."

Life in Lower Galilee

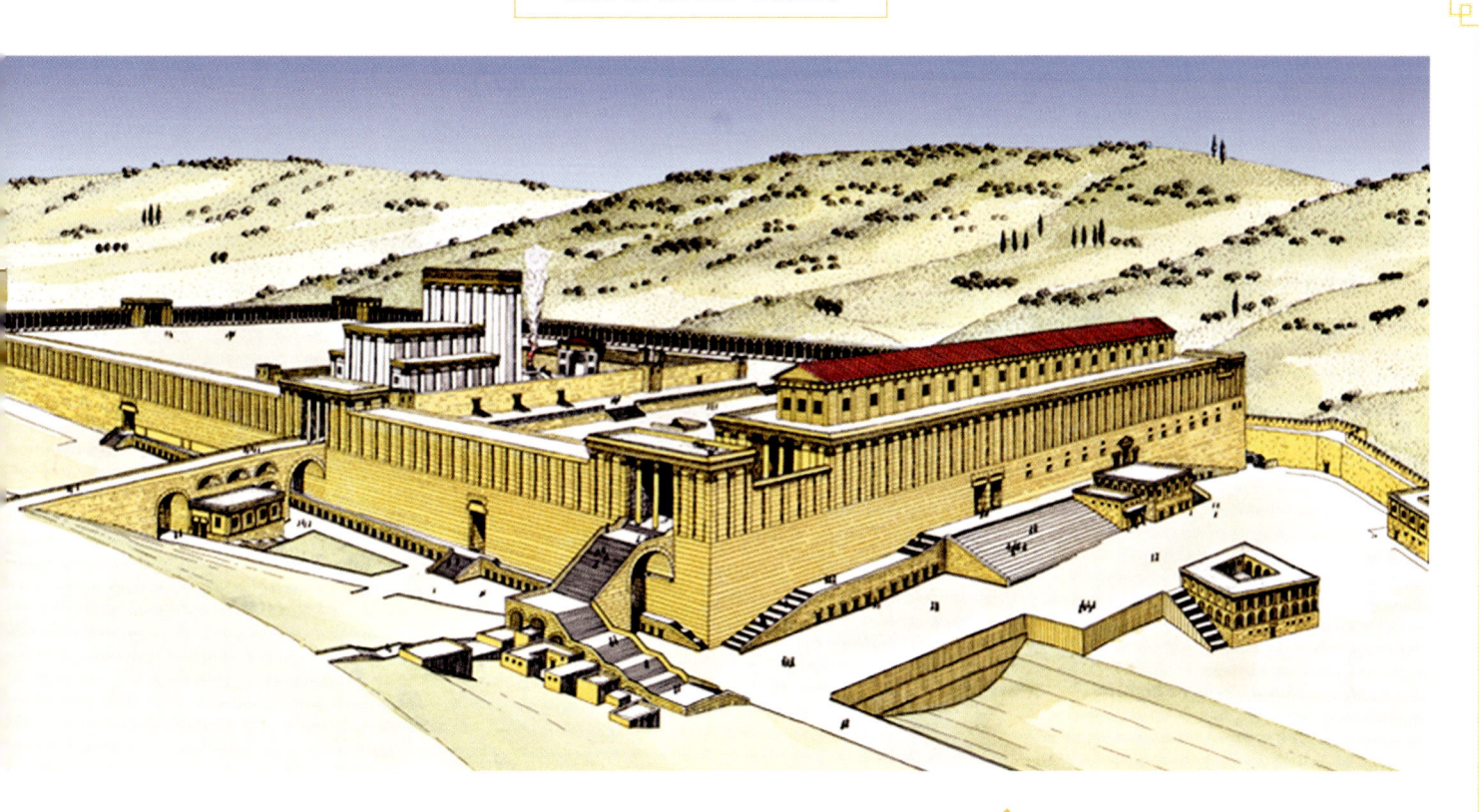

Not to be outdone, a former slave in Herod's employ named Simon decided to crown himself king and burn down Herod's sumptuous palace in Jericho, while a shepherd called Athronges began to conduct terror raids on his own. The country was falling apart at the seams. Commerce ground to a halt as the roads became unsafe, and peasants refused to take their produce to market in the townships for fear of being raided by bandits.

Back in Syria, Varus grasped the severity of the situation and ordered a full military response. He had, however, only a limited amount of legions at his disposal. The record is not clear, though it is possible that Roman strength in Syria included the III Gallica, the X Fretensis, and either the VI Ferrata or the XII Fulminata. Not all of these could be deployed, for Varus was responsible for one of the most strategic flanks of the Roman Empire: its frontier with the powerful Parthians. Were Varus to send all of his legions out of Syria, he would leave the portal to Rome's Southwest Asian possessions vulnerable to attack. Moreover, based on the reports provided by Sabinus, he probably would need more than three legions—a force of some 15,000 men—to restore Roman control over Herod's former kingdom.

Varus called upon all vassal kings in the region to contribute auxiliary forces, as by treaty they were required to do. His call to arms was received with enthusiasm. Many local princes may have welcomed the idea of invading the kingdom of their former adversary, King Herod, and to loot and plunder to their hearts' content. One of the vassal kings who rushed to arms was King Aretas IV Philopatris of Nabatea, the father-in-law of Herod's son Antipas, since he had married his daughter Phasaelis; perhaps Aretas hoped to buttress Antipas's claim. Unopposed by any

Herod's sanctuary platform, built between 20 B.C.E. and 62 C.E., surrounded the Second Temple as shown in this reconstruction, seen from the southwest.

The so-called Apollo Barberini (opposite) is probably a copy of the Apollo statue that once stood in the Temple of the Palatine Hill, where Augustus received the delegations from Judea.

PART I | THE WORLD OF JESUS

These remains of the Temple of Apollo on the Palatine Hill—facing the Circus Maximus, excavated in the 1960s—mark the location where Augustus received the delegations from Judea.

> AND NOW ARCHELAUS FACED A NEW SOURCE OF TROUBLE AT ROME, FOR AN EMBASSY OF JEWS HAD ARRIVED, WITH THE PERMISSION OF VARUS, IN ORDER TO PETITION FOR THE LIBERTY OF LIVING BY THEIR OWN LAWS.
>
> JOSEPHUS, *ANTIQUITIES OF THE JEWS*
> *Circa 95 C.E.*

significant military forces, the Nabatean king invaded Galilee, but refrained from pursuing the guerrilla bands in the hill country, their natural hiding places. Instead, Aretas embarked on a series of reprisals among the unarmed peasantry, moving from village to village in an orgy of rape, looting, and burning. "All places were full of fire and slaughter," says Josephus. When a short while later Roman general Gaius arrived with his legions, he was astonished to find that most villages had been burned to the ground.

Aretas's ultimate objective was Sepphoris, so his forces would have passed through the fields and homes of most villages in the immediate vicinity, including Nazareth. And indeed, Sepphoris was burned to the ground; its population was sold into slavery. During excavations of Sepphoris, the archaeologists found little evidence of the destruction wrought by Varus's forces, which either suggests that the city was small and predominantly built of wood, or that most traces were eradicated as part of the initial destruction by the Romans and, later, its rebuilding by Antipas.

The Breakup of Herod's Kingdom

As reports of the brutal suppression filtered into Rome, a third delegation arrived from Judea. They represented neither the Hasmonean nor the Herodian factions; they were simply a group of concerned citizens who, with Varus's permission, had come to present Augustus with quite a different proposal for the future disposition of Herod's kingdom. The embassy was received in the temple of Apollo, the patron god of Augustus, which the emperor had recently built on the Palatine Hill. This temple was dedicated to the victories by Augustus over both Pompey in 36 B.C.E. and Mark Antony in 31 B.C.E. The delegation's proposal was simple: The Emperor should appoint neither Archelaus nor Antipas, and in fact abandon all pretense of a Herodian kingdom altogether. Instead, Herod's lands should be added to Roman Syria, to be governed by the Roman legate—*as long as the Jews would be allowed to live according to their laws*. To press their case, the delegation had rallied the support of 8,000 members of Rome's Jewish community.

Augustus did not heed their advice. He remembered Herod's loyalty, and for Augustus loyalty was a paramount virtue. Thus, Herod's will was confirmed, granting Archelaus, Antipas, Philip, as well as Salome their individual territories. But Augustus added one caveat: no one, not even Archelaus, would be allowed to inherit Herod's title of "king." Instead, Archelaus would be known as *ethnarch*, "ruler of the people," whereas Antipas had to satisfy himself with an even lesser title, *tetrarch*, meaning "ruler of a one-quarter kingdom." Antipas had little choice but to accept the Emperor's decision.

This, then, is the place in which Matthew and Luke set their stories.

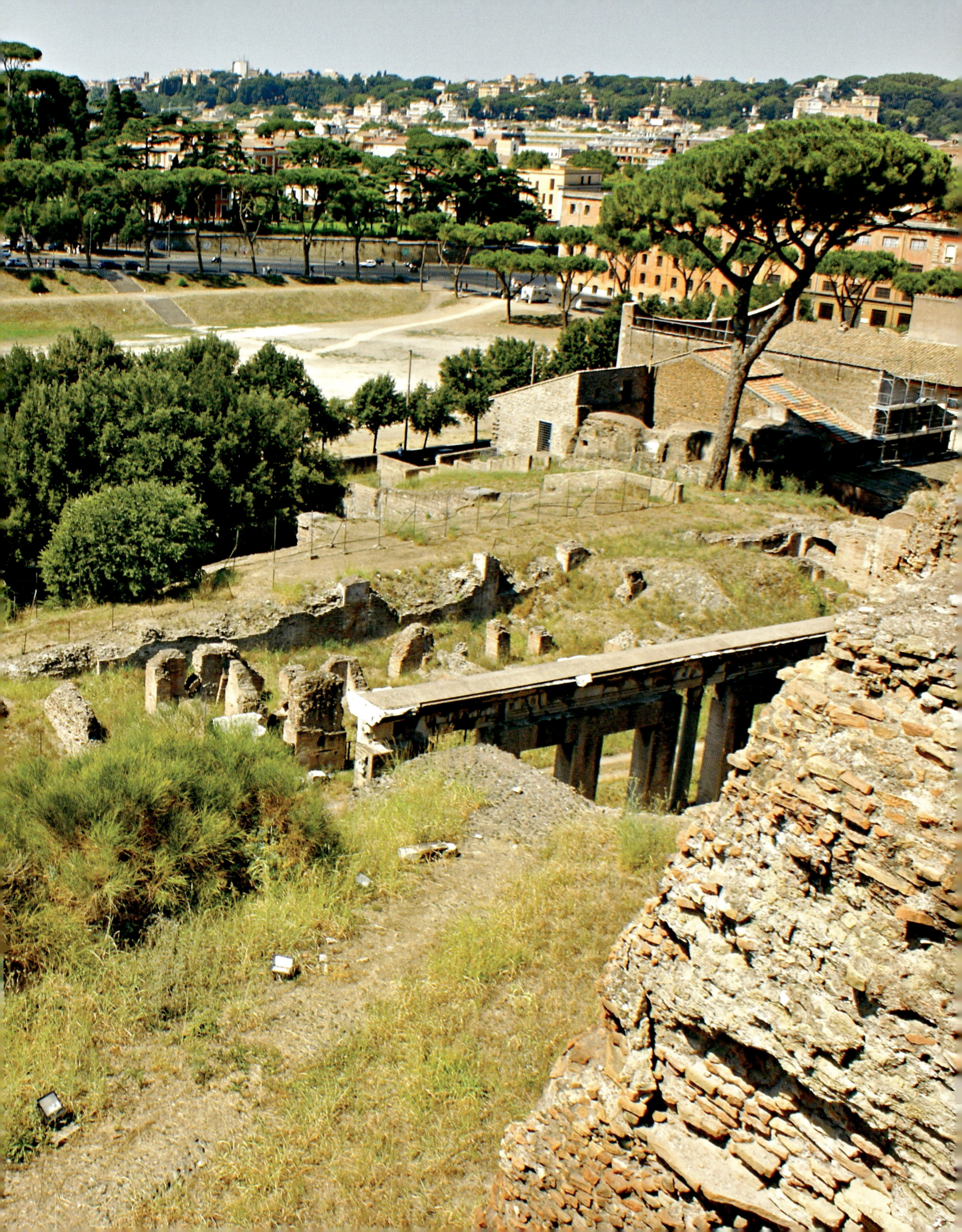

PART II

CIRCA 4 B.C.E. TO 30 C.E.

A child is born to Mary and Joseph of Nazareth. When Jesus is about 30 years old, he joins John the Baptist in the Jordan, prior to launching his ministry in Capernaum, on the shores of the Sea of Galilee. The overwhelming response to his teachings takes him to towns and villages throughout Galilee, Phoenicia, and the Decapolis, before he embarks on his fateful journey to Jerusalem.

THE LIFE OF JESUS

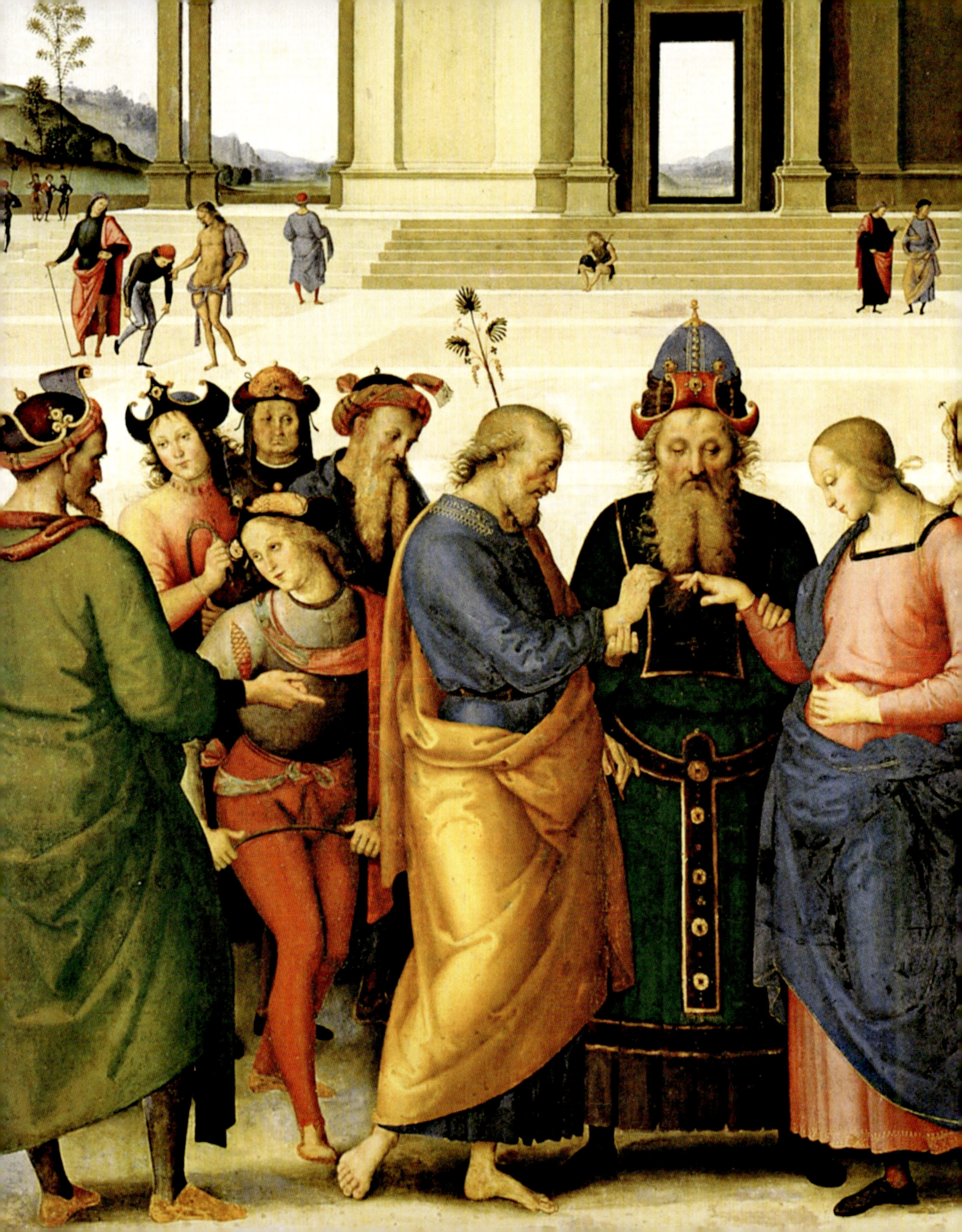

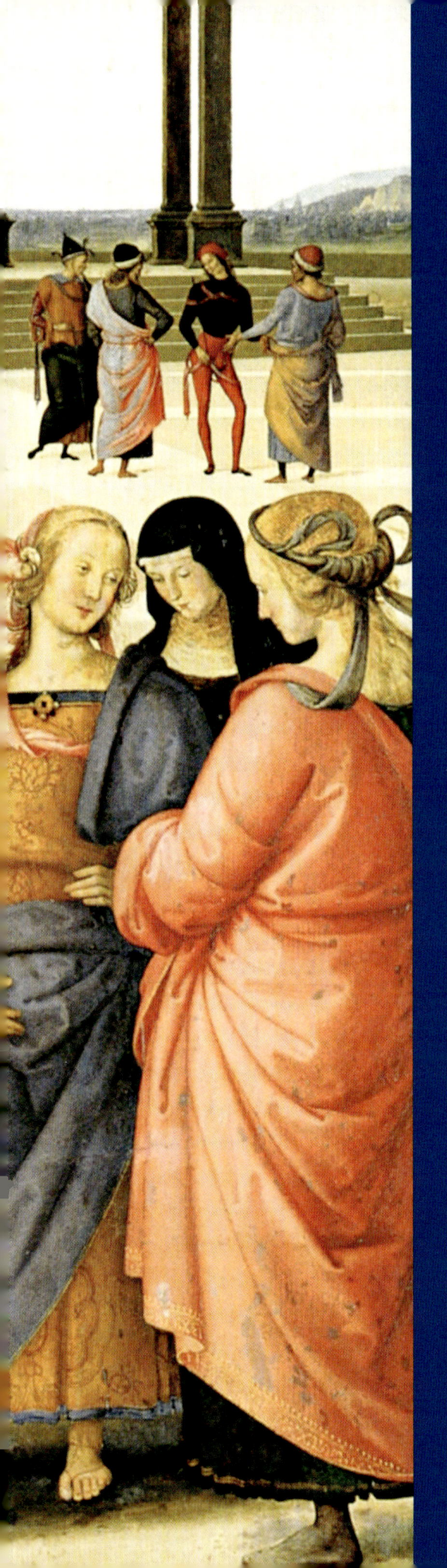

CHAPTER 4

MARY and JOSEPH

IN THE SIXTH MONTH
THE ANGEL GABRIEL WAS SENT
BY GOD TO A TOWN IN GALILEE
CALLED NAZARETH,
TO A VIRGIN ENGAGED TO A MAN
WHOSE NAME WAS JOSEPH,
OF THE HOUSE OF DAVID.

GOSPEL OF LUKE 1:26-27
Circa 75–90 C.E.

This panel by the Italian Renaissance artist Pietro Perugino (ca 1446/1450–1523) depicts either the betrothal or the marriage of the Virgin, painted around 1500–1504.

PART II | THE LIFE OF JESUS

Perched high on a hill, sweetened by the scent of honeysuckle and jasmine in springtime, was a small hamlet called Nazareth. It was located some 16 miles from the area's main source of water, the Sea of Galilee, and just 6 miles southeast of the regional capital, the city of Sepphoris. The Nazareth Ridge, on the chalky slopes of which the hamlet had been built, rose to well higher than 1,200 feet, high enough to catch the cool breeze from the Mediterranean as it came down the Beit Netofa and Nahal Sippori valleys.

While it slumbered in the waning days of King Herod's reign, Nazareth was a tiny village, small enough to escape the discerning eyes of generations of scribes who had written about Galilee since the days of David and Solomon. Like hundreds of other anonymous peasant villages and hamlets that dotted the Galilean countryside, it survived because of the moist fecundity of the fields that surrounded it. On market days—Mondays and Thursdays—the farmers of Nazareth traveled to Sepphoris to sell what these fields had yielded them, their olives and olive oil, their wheat and their dates. We may infer as much because during excavations underneath the Basilica of the Annunciation in modern-day Nazareth—traditionally the site associated with the paternal house of Mary—the Franciscan archaeologist Bellarmino Bagatti found granaries, olive presses, and wells, which he dated to the first or second centuries C.E. Still, the size of these and other archaeological finds suggest that Nazareth was a community of not more than 500 inhabitants.

According to Luke, among those inhabitants was a young girl named Miriam, or Mary, who had recently been betrothed to a man named Josef, or Joseph. Whether Joseph lived in Nazareth as well is not clear. Luke tells us that he was "of the house of David," and his Gospel later offers a detailed genealogy of his family, as authors in Antiquity often did when introducing the principal male characters of their story. Joseph is thus identified as "the son of Heli, son of Matthat," followed by a list of more than 50 generations, which end with Adam. Matthew's Gospel also offers a genealogy, but his list is different, inspired by the opening of the first book of Chronicles and the Book of Ruth.

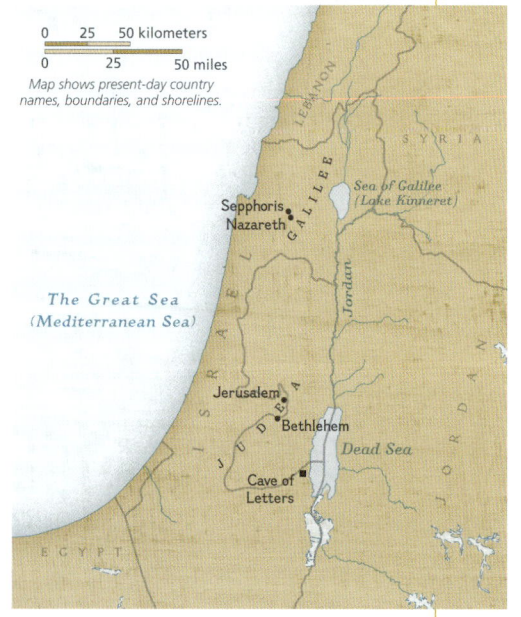

For both Luke and Matthew, the purpose of their genealogies was to anchor Jesus within the continuous narrative of Scripture. In Matthew's elegant and poetic design, for example, 14 generations separate Abraham and David; 14 generations lie between David and the Babylonian Exile; while 13 generations separate the Exile from Jesus, so as to denote the generation of Jesus' followers, the first Christians, as the 14th generation. Where Joseph lived is not specified; in fact, for reasons we shall see shortly, Matthew implies that Joseph lived in Bethlehem, rather than Nazareth. Only John specifically states that Joseph was "from Nazareth," but he offers no further details.

Negotiating the Marriage Contract

Marriage was a highly praised institution in Jewish Palestine, and indeed in the Roman world altogether. It was considered a cornerstone of the social relations that both sustained and perpetuated the cultural identity of a community. The Book of the Wisdom of Sirach, dating to the third century B.C.E., argues that "where there is no fence, the property will be plundered; and where there is no wife, a man will become a fugitive." (Sirach 36:30) Consequently, the book urges

The rolling fields of the Beit Netofa Valley near Nazareth appear to be as lush as they were in the days of Jesus.

PART II | THE LIFE OF JESUS

fathers to "discipline [your sons], and marry them off to women while they are still youths." (Sirach 7:33) Rabbinic texts of later centuries would stress marriage as both a blessing and a divine command.

The betrothal of a young man to a woman in ancient Galilee, however, could only come about after negotiations between their families. Part of the reason is that traditionally, marriage involved the transfer of some parcel of land from the bride's family to the groom's family as part of the dowry. Only by having a plot of their own could the young couple make a living and sustain a growing family of their own, and each family was expected to contribute its share.

A marriage tract bound two families together and made them kin, made them relatives of one another. Kinship was a cornerstone of all ancient society. People looked to their relatives first and foremost for their social and economic needs. Therefore, before any *Ketubot* or marriage contracts could be entered into, the parents of the young couple needed to verify that their families were compatible, honorable, and worthy of the trust that they were about to place in each other.

Many marriages in ancient Palestine were arranged by the couple's parents, who would often begin the search for suitable candidates while their children were still young. As Douglas Oakman has argued, they would often start with their own circle of relatives so as to keep their land holdings within the greater family or clan. Endogamy has a long tradition in the Hebrew Scriptures. Abraham, for example, sent a servant to Haran, where his brother's family dwelt, in order to find a suitable bride for his son Isaac. Later, Isaac's son Jacob would also travel to Haran to find a spouse among his kin. Much closer to the age of Jesus, the apocryphal books of Tobit and Judith, as well as the book of Jubilees (all dating to the second century B.C.E.) refer to several endogamous marriages, including that of Tobias and Anna, as well as Manasseh and Judith.

Once a match had been arranged, the families would sit down to negotiate the marriage contract in earnest. The most important clause dealt with the dowry that the bride would bring with her, so as to compensate the groom's family for the fact that the bride's maintenance was now their responsibility. A dowry usually consisted of the girl's personal items such as clothing or simple jewelry; parcels of land; and perhaps some sheep, goats, and fowl. In wealthier households, gold, silver, and even slaves would be added, but such was far beyond the means of most Galilean peasants.

Mary and Joseph

In return, the groom's family could offer the bride a pension known as bride price or bridewealth. This would be released to the wife in the event that her husband divorced her or died prematurely, leaving her a widow and their children orphans. The source of this pension was rooted in the old Hebrew tradition of the *mohar*, but had gained new currency during the Hasmonean period as a result of Hellenistic influences. A first-century marriage contract between Isadora and Dionysios, a Gentile couple from Alexandria, for example, states that in the event the husband engaged in "wanton" behavior, threw his wife out of the house or brought in another woman, the marriage would be dissolved, and the husband would owe his wife one and a half times the original dowry that she brought to the marriage.

Rabbinic texts dating from the third century suggest that a woman's pension would range between 100 and 400 *denarii*. Jesus alludes to the frugality of women when he asks in Luke's Gospel, "What woman, having ten silver coins, if she loses one of them, does not light a lamp, sweep the house, and search carefully until she finds it?"

The Church of the Annunciation in Nazareth, completed in 1969, marks the location where tradition holds that the archangel Gabriel visited Mary.

The British artist William Beattie (1810–1870) created this delicate porcelain composition of Isaac and Rebekah (opposite) for Wedgwood in 1865.

PART II | THE LIFE OF JESUS

Mary and Joseph

With both the dowry and bridewealth sums established, a marriage contract would next define the marital rights of husband and wife. In one second-century contract that has survived, a Jewish groom faithfully promises his bride that "you will be my wife according to the law of Moses and the Judeans, and I will feed you and clothe you and I will bring you [into my house] by means of your *ketuba* and I owe you the sum of 400 denarii . . . together with the due amount of your food and your clothes and your bed, provision fitting for a free woman." The same concern for proper food and clothing is reflected in the Mishnah, where husbands are told "not to give [their wives] fewer than two *kabs* of wheat or four *kabs* of barley [every week]." A *kab* was roughly equivalent to 1.1 kilograms, or 2.4 pounds. In addition, husbands are urged to clothe their spouses properly, including "a cap for her head and a girdle for her loins and shoes at each of the three feasts," meaning the festivals of Passover, Shavuot, and Succoth. Provisions such as these hew closely to Covenant Law, which states that "if [a man] takes another wife to himself, he shall not diminish the food, clothing, or marital rights of the first wife." (Exodus 21:10)

A Young Woman's Education

The need to specify what for us are rather obvious provisions, such as food and clothing, gains a new significance when we consider that a peasant woman in first-century Palestine did not have the rights we would take for granted today.

Throughout the ages, Jewish marriage contracts were often richly adorned, as in this 17th-century Ketubbah from Holland.

A DENARIUS

A denarius, a coin that figures prominently in the Gospels (for example, Matthew 20:2), was the most common form of currency in the Roman Empire. The name denarius, meaning "holding ten," stemmed from the fact that it was worth ten *asses*, an *ass* being the smallest coin in circulation, made of bronze. It was also worth four sesterces. In Jesus' time, a denarius was most often a silver coin, sometimes stamped with the image of the reigning emperor, Tiberius, though since Augustus its actual silver content was less than 3.9 grams. A denarius was equal to a day's wages of a serf or farmhand, or that of a soldier, roughly the equivalent of $18 in modern currency. By comparison, a "scribe"—essentially a notary public who filled out forms of marriage, divorce, sale, credit, or rent—made twelve denarii per week, roughly double a worker's wages. For a single denarius, one could buy a large meal or a jar of olive oil of average quality. According to Luke, a stay in an inn cost two denarii (Luke 10:35). When Jewish worshippers wanted to purchase sacrificial doves or lambs in the Temple, they first had to change their denarii into Temple shekels, at an exchange rate of four denarii to a shekel. Temple shekels were special coins of greater metallic purity than normal shekels, minted in Tyre.

A Roman silver denarius depicts the Roman emperor Trajan (98–117 c.e.).

PART II | THE LIFE OF JESUS

Olive groves such as this orchard outside Nazareth evoke the timeless beauty of ancient Galilee.

This portrait of the young Virgin Mary (opposite) is a detail from the "Holy Family with St. Anne and the infant St. John the Baptist" from around 1550, painted by Renaissance artist Agnolo Bronzino (1503–1572).

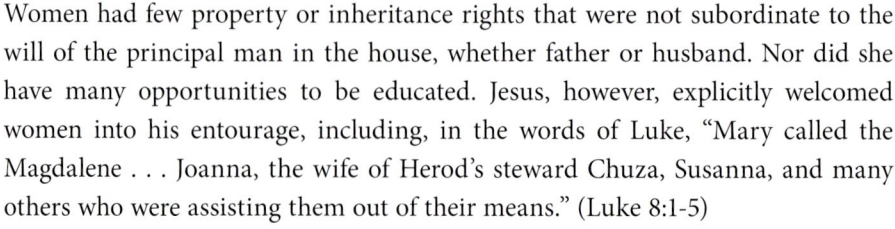

Women had few property or inheritance rights that were not subordinate to the will of the principal man in the house, whether father or husband. Nor did she have many opportunities to be educated. Jesus, however, explicitly welcomed women into his entourage, including, in the words of Luke, "Mary called the Magdalene . . . Joanna, the wife of Herod's steward Chuza, Susanna, and many others who were assisting them out of their means." (Luke 8:1-5)

After a marriage was confirmed, wedding preparations began in earnest when the bride had her first menses, usually at age 13 or 14. This may seem very young, but in Antiquity a woman typically experienced the onset of menopause in her late 30s and was not expected to live beyond her 40s, in part because of the burden of her household and child-rearing duties, in addition to the effects of multiple childbirths.

Knowing this, Mary's mother would have prepared her daughter for the manifold duties of a wife early on. From age six or seven onward, Mary would have helped her mother with simple duties involving cooking, kneading dough for bread, washing, feeding the animals, and taking care of the younger children. At harvest time, she was expected to help her parents pick the fruits from their orchard and learn to carefully crush the olives for the production of olive oil. On market day, Mary would have accompanied her mother to the nearest market to help sell their surplus yields. Here, she may have picked up a few words of Greek, in addition to her native tongue of Aramaic, though this suggestion is subject to scholarly debate.

Most important, as soon as her fingers were sufficiently developed, Mary would have been introduced to the loom, since women were expected to produce most of the clothing worn by her family, including her husband's. In fact, weaving was perhaps the most important skill her mother needed to teach her. First, she would have been trained in rolling coarse strands of wool or flax into spinning yarn. This yarn would then be used to weave straight strips of wool, using a simple upright loom of vertical threads. These threads, known as the warp, could be suspended from a beam, or the branch of a tree, with small wooden or clay weights so as to keep them taut, allowing the weaver to move the woof thread in and out. During the first century C.E., the warp-weighted loom was gradually replaced by the more sophisticated two-beam loom, in which the warp was stretched from a bar on top to a beam on the bottom. This arrangement not only increased the tension on the warp threads but also eased the movement and integrity of the woof thread. A woman working a two-beam loom could sit comfortably on a stool, rather than standing for hours at a time while using a weighted loom.

Rabbinic texts, dating from the second century, only refer to the two-beam loom, but the earliest references in Roman text come from Seneca, probably dating to the middle of the first century C.E. It is probably safe to assume that Mary was instructed in the old warp-weighted loom, a sample of which has been excavated near En Gedi.

Mary and Joseph

PART II | THE LIFE OF JESUS

A Bedouin woman weaves a rug near the El-Farafra Oasis in Egypt using some of the same techniques that mothers would have taught their daughters in the time of Jesus.

This impression of women hauling water (opposite) from Nazareth's village well was painted by Russian artist Vasilij Dmitrievich Polenov (1844–1927).

Once a loom yielded two strips of cloth, about three feet long, these could then be joined to create a sleeveless garment. Mary's mantle would have fringes on the bottom and be tightened around her waist with a blue ribbon. Underneath this tunic, Mary would have worn a simple linen undergarment, which she also wore when she slept. A man's mantle was very similar, but girded with a leather belt, or one made of cloth. Mark tells us that "John was clothed with camel's hair, and with a girdle of a skin about his loins." When in the Gospel of Luke, Jesus tells his followers to "gird your loins" (Luke 12:35), he meant that they should lift their tunic and tuck it under their belt, which was the first-century way of saying that they should "roll up their sleeves" and get to work.

For footwear, Mary would have worn sandals made of palm bark, fastened with straps of flax, rope, or leather. Whenever she left the house, she would drape a white cloth over her head, not only to cover her hair but also to protect her against the sun. All respectable women kept their heads covered in public.

Joseph's Education

Given the very little information we can glean about Joseph's background, it is difficult to determine whether Joseph was in any way educated or not. Rabbinic sources from the late second and third century C.E. suggest that larger villages and townships typically maintained a synagogue where young boys received some schooling, starting at age six. The

> [JUDAH, SON OF ANANIAS] OWES TO SHELAMZION HIS WIFE THREE HUNDRED DENARII WHICH HE PROMISED TO GIVE HER IN ADDITION TO THE SUM OF HER DOWRY . . . [TO BE USED] IN THE UNDERTAKING OF FEEDING AND CLOTHING BOTH HER AND FUTURE CHILDREN.
>
> MARRIAGE CONTRACT FROM EN GEDI
> *Early second century C.E.*

Palestinian and Babylonian Talmuds, for example, tell us that Simeon ben Shetach (120–40 B.C.E.) decreed that every district and town should have a *Bet ha-Sefer,* or House of the Book. The main purpose of this schooling was not to teach young boys to write, but to give them a rudimentary understanding of the Hebrew Scriptures and the precepts of the Law. Many scholars believe, however, that such instructions reflect more of a pious ideal than actual practice, certainly in the smaller and less affluent communities. It is unlikely that any such schools would have existed in the Galilean countryside *before* the destruction of the Temple in 70 C.E.

Luke tells us that Jesus returned to Nazareth at the beginning of his ministry and "went to the synagogue on the Sabbath day, as was his custom," but whether this was a purpose-built synagogue of the type that became common after the destruction of the Temple (when Luke is believed to have written his Gospel) is uncertain. During his excavation campaign underneath the Church of the Annunciation, Bagatti uncovered a number of architectural fragments from the second century C.E. that he identified as the remains of a village synagogue, but this interpretation is not universally accepted.

PART II | THE LIFE OF JESUS

In this so-called Cave of Letters in the Judea desert, archaeologist Yigael Yadin found numerous records of refugees from the Bar Kokhba Revolt of 132–135 C.E., including the documents of a woman named Babatha of Maoza.

JEWISH FAMILY LIFE

Based on Biblical accounts as well as other sources, including documents related to a second-century Jewish woman named Babatha of Maoza recovered from a cave near the Dead Sea, it is possible to reconstruct, to some degree, Jewish family life in the time of Jesus. These records show that even though the Law allowed men to have several wives, most husbands in first-century Judea and Galilee were monogamous. Since men were usually older than their brides, and mortality rates were high, a woman was often married more than once. Ross Kraemer has argued that, while her first marriage was usually arranged by her parents, a woman would typically have a greater say in her second marriage. Some references in the Mishnah would indicate that only husbands could initiate a divorce, but there is evidence that in practice, a woman could obtain a get or divorce certificate as well. This resulted in large households, which could number children from multiple fathers, their spouses, and even their children. This arrangement appears to be reflected in several residential structures from the first century C.E., which feature a number of dwellings, conceivably on two levels, grouped around a common courtyard. Once married, a young woman was responsible for the home, her family's clothing, the washing and the cooking, as well as tending to her children. During harvest time, she often helped her husband in the fields or orchards. Some women may also have been adept at making pottery, though such would depend on the availability of good clay in the vicinity of the village.

Mary and Joseph

This does not mean that the villagers of Nazareth would not gather for communal prayers and other religious or civic functions. It merely suggests, as most archaeologists have concluded, that since only a few purpose-built synagogues from the first century have been found in Galilee, such gatherings could have taken place in the village center, near the communal well, or in one of the larger homes. It also indicates that most village boys in the time of Jesus would have received their primary religious and vocational training at home. By age 13, a boy was deemed to have reached adulthood, ready to begin work alongside his father.

A Jewish boy in Palestine was ready to enter matrimony when he reached the age of 18 years. Even then, he would not have been allowed to "date" Mary in a modern sense. With the conclusion of the marriage contract, the young couple would certainly have been introduced to each other, if they didn't already know each other from prior family gatherings; but any such encounters would have been carefully supervised by their parents. Especially as a young girl approached her wedding day, it fell on her brothers and her father to protect her chastity, and thus the honor of her family, as was common in many other cultures throughout the empire.

Meanwhile, the mothers and other female members of the household would have plunged into preparations for the wedding feast. Even in a small hamlet like Nazareth, a wedding could stretch over several days. All the people of the village, as well as relatives from surrounding villages, would be invited. The ceremonies would begin with a formal procession of the groom and his relatives to the house of the bride on the eve of their wedding. The groom would take his veiled bride by the hand and lead her back to the house of the groom's family, where she was given separate sleeping quarters, carefully guarded by her bridal attendants. The next day, the marriage ceremony would take place, followed by a great village feast. This was one of the rare occasions when Jewish peasant families could indulge in the luxury of roasted meat, so several goats or sheep would be slaughtered for this purpose. All through the evening, the happy couple would be showered with seeds and flowers, until it was time for the bride and groom to be escorted to their new home, which usually involved a room, or a group of rooms, within the family compound. While the young couple consummated their union for the first time, the wedding party outside their window continued with renewed vigor.

But then something happened that upended all these carefully laid plans, and indeed changed the course of Mary's life forever. For Mary was found to be pregnant.

Mary's Pregnancy in the Gospels

The discovery of Mary's condition is described by Luke and Matthew, and while both Gospels agree on the principal features, each evangelist approaches the story from a distinct perspective. They both state that Mary and Joseph were betrothed; that Joseph descended from the house of King David; and that Mary, while a virgin and not yet wed, conceived a child by the Holy Spirit. Furthermore, both writers use stories from

This pair of carved wooden dolls probably belonged to a young child living in the late third century C.E.

PART II | THE LIFE OF JESUS

A pair of leather sandals from the late first century C.E. are superimposed over an oil press from a house in Hazor in northern Galilee.

These gently undulating hills (opposite) near the Sea of Galilee lead to the modern city of Tiberias.

the Hebrew Scriptures as the literary model for their account, so as to emphasize the birth of Jesus as a continuation—and indeed, a fulfillment—of Scripture.

Luke's so-called "Annunciation" is modeled on the story in Genesis of the angel's prophecy to Abraham, who was married to Sarah. Luke adds a refinement by also using the angel's appearance to Sarah's slave, Hagar, who had previously borne Abraham a son. Because of tensions between her and Sarah, Hagar was sent away into the desert. There, an angel appeared to Hagar, telling her

Now you have conceived and shall bear a son,
you shall name him Ishmael, for the Lord has given heed to your affliction
. . . and he shall live at odds with all his kin.

Soon thereafter, God appeared before Abraham, and said

Sarah your wife shall bear you a son,
and you shall call him Isaac;
I will establish my covenant with him.

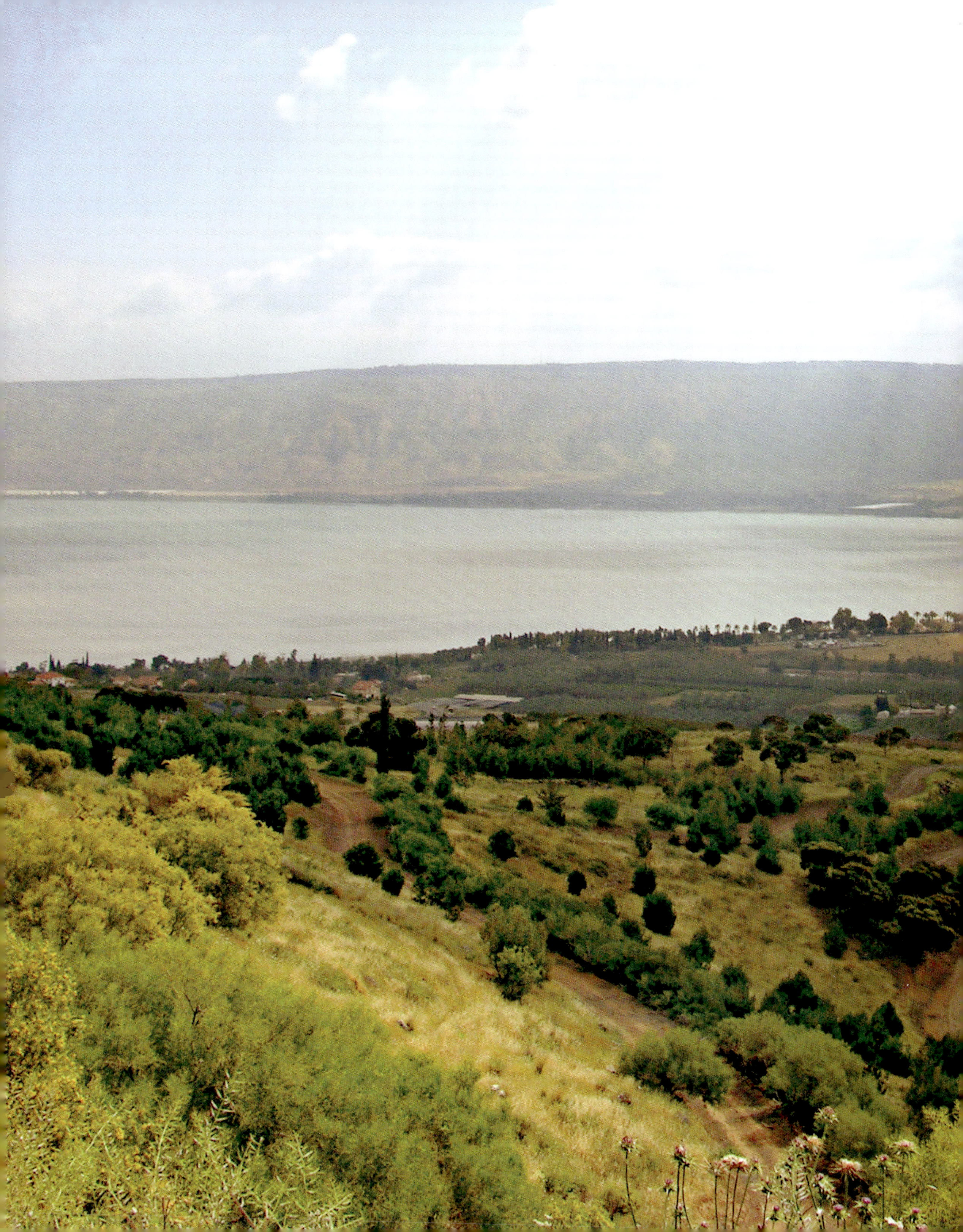

PART II | THE LIFE OF JESUS

In Dante Gabriel Rossetti's (1828–1882) depiction of the Annunciation (1850), Mary is a frightened young woman who is reluctant to accept Gabriel's charge.

In both instances, it is God who names the child, thus indicating the divinely ordained role that the child is destined to play. In Luke's story, then, the angel Gabriel appeared before Mary in her house in Nazareth, and said, "Do not be afraid, Mary, for you have found favor with God." And the angel continued:

And now, you will conceive in your womb and bear a son,
and you will name him Jesus.
He will be great, and will be called the Son of the Most High.

THE ANNUNCIATION IN WESTERN ART

The story of the Annunciation has inspired countless artists from the Middle Ages through modern times. Byzantine artists showed the scene according to the highly stylized canon of the period, with Mary enthroned as the exalted Virgin against a golden background. In the wake of the Renaissance, artists sought to imagine the event in more naturalistic terms. The Flemish artist Rogier van der Weyden sets the scene in the comfortable surroundings of an affluent burgher's home in Flanders. In Leonardo da Vinci's vision, Mary is a young woman who receives the news proudly and full of self-confidence. By contrast, in the hands of the 19th-century Pre-Raphaelite artist Dante Gabriel Rossetti, Mary is a fearful young girl who appears to recoil from the flower that the angel Gabriel extends to her, as if mindful of the great suffering to come.

Leonardo da Vinci (1452–1519) painted the "Annunciation" in 1472, as one of his first completed works.

Mary and Joseph

Like "Joshua" or "Hosea," the name Jesus, or "Yeshua" in Aramaic, is a contraction of *Yehoshuah*, meaning "YHWH is salvation"; as such it was a very common name in Judea and Galilee. When Mary protested that she was still "a virgin," the angel Gabriel replied that "the Holy Spirit will come upon you, and the power of the Most High will overshadow you." (Luke 1:34-35) So as to underscore God's power, the angel added that "your relative Elizabeth in her old age has also conceived a son . . . for nothing will be impossible with God."

Indeed, Luke also relates how the angel Gabriel had previously appeared to Elizabeth's husband, the elderly Zechariah, who is identified as a member of the "priestly order of Abijah." (Luke 1:5) At first, Zechariah was taken aback by the angel's appearance, so Gabriel put him at ease, using almost the same words as spoken to Mary: "Do not be afraid, Zechariah, for your prayer has been heard." And Gabriel continued:

Your wife Elizabeth shall bear you a son,
and you will name him John.
You will have joy and gladness, for he will be great in the sight of the Lord.
(Luke 1:13-15)

Zechariah was incredulous, just as Abraham and Sarah had been. "How will I know that this is so?" he asked. "For I am an old man, and my wife is getting on in years." The angel replied: "I stand in the presence of God."

Luke then adds a further narrative layer, using as his source the story of Hannah and Elkanah from the Book of I Samuel. Like Sarah, Hannah had been unable to give her husband a child. In her prayers, she promised that if God granted her a son, she would raise him to become a *nazirite*—a person devoted to the service of God. And as a nazirite, Hannah pledged, "he shall drink neither wine nor intoxicants, and no razor shall touch his head." (I Samuel 1:11) Hannah's prayers were answered, and she gave birth to the prophet Samuel.

In Luke's story of Elizabeth and Zechariah, the angel Gabriel uses the same words to admonish Zechariah about *his* future son: "He must never drink wine or strong drink." By doing so, Luke establishes a parallel between Scripture and Gospel. Just as Hannah gave birth to the prophet Samuel, so in the New Testament will Elizabeth give birth to John the Baptist. And just as Samuel once anointed David, the king of Israel, so too will John the Baptist baptize Jesus as the Davidic Messiah in the waters of the Jordan.

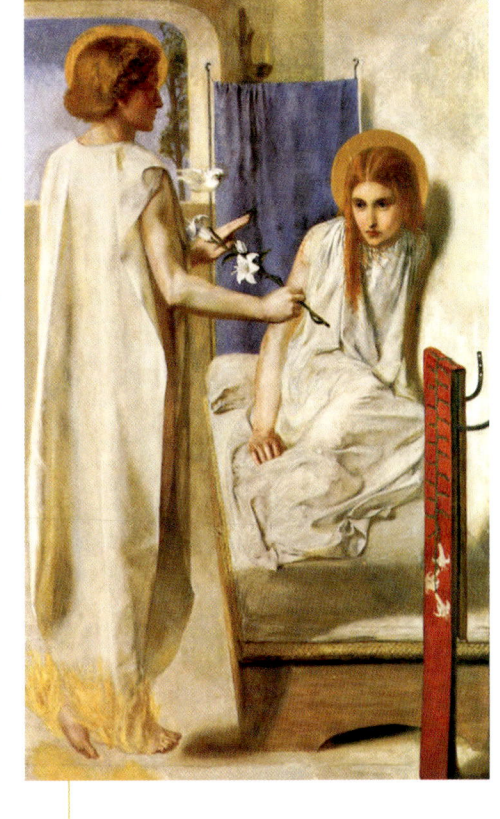

> DO NOT BE AFRAID, MARY, FOR YOU HAVE FOUND FAVOR WITH GOD. AND NOW, YOU WILL CONCEIVE IN YOUR WOMB AND BEAR A SON, AND YOU WILL NAME HIM JESUS.
>
> GOSPEL OF LUKE 1:30-31
> *Circa 75-90 C.E.*

THE GROTTO OF THE ANNUNCIATION

Since the third century C.E., a grotto carved out of the soft chalk hills of Nazareth has been associated with the place of the Annunciation. This is where,

PART II | THE LIFE OF JESUS

Artist Rogier van der Weyden (ca 1400–1464) sets this visualization of the Annunciation in the richly appointed home of a Flemish burgher.

according to tradition, Mary lived when she received the Annunciation from the angel Gabriel. A basilica-type church was built on top of the grotto in the fourth century by a certain Joseph of Tiberias on behest of the mother of Constantine the Great, the Empress Helena, after Christianity became a licensed religion in the Roman Empire. A small monastery was added later, but it was destroyed during the Persian invasion of 614. A third church in the form of a Crusader basilica was then built in the 12th century, only to be destroyed once again in 1263. In 1730, the Franciscans obtained permission from the Ottoman rulers to build yet another church, again incorporating the original grotto. In 1955, the Franciscans purposefully demolished this building in order to make room for the current imposing edifice, which is the most modern church building in Israel today. Designed by the Italian architect Giovanni Muzio, it was inaugurated by Pope Paul VI in 1964 and completed in 1969. This church remains faithful to the Crusader church plan, and it is divided into two floors; the lower floor gives access to the grotto, in front of which Masses can be said.

> **WHEN HIS MOTHER MARY HAD BEEN ENGAGED TO JOSEPH, BUT BEFORE THEY LIVED TOGETHER, SHE WAS FOUND TO BE WITH CHILD FROM THE HOLY SPIRIT.**
>
> GOSPEL OF MATTHEW 1:18
> *Circa 75–90 C.E.*

Matthew's Version

Matthew's narrative announcing Mary's pregnancy unfolds through the eyes of Joseph, and here we get a sense of the tremendous impact that Mary's premarital pregnancy would have had on her family. Honor was the essential quality by which a family in Antiquity established its reputation within the community. Mary's pregnancy would have brought great shame on her relatives.

In Matthew's Gospel, Joseph is fully aware of the consequences. Since he hasn't had conjugal relations with Mary yet, and therefore cannot be the father, he knows the marriage contract is invalid; but he doesn't want to humiliate Mary and make a scandal. "Her husband Joseph," says Matthew, "being a righteous man and unwilling to expose her to public disgrace, planned to dismiss her quietly." (Matthew 1:19) But then, "an angel of the Lord appeared to him in a dream and said, 'Joseph, son of David, do not be afraid to take Mary as your wife, for the child conceived in her is from the Holy Spirit.' " And the angel continued:

She will bear a son,
and you are to name him Jesus,
for he will save his people from their sins. (Matthew 1:21)

And, says Matthew, when "Joseph awoke from sleep, he did as the angel of the Lord commanded him; he took her as his wife, but had no marital relations with her until she had borne a son." (Matthew 1:24-25)

Mary and Joseph

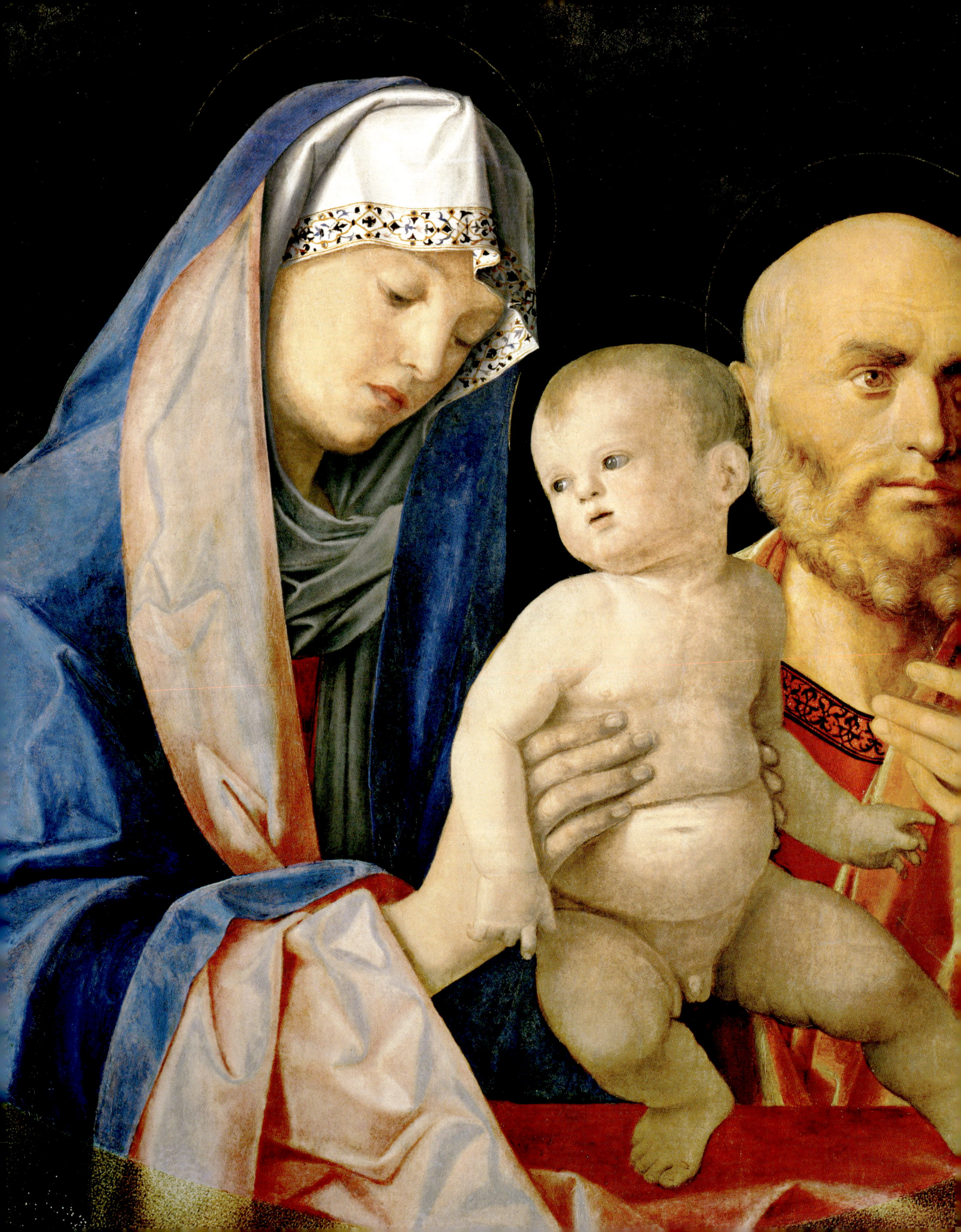

[CHAPTER] 5

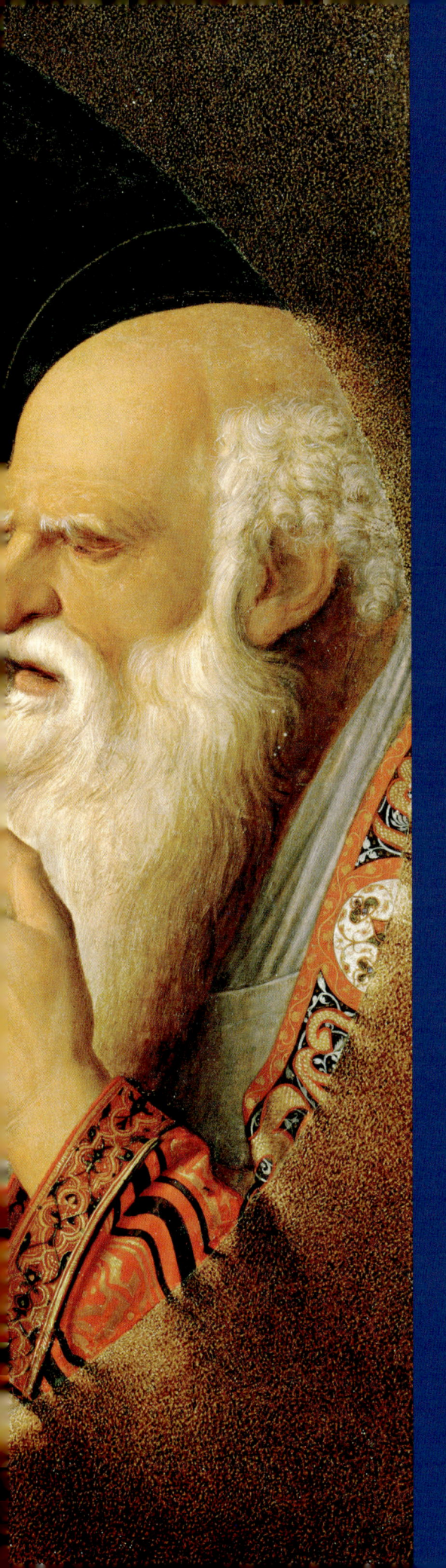

The EARLY YEARS of JESUS

IN THOSE DAYS
A DECREE WENT OUT
FROM EMPEROR AUGUSTUS
THAT ALL THE WORLD
SHOULD BE REGISTERED.

GOSPEL OF LUKE 2:1
Circa 75–90 C.E.

The Venetian artist Giovanni Bellini (1430–1516) painted this depiction of Jesus' "Presentation in the Temple" around 1490–1500.

PART II | THE LIFE OF JESUS

No Gospel account has so fastened itself on our imagination as Luke's Nativity story. It is his narrative that forms the basis for the way Christians around the world celebrate Christmas, the annual celebration of Jesus' birth.

Luke sets his story "in the days of King Herod of Judea." The nomenclature is important because the evangelists often refer to "King Herod" without clearly distinguishing between Herod the Great, ruler of the former Hasmonean kingdom, and his son Herod Antipas, who would rule Galilee and Perea as a mere tetrarch after his father's death. In this case the attribute "of Judea," which the Romans used as *pars pro toto* to designate all of Palestine, is a clear indication that Luke is referring to King Herod. Matthew agrees; he also refers to "the time of King Herod, after Jesus was born." Later on, this same Herod is mentioned in Matthew's account of the massacre of the innocents in Bethlehem, which confirms that Matthew is talking about Herod the father, since his son Herod Antipas had no jurisdiction over Judea, where Bethlehem was located.

If it is true that Jesus was born during the king's reign, then we must change the assumption that Jesus was born in the year 0. King Herod died in March or April of 4 B.C.E., so Jesus' birth must have occurred before that date. The situation is complicated by additional information provided in the Gospel of Luke. "In those days," says Luke, "a decree went out from Emperor Augustus that all the world should be registered." (Luke 2:1) Luke is correct that Roman emperors and governors did periodically order a comprehensive census of the subjects in their territories. The purpose of such a census was not to gauge the demographic makeup of a province, but to establish a detailed inventory of individuals and their property. Without such an inventory, Rome could not arrive at a reasonably accurate assessment of what a given region was worth, and what it could be expected to yield in taxes. This was important, since Roman governors did not collect the taxes themselves; they lacked the administrative apparatus to do so. Instead, tax collection was outsourced to free agents known as tax collectors—the *telones* or publicans of the Gospels. The only way to determine whether these tax collectors were cheating or not was if one knew beforehand what the tax base should yield in any given year. That is why a census operation was of vital importance to Rome's imperial budget.

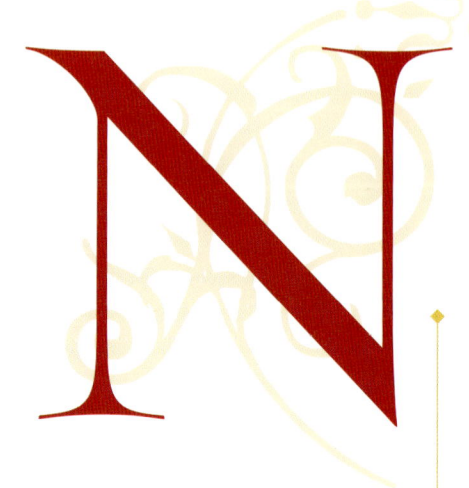

Luke goes even further and states that this census "was the first registration," meaning it was the first time the Romans ever conducted such a census in Judea. That is also true, because in the past all taxes had been collected by

Herod's regime. The king, keen to please Rome, always paid his tribute on time, and even sent personal gifts to Augustus and other highly placed officials. While Herod was alive, therefore, there was no need for a Roman census, not in the least because Judea was technically still an autonomous kingdom. Even after—with Augustus's blessing—Herod's kingdom was carved up between his sons and sister, these individual territories were governed as before. In other words, it was up to Archelaus, Antipas, Philip, and Salome to collect the taxes in their allotted fiefdoms, and to remit their share of the tribute to Rome—without the need for Roman tax officials to get involved.

But this changed in the year 6 C.E., when Archelaus, ethnarch of Judea and Samaria, was removed from office, after a delegation from Judea had asked Augustus to intervene because of the ethnarch's misrule. Augustus ordered Archelaus banned to Vienne, the Roman city on the Rhône in Gaul, and resolved that Judea should be annexed as a Roman possession. This was a grave disappointment for

An orchard in the vicinity of Sepphoris in Galilee has olives ripe for the plucking.

PART II | THE LIFE OF JESUS

Herod Antipas, who had hoped that Augustus would now declare *him* as the rightful heir of his father's kingdom, including the right to be called king.

This was not to be. Augustus considered Judea (and Samaria) to be of so little consequence that he did not even give it the designation of a Roman province, to be ruled by a governor. Instead, it was to be treated as an appendage to Roman Syria, to be governed by a *prefectus,* or prefect, who in turn would report to the governor in Antioch, Syria, rather than to the emperor or the Senate. Given the lower diplomatic status, the position of prefect was usually filled by a Roman *eques,* or knight, whereas a governorship was reserved for senators.

As it happened, the position of governor in Antioch was also vacant at the time. Therefore, two new Roman diplomats soon set sail for the Near East. One was the first prefect of the newly minted territory of Roman Judea (Iudaea), a man called Coponius, suitably drawn from the equestrian ranks in Rome. His new superior was a senator named Gaius Publius Sulpicius Quirinius, a longtime friend of Julius Caesar. Quirinius had served under Augustus in the legion that defeated the emperor's longtime nemesis, Mark Antony. He had also finished a term as governor in Galatia and

The Early Years of Jesus

Pamphylia in Asia Minor—the same region where, some 50 years later, Paul would conduct some of his most successful missionary work.

Since Quirinius was new to the job in Syria, and since Judea had only recently been added as Roman-occupied territory, his first decision was to order a census to assess the property values in all of the regions now under his control, not only Syria but also Judea and Samaria. Rome could no longer rely on a Herodian to remit the tribute; hence, this now became *his* responsibility, or better still, that of his subordinate, the prefect Coponius. And this brings us back to the Gospel of Luke, who confirms that "the first registration . . . was taken while Quirinius was governor of Syria." (Luke 2:2)

The dating used by Luke's narrative, however, creates a problem with the chronology. As we saw, Judea was not annexed and Quirinius did not assume his new position as governor until 6 C.E., some ten years *after* the death of King Herod. Jesus would have been at least ten years old at that time. We should therefore look for other indications in the Gospels that can help us determine the exact year of Jesus' birth.

The Magi from the East

In Luke's story, the newborn Jesus is attended by shepherds, but in Matthew's narrative the birth summons the arrival of three "wise men from the East" (*magoi*

A modern photo of Jericho evokes the lushness of its palm groves, which were renowned in the days of Herod the Great.

In this Byzantine 14th-century mosaic (opposite), Governor Quirinius is receiving the roll calls from the census in Bethlehem.

PART II | THE LIFE OF JESUS

apò anatoloon; Matthew 2:1). The Greek word *magoi* used by Matthew has been translated as either magicians or astrologers. At many courts in the East, including ancient Babylon and Persia, learned astrologers often served as highly placed priestly advisers, practiced in the art of magic. During the centuries, the three magi have also been interpreted as kings, particularly given Matthew's frequent use of prophetic symbolism inspired by Hebrew Scripture. Psalm 72, for example, extols the wise and righteous ruler, praying that "all kings fall down before him, and all nations give him service." (Psalms 72:11) Matthew also relates how the magi knelt down for the baby Jesus and "offered him gifts of gold, frankincense, and myrrh," which may reflect Isaiah's vision of nations rendering tribute to Jerusalem: "A multitude of camels shall cover you . . . they shall bring gold and frankincense, and proclaim the praise of the Lord." (Matthew 2:11; Isaiah 60:6) Others, however, see the reference to "frankincense and myrrh" as a foretelling of the funerary unguents that will be carried to Jesus' tomb after his Crucifixion.

> WISE MEN FROM THE EAST CAME TO JERUSALEM, ASKING, "WHERE IS THE CHILD WHO HAS BEEN BORN KING OF THE JEWS?"
>
> GOSPEL OF MATTHEW 2:1-2
> *Circa 75-90 C.E.*

Matthew also mentions that the three magi embarked on their journey when they "observed his star at its rising." (Matthew 2:2) This may be another symbolic allusion to Hebrew Scripture, in particular to a "magician" named Balaam, who was asked by the king of Moab to put a curse on Moses and the Israelites on their way to the Promised Land. According to the Book of Numbers, Balaam obeyed an angel of the Lord and offered an oracle of blessing instead, saying "I see him, but not now; I behold him, but not near—a *star* shall come out of Jacob, and a scepter shall rise out of Israel." (Numbers 24:17)

Other authors, however, have interpreted the reference to the "star of Bethlehem" as a historical event that could provide a clue to Jesus' birth date. One example is when the 17th-century astronomer Johannes Kepler, on the evening of December 17, 1603, discovered a bright conjunction of the planets Jupiter and Saturn in the constellation of Pisces. Working his way back, he postulated that a similar conjunction would have occurred in 7 B.C.E. Modern calculations, however, indicate that the closest approach of these planets would have been 0.98 degrees, not enough to make them appear as "one bright star." Nevertheless, an interesting twist on the conjunction theory is that the 15th-century rabbinical sage Isaac Abravanel prophesied that the conjunction of Saturn and Jupiter in Pisces in 1464 would herald the coming of the Messiah.

Another candidate that has been put forward as Matthew's star is Halley's Comet, which appeared in 12 B.C.E. and was widely observed throughout

The Early Years of Jesus

the Roman Empire. As a comet, this celestial phenomenon had a long tail, which in the unspoiled, crystal-clear nights of Antiquity would have been visible to the naked eye. What's more, it *moved;* hence, it could conceivably lead people in a given direction. As Matthew states, it went "ahead of them . . . until it stopped over the place where the child was." (Matthew 2:9)

Halley's Comet visits the earth every 74 to 79 years. In 66 C.E., Josephus reported the comet's appearance over Jerusalem, indirectly confirming its previous showing in 12 B.C.E.

Yet another explanation for Matthew's "star from the East" is provided by Chinese astronomers during the Han dynasty. They recorded what some astronomers have assumed was a supernova in late March or early April in the year 5 B.C.E. A supernova is a stellar explosion of such power that it can briefly outshine its galaxy for several weeks or months, easily visible to the naked eye.

Mindful of the fact that Jesus must have been born before the death of King Herod in 4 B.C.E., and the possibility that Matthew's "star from the East" may

This sixth-century mosaic of the Three Magi is visible in the S. Apollinare Nuovo in Ravenna, Italy.

This gold rhyton, or drinking cup (opposite), in the shape of a winged lion, dating from the fifth century B.C.E., attests to the virtuosity of Achaemenid Persia in precious metals.

PART II | THE LIFE OF JESUS

have either been Halley's Comet or the Chinese-observed supernova event, we should therefore place the date of Jesus' birth sometime before the year 4 B.C.E.

The Fields of Bethlehem

Where was Jesus born? At first glance this appears to be an easy question: in Bethlehem, of course. Both Luke and Matthew place the birth in this small town located just five miles south of Jerusalem. But why Bethlehem? Did Mary not live in the village of Nazareth in Lower Galilee? What brought her and her husband Joseph to Bethlehem, a journey of more than 100 miles by foot, even though Mary was in the final stages of her pregnancy? Both Luke and Matthew present a different explanation, which again has provoked intense scholarly debate.

Luke links the journey to the census ordered by Quirinius. Because of this mandatory registration, says Luke, "all went to their own towns to be registered." Indeed, the Romans wanted to document the population in their place of residence, not only to verify their property values but also to ensure that they knew where the tax collectors could find them. "Joseph," Luke continues, "also went from the town of Nazareth in Galilee to Judea, to the city of David called Bethlehem." Luke however doesn't tell us where Joseph actually lived. Given the endogamous nature of marriages in first-century Galilee, we would expect Joseph to live in the region of Nazareth. Luke indicates as much when he says that Joseph had to go to Bethlehem "because he was descended from the house and family of David." (Luke 2:4) In other words, while Joseph didn't actually reside in Bethlehem, this is where traditionally his family had come from. The Romans however didn't care about the place of ancestry; they wanted to see where one lived at that very moment. What's more, if Joseph indeed resided in Galilee, then the Quirinius census would not have applied to him and Mary, since Galilee was still an autonomous region ruled by Herod Antipas, not Roman-occupied land.

Luke tells us that once Joseph and Mary arrived in Bethlehem, they found that "there was no place for them in the inn." So they sought shelter in a stable, and while there, "the time came for her to deliver her child. And she gave birth to her firstborn son and wrapped him in bands of cloth, and laid him in a manger." (Luke 2:6-7)

Matthew, on the other hand, offers a different reason why Joseph and Mary found themselves in Bethlehem. He suggests that this is actually where Joseph and Mary lived. The star that leads the magi from the East stopped "over the place where the child was," and "upon entering the house" (*oikian*) "they saw the child with Mary his mother." *Oikos* means both "house" and "household," which

A photo of Halley's Comet taken in 1986 clearly shows the lower and upper tails, consisting of plasma and dust.

The star near the top of this fresco of "The Adoration of the Magi" (opposite) by Italian artist Giotto di Bondone (1266–1337) is believed to be inspired by Halley's comet.

> AND YOU, BETHLEHEM, IN THE LAND OF JUDAH... FROM YOU SHALL COME A RULER WHO IS TO SHEPHERD MY PEOPLE IN ISRAEL.
>
> Gospel of Matthew 2:6
> *Circa 75–90 C.E.*

PART II | THE LIFE OF JESUS

implies that Matthew is talking about the couple's principal residence. In Matthew's Gospel, Mary and Joseph are already married at this time and thus living in the same house ("he took her as his wife" before she gave birth), whereas Luke states that Joseph "went to be registered with Mary, to whom he was engaged." (Matthew 1:24, Luke 2:5)

Later on in Matthew's story, after Joseph and Mary have fled to Egypt to escape King Herod, an angel appeared to Joseph, telling him it was safe to return. "But," says Matthew, "when he heard that Archelaus was ruling over Judea in place of his father Herod, he was afraid to go there. And after being warned in a dream, he went away to the district of Galilee." The fact that Archelaus succeeded Herod as ruler of Judea fits with the historical record, but it implies that Joseph and Mary were actually residing in Bethlehem before the turmoil surrounding the Herodian succession compelled them to move up north, to Galilee, which was outside Archelaus's jurisdiction.

The Role of Bethlehem in Scripture

Do the differences in Luke and Matthew matter? From a devotional point of view, they do not. The fact is that both evangelists are very careful to set the birth of Jesus in the village of Bethlehem, because many centuries earlier the prophet Micah had decreed that that's where the son of David would be born. Matthew, whose gospel is rich with allusions to Hebrew Scripture as instances of fulfillment, even paraphrases Micah's prophecy in full:

And you, Bethlehem, in the land of Judah,
are by no means least among the rulers of Judah;
for from you shall come a ruler
who is to shepherd my people in Israel
(Matthew 2:6; paraphrasing Micah 5:2 and II Samuel 5:2)

Lately, however, some scholars have become intrigued by another possibility. Seven miles northwest of Nazareth was a small village that was likewise called Bethlehem, or "Bethlehem-in-Galilee." As such it appears among 19 names in Joshua's description of the boundaries of the tribe of Zebulun (Joshua 19:15). The presence of a village by the name of Bethlehem in such close proximity to Nazareth, which was a tiny hamlet at the time, is certainly interesting. Bruce Chilton has argued that this is where Mary went to give birth, possibly because her pregnancy was under a cloud of uncertain

A BIRTH IN ANTIQUITY

As in many other cultures, childbirth in Galilee was the preserve of women, usually supervised by a midwife. A Greek physician named Soranus has left us a detailed record of birthing procedures. Prenatal care reportedly began around the seventh month, when linen bandages would have been tied around a woman's back to help her carry the burden of her growing belly. After the eighth month, the support bandages were removed in order to let gravity take effect and allow the child to drop. When the contractions began, she was seated on a birthing stool—a comfortable chair, sometimes with arm rests and back, with an opening in the seat for the delivery of the child. The newborn baby was rinsed with warm water and sprinkled with powdered salt as a disinfectant. Interestingly, Soranus recommended the use of "feeding troughs" or "mangers" as cradles, since they were slightly inclined and thus lifted the baby's head.

The Early Years of Jesus

paternity, and Mary wanted to get away from wagging tongues. It is also possible—though not proven—that either Mary or Joseph had family there. The putative birth of Jesus in a *Galilean* village called Bethlehem, then, may have inspired the evangelists to link it to Micah's prophesy.

Circumcision and Purification

For seven days after the birth of her male child, Mary was considered ritually impure (Leviticus 12:2). This enabled her body to slowly recover from the strain of birth. If her baby had been a daughter, the period of impurity would have been 14 days (Leviticus 2:5). Then, on the eighth day after birth, a joyful moment arrived: the baby Jesus was now considered strong enough to undergo *berit*, or ritual circumcision (Genesis 17:10-12). "After eight days had passed," Luke says, "it was time to circumcise the child." (Luke 2:21) Such a rite usually took place with all elders present. According to ancient Jewish practice, Joseph marked this

Dutch artist Gerard van Honthorst (1592–1656) cast this Nativity scene of 1620 in a romantic light, which was made popular during the Baroque era.

A midwife assists a young woman (opposite) in childbirth, in this Roman stone relief from Ostia.

> THE CHILD GREW
> AND BECAME STRONG,
> FILLED WITH WISDOM;
> AND THE FAVOR OF GOD
> WAS UPON HIM.
>
> GOSPEL OF LUKE 2:40
> *Circa 75–90 C.E.*

moment by naming the child. By bestowing his chosen name and his patronymic on Jesus, Joseph accepted the child as his legitimate offspring.

The name he chose was Jesus. As we noted, *Yeshu* or "Jesus" was a very common name in first-century Palestine, comparable perhaps to the popularity of "John" or "Joe" in our modern day. In the books written by Josephus, there appear at least 20 different men who are alternatively called "Jesus" or "Joshua"—ten of whom are Jesus' contemporaries.

Once the circumcision and naming ritual was completed, a feast was held to usher the newborn into the village community. The women would be busy laying out tables with fruits, barley cakes, and wine. If the harvest had been good and plentiful, perhaps a lamb or a sheep would have been slaughtered to heighten the festivities.

As prescribed in the Book of Leviticus, for the next 33 days Mary was not allowed "to touch any holy thing, or come into the sanctuary"; some scholars have interpreted this to mean that she would also be exempt from most household work (Leviticus 12:4). As Leviticus may have intended, this would have been

The Early Years of Jesus

a very special time for the young mother to bond with her newborn, to experience the unfamiliar pangs, anxieties, and joys of motherhood without having to worry about her housekeeping duties. During this blissful time, the women in the village took care of her and her husband's needs. She was, however, allowed to touch nonsacred objects or humans, such as hugging or kissing her husband, though she and Joseph knew that they had to abstain from any sexual relations during this period. According to Matthew, the couple had abstained from any intercourse up to this point, even though they were married, since the child was conceived "from the Holy Spirit." "Joseph," says Matthew, "had no marital relations with her until she had borne a son." (Matthew 1:25)

Once the 33 days were complete, Mary resumed her duties as spouse and mother. To restore her state of purity, she offered a sacrifice to God. Leviticus required a first-year lamb to be sacrificed as a burnt offering and a pigeon or dove for a sin offering. The word "sin offering" in this context means an "offering of purification." A lamb was beyond the means of most peasant families, but Leviticus had allowed for this, enabling poor families to suffice with only "two turtledoves or two young pigeons" as both a burnt offering and sin offering (Leviticus 12:6-8). Luke thus confirms that Mary and Joseph were "poor" when he states that after "they brought him up to Jerusalem . . . they offered a sacrifice according to what is stated in the law of the Lord, "a pair of turtledoves or two young pigeons." (Luke 2:22-24)

For Luke, however, the purpose of the journey to Jerusalem is not only to offer the purification sacrifice, but to also "present him to the Lord," quoting the book of Exodus, that "every firstborn male shall be designated as holy to the Lord." (Luke 2:23; Exodus 13:2) Just as Hannah presented her son Samuel at the Lord's shrine in Shiloh, so did Mary present her son Jesus in the Temple in Jerusalem (I Samuel 24-28). Luke reinforces the designation of Jesus as the Divine instrument of salvation, as Samuel once was, through the appearance of Simeon, a man filled with "the Holy Spirit," who recognizes Jesus "as your salvation which you have prepared in the presence of all the peoples." (Luke 2:25-31)

Growing Up in Nazareth

Both Matthew and Luke agree that Jesus grew up in his parents' home in Nazareth (Matthew 2:23; Luke 2:39). This would have been a humble dwelling built of rocks and stones, mortared with mud and then coated with clay, to ward off the sun in summer and the chill and rain in winter. This structure would have been roofed over with a latticework of wooden beams, interwoven with branches and palm fronds, and covered with hardened mud. The roofing technique of placing tiles on a crossbeam frame, often practiced in urban areas, was well beyond the means of the peasantry.

This humble home would have been large enough to accommodate Joseph, Mary, and their newborn baby. Mark suggests that Mary had more children by

This unusual polychrome figure of Mary breast-feeding the baby Jesus was carved in Austria in the 14th century.

The Church of the Nativity (opposite) in Bethlehem, built by Byzantine emperor Justinian in 565 C.E., is one of the oldest continuously operating churches in the world.

PART II | THE LIFE OF JESUS

This reenactment of a family from first-century Galilee shows the type of garments that adults and children in Nazareth would have worn at that time.

The village of Kazrin, in the North Golan, features a reconstruction of a typical single-family dwelling in northern Palestine of the first century C.E. (opposite).

Joseph, and that Jesus ultimately had four brothers, "James and Joses and Judas and Simon," as well as at least two sisters (Mark 6:3). Some scholars, however, defend the Catholic tradition of the perpetual virginity of Mary by noting that the term "brother" (*adelphos* in Greek) was often used within a clan to refer to close relatives or cousins.

Whenever the home needed additional space, most peasants simply built a second story on top of the first one—as is still the custom in many parts of the Middle East. As we saw, peasant homes of this type were usually clustered as multifamily dwellings around a common courtyard, sheltering members of a greater family. This arrangement offered a measure of protection and enabled the inhabitants to share milk from goats, eggs from chickens, as well as a grain mill and a clay oven, used for baking bread. Ze'ev Safrai has found the remains of such multifamily dwellings in a number of locations including Hirbet Najar, Hirbet Susyah, and Meiron.

Each morning before dawn, the women would rise to fetch fresh water from the village well. They would then sit down to make their "daily bread." Each would draw a measure of grain from a lidded jar and pour it into the grain mill. This mill consisted of two round slabs of stone, anchored on a central wooden spike, which allowed the top to be rotated across the bottom by way of a wooden handle. The

The Early Years of Jesus

motion crushed the kernels and ground them into fine flour that sifted down to the bottom. The women would gather the flour in a bowl and add a bit of salt, olive oil, half a cup of water, and yeast, and knead it into the consistency of dough. The dough would then be rolled out into thin round cakes, since these rose more quickly and thus saved time and fuel.

Next, the oven would be fired with kindling, branches, and animal dung. Once the clay chamber was sufficiently hot, the dough patties were inserted and baked until the bread rose and was ready for consumption. Soon, the heady scent of freshly baked bread would waft through the compound, drawing all family members to the courtyard. If the air were cool and fresh, they would sit around the oven and enjoy the bread cakes with a sprinkling of olive oil, washed down with water, while the young women chattered in the light of the rising sun. Jesus would later pay homage to this quintessential ritual of Galilean life with the words "give us this day our daily bread" in the prayer he taught his disciples.

> HEROD ALSO BUILT A WALL ABOUT SEPPHORIS (WHICH IS THE SECURITY OF ALL GALILEE), AND MADE IT THE METROPOLIS OF THE COUNTRY.
>
> JOSEPHUS, *ANTIQUITIES OF THE JEWS*
> Circa 95 C.E.

PART II | THE LIFE OF JESUS

Olive trees such as this one in northern Galilee yielded one of the most valuable products in Antiquity: olive oil, to be used for cooking, for skin care, for lighting fluid, or as a condiment.

AT WORK IN THE FIELDS

Once breakfast was completed and the women gathered the remaining cakes for dinner, the men kissed their families and prepared to go to work. In an agricultural society like Lower Galilee, this meant a trip to the nearby fields. In ideal circumstances, family plots would be adjoining, so that a helping hand was always close by if one needed it, and draught animals and farming implements could be shared. In some cases, however, plots were scattered across a patchwork of fields because of intermarriage with other families and clans; in that case, individual lands were marked with boulders. Olive orchards and grapevines, by contrast, were bordered by walls to deter roving animals or even thieves. Was Joseph a farmer as well? Mark tells us that when Jesus returned to his native Nazareth after the beginning of his ministry, the people of his hometown were amazed by his words. "Is this not the carpenter, the son of Mary and brother of James?" they asked (Mark 6:3). The word *tektōn,* which in the King James Bible is translated as "carpenter," actually means something else: a skilled worker in either stone, wood, or metal. Good, workable wood was expensive in Lower Galilee, so wooden furniture—with the exception of farming tools—was beyond the reach of most peasants. In fact, the rich parables that Jesus uses later to describe his vision of the Kingdom of Heaven often use the metaphors of the field. Time and again, we hear him talk about seeds and sowing, the joys of a full orchard, or the frantic urgency of harvest time. Luke quotes the parable of a gardener, who counseled the owner of a fig tree to "let it alone for one more year, until I dig around it and put manure on it. If it bears fruit next year, well and good; but if not, you should cut it down." (Luke 13:6-8) Arguably, these are the words of a man who observed the seasonal cycle of orchards and fields since childhood. So why would Mark call Jesus a *tektōn*? A possible answer may be found in the political developments within Galilee proper.

THE TAX REVOLT

The census instigated by the Roman governor Quirinius and executed by the prefect Coponius in Judea and Samaria was not well received. One reason might be that the Romans expected the population to declare their property in currency value, rather than in kind—as a share of projected harvest yields as had been the custom for centuries. Josephus tells us that many Jews—specifically the urban elites—gave "a full account of their estates without protest." But the peasantry at large was not so amenable. Once again, unrest erupted into a protest movement, this time led by a man known as Judas the Galilean. Josephus does not say whether this man is the same as Judas, the son of Hezekiah, who led a revolt after the death of Herod the Great. Given the frequency of the name "Judas" in first-century Palestine, this is probably not the case.

HUNGER AND POVERTY

In his Sermon on the Mount, Jesus specifically addresses the poor and the hungry. How poor was a Galilean peasant? The typical land holdings of a peasant family probably ranged around four acres. Julius Caesar granted his legionnaires ten *jugura* of land, some six acres, which was considered the minimum to sustain a family. A farmer in Antiquity probably realized a return of 1:5, that is, five times the original seed planted. Ze'ev Safrai has calculated that the annual yield of a single acre was around 600 kilograms, or around 1,320 pounds. Allowing for crop rotation, this means that the average farmer would have needed at least 0.625 acre per person in his household. Douglas Oakman estimated it probably took 11 bushels of wheat to feed an adult person for one year. William Arnal agrees that Galilean families of four or five needed at least 5.5 to 6.5 acres of land to feed their families, and this *before* taxes. Recent U.N. estimates of peasant lands in developing countries have reached the same conclusion. This underscores the sense that most rural families in Galilee labored below subsistence levels.

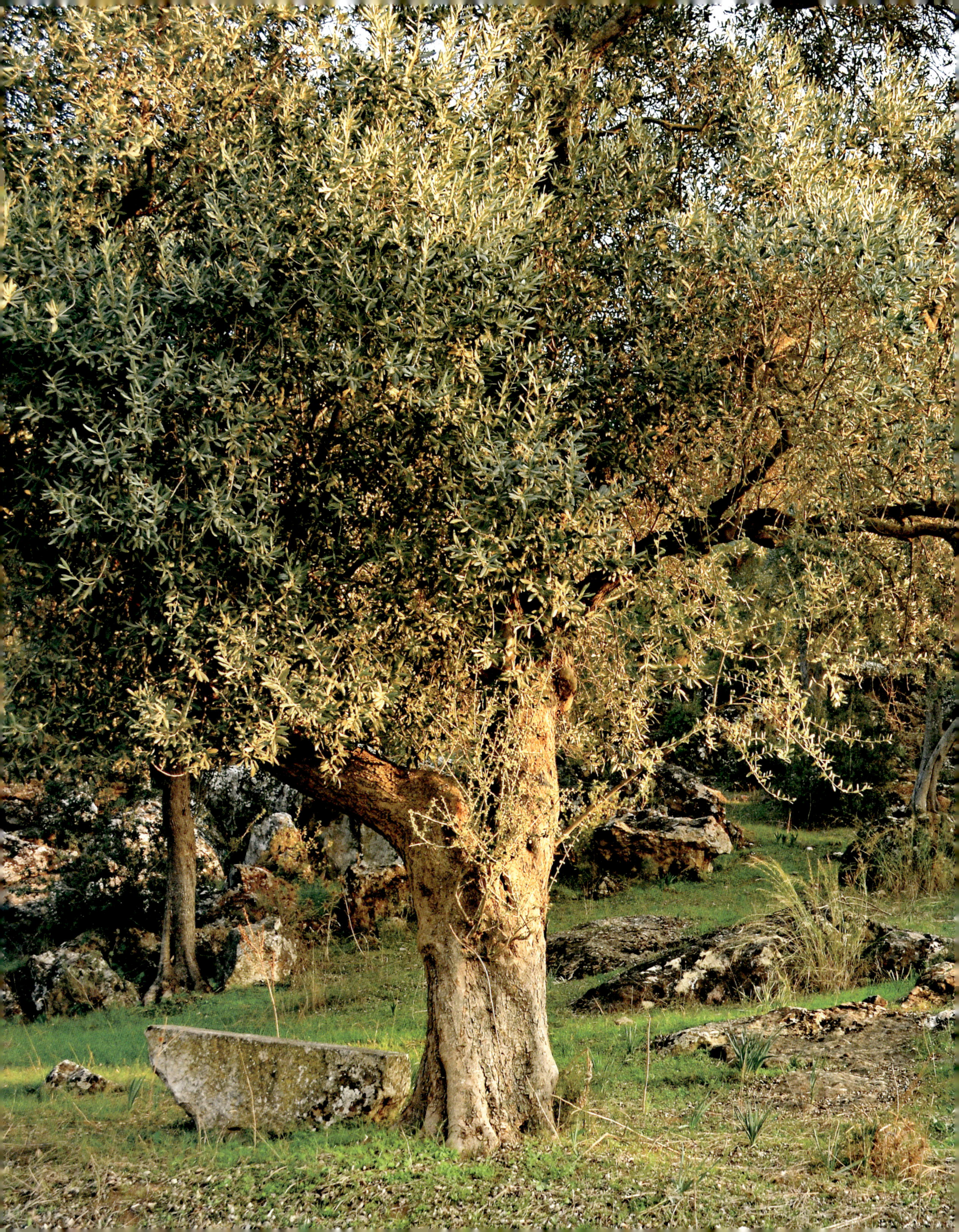

PART II | THE LIFE OF JESUS

THE BUILDING OF TIBERIAS

In 14 C.E., Augustus was laid to rest and succeeded by his stepson, Tiberius. The news would have been welcomed by Herod Antipas, whose relationship with Augustus was strained. It is also possible that Antipas, who was educated in Rome, had cultivated contacts with the Tiberius party; Josephus later wrote that "the tetrarch was in great favor with Tiberius." Antipas then began the construction of a second city dedicated to his new patron and named Tiberias. Located on the western shore of the Sea of Galilee, it was a true Greco-Roman city, including Roman baths, temples, and a gymnasium—institutions detested by observant Jews, since they were frequented by people in the nude. He also ordered a palace built for himself, which was destroyed after the outbreak of the Jewish War by vengeful Zealots. That the city was spared during the Roman reprisals that followed is evidence of the population's pro-Roman stance. Tiberias was built on the site of an old Jewish cemetery, which would have made it ritually unclean. Many Jews would have refused to work on the city, unless they were forced to. After the second Jewish Revolt led by Bar Kokhba, the rabbi Shimon bar Yochai cleansed the city, and eventually it became the center of a flourishing Jewish community and seat of the Sanhedrin.

The ruins of ancient Tiberias are still visible today on the southwestern shore of the Sea of Galilee.

The Early Years of Jesus

A detail of a third-century mosaic, known as the "Mona Lisa from Galilee," was discovered in a Roman villa of Sepphoris in the 1980s.

This olive lamp (below) with a scene from Homer's Odyssey *is typical of the type of terra-cotta lamps that were in use throughout the Roman Empire.*

But this resistance movement was very different from preceding revolts. Led by this Judas and a Pharisee named Zaddok, the movement urged noncompliance with any decree issued by the Romans, including their demand for people to report their property. As such it practiced a rather modern form of passive resistance that eschewed violence but refused to abide by what its adherents considered unlawful behavior. And in their eyes, the Roman census *was* unlawful, for the land it meant to assess belonged to God, not to Rome. For Judas and his followers, therefore, to accept the census was tantamount to submission to slavery. Josephus reluctantly admits Judas's ideological motives when, in his book *The Jewish War*, he called Judas a "teacher" rather than a "bandit." Some scholars believe that this resistance movement would ultimately coalesce into the party of the Zealots—the group that launched the disastrous Jewish War some 60 years later.

Sepphoris Is Rebuilt

In Sepphoris, the provincial capital of Galilee, the tetrarch Herod Antipas had reluctantly come to the conclusions that the Romans were in Judea to stay and he would *not* inherit his father's kingdom. This is when, some scholars believe, Antipas decided that if he couldn't be his father's successor, he would *act* as if he were. He too would start building cities from scratch.

The first city he ordered built was Sepphoris. Since the town's destruction by Aretas in 4 B.C.E., Antipas had merely restored the city's defensive walls and

PART II | THE LIFE OF JESUS

Discovered in Sepphoris, this colorful mosaic featuring geometric motifs probably dates from a later phase of this Galilean city, possibly around the third century C.E.

towers. Now, he resolved to rebuild Sepphoris as a new and splendidly Greco-Roman city, "the ornament of all Galilee," in Josephus's words. For Galilee, this was unprecedented. King Herod had never bothered to build anything of note in the province, and neither had the Hasmoneans. Galilean towns were usually a bewildering cluster of alleyways; a *planned* city was unheard of.

A major enterprise such as this would have deeply affected the neighboring villages, including Nazareth, just six miles distant. Most able-bodied men, including young boys older than 12, would have been conscripted to the work pits of Sepphoris. King Herod had done the same while building his glittering cities of Caesarea and Sebaste, and so did the Romans, who habitually recruited forced labor *ad opus publicum,* as letters by Pliny attest. Some authors have suggested that Jesus—and possibly, his father Joseph—spent many years in Sepphoris as workers in stone, wood, or metal—as *tektoi,* in short.

Eventually, the new Sepphoris would be equipped with several multistory buildings connected by well-paved streets and sidewalks. Shirley Case of the University of Chicago has speculated that Joseph and Jesus may have worked on building the theater. The dating of this theater is disputed, since Sepphoris was expanded considerably after the second century C.E. But some scholars still believe that the core of the theater, accommodating some 1,500 spectators, could have been built in the time of Herod Antipas.

Antipas had to tread carefully, however. He did not build structures that would give offense to the Jewish population, such as Roman baths, a gymnasium, or any temples dedicated to pagan gods. The coins struck in the city piously avoided any representation of living things. After the second century, the character of Sepphoris changed as it became more overtly Roman; but as Mark Chancey and Eric Meyers have shown, in the time of Jesus, Sepphoris was predominantly Jewish, given the presence of ritual baths, *mikva'ot,* and of stone vessels. As a result of Antipas's efforts, by about 20 C.E., Sepphoris was once again a sizable city, ranging anywhere from 12,000 to 30,000 inhabitants.

Sometime along the way, Jesus learned to read Scripture, though it is unclear where he would have received such an education. Nazareth was a very small hamlet at the time, though it is possible that Jesus received some form of synagogue schooling elsewhere. As we saw, the Talmud suggests that during the era of Rabbinic Judaism—after the destruction of the Temple in 70 C.E.—rabbis sought to provide every boy, even peasant boys, with some rudimentary training in the Law, but opinions vary as to what extent this program was carried out. While by the third or fourth centuries, some teachers, or rabbis, may have visited villages to teach Scripture to children of the local peasantry, it is unlikely that such would already have been the case in Jesus' time. Nevertheless, Jesus' own knowledge of Scripture must have been considerable because in the Gospels he is often referred to as *rabbi* himself.

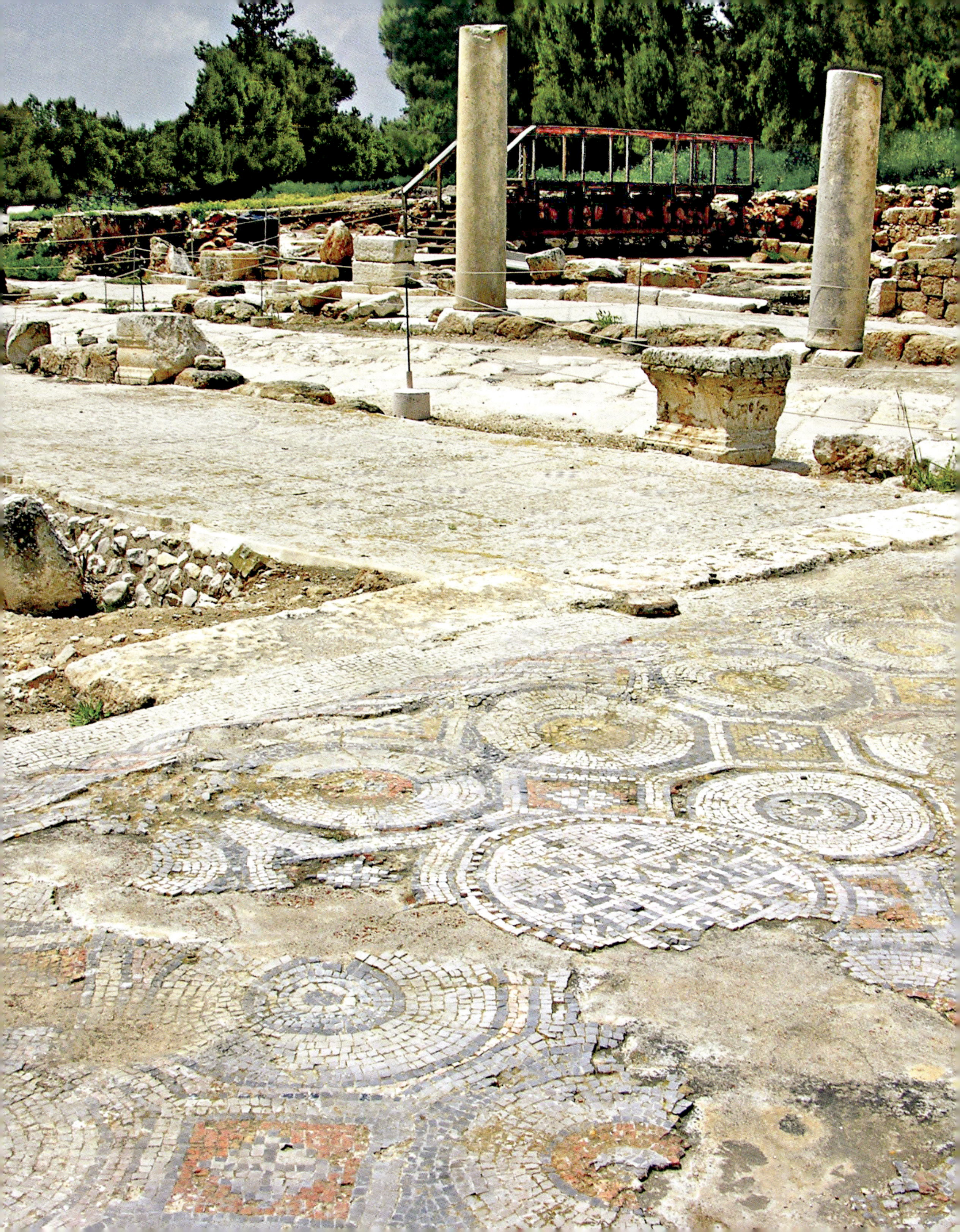

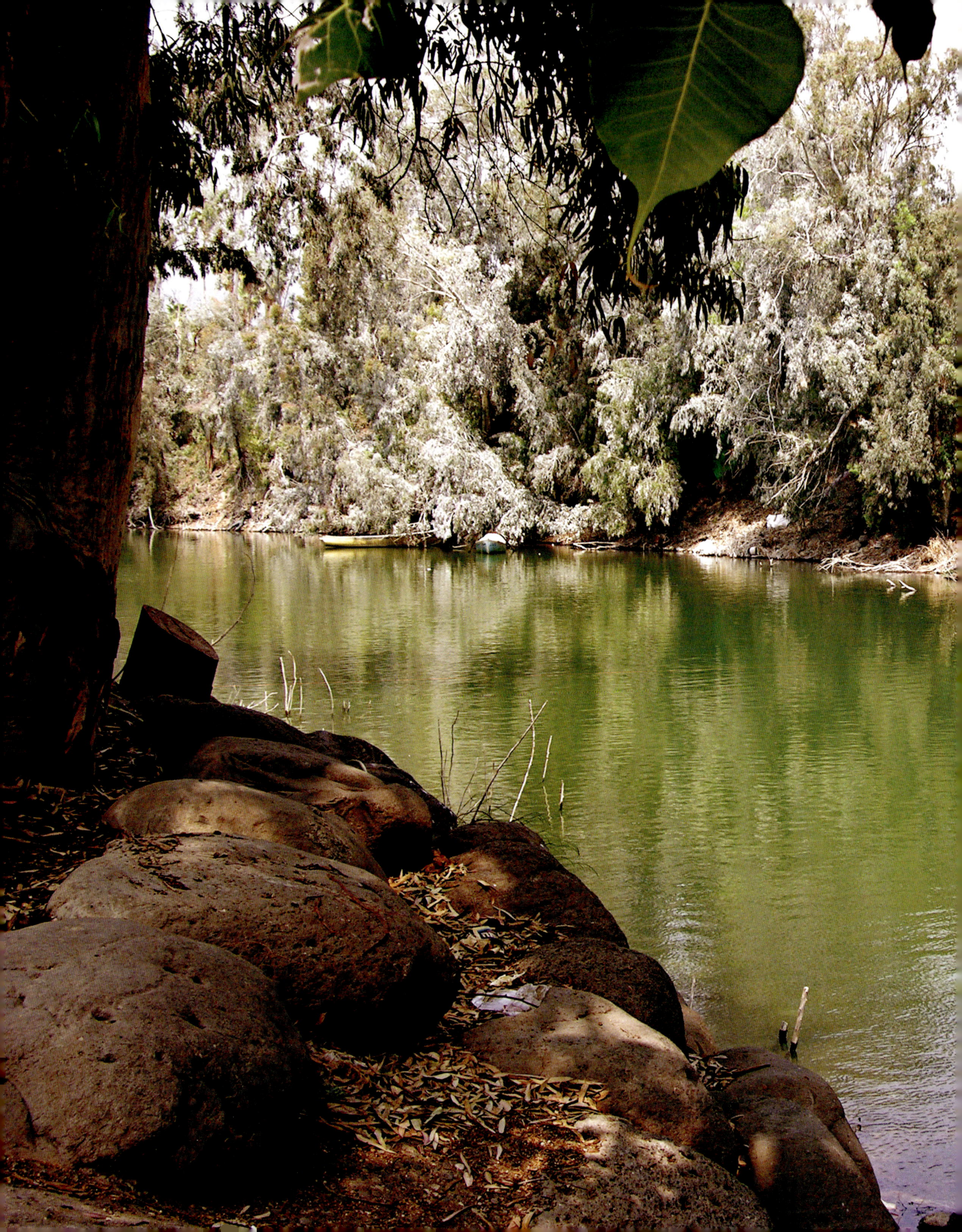

[CHAPTER] 6

JOHN THE BAPTIST *in the* JORDAN

IN THOSE DAYS
JOHN THE BAPTIST APPEARED
IN THE WILDERNESS OF JUDEA,
PROCLAIMING "REPENT,
FOR THE KINGDOM OF HEAVEN
HAS COME NEAR."

GOSPEL OF MATTHEW, 3:1-2
Circa 75–90 C.E.

The Jordan River flows near one of the places identified with Jesus' baptism by John the Baptist. From here, it descends down to the Dead Sea, located at 1,300 feet below sea level.

PART II | THE LIFE OF JESUS

Sometime after 26 C.E., about 20 years after the rebuilding of Sepphoris began, Jesus left his native Galilee and headed south, to Judea. For much of the way he would have followed the Jordan, a river that plunges headlong from its highest perch at 9,200 feet near Mount Hermon to just 700 feet below sea level over a distance of only 60 miles, before joining the Sea of Galilee as the lowest freshwater lake in the world. Along the way it is fed by streams, including the Hasbani (from Lebanon), the Dan, and the Banyas, which both spring from the foot of Mount Hermon. Exiting the Sea of Galilee just below Philoteria, past the Roman resort of Hamat Gader, the Jordan gains new impetus after it is joined by the Yarmouk River. It then meanders its way down the Jordan Rift Valley, the lowest land depression on Earth, and into the wide Jordan plain.

Well before this point, the soft green hills of Galilee, carpeted with the hues of apricot and lemon, are replaced by the stark, red ochre hills of the Judean desert, blazing against the deep blue sky. The river is then joined by another set of tributaries, the streams of Nahal Yaboq and Nahal Tirza, before beginning its last run down to Jericho and the Dead Sea, just 1,365 feet below sea level. At this point, in southern Judea, the river carves a narrow ribbon of luscious green, in stark contrast to the barren landscape on either side of the valley. It teems with cane, oleander, tamarisk, and brush—an unfettered "wilderness," as the Gospel of Matthew calls it, in the heart of the Judean Desert.

John in the Jordan

Jesus had embarked on this journey to meet one of the most charismatic religious dissidents of his day, a man named John. All the Gospels describe this pivotal encounter, which in many ways marks the beginning of Jesus' ministry. In his usual laconic style, Mark reports that "in those days Jesus came from Nazareth of Galilee and was baptized by John in the Jordan." (Mark 1:9) With his eye for historical context, Luke sets the scene "in the fifteenth year of the reign of Emperor Tiberius, when Pontius Pilate was governor of Judea, and Herod was ruler of Galilee." (Luke 3:1) Tiberius succeeded Augustus in 14 C.E., and Pontius Pilate assumed his office as Roman Prefect in Judea in 26 C.E.; by modern reckoning, Luke is probably talking about the year 28 C.E.

126

Matthew gives us a vivid portrait of John the Baptist. "Now John wore clothing of camel's hair with a leather belt around his waist, and his food was locusts and wild honey," the evangelist tells us, evoking the image of Elijah, who was likewise described as "a hairy man, with a leather belt around his waist." (Matthew 3:4, II Kings 8) The allusion to Elijah was probably deliberate, for it reminded Matthew's audience of God's promise that "I will send you the prophet Elijah before the great and terrible day of the Lord comes." (Malachi 4:5) In Matthew's elegant allegory, John is the harbinger of the Messiah, just as Elijah had once foretold the Lord's coming.

The Gospel of John continues the metaphor; at one point, the Baptist is asked by "priests and Levites from Jerusalem" whether he is Elijah, or even the Messiah himself (John 1:20-21). John assured them that he was not, and then paraphrased Isaiah, saying that "I am the voice of one crying out in the wilderness, Make straight the way of the Lord." (Isaiah 40:3)

The Jordan Rift Valley, the lowest land depression on Earth, is a 230-mile fault zone that runs from Syria through Israel, Jordan, and the Palestinian Territories to the Dead Sea, and on to East Africa.

PART II | THE LIFE OF JESUS

French artist Antoine de Favray (1706–1792) painted this impression of "St. John the Baptist in the Wilderness Indicating Christ" around 1759.

Who was John the Baptist? Luke depicts him as a powerful orator who urged his listeners to repent and plead forgiveness of sins, for a great cataclysm was coming that would herald the coming of the Messiah. John was not alone in espousing such eschatological ideas. During the previous century, the Jewish nation had become increasingly polarized over the Hasmonean decision to combine the office of the high priest with that of the secular monarch. Things didn't improve when Herod, though not assuming the title of high priest himself, appointed priests to the office from among families he could trust and control. The popular revulsion against this cronyism led to a fragmentation into factions, each determined to restore observance and piety according to the Law. On the one hand, the Sadducees insisted that the sacrificial cult at the Temple was the principal conduit to repentance and salvation, while on the other, the Pharisees wanted to extend the possibility of holiness beyond the priestly caste to the ordinary people. Through constant debate of the Law, the Pharisees sought for ways to make observance more accessible for ordinary Jews.

There was also a third group, which was called the Essenes. They agreed with much of what the Pharisees were saying, but pushed the practice of physical and spiritual purity to the extreme—even to the point of abstaining from bowel movements on the Sabbath, lest they defile this holy day. Living in a monastic community of sorts, wearing linen shifts and bathing often, they practiced an ascetic lifestyle so as to come closer to God. "They despise riches," Josephus wrote, claiming that the movement numbered around 4,000 members, "and it is a law among them, that those who join must let whatever they have be shared with the whole order." In addition, Josephus added, "they reject pleasures as an evil, but esteem continence and the conquest over our passions to be a virtue."

The Hellenization of the Jewish kingdom under the Herodians and the subsequent Roman occupation produced a fourth and more radical group, possibly as the result of a split from the Pharisaic faction, which sought full religious and political freedom without any compromise. This group, which was implicated in the tax revolt of 6 C.E., would later assume more militant overtones and become known as the Zealots.

Eschatological Ideas

What these factions had in common was a firm belief that the nation was on the wrong track, and that its sins, as well as the sins of its foreign occupier, were bound to invite the wrath of the Lord. This, they believed, would be a cataclysmic

PONTIUS PILATE

The Pontii were a minor family of Roman *equites,* or equestrian class, as distinct from the true aristocracy of Rome, the senatorial class. For a knight to gain the rank of senator, he not only had to have a distinguished military and political career, but also show assets in excess of a million sesterces (roughly the equivalent of $4 million today). By law, senators (and aspiring senators) could not engage in commerce, trade, or financial speculation. Hence, for most knights the diplomatic service was often the only route to advancement. While serving as a prefect or governor, a man could make a fortune selling monopolies and franchise licenses, while skimming from mining and taxation proceeds. In one notorious case exposed by Cicero, Gaius Verres, the governor of Sicily, had amassed a huge fortune by extorting large sums from wealthy Sicilians—simply by threatening his victims with crucifixion. In 26 C.E., the year when Pontius Pilate was appointed prefect to Judea, the emperor Tiberius chose to retire from active rule, leaving the government in the hands of the commander of the Praetorian Guard, named Lucius Aelius Sejanus. Some scholars have speculated that Pilate was a close friend of Sejanus, which may explain why Pilate was awarded the appointment in Judea, even though there is no record of him having served in any diplomatic or military capacity before this date.

A stone from the Roman theater in Caesarea bears the dedication "[to the gods this] Tiberium [has been dedicated by] Pontius Pilate, Prefect of Judea."

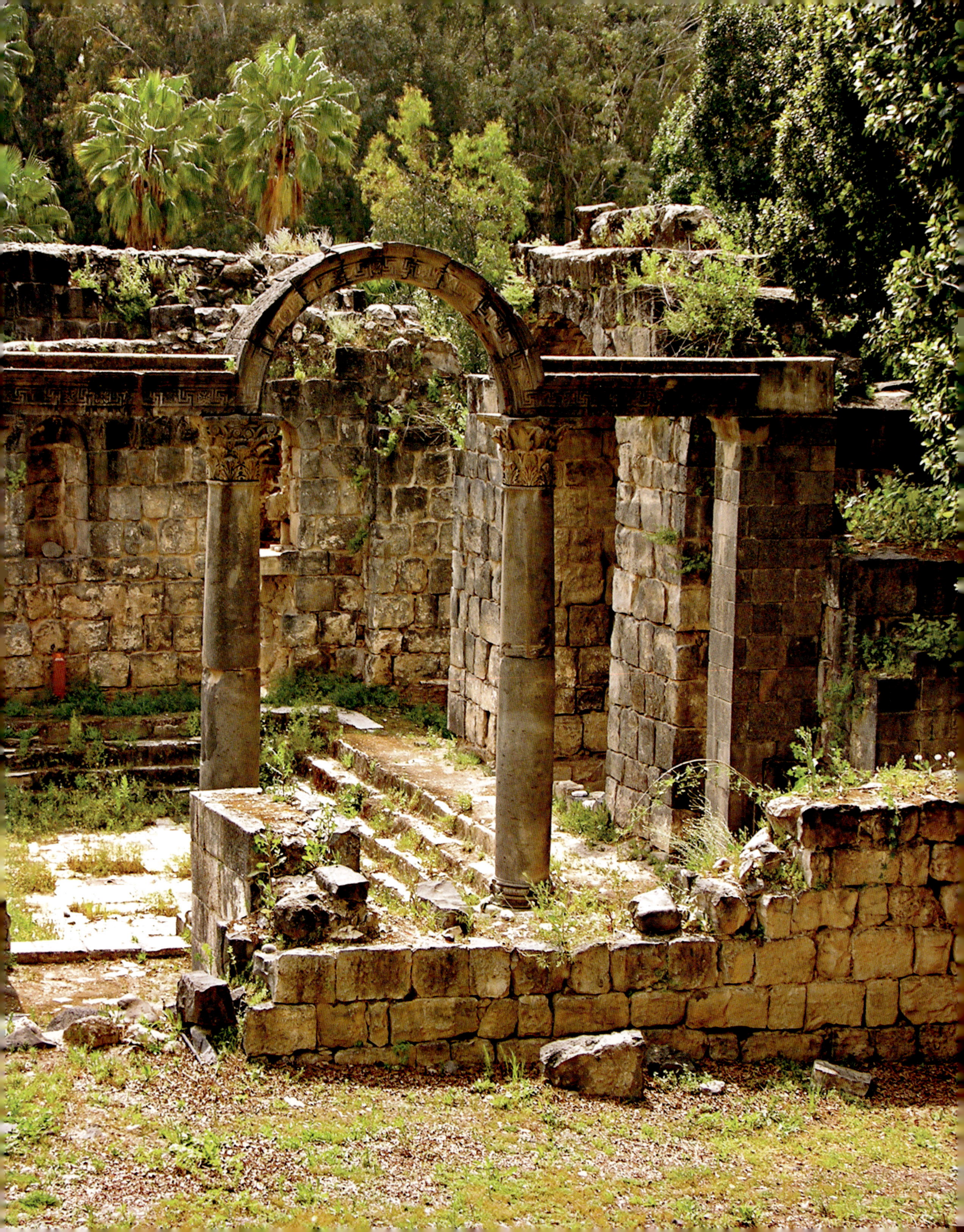

transformation, brought about by a divinely appointed savior—the *Mashiach* or Messiah—which would herald a true reign of God.

As several scholars including David Levenson have shown, these eschatological ideas originated as early as the mid–second century B.C.E. One example is the Book of Daniel, which laments to God how "all Israel has transgressed your law and turned aside, refusing to obey your voice." Only if the nation repents, the book says, will God's control be restored over the Jewish nation (Daniel 9:11). The Psalms of Solomon, written about 50 years before the birth of Jesus, also anticipates a spiritual "cleansing" of the Jewish nation. "May God cleanse Israel against the day of mercy and blessing," the book states, "against the day of choice when He brings back His Anointed" (the literal translation of the Hebrew word *Mashiach* or Messiah). (Psalms of Solomon 18:6-8)

At this stage in Jewish thought, however, there was no agreement as to who this Messiah would be. Some saw him as a descendant of King David, and the reign of God as a restoration of the former Davidic Kingdom. The book of Daniel sees the deliverer as, alternatively, an angel (Michael) or by contrast, "one like a son of man," a normal human being. In some cases, the Messiah was cast as a military commander; many believed that Simon bar Kokhba, the leader of the Second Jewish Revolt against the Romans in 132 C.E., was the Messiah. The Dead Sea Scrolls, by contrast, speak of *two* messiahs; a warrior king and "Branch of David," who is subordinated to a priest, the "Messiah of Aaron."

Seen in this context, John the Baptist was very much a man of his time. He too preached the coming of a Messiah and warned his audience that "even now the ax is lying at the root of the trees; every tree therefore that does not bear good fruit is cut down and thrown into the fire." (Luke 3:9) John's militant language would suggest that he saw the *mashiach* in a military sense, one who would reconquer the Jewish nation through force of arms. "The winnowing fork is in his hand, to clear his threshing floor and to gather the wheat into his granary," the Baptist threatens in the Gospel of Luke; "but the chaff he will burn with unquenchable fire." (Luke 3:17) To prepare for this event, John urged his listeners to repent, to abandon their sinful ways, and to signify this transformation with a ritual of purification: the rite of baptism.

The Place of Baptism

Where was John's principal base of operations? The Gospel of John says that the first encounter between Jesus and John "took place in Bethany across the Jordan." (John 1:28) For years, scholars have been trying to locate a village called Bethany in the Transjordan—that is, on the east bank of the Jordan, in what was then the territory of Perea. The Gospels also refer to another village of Bethany, but this was located just a few miles away from Jerusalem. The famous

This cooking pot, dating from the Late Second Temple period (first century B.C.E. to first century C.E.) was found in an individual grave of a mysterious male skeleton at Qumran.

These impressive remains of a Roman baths complex (opposite), begun in the second century C.E., were excavated in Hamat Gader, near the eastern shore of the Sea of Galilee in the Yarmouk Valley.

The Dead Sea Scrolls were found in 1947 in a group of caves, including Cave 4 shown here, located just outside the ancient settlement of Qumran, close to the Dead Sea.

In this ancient cave town (opposite) in Jordan, refugees from the Second Jewish Revolt (131–135 C.E.) found refuge.

Byzantine Madaba Map, dating from the sixth century, refers to a village called Beth Araba west of the Jordan, which some Church fathers, including Origen and Eusebius, identified with Bethany-across-the-Jordan. But other authorities suggest that John operated on the river's *eastern* banks, not in the least because Perea was ruled by Antipas from his palace in faraway Sepphoris, well outside the jurisdiction of the Roman Prefect of Judea.

During her journey to the Holy Land in the fourth century C.E., Empress Helena, the mother of Constantine the Great, reportedly identified a spot on the eastern shore that she believed was the location of John's baptism and decided to build a church there. The location of this church remained a mystery until the 1994 Peace Treaty between Israel and Jordan allowed the Jordanian Army to clear the region of land mines. Archaeologists eagerly followed in their wake, and soon discovered remains that they tentatively identified as John's Bethany—some seven miles north of the Dead Sea. Starting in 1996, the Jordanian Department of Antiquities conducted a six-year excavation campaign led by Mohammad Waheeb, which brought to light various remains from the Early Roman Period as well as the ruins of a Byzantine monastery. The presence of stone jars, prized for their properties of preserving cultic purity, clearly suggest the place was once an observant Jewish community. Nearby the excavators discovered the remains of an early Byzantine church, which could well be the edifice originally built by Empress Helena.

If the identification of this location as John's village of Bethany is true, then its proximity to another famous spot close to the Dead Sea—the community of Khirbet Qumran—is certainly intriguing.

The Community of Qumran

Qumran is the location of many steep cliffs and crags, bordering on the Dead Sea, where in the winter of 1947 a Bedouin shepherd named Muhammad el-Hamed went looking for a lost goat. The hills are permeated with caves; in one of these, now known as Cave 1, the shepherd found several jars containing ancient scrolls, among which are the oldest known versions of the Hebrew Scriptures. As archaeologists—as well as eager Bedouin—descended on the hills, scores of other ancient "Dead Sea Scrolls" were found, spread over 40 of the 260 caves that dot the limestone cliffs. Some of the rolls, mostly written in Hebrew, have been carbon-dated to between 20 B.C.E. and 60 C.E.—exactly the time of Jesus, right before the outbreak of the Jewish War of 66–70 C.E.

What is remarkable about the Dead Sea Scrolls is their age; before their discovery, the oldest known manuscripts of Hebrew Scripture in *Hebrew* included the Aleppo Codex from the tenth century C.E., while the oldest *Greek* version of segments from the Old and New Testament, the Codex Sinaiticus, was probably written in the fourth century C.E. What's more, the Dead Sea Scrolls contain almost all of the books included in our modern Hebrew Bible, with the exception of the Book of Esther. But the cache also included other texts not related to the Bible, some of which purport to be the rules of some sort of cultic community. These include the so-called Community Rule document (*Serekh ha-Yahad,* referred to by scholars as 1QS) and a foundational text known as the Cairo-Damascus Document. It is likely that this mysterious sect was probably involved in the copying and safekeeping of the Dead Sea Scrolls.

The discovery launched an intensive search to see where this community could have lived.

> **ALL WHO PRACTICE RIGHTEOUSNESS ARE UNDER THE DOMINATION OF THE PRINCE OF LIGHTS, AND WALK IN WAYS OF LIGHT; WHEREAS ALL WHO PRACTICE PERVERSITY ARE UNDER THE DOMINATION OF THE ANGEL OF DARKNESS.**
>
> "The Community Rule"
> (1QS), Qumran
> *Circa 150 B.C.E.–70 C.E.*

PART II | THE LIFE OF JESUS

In 1951, Roland de Vaux began excavating the remains of a large settlement near Khirbet Qumran, right in front of the rocky outcroppings where nearly 900 scrolls were found. He eventually laid bare an elaborate complex, guarded by a tower, which includes what appears to be a library, a dining hall, and a potter's workshop with kilns and ovens. He also found an elaborate system of stepped cisterns that could have been used for ablutions or water storage. Potsherds and other artifacts suggest that the community was established around 150 B.C.E. and lasted until the onset of the Jewish War, sometime between 66 and 70 C.E.

As many as six inkwells were found on the site, a very large number by archaeological standards, which clearly points to extensive scribal activity. Though some scholars continue to insist that the settlement was a private villa, a military fortress, or even a caravanserai, most scholars accept that this was the place, or one of the places, where the Dead Sea Scrolls were written. Scholars theorize that the Qumranite scribes hid the scrolls in the nearby caves in order to save them from the advancing Roman army during the Jewish War of 66–70 C.E.

Teacher and Prophet

According to the so-called Cairo-Damascus Document, the Qumran community was formed under the leadership of a "Teacher of Righteousness," who derived his authority from his knowledge and interpretation of "the Torah and the Prophets"—the canon of the Hebrew Scriptures as the age of Jesus knew it. It was the "Teacher of Righteousness," says one document, "to whom God has disclosed all the mysteries of the words of his servants the prophets." The documents present this Teacher of Righteousness (*Moreh Tzedek*) as both a prophet, a teacher, and an agent of salvation. By following his example, the Qumran community devoted itself repentance and scriptural study in expectation of the coming reign of God.

What kind of a sect was this Qumran group? The presence of what appear to be ritual baths or *mikva'ot*, indicating a concern for physical purity, combined with an obvious interest in studying biblical texts would suggest that they were Pharisees. However, Pharisees usually lived in urban areas, not in the desert. Some experts have associated the group with Sadducees, given that the Qumran community was led by a priest, or a hierarchy of priests; on the other hand, the Qumran community clearly rejected the cult of the Temple so prized by Sadducees (though it is believed that they did remit their annual tithes). Many scholars, therefore, see a link to the third cult group described by Josephus, namely the Essenes.

When we take Josephus's description of the Essenes and compare it with the archaeological evidence found at Qumran, a number of parallels are apparent. Josephus said that at the fifth hour, after "they have clothed themselves in white veils, they then bathe their bodies in cold water." This would

---

JESUS' SPEECH

Like virtually all other Jewish peasants in Galilee, Jesus spoke Aramaic, the common language in Palestine. A Semitic language closely related to Hebrew and Phoenician, it is also the language of later books in the Hebrew Scriptures, such as the Book of Daniel. The Gospels contain no fewer than 26 words in Aramaic spoken by Jesus. For example, Jesus refers to God the Father as *Abba*, an Aramaic term of endearment. While on the cross, Jesus cries out, "*Eloi, Eloi, lama sabachthani?*"—a quote in Aramaic from Psalm 22, which means "My God, my God, why have you forsaken me?" Some scholars infer that Jesus spoke Aramaic with a Galilean accent. While Peter was warming his hands by a fire in the courtyard of Caiaphas's palace, he was promptly recognized as one of Jesus' followers by his speech. "Certainly you are also one of them," a servant girl told Peter, "for your accent betrays you." (Matthew 26:73) It is possible that Jesus also picked up a few words of Greek in places like Sepphoris. The Gospels suggest that he could converse with a centurion, as well as the prefect, Pontius Pilate, who would have spoken Greek—the diplomatic language of the time.

explain the network of cisterns at the site, designed to catch sufficient rainfall to allow members to ritually immerse themselves at set times of the day. After this ritual ablution, Josephus claims, the Essenes entered a communal "dining room, as into a certain holy temple," where they say grace and share their meal. Exactly such a "refectory" has been tentatively identified in Qumran.

Furthermore, Josephus tells us, the Essenes "take great pains in studying the writings of the ancients, and choose out of them what is most for the advantage of their soul and body." This would strongly argue for an identification of the Essenes with the authors of the Dead Sea Scrolls. Josephus also claims that "[the Essenes] equally preserve the books belonging to their sect," which could refer to the "Community Rule" documents found among the Dead Sea Scrolls.

And yet, the question of whether the Qumran community should be considered Essene or not continues to occupy scholars. Some have argued that in the works of Josephus, the Essenes are described as an urban phenomenon, rather than a community of hermits in the desert. The Jewish philosopher Philo seems to agree, writing that the Essenes lived "in many cities of Judea, and in many villages and grouped in great societies of many members."

Among these remains of the Qumran settlement, Roland de Vaux found potsherds and other artifacts dated between 150 B.C.E. and 70 C.E.

These terra-cotta and copper ink pots (opposite), dating from the Late Second Temple period (first century B.C.E. to first century C.E.), were found at Qumran.

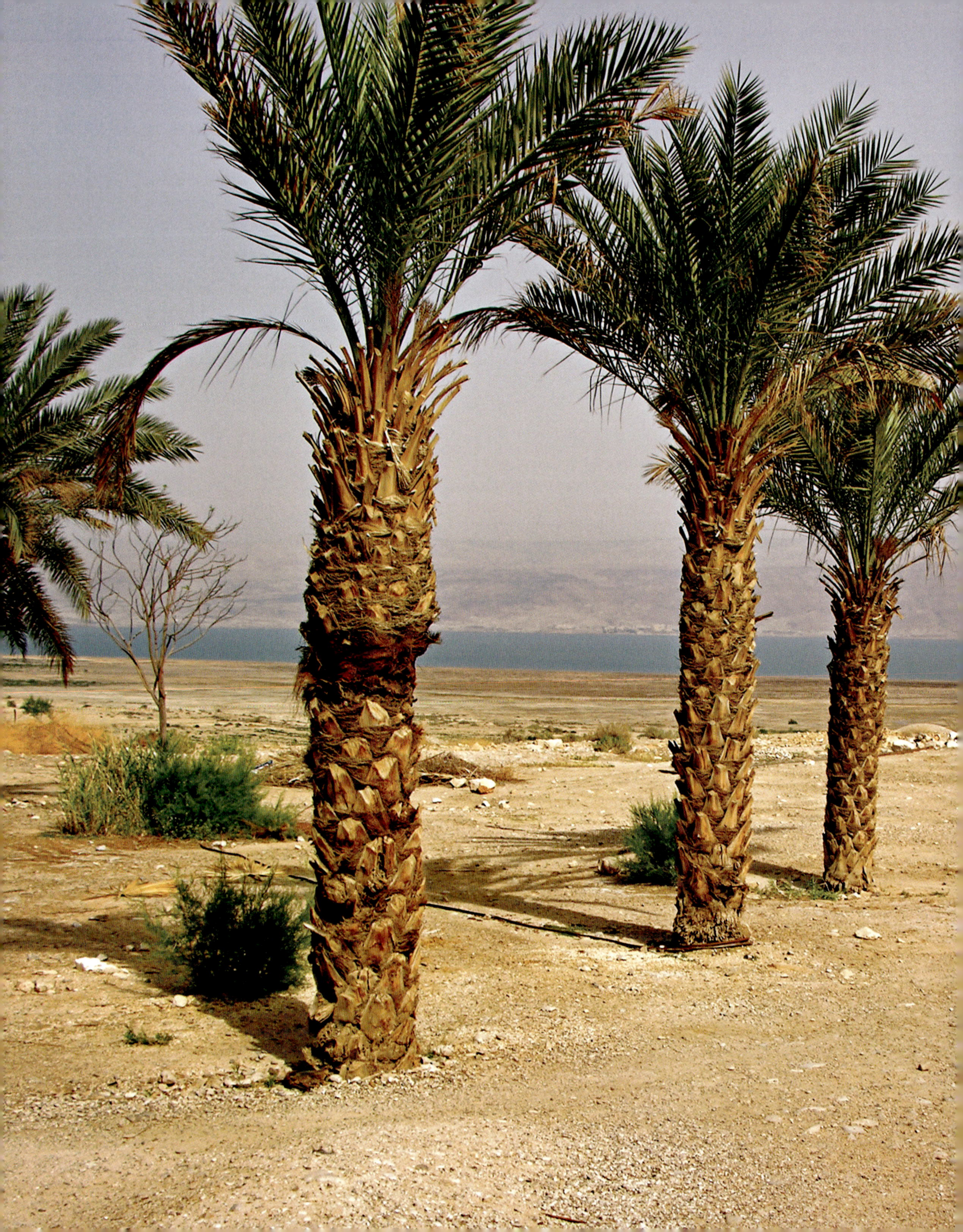

John the Baptist in the Jordan

Many scholars now believe that the Qumran community was an Essene breakaway group that sought the solitude of the desert—perhaps as a symbolic return to the wilderness, to prepare for the coming of the reign of God. Josephus himself tells us that there was at least "another order of Essenes."

Qumran and John the Baptist

Is there a possible connection between John the Baptist and the Qumran community? According to the Community Rule document, the mission of the sect was to prepare for the final struggle between the forces of good and evil, of "Darkness" and "Light"—metaphors that would later return in the Gospel of John—while anticipating the arrival of the Messiah, "the Prince of Light."

The Qumranite community texts also instruct each member that "his property and his possessions shall be given to the hand of the man who is the examiner over the possessions of the many." Similarly, John the Baptist told a crowd that "Whoever has two coats must share with anyone who has none; and whoever has food must do likewise." (Luke 3:10-11) Both the Qumranites and John the Baptist lived in isolation, far from Judea's urban centers, in search of an ascetic lifestyle, subsisting on a Spartan diet.

In addition, the Qumran concept of a Teacher/Prophet who leads his people to repentance, guided by the spirit of God, resonates strongly with the portrayal

This detail of the Community Rule scroll (1QS), found in Cave 1 in Qumran, includes rules for the disposition of property within the community.

These palm trees (opposite) mark the boundary of the Qumran archaeological area, located close to the Dead Sea.

of John the Baptist and Jesus in the Gospels, who are also referred to as Teachers (Luke 3:12 and John 3:26).

There are, however, also important discrepancies. The Qumran sect formed what appeared to be a fairly closed community to which one had to be initiated; the Baptist, on the other hand, welcomed whomever was willing to cleave to his words—even Sadducees and Pharisees, according to Matthew (Matthew 3:7). The Qumran group practiced ritual immersion, but only in private baths or *mikva'ot*, in order to achieve physical and moral purity. For John, however, immersion was not a daily cleansing ritual but a symbolic token of repentance. In John's hands, "baptism" became an instrument of personal empowerment, of individual transformation. Last but not least, John didn't use a private *mikveh* for his baptisms, but the flowing waters of the River Jordan, available to all.

One way to explain both the similarities and the discrepancies between John and the Qumran sect is that John may have been a member of the group who eventually chose to go his own way. Perhaps he desired to minister to *all* of Judea, rather than to a closed circle of members. Interestingly, Luke suggests at the beginning of John's infancy narrative that "the child was *in the wilderness* until the day he appeared publicly to Israel." (Luke 1:80)

> FOR IT SEEMED TO [JOHN] THAT BAPTISMAL WASHING WOULD BE ACCEPTABLE, NOT ONLY FOR THE REMISSION OF SINS, BUT ALSO FOR THE PURIFICATION OF THE BODY, BELIEVING THAT THE SOUL WAS THOROUGHLY CLEANSED BY RIGHTEOUS CONDUCT.
>
> JOSEPHUS, *ANTIQUITIES OF THE JEWS*
> *Circa 95 C.E.*

JOHN AND HEROD ANTIPAS

While the Gospels depict John the Baptist in predominantly religious terms, Josephus—who devotes almost half a page to John the Baptist—explains John's prominence from a more political point of view. We should remember that Josephus wrote for a Roman audience, who had little understanding of Jewish messianic aspirations but who, in the wake of the Jewish Rebellion of 66 C.E., were more concerned about the political stability of Judea. John "the Baptizer," says Josephus, "was a good man, who exhorted the Jews to exercise virtue, both in terms of righteousness toward one another and piety toward God, and so come to baptism." In fact, Josephus adds, John's movement became so successful that "crowds flocked to him, and they were greatly moved by his words."

The Baptist's popularity soon raised the suspicions of Herod Antipas, who as we saw ruled over both Galilee and Perea—including the eastern bank of the Jordan. The reason was that, as Josephus suggests, John's followers "seemed ready to do anything he should advise." In first-century Palestine, where religious passions and political aspirations were always closely intertwined, John's mass following would have been a source of concern. Moreover, John's vocabulary was rather shocking and abusive—even to those who came to hear him. In the Gospel of Luke, for example, a group of newly arrived pilgrims is promptly greeted as "a brood

John the Baptist in the Jordan

of vipers." "Do not begin to say to yourselves, 'We have Abraham as our ancestor,'" John rails; "even now the ax is lying at the root of the trees!" (Luke 3:8-9) In the politically charged atmosphere of the moment, this strong language was bound to elicit some form of response from the authorities. For John, it may have been a calculated ploy to shake his listeners from their complacency and urge them to repentance. Later we will see that Jesus sometimes used the same tactic, particularly when addressing the wealthy or the powerful, rather than the Galilean poor.

John reserved special scorn for corruption among the elites, such as tax collectors and soldiers. In the Gospel of Luke, John orders the "publicans" to "collect no more than the amount prescribed to you"—meaning the target amount that the Roman census had assigned to each property. Soldiers are warned not to "extort money from anyone by threats or false accusation, and [to] be satisfied with your

Flemish artist Joachim Patinir (1480–1524) created this panel of "The Baptism of Christ" around 1515.

This colored depiction (opposite) of a soldier was found on a gravestone near Sidon, Lebanon. Soldiers were one of the groups targeted by John the Baptist for their corrupt practices.

PART II | THE LIFE OF JESUS

wages"—implying that such extortion was probably common practice at the time (Luke 3:12-14).

It is perhaps not surprising that Herod Antipas began to see John's growing prominence as a threat. He "feared that the great influence John had over the people might empower him to raise a rebellion," Josephus explains, which given the recent memory of peasant revolts in Judea and Galilee was not an unreasonable assumption. Even the Gospels, which are careful not to exalt John above Jesus, acknowledge that "the people of Jerusalem and all of Judea were going out to him, and all the region along the Jordan." (Mark 1:5; Matthew 3:5)

{ THEN JESUS CAME FROM GALILEE TO JOHN AT THE JORDAN, TO BE BAPTIZED BY HIM.

GOSPEL OF MATTHEW 3:13
Circa 75–90 C.E. }

Jesus' Baptism

This, then, is the moment when Jesus arrives on the scene. Why did Jesus decide to join John's movement? Why now, around 28 C.E., when Jesus—if our calculations are correct—would have been at least 32 years old, and by the standards of

John the Baptist in the Jordan

his time, approaching middle age? The evangelists do not tell us, which is rather remarkable, given that Matthew and Luke are often at pains to provide motive for events in Jesus' life. One explanation would be that Jesus gravitated to John because of his dramatic message of religious reform. John urged repentance and the rejection of sinful living in anticipation of a future kingdom of God—ideas that would later become key themes in Jesus' ministry. Another reason may be found in Josephus's book *Antiquities of the Jews.* One or two years before Jesus' journey to the Jordan, in 26 C.E., the new Roman Prefect of Judea—a man named Pilate, member of the knightly family of the Pontii—had embarked on a deliberate policy of provocation and confrontation with his Jewish subjects. In this he had considerable freedom of movement because his nominal superior, Lucius Aelius Lamia, governor of Greater Syria, was not in Antioch but in Rome, having left for an extended stay in the Roman capital.

Pilate's escalating provocations eventually led to mass protests in Jerusalem. These demonstrations were prompted by rumors that Pilate was planning to seize funds from the Temple treasury in order to build a Roman aqueduct. As a large crowd began to form near the Temple, Pilate ordered his soldiers to don civilian cloaks and infiltrate the crowd. At his signal, they threw off their mantles and raised their swords on whoever happened to be standing nearby. "They slew not only those that had participated in the demonstration," says Josephus, "but even innocent bystanders, who had nothing to do with it." Before the day was out, thousands lay dead or dying in the twisting alleys of Jerusalem. A wave of revulsion swept over Judea. This may have induced many Jewish men and women to leave their homes and turn to one of the most famous religious orators of their day, in search of succor and guidance.

Sometime after his arrival in the wilderness, Jesus was baptized by John in the Jordan River. The Gospels are aware of the subtle incongruity of this event, because John's baptism was designed for sinners, as an instrument of repentance. What type of sins would have been attached to Jesus? In Matthew's story, John actually resists Jesus' request to be baptized, saying, "I need to be baptized by *you*, and (yet) you come to me?" But Jesus answered him, "Let it be so now; for it is proper for us in this way to fulfill all righteousness." (Matthew 3:14-15) John then proceeds with the baptism, but as Jesus emerges from the water, says Mark, "he saw the heavens torn apart and the Spirit descending like a dove on him. And a voice came from heaven, "You are my Son, the beloved; with you I am well pleased." (Mark 1:10-11) This verse, which appears to combine a citation from the Psalms ("You are my Son," Psalms 2:7) with Isaiah ("My chosen, in whom my soul delights," Isaiah 42:1) is repeated almost verbatim in the other Gospels (Matthew 3:17, Luke 3:22, and John 1:32-33).

The vision of the dove illustrates the true allegorical meaning of John's baptism: Instead of symbolizing the rejection of sin through the cleansing water of

This elegant terra-cotta dancer from the Early Roman Period is typical of votive statuettes that were often found at sanctuaries.

This impression of "Herod's Birthday Feast" (opposite) from 1868 was painted by British Victorian artist Edward Armitage (1817–1896), who specialized in historical and biblical subjects.

JOHN'S PLACE OF EXECUTION

The fortress of Machaerus was a Hasmonean fortification, located on the eastern banks of the Dead Sea in the territory of Perea. Archaeologists believe it was originally built by the Hasmonean king Alexander Jannaeus (r. 103 to 76 B.C.E). Thirty years later, during Pompey's invasion of Palestine, it was destroyed by Roman forces, but rebuilt by Herod because of its excellent natural defenses. Like Masada and the Herodion, two other natural strongholds expanded by Herod, Machaerus rose high above the surrounding countryside to an altitude of 3,000 feet above the level of the Dead Sea. Surrounded by ravines on all sides, the location offered protection to a sumptuous palace built within its center. It was here, according to Josephus, that John the Baptist was executed on orders of Herod Antipas, since Perea formed part of Antipas's territory. During the Jewish War, Zealots occupied the fortress, which prompted the Roman general Lucilius Bassus to besiege the stronghold and start building a ramp, as was done at Masada in 73 C.E. Unlike the defenders of Masada, however, the occupying force of Machaerus capitulated to the Romans before the siege engines could be brought in place. Machaerus was first excavated in 1968, though the actual remains of the Herodian palace were discovered by Virgilio Corbo of the Franciscan Biblical Institute in Jerusalem between 1978 and 1981.

The citadel of Machaerus, about 15 miles southeast of the River Jordan, was rebuilt by Herod the Great around 30 B.C.E. and later passed to his son Herod Antipas.

the Jordan, Jesus is being *anointed* by the Spirit of the Lord for his ministry as the Messiah, the Anointed One. In describing the scene, the evangelists may once again have been inspired by Hebrew Scripture. "The spirit of the Lord God is upon me," says Isaiah; "because the Lord has anointed me; he has sent me to bring good news to the oppressed, to bind up the brokenhearted, to proclaim liberty to the captives." (Isaiah 61:1) Sometime later, in Capernaum, Jesus will read from this very verse to proclaim the beginning of his ministry (Luke 4:18).

In his later teachings, Jesus would often pay homage to John the Baptist. In the Gospel of Luke, for example, Jesus asked the crowds, "What did you go out into the wilderness to look at? . . . A Prophet? Yes, I tell you, and more than a prophet." (Luke 7:24, 26) And he added, "I tell you, among those born of women no one is greater than John." (Luke 7:28) In the Gospel of Matthew, Jesus calls John "the Elijah who is to come. Let anyone with ears listen!" (Matthew 11:14)

John's Arrest

Sometime after 28 C.E., Herod Antipas decided that he could no longer tolerate John's activity as a preacher, and ordered his arrest. The Gospels provide religious motives for this decision, whereas Josephus explains it in political terms.

Antipas was originally married to the daughter of King Aretas IV Philopatris—possibly the same Aretas (or the son thereof) who had devastated Galilee during the peasant revolt. During one of his visits to Rome, Antipas had been introduced to the wife of his half-brother Philip, named Herodias. Scholars do not agree whether Josephus is referring to Philip, the Tetrarch of the Gaulanitis, or Herod Philip I, but either way the family association was uncomfortably close. What's more, Herodias herself was *also* related to Antipas, for she was the daughter of Antipas's half-brother, Aristobulus (son of Herod the Great and Mariamne). This in itself wasn't exceptional; of the 39 members of the Herodian line who were married, no fewer than *17* marriages were concluded between blood relatives.

Antipas then decided to ask for Herodias's hand in marriage. Herodias accepted, provided that Antipas divorce his first wife, the daughter of King Aretas. The first wife, however, found out about her predicament. She promptly fled to the fortress of Machaerus, where the Nabatean army collected her. King Aretas was deeply displeased and would soon exact his revenge.

John the Baptist took great umbrage at Antipas's marriage to Herodias. He told the tetrarch that "it is not lawful for you to have your brother's wife." (Mark 6:18) This is an obvious reference to Leviticus, which specifies that "you shall not uncover the nakedness of your brother's wife; it is your brother's nakedness." (Leviticus 18:16) Mark says that Antipas, stung by John's criticism, threw the Baptist in prison, but still the tetrarch feared him, "knowing that he was a righteous and holy man, and he protected him."

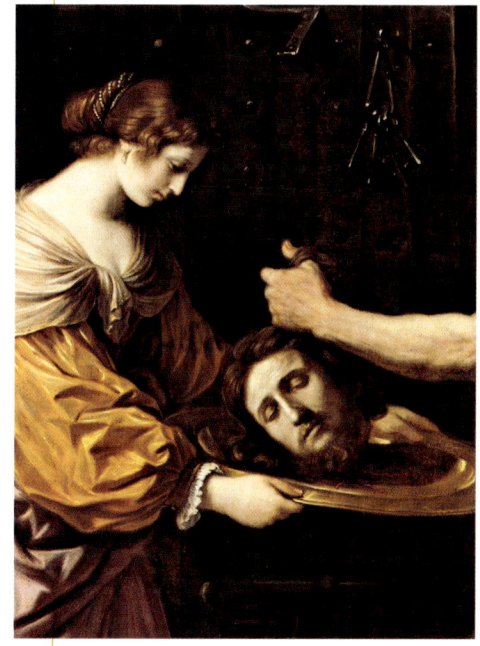

Italian Baroque artist Giovanni Francesco Barbieri, better known as Guercino (1591–1666), painted this canvas of "Salome Receiving the Head of St. John the Baptist" in 1637.

PART II | THE LIFE OF JESUS

A waterfall flows into the River Banyas, one of the source streams of the Jordan in Upper Galilee, located close to Mount Hermon.

Herodias herself, however, was not so well disposed. When Herodias's daughter (by her first marriage) delighted her stepfather on his birthday with her seductive dancing, Antipas offered her "whatever she wished," even "half of my kingdom." The daughter—whose name, according to Josephus, was Salome—conferred with her mother, who told her daughter to ask "for the head of John the Baptist on a platter." Antipas, says Mark, was "deeply grieved; yet out of regard for his oaths and for the guests, he did not want to refuse her." (Mark 6:17-28)

Thus, John the Baptist was beheaded.

For Josephus, however, the motive for John's murder is obvious: Antipas was afraid of John's power because his growing following appeared ready to do "anything that he would tell them to." Antipas feared that unless he intervened, John might be tempted to exploit the tensions in the region, with the "power and inclination to raise a rebellion." Matthew appears to agree with this assessment when he says that "[Antipas] feared the multitude, because they counted [John the Baptist] as a prophet." (Matthew 14:5) Hence, Josephus explains, Antipas "thought that by putting [John] to death, he would prevent any mischief he might cause."

It is remarkable that Antipas felt authorized to order John's death without some form of legal proceeding. For example, the Mishnah tractate *Sanhedrin* describes the conditions under which a "false prophet" may or may not be put on trial. Scholars debate, however, whether the Sanhedrin's reach beyond Judea was already in effect in the early first century.

What we do know is that Antipas's swift dispatch of John the Baptist, on his own authority, stands in sharp contrast to the lengthy proceedings required to bring Jesus to the cross. Mark adds that after John was killed, "his disciples heard about it, . . . took his body and laid it in a tomb." (Mark 6:29) This tomb has never been found, although in 2005 the archaeologist Shimon Gibson claimed that he had discovered a "cave" near the Tzova Kibbutz at Ain Karim. Based on various potsherds and markings, he identified the tomb with John's baptism. It is true that John's movement continued well into the second century and even penetrated as far as Asia Minor (Acts 19:1-4). However, Gibson's identification of the "Cave of John the Baptist" has not found broad support.

As a postscript, around 35 C.E., King Aretas invaded Perea, the territory ruled by Antipas, in order to seek revenge for the tetrarch's disgraceful divorce from his daughter. Herod Antipas sent an army to meet the invaders, but it was destroyed. Josephus adds that when word of the defeat spread in Palestine, many people were pleased, for they "thought that the destruction of Herod's army came from God, as just punishment for what he had done to John [the Baptist]."

> HEROD . . . THOUGHT THAT BY PUTTING [JOHN] TO DEATH, HE WOULD PREVENT ANY MISCHIEF HE MIGHT CAUSE, RATHER THAN GET HIMSELF IN DIFFICULTY BY SPARING THE MAN AND REGRETTING IT WHEN IT WOULD BE TOO LATE.
>
> JOSEPHUS, *ANTIQUITIES OF THE JEWS*
> Circa 95 C.E.

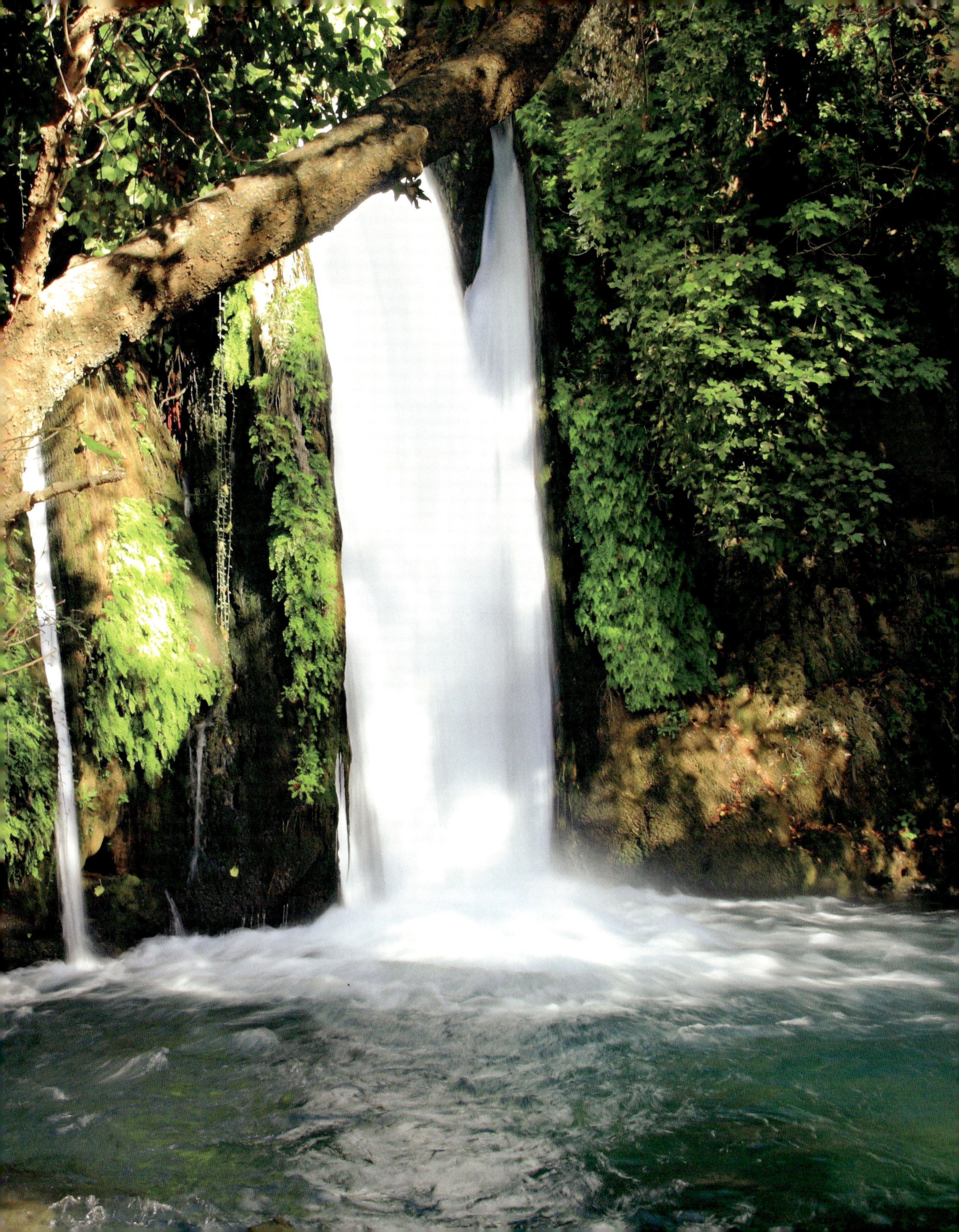

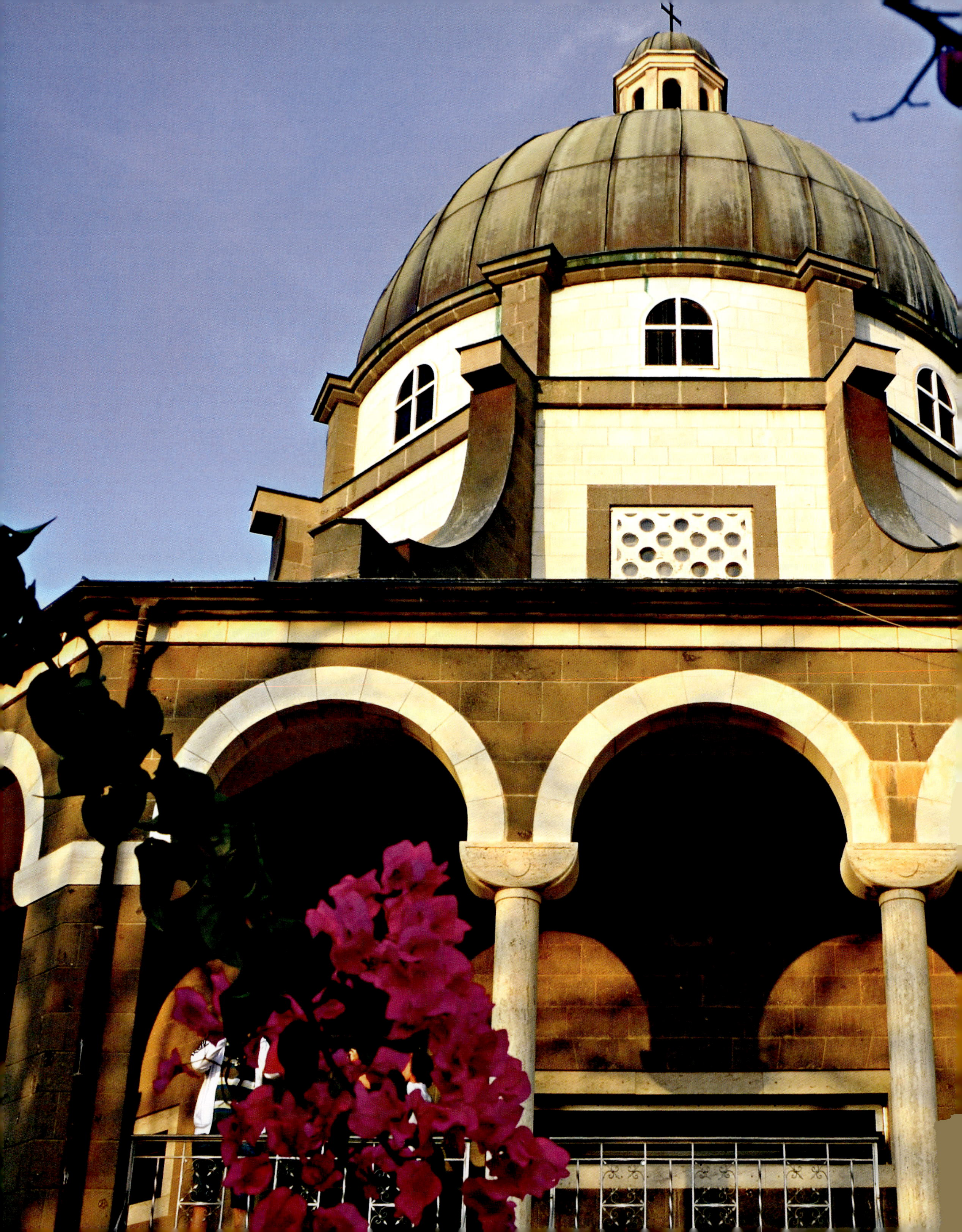

CHAPTER 7

JESUS' MINISTRY BEGINS

NOW AFTER JOHN WAS ARRESTED, JESUS CAME TO GALILEE, PROCLAIMING THE GOOD NEWS OF GOD, AND SAYING, "THE TIME IS FULFILLED, AND THE KINGDOM OF GOD HAS COME NEAR; REPENT, AND BELIEVE IN THE GOOD NEWS."

GOSPEL OF MARK 1:14-15
Circa 66–70 C.E.

The Church of the Beatitudes, built with Italian assistance in 1937— and inspired by the central church in Raphael's painting "The Marriage of the Virgin" (1504)—marks one of the locations associated with Jesus' Sermon on the Mount.

PART II | THE LIFE OF JESUS

Anyone who has ever read the Gospels will realize that the Gospel of John is different from the "Synoptic Gospels" of Matthew, Mark, and Luke. The Gospel is more symbolic and literary in scope; it dwells, for example, on long discourses by Jesus that are missing from the other Gospels. John's Gospel was probably written near the end of the first century C.E.; most scholars assume a date in the late eighties or nineties.

Nevertheless, the Gospel features some very specific characters and events—the wedding in Cana, for example—that do not appear in any of the other canonical texts. This would suggest that John's Gospel represents a parallel historical stream of tradition—one that may have had some contact with the Synoptic traditions but evolved independent of them. Indeed, John himself—or the author of the Gospel writing under John's name—claims that the document is based on "testimony" by a "disciple who is testifying to these things and has written them." (John 21:24)

Matthew and Luke state that after his baptism by John, Jesus withdrew into the desert where "he fasted forty days and forty nights." (Matthew 4:2) Their Jewish audience would have recognized this passage as a symbolic allusion to the 40 years that Moses spent in the desert, in preparation for entry into the Promised Land. The Gospel of Mark merely states that "Jesus withdrew to Galilee after John had been arrested." (Mark 1:14)

The Gospel of John, on the other hand, indicates that several of John's disciples gravitated to Jesus. Already, John's followers were calling Jesus "Rabbi" (which, John explains helpfully for his Greek-speaking audience, "means Teacher"), while the Baptist himself, in John's account, referred to him as "the Lamb of God." One day, John's disciple Andrew said to his brother Simon Peter, "We have found the Messiah." (John 1:38-41) The two brothers then shifted their loyalty to Jesus, who welcomed them and said to Simon, "You are Simon son of John."

It is not clear whether this means that Jesus knew Simon or his family. Jesus did however recognize Simon's steady and resolute character, for he promptly gave him a new name: "You are to be called Cephas." The Greek word *kephas* is a transliteration of the Aramaic word *kêfa*, which means "stone" or "rock"; in Christian literature it would be translated into the more familiar *Petros*, or Peter. In this, Jesus followed biblical precedent whereby figures are given new names the moment they embark on their divine mission. So, for example, did Abram become *Abraham,*

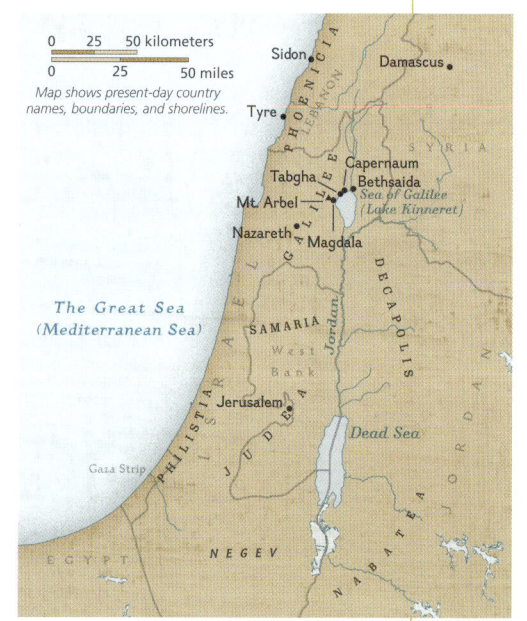

148

and Jacob was renamed *Israel*. Simon Peter and Andrew were soon joined by a third disciple named Philip. As it turned out, Philip—like the two brothers—hailed from the Galilean town of Bethsaida, and in first-century Palestine, village and kinship roots ran deep.

Jesus Leaves for Galilee

Jesus and his new followers then set out for Galilee. John's Gospel doesn't explicitly correlate Jesus' departure to the arrest of the Baptist, but Matthew does: "When Jesus heard that John had been arrested," his Gospel says, "he withdrew to Galilee." (Matthew 4:12) John's Gospel states that on the way to Galilee, Philip met a man named Nathanael and told him that "we have found him about whom Moses in the law and also the prophets wrote, Jesus son of Joseph from Nazareth." Nathanael was not impressed. He scoffed, "Can anything good come out of Nazareth?" Jesus found out about Nathanael's comment, because when

The northern shore of the Sea of Galilee, close to the ancient city of Capernaum, has changed little from the days of Jesus' ministry.

PART II | THE LIFE OF JESUS

This Roman fish hook is typical of the type used by fishermen in the Early Roman Period (first century B.C.E.–first century C.E.).

> **AS JESUS PASSED ALONG THE SEA OF GALILEE, HE SAW SIMON AND HIS BROTHER ANDREW CASTING A NET INTO THE SEA—FOR THEY WERE FISHERMEN. AND JESUS SAID TO THEM, "FOLLOW ME AND I WILL MAKE YOU FISH FOR MEN."**
>
> GOSPEL OF MARK 1:16-17
> *Circa 66-70 C.E.*

Nathanael reluctantly went to see Jesus for himself, Jesus mockingly said, "Here is truly an Israelite in whom there is no deceit!" (John 1:45-47) Jesus' use of the term "Israelite" was a deliberate pun on Israel, originally called Jacob, who in the book of Genesis had stolen the birthright from his brother Esau by subterfuge. Nathanael is usually identified with the man known as Bartholomew in the other Gospels, who was one of the 12 Apostles.

It is possible that Jesus first led the group to Bethsaida, where the three disciples could find shelter with relatives. Bethsaida was located *east* of the Jordan River, on the northeastern shore of the Sea of Galilee, and just inside the Gaulanitis—territory ruled by the tetrarch Philip. As such, Jesus and his new group of followers would have been safely beyond the reach of Herod Antipas, since no one knew whether Antipas was planning to arrest any of the Baptist's followers as well. They may have remained there until it was clear that Antipas was satisfied that John's movement had been fully suppressed.

Beth-tsaida literally means "house of fishermen," which denotes the town's principal trade; indeed, even Emperor Hadrian would later extol the abundance of its fish. Despite its renown, however, scholars have had trouble locating this ancient city. Some believe that there actually may have been two cities by that name. The Gospel of John, however, only refers to one Bethsaida, and it was unusual in Antiquity for two places by the same name to be in close proximity with each other. What's more, the city would figure prominently in the Gospel of Mark (Mark 8:22-26) and Luke (Luke 9:10-17) as one of the three cities that formed Jesus' "ministry triangle," which suggests it was at least within a day's journey by foot from Capernaum and Chorazin.

In 1987, the Israeli archaeologist Rami Arav decided to investigate one of the proposed sites of Bethsaida, at a *tell* or mound about a mile or so inland from the Sea of Galilee. This led to a major excavation project involving the University of Nebraska at Omaha and 14 other American universities and colleges, as well as universities in Germany and Poland. This international team discovered a small town with structures built using the local, charcoal-colored basalt stone, including remains from the Early Roman Period. These could have been the dwellings that Jesus saw when he arrived here in late 28 or 29 C.E. More discoveries await, since the campaign is expected to continue well past the 2012 and 2013 season.

JESUS GATHERS HIS DISCIPLES

Eventually, Jesus and his new followers moved across the Jordan into Galilee and settled in a town named Nahum's Village, or Capernaum. Some scholars infer from Mark that it was the hometown of Peter's wife (Mark 1:29-30), so Jesus

THE FISHERMEN OF GALILEE

Modern research suggests that the traditional community of professional fishermen around the Sea of Galilee was inundated with untrained peasantry who were dislocated from their ancestral land and no longer had any homes or means of support. At the Sea of Galilee, they may have reasoned, was still a harvest to be had, a harvest of fish. Many of these new arrivals may have first tried to catch fish from the shore, which would have had little effect. To get to the principal fishing grounds, one needed a boat—specifically, a boat big enough to hold several men able to cast and draw nets—and an expert mariner experienced in navigating the sometimes treacherous waters of the lake. Boats were expensive, but they could be leased out to multiple teams working in shifts. As documented by John Dominic Crossan, low water levels in the Sea of Galilee have exposed the levees of no fewer than 15 first-century fishing harbors. Inevitably, this vast increase in activity would have led to over-harvesting and the gradual depletion of the fish stocks. In the Gospel of Luke, Simon Peter tells Jesus that they have "toiled all night long, and not caught anything." Jesus urges him to throw his nets once again. Their nets then found such a huge catch that "many ships from nearby" rushed to the scene to help and to get their share of this unexpected boon, suggesting that even during the night many fishermen were out, casting their nets (Luke 5:4-7).

An anonymous sixth-century artist created this mosaic of **St. Andrew and St. Peter** responding to the call of Jesus in the church of **St. Apollinaire Nuovo** in Ravenna, Italy.

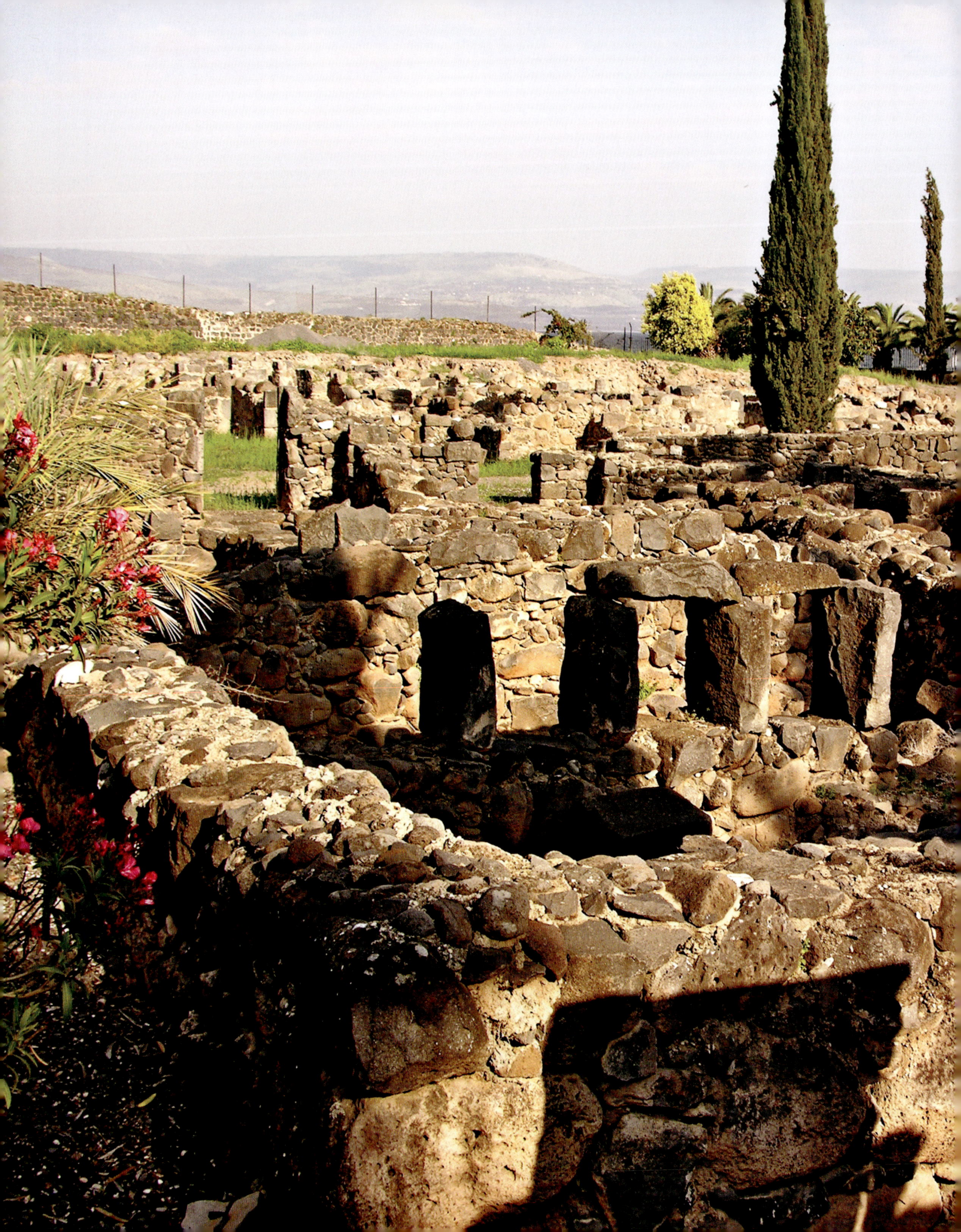

Jesus' Ministry Begins

would have been assured of a place to live while he prepared for the beginning of his ministry. In those days Capernaum was larger than Bethsaida, for it straddled one of the principal trade routes between Damascus and Jerusalem, and therefore featured toll booths as well as a modest military garrison. In addition to its access to good roads, it also served as a port for extensive shipping traffic across the Sea of Galilee. For that reason, Jesus may have chosen Capernaum with care, for his career as a preacher would be quite unlike that of John. Jesus had decided to become an *itinerant* preacher, a rabbi who would actively seek out towns and villages to spread his good news, rather than wait for his listeners to come to him. In that respect, he could not have chosen a better location than Capernaum.

To make use of the many connections across the Sea of Galilee, Jesus had to enlist the help of fishermen. Indeed, the Gospel of Matthew depicts him walking along the shore of the Sea of Galilee until he saw two brothers, "James (the) son of Zebedee and his brother John, in the boat with their father Zebedee, mending their nets." (Matthew 4:18-21) "And," says Mark, "they left their father Zebedee in the boat with the hired men, and followed him." (Mark 1:20) This episode reveals another novel aspect of Jesus as Teacher; unlike John, or unlike most teachers and tutors in Antiquity, he also went out to *handpick* his followers. This, too, suggests that in Jesus' mind, the contours of his coming campaign were beginning to take shape.

The Gospel of Mark tells us that Jesus would go out before dawn, "while it was still very dark," to find a quiet place to pray. This is where Simon and the other disciples eventually found him. "Everyone is looking for you," Peter said. Jesus then revealed what he was planning to do. "Let us go into the neighboring towns, so that I may proclaim the message there also," he said, and added, "for that is what I came out to do." (Mark 1:35-38)

Since Jesus planned to become a preacher "on the move," he would need *delegates,* rather than followers—men and women who could serve as his advance party, who could organize public events, manage crowds, and look after their needs as well as his own. As it happens, a "delegate" is called *shaliach* (literally, "one sent") in Hebrew and Aramaic, which in the Gospels would be translated as *apostolos,* or Apostle.

Eventually, Jesus collected 12 Apostles, a number inspired by the 12 tribes of Israel. Later, Jesus would promise them that "you will sit on thrones judging the twelve tribes of Israel." (Luke 22:30) In addition to the five we met earlier—Simon Peter, Andrew, Philip, as well as James and John, the sons of Zebedee—he also recruited "Bartholomew, and Matthew, and Thomas, and James son of Alphaeus, and Thaddaus, and Simon the Cananaean, and Judas Iscariot, who betrayed him." (Mark 3:18-19) It is Mark who provides this list of Apostles, and as such it would be repeated in the Gospels of Matthew and Luke (Matthew 10:2-4; Luke 6:13-16). In the Synoptic Gospels, however, Peter, James, and John stand out. They

A third-century Roman terracotta bowl shows two fishermen hauling in their nets, surrounded by various fish types, molded in a delicate bas-relief.

These remains of residential structures (opposite) in ancient Capernaum were built using basalt stones that were quarried locally.

The shores of the Sea of Galilee near Tabgha evoke the setting of Jesus calling his disciples.

This modern fisherman's vessel (opposite) is an approximation of the type of boats that would have plied the Sea of Galilee in Jesus' time (opposite)

are present at the Transfiguration, and they will be with Jesus in the final hours in Gethsemane, before his arrest. The Gospel of John, on the other hand, has a different emphasis; in this story, Andrew and Philip appear to have considerable prominence.

The Demands of Discipleship

There is little doubt that Peter was the senior Apostle, who served as Jesus' "right-hand man." It is also quite possible that Peter used his connections among the local network of fishermen to pick those he believed would be suitable for the task. This recruitment effort may also have been facilitated by the fact that most fishermen around the Sea of Galilee worked in cooperatives. Luke's Gospel confirms this when he refers to "James and John, sons of Zebedee, who were partners (*koinōnoi*) with Simon." Cooperatives were necessary, for only by pooling their funds could fishermen borrow the necessary capital to buy or lease a boat with all the requisite equipment and nets, using their future catch as collateral. Such capital could be obtained from the same brokers who also happened to sell the

Jesus' Ministry Begins

fishing licenses (which were rigidly controlled by Herod Antipas) and extracted polls—in sum, the tax collectors.

The Gospels tell us that Jesus demanded total commitment from his chosen ones. James and John dropped their nets where they were and abandoned their father, Zebedee; Levi, the son of Alphaeus, promptly walked away from his toll booth without giving it another look (Mark 1:20; 2:14). Even family and relatives were of no account. "I tell you solemnly, there is no one who has left house, wife, brothers, parents or children for the sake of the kingdom of God who will not be given repayment many times over," Jesus says in the Gospel of Luke (Luke 18:28-30). Elsewhere in the same Gospel, Jesus reiterates his demands in even stronger terms: "Whoever does not hate his father and his mother cannot become a disciple to me. And whoever does not hate his brothers and sisters . . . will not be worthy of me." (Luke 14:26-27)

Other references, however, suggest that discipleship with Jesus was not a full-time engagement. Throughout the Gospels, we see the Apostles back at their *métier,* fishing on the Sea of Galilee. Not doing so would have put their families at risk of poverty and starvation. On some occasions Jesus would join them in their boats to boost a catch, or to calm a sudden squall.

Why, then, would the Gospels depict the recruitment of Apostles as an "all or nothing" proposition? The evangelists may have been inspired by the example of Elisha and Elijah, two prophets who figure prominently in the Gospel stories. According to the Book of I Kings, Elijah came across Elisha while the younger man was busy plowing in the field, and decided to take him on as his disciple. Elisha accepted, but said that he should first go back and kiss his father and his mother, before he could follow the prophet. Astounded, Elijah rebuked him. "Go back again?" he said; "What have I done to you?" (I Kings 19:19-20) An almost identical episode appears in the Gospel of Matthew. An aspiring disciple agrees to follow Jesus, but says, "First let me go to bury my father," a holy obligation in Judaism. Jesus answers him brusquely, "No, follow me [*now*], and let the dead bury their dead." (Matthew 8:22) Perhaps these and other stories of spontaneous surrender to Jesus serve as allegorical instruction, impressing the need for unconditional faith and commitment—certainly in the latter part of the first century when much of the Early Christian church began to face persecution. Or perhaps, as some have suggested, Jesus merely

> [JESUS] MADE HIS HOME IN CAPERNAUM BY THE SEA, IN THE TERRITORY OF ZEBULUN AND NAPHTALI, SO THAT WHAT HAD BEEN SPOKEN THROUGH THE PROPHET ISAIAH MIGHT BE FULFILLED.
>
> GOSPEL OF MATTHEW 4:12-14
> *Circa 75–90 C.E.*

PART II | THE LIFE OF JESUS

This fragment of a bas-relief showing a wagon, possibly the Ark of the Covenant, was excavated in close proximity to the fourth-century synagogue of Capernaum.

demanded the same type of dedication that other religious leaders and movements of his time would have insisted on—including John the Baptist and the community of Qumran.

Capernaum

In Capernaum, Jesus decided to formally declare himself as a teacher and healer. "When the Sabbath came," says Mark, "he entered the synagogue and taught." The congregation was "astounded at his teaching, for he taught them as one having authority, and not as the scribes." (Mark 1:21-22) These "scribes" were professional writers skilled in preparing a variety of legal documents, who catered to the vast majority of illiterate peasants in Palestine. Given that people in these areas followed the Torah, the Jewish Law, scribes were of necessity also steeped in the precepts of Mosaic legislation. As such, they are often presented by Mark as the educated opposition to Jesus, together with the Pharisees and Sadducees.

Jesus' presentation is immediately followed by an exorcism. Among the synagogue assembly, Mark tells us, was a man "with an unclean spirit, and he cried out: "What have you to do with us, Jesus of Nazareth?" "Have you come to destroy us?" Jesus rebuked him sternly, saying, "Be silent, and come out of him!" In that moment, the "unclean spirit" left the man. The purpose of this event is to authenticate the launch of Jesus' divine mission by showing a sign (*semeion* in Greek). Based on examples cited by Josephus, it appears that many people of the time were only prepared to accept a prophet's *bona fides* if he was able to perform a supernatural act—preferably an exorcism. "The ability to [exorcise] remains very strong among us even to this day," Josephus writes in *Antiquities of the Jews*, and adds that he himself had once witnessed an exorcism, performed by a Jew named Eleazar.

Jesus' sermon and his subsequent exorcism astounded the Capernaum congregation. "They kept on asking one another, 'What is this? A new teaching—with authority?'" And, Mark adds, "At once his fame began to spread throughout the surrounding region of Galilee." (Mark 1:27-28)

In 1905, two German archaeologists began to excavate near Tell Hum, the location associated with the biblical Capernaum. They uncovered what appeared to be an ancient Jewish synagogue, built as a basilica and supported by two rows of columns, in addition to a two-column row in the back. Stone benches lined the walls of the prayer hall, as is common with synagogues of this type, while much ornamentation was lavished on the exterior. Its columns were crowned with expertly carved Corinthian capitals, and the main portal featured a frieze

The synagogue of ancient Capernaum, built of blocks of white limestone, has been dated to the early fourth century C.E., although some scholars believe it was built on top of an older synagogue structure.

THE SYNAGOGUES OF GALILEE

A number of synagogues from the third through the fourth centuries C.E. have been excavated throughout Galilee, and some of these are quite impressive. But recent research by Anders Runesson, Donald Binder, and Birger Olsson has now established that there were synagogues before the Jewish War of 66–70 C.E. and possibly in Jesus' time as well. The word "synagogue" comes from the Greek *synagogē*, which doesn't denote a particular building, but rather an assembly or gathering. Josephus refers to synagogues as *proseuchai* (singular *proseuchè*), which means prayer house. Archaeologists have discovered prayer houses in several places in the Diaspora, usually in affluent Jewish communities such as the one on the Greek island of Delos, built as early as the second century B.C.E. Other early synagogues have been found in Jericho and Gamla, which some scholars believe date to the first century B.C.E., and on Masada. In Galilee, seven synagogues from the pre-70 C.E. era have now been excavated, including one at Magdala, which we will discuss shortly. In smaller villages, however, Sabbath services may have taken place in a prominent location out in the open, in the village square, or in one of the homes—usually the larger one—of a village elder. The Book of Acts confirms this when it relates how Paul and his companions "went [on the Sabbath day] outside the gate by the river, where we supposed there was a place of prayer." (Acts 16:13) Some of the most prominent Galilean synagogues, including the ones in Capernaum and Chorazin, appear to have been built in the third or fourth centuries C.E., during the heyday of Rabbinic Judaism in the region.

PART II | THE LIFE OF JESUS

The remains of this fourth-century Byzantine church, consisting of two concentric octagonal structures surrounded by a colonnade, has traditionally marked the location of Peter's house in Capernaum.

French artist James Jacques Joseph Tissot (1836–1902) painted this impression (opposite) of "The Palsied Man Let Down through the Roof" around 1894.

decorated with vine branches, grapes, and palm trees. Equally impressive was the fact that the synagogue was built of limestone, which in Galilee was far more expensive than the locally quarried basalt.

Excitement gripped the world. Was this the synagogue in which Jesus had exorcised the demon-possessed man? The building, now lovingly restored and screened by picturesque palm trees, certainly fit everyone's idea of what a synagogue from the time of Jesus should look like. But other scholars were not convinced, and pushed the date of the synagogue into the late second or early third century C.E. The controversy prompted Virgilio Corbo to begin a new round of excavations in 1969, digging underneath the present synagogue. Here, he discovered the remains of another building, with coins and potsherds that were dated to the fourth century. Stylistically the Capernaum synagogue is very close to the synagogue of Chorazin, which has been reliably dated to 300 C.E.

But then came a new twist: Perhaps the building *underneath* the present synagogue was the synagogue in which Jesus taught. This argument is compelling; new synagogues were usually built on top of old ones. But the latest analysis suggests that the structures found underneath the Capernaum synagogue are probably a group of private homes. That doesn't disprove the fact that one of them could have been used as a prayer hall (*proseuchè*), since this appears to have been the case in many other towns and villages in pre-70 C.E. Galilee. But such a prayer hall may not have looked like the synagogue we see today.

THE HOUSE OF PETER

Just a few steps away from the synagogue, the 1969 excavation team also dug underneath an unusual octagonal building first discovered in the 1920s, which resembles descriptions in medieval pilgrims' accounts. This structure actually held three octagons, the smallest of which, only 26 feet wide, was reputed to straddle the house of Peter. Both Mark and Matthew confirm the presence of such a house. "When Jesus entered Peter's House," Matthew says, "he saw his mother-in-law lying in bed with a fever." (Matthew 8:14) Jesus healed her, and soon the house was visited by those who were sick or possessed.

In the early Byzantine era, octagonal churches usually marked the location of places associated with important events in the New Testament. Indeed, underneath the octagonal church the excavators found the remains of another, even earlier church, built of sturdy basalt blocks and featuring more than 100 examples of graffiti in Greek or Syriac, scratched by pious pilgrims. One reads, "Lord Jesus Christ help thy servant . . . "; another says, "Christ have mercy." Pottery sherds and coins indicated that the oldest church was originally a private residence dating to the Early Roman Period—possibly even the time of Jesus. This residence followed the Galilean precedent of grouping multiple single-family dwellings around a central courtyard; in this case, the courtyard even featured an oven for common use.

The central room is rather large—some 21 by 20 feet—which prompted the excavators to theorize that it formed the core of an early church. This theory is corroborated by the fourth-century pilgrim Egeria, who wrote that "in Capernaum the house of the prince of the Apostles [i.e., Peter] has been made into a church, with its original walls still standing." What's more, on one plaster fragment an inscription, according to one epigrapher, reads "Peter, the helper of Rome." However, the inscription is so scratchy and jumbled that this interpretation is still controversial.

> A REPORT ABOUT [JESUS] SPREAD THROUGH ALL THE SURROUNDING COUNTRY. HE BEGAN TO TEACH IN THEIR SYNAGOGUES AND WAS PRAISED BY EVERYONE.
>
> GOSPEL OF LUKE 4:14
> *Circa 75–90 C.E.*

PART II | THE LIFE OF JESUS

The Sea of Galilee is relatively shallow at 200 feet deep; even so, winds coming down from the Golan often produce storms without warning because of the temperature contrast between the sea and the mountains beyond.

A tenth-century ivory miniature depicts Jesus driving out the unclean spirit (below).

The walls of the dwelling were too thin to have supported a pitched roof with terra-cotta tiles. It is more likely that the house was covered with a latticework of thin beams and subsequently covered with palm fronds and leaves, packed with mud. If true, then this would confirm the story in the Gospel of Mark of how Jesus, upon returning to Peter's house, was mobbed by crowds. Four people came, carrying a paralyzed man. When they saw that "they could not bring him to Jesus because of the crowd, they removed the roof above him; and after having dug through it, they let down the mat on which the paralytic lay." (Mark 2:1-4) Egeria agrees, writing, "This is where the Lord healed the paralytic."

JESUS RETURNS TO NAZARETH

As rumors of the events in Capernaum spread by word of mouth to the surrounding villages, Jesus was invited to come and address their prayer houses as well. In these early days, Jesus did not stray too far from his base, and most of his appearances took place in synagogues, rather than in front of large crowds. It may also indicate that his presentations took place during services on the Sabbath, since at other times most of the peasants, fishermen, or tradesmen would be at work. "He went to the synagogue on Sabbath day," Luke confirms, "as was his custom." (Luke 4:16)

According to the same Gospel, Jesus eventually made his way to Nazareth—the village of his youth. This would have been an auspicious event, for Jesus as well as his family. "He stood up to read," says Luke, "and the scroll of the prophet Isaiah was given to him." It was the responsibility of an attendant, such as a village elder, to select a particular scroll and hand it to the reader.

Jesus then located the verses of Isaiah's commission: "The Spirit of the Lord is upon me, for he has anointed me; he has sent me to bring good news to the oppressed, and heal the brokenhearted." (Isaiah 61:1-2) Having finished his reading, Jesus sat down and said, "Today this scripture has been fulfilled in your hearing." (Luke 4:21) And, says Mark, "many who heard him were astounded. They said, 'Where did this man get all this? What is this wisdom that has been given to him?'" (Mark 6:2) Their astonishment is understandable, given that rural children such as Jesus would have had very little opportunity to be educated in Scripture. Quite possibly, Jesus' family was equally amazed. After the infancy narratives, Joseph is no longer mentioned in any of the Gospels, which could mean that Joseph died sometime during Jesus' adolescence or early adulthood. His mother Mary, on the other hand, was certainly still alive, since she is featured in the Gospel stories later on. Indeed, as the Nazareth congregation turned to one another to express their wonder, they said, "Is this not the carpenter *(tektōn)*, the son of Mary and brother of James and Joses and Judas and Simon, and are not his sisters here with us?" (Mark 6:3)

Jesus understood the astonishment of his audience. "You will say, 'Do here also in your hometown the things that we have heard you did at Capernaum,'" he told them, and added wistfully, "Truly I tell you, no prophet is accepted in the prophet's hometown." (Luke 4:23-24) He then continued to expound on the theme of alienation by quoting from the books of I and II

THE EXORCISMS

Exorcism (*exorkismos* in Greek) is the practice of forcefully excising demons or spirits from the person whom they appear to possess. The exorcism in the Capernaum synagogue seals Jesus' new role as not only a teacher, but also a divinely ordained prophet with power over *demons*—the pawns of Satanic power. By exorcising evil spirits, Mark tells us, Jesus demonstrates his ability for fighting the great eschatological battle between good and evil. E. P. Sanders has argued that Jesus' exorcisms are a direct challenge to the ruling political and religious authorities for his apparent ability to manipulate and exorcise Satanic powers, and attract huge crowds in the process. Exorcisms continue to be practiced to this day, although the Roman Catholic Church insists that one can only be performed by an ordained priest with the permission of the local bishop.

PART II | THE LIFE OF JESUS

A colorful sixth-century mosaic from the St. Apollinaire Nuovo in Ravenna, Italy, depicts Jesus delivering the Sermon on the Mount.

Some scholars believe that this gently sloping hill (opposite) on the shores of the Sea of Galilee near Tabgha served as the location of Jesus' Sermon on the Mount.

Kings. These verses revealed how in times of deprivation and crisis, the prophets Elijah and Elisha were not sent to help the people of Israel, but to assist foreigners, who were more susceptible to their aid. This theme of estrangement, of feeling rebuffed by one's kin and clan while being embraced by others, is a frequent motif in Mark's Gospel, as we will see.

Jesus' discourse changed the mood in the prayer hall. The pleasant surprise that had greeted his readings now turned to indignation and anger. "They took offense at him," says Mark (Mark 6:3). Luke puts it even stronger: "They got up, drove him out of the town, and led him to the brow of the hill on which their town was built, so that they might hurl him off the cliff." (Luke 4:29) But in the end, no one dared to touch him, and "he passed through the midst of them and went on his way."

162

Jesus' Ministry Begins

In Capernaum, on the other hand, his fame was by now firmly established. Having previously healed Peter's mother-in-law and the paralytic man who was lowered through the roof, his renown as a faith healer had begun to spread, attracting a steady stream of sick and crippled people. "And they brought to him all the sick," says Matthew, "those who were afflicted with various diseases and pains, demoniacs, epileptics, and paralytics." (Matthew 4:24) Soon, the stream of patients became a veritable flood. Jesus was compelled to tell his disciples "to have a boat ready for him because of the crowd, so that they would not crush him." Indeed, says Mark, he had cured so many people that "all who had diseases pressed upon him to touch him." (Mark 3:9-10)

Healing the sick—some of the "diseases" reported in the Gospels may in fact have been brought about by hunger and malnutrition as a result of the land foreclosures by the Herodians—was an important aspect of Jesus' ministry, for it served to illustrate the "good news" (*good-spell* in old English, or "gospel") of the kingdom of God as Jesus envisioned it. As we saw, many Jewish groups had talked about a "kingdom of God" in the preceding decades. Many saw it as a nation governed by Jewish Law and ruled by a true and legitimate Davidic king, rather than a Herodian tyrant or a Roman despot. But to Jesus, the "kingdom of God"—or "kingdom of Heaven," a term that piously avoids using the name of "God"—would mean something different.

The Sermon on the Mount

One day, when Jesus once again saw large crowds streaming toward him "to be healed of their diseases," he decided instead to preach to them. It was time to present his great vision and articulate his *halakha*, his legislative teachings. This speech would become known as the Sermon on the Mount, which contains eight blessings known as the Beatitudes. The Greek expression *Makarioi* ("Blessed are . . .") as used in Matthew was a popular rhetorical flourish that frequently appears as *ashrei* ("Happy are . . .") in the Hebrew Scriptures (Psalms 1:1; Job 5:17; Daniel 12:12). Another close parallel to the beatitude "Blessed are the meek, for they will inherit the earth" is Psalm 37: "But the meek shall inherit the land." (Psalms 37:11)

PART II | THE LIFE OF JESUS

Or in Jesus' words:

Blessed are the poor in spirit, for theirs is the kingdom of heaven.
Blessed are those who mourn, for they will be comforted.
Blessed are the meek, for they will inherit the earth.
Blessed are those who hunger and thirst for righteousness, for they will be filled. (Matthew 5:3-6)

> HE CAME DOWN WITH THEM AND STOOD ON A LEVEL PLACE, WITH A GREAT CROWD OF HIS DISCIPLES AND A GREAT MULTITUDE OF PEOPLE FROM ALL OVER JUDEA, JERUSALEM, AND THE COAST OF TYRE AND SIDON.
>
> GOSPEL OF LUKE 6:17
> *Circa 75-90 C.E.*

This theme, of a *kingdom of God* that is within the grasp of those who cleave to Jesus' words, would dominate Jesus' teaching for much of his subsequent ministry in Galilee and beyond. Whereas most of Jesus' contemporaries saw the reign of God as a future promise to be realized by a redeemer or Messiah, many Gospel passages suggest that Jesus saw the kingdom as present in his lifetime (Mark 1:15; Luke 17:21). Arguably, Jesus' kingdom concept was not a new Davidic polity (though some scholars have tried to portray it in such terms), but a radically new way in which society would operate. Its realization would require a new social covenant whereby Jews pledged to return to the quintessential virtues of the Law: compassion toward one another, solidarity within one's community, and love and faith in God.

In this, Jesus may have found inspiration in prophets such as Micah, Hosea, and particularly Jeremiah, who also admonished the Jews of their time on the biblical commandment for social justice. "Behold," Jeremiah had said, "if you truly amend your ways, if you truly act justly with one another, if you do not oppress the alien, the orphan, and the widow, or shed innocent blood," then God "would dwell in this land." (Jeremiah 7:1-7)

One interpretation of Jesus' kingdom of God, then, is that it was both a social and a spiritual revolution, to be brought about as a grassroots movement of people power. "The kingdom of God is not coming with things that can be observed," Jesus says in the Gospel of Luke; "Nor will they say, 'Look, here it is!' or 'There it is!' For in fact, the kingdom of God is *among you.*" (Luke 17:20-21)

There is, however, some ambiguity in Jesus' parables about the kingdom, and it is questionable whether his disciples ever truly grasped the meaning of Jesus' vision. But one thing is clear: Jesus never imagined a break from contemporary Judaism. Rather, he sought a redefinition of its most essential values—social responsibility and faithfulness to God. "Do not think that I have come to abolish the law or the prophets," Jesus states emphatically at the end of the Beatitudes, referring to the two principal divisions of the Hebrew Bible—the Law *(Torah)* and the Prophets *(Nevi'im)*—of his time; "I have come not to abolish, but to fulfill." (Matthew 5:17) And to underscore that notion, he added, "Not one letter, not one stroke of a letter will pass from the Law until all is accomplished."

The Mount of Beatitudes

There are several places that tradition has marked as the place where Jesus delivered his seminal speech at the beginning of his campaign of social and spiritual renewal. Some suggest it took place near Bethsaida; other traditions point to Mount Arbel near Tiberias, the highest hill in walking distance of the Sea of Galilee, at an altitude of more than 1,000 feet above the level of the lake. But the location with the longest claim is undoubtedly the so-called Mount of Beatitudes (or Mount Eremos) close to Tabgha and ancient Capernaum, on the northern

The Church of the Multiplication of Loaves and Fishes, built in 1982 based on the design of an early Byzantine basilica, incorporates a number of fifth-century mosaics, including the one on the opposite page.

This well-known fifth-century mosaic of a bread basket and two fishes (opposite) commemorates the miraculous multiplication of loaves and fishes by Jesus as described in all four Gospels.

PART II | THE LIFE OF JESUS

This old anchorage on the Sea of Galilee near Tabgha is similar in design to ancient anchorages found all along the lake for use by fishermen of the time.

shore of the Sea. As early as the fourth century C.E., a Byzantine church was built there, later expanded into a monastery, of which some remains have been excavated. In 1937, the Italian dictator Benito Mussolini commissioned a new church on the site, which was designed by Antonio Barluzzi, loosely inspired by the centralized church in Raphael's painting "The Marriage of the Virgin" (1502). The result is a lovely octagonal church, each side of which is dedicated to one of the eight beatitudes. From here, one has a stunning view of the softly undulating hillside that once reportedly served as the sounding board for Jesus' words.

Just a short walk away is Tabgha, traditionally associated with Jesus' miraculous multiplication of loaves and fishes. This miracle, also known as the "Feeding of the Five Thousand," is the only miracle described in all four Gospels (Matthew 14:13-21; Mark 6:31-44; Luke 9:10-17; John 6:5-15). According to the story, Jesus felt compassion for the crowds that had come from afar to see him, "because they were like sheep without a shepherd." (Mark 6:34) Jesus charged his Apostles to go and find something to feed them with. They answered incredulously, "Are we to go and buy two hundred denarii worth of bread, and give it to them?"—implying that this would have severely strained the movement's modest funds.

> HE BROKE THE LOAVES, AND GAVE THEM TO HIS DISCIPLES TO SET BEFORE THE PEOPLE; AND HE DIVIDED THE TWO FISH AMONG THEM ALL. AND ALL ATE AND WERE FILLED.
>
> GOSPEL OF MARK 6:41-42
> *Circa 66-70 C.E.*

Jesus replied, "How many loaves have you? Go and see." They did so, and reported back that they had "five (loaves), and two fish." Jesus then ordered everyone to "sit down in groups on the green grass." And "taking the five loaves and the two fish, he looked up to heaven, and blessed and broke the loaves, and gave them to his disciples." And, says Mark, "all ate and were filled." And when everyone was finished, "they took up twelve baskets full of broken pieces and of fish." (Mark 6:37-43)

The traditional spot associated with this miracle was marked in the fourth century by a small church, which was later replaced by a fifth-century Byzantine basilica. In 1932, the remains of this basilica were excavated. This in turn inspired the current structure, built by the German Foundation for the Holy Land in the late 1970s, which in many ways attempts to re-create the elegant simplicity of the original. The new walls were rebuilt on the old wall remains whenever possible, while columns were restored in their original positions; the overall effect is exceptionally peaceful. In the pavement just before the altar, the builders retained a beautiful mosaic of a basket of loaves with two fishes, which the pilgrim Egeria described in her fourth-century notebook.

Luke tells us that this was also the place where Jesus formally commissioned his Apostles. For the roughly 12 months that remained to him, Jesus then set out to propagate his great vision—not only in Capernaum and surrounding villages, but in all of Galilee, and even the towns and cities beyond, in foreign lands.

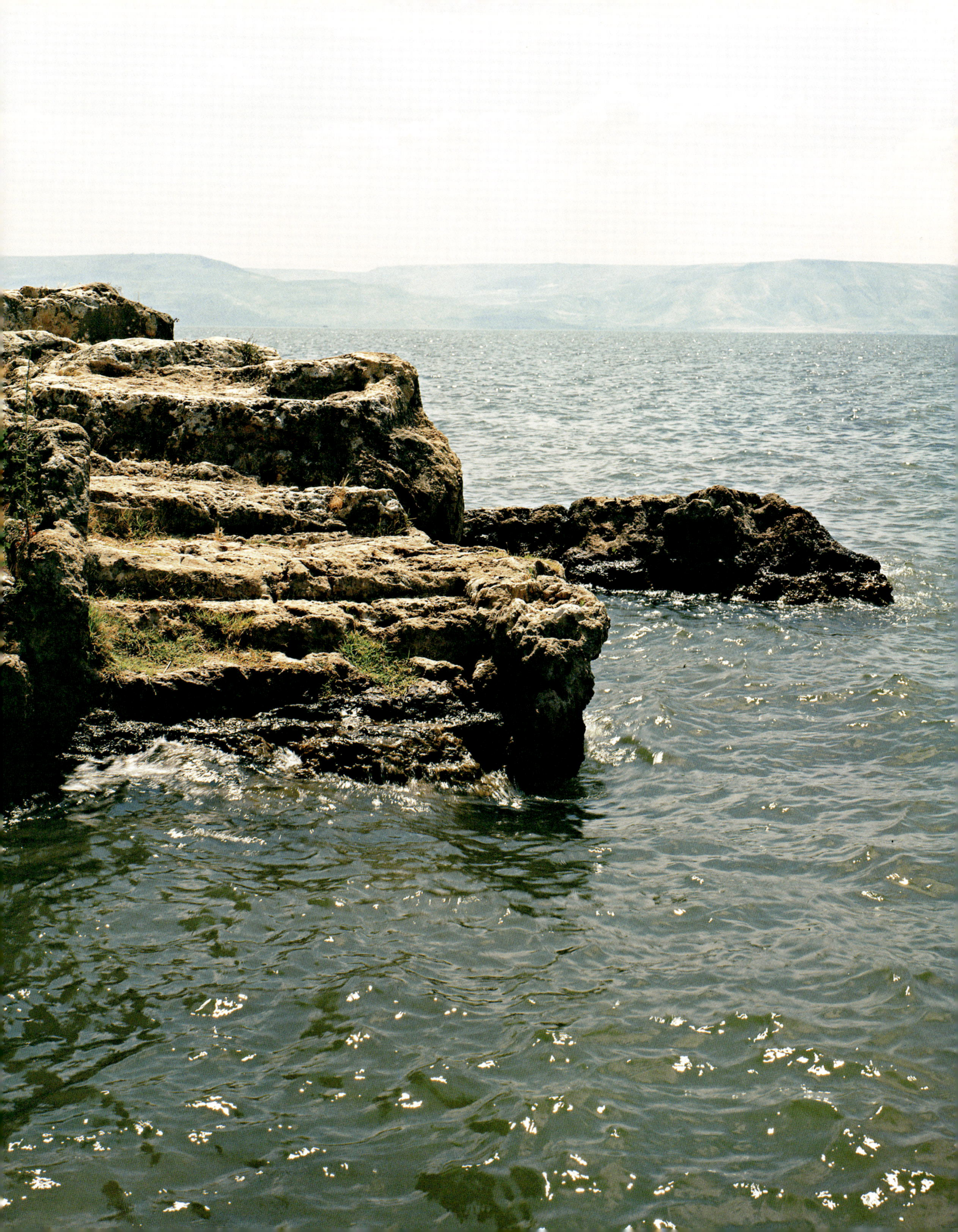

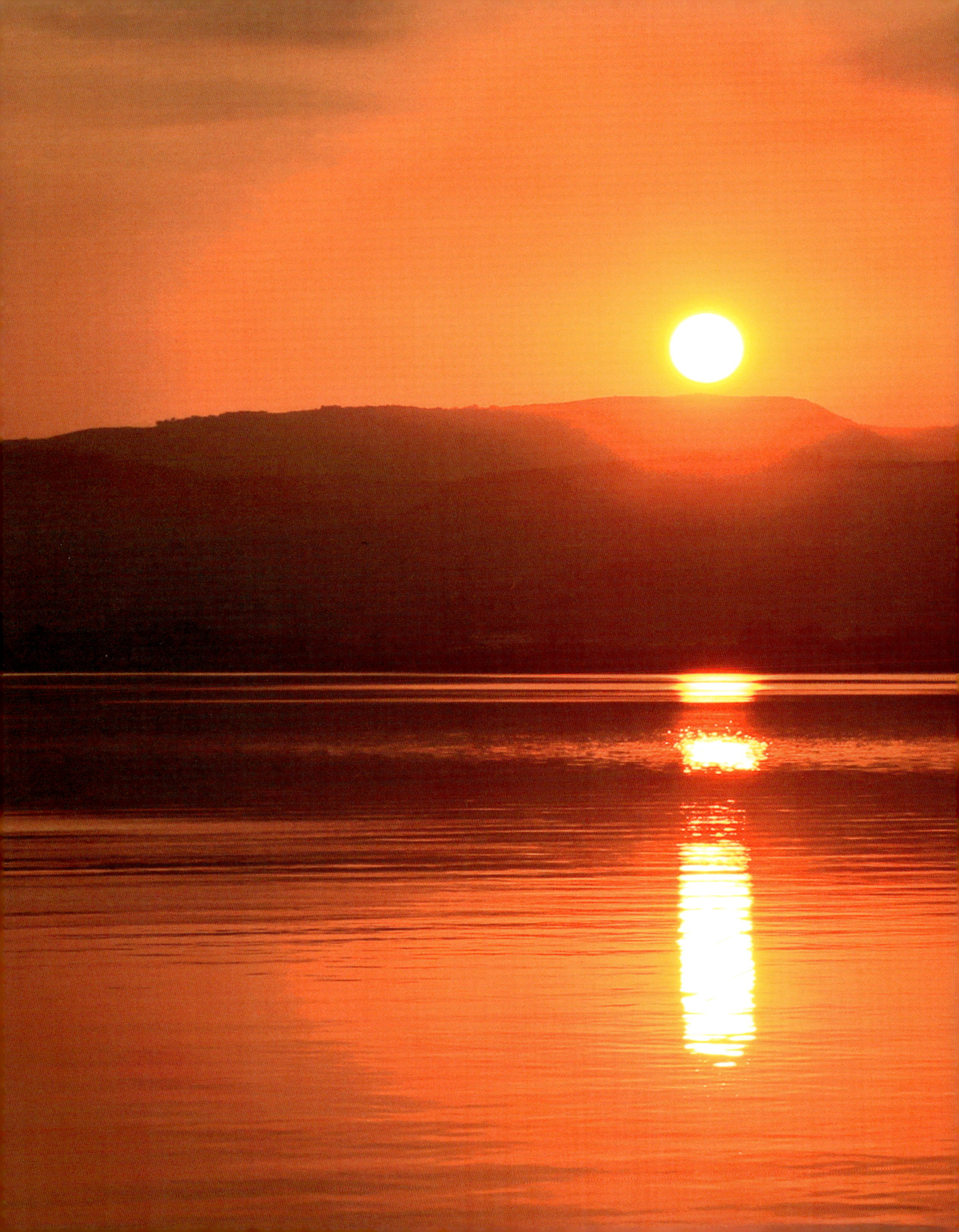

CHAPTER 8

The GALILEAN CAMPAIGN

THE BLIND RECEIVE THEIR SIGHT,
THE LAME WALK, THE LEPERS
ARE CLEANSED, THE DEAF HEAR,
THE DEAD ARE RAISED, AND
THE POOR HAVE GOOD NEWS
BROUGHT TO THEM.

GOSPEL OF LUKE 7:22
Circa 75–90 C.E.

The sun rises over the calm waters of the Sea of Galilee, bathing the hills on the eastern shore in a golden glow.

PART II | THE LIFE OF JESUS

Buoyed by the enthusiasm of the crowds streaming to Capernaum, Jesus gradually expanded his movements beyond the radius of a day's march on foot. He left the boundaries of the coastal triangle of Capernaum–Bethsaida–Chorazin and began to travel throughout Galilee, to spread his vision for the kingdom of God.

It is difficult to reconstruct the exact shape of the itineraries that Jesus undertook, since the principal source of the Synoptic Gospels—the Gospel of Mark—is not arranged in chronological order. This, as we saw, was typical of Antiquity; many scribes and authors were less concerned with an objective arrangement of facts than with organizing the story in such a way that it sustained its principal message. This was recognized as early as the second century C.E., when Bishop Papias, our earliest witness to the Gospel of Mark, said, "Mark wrote accurately what he remembered the Lord said and did, though not in order." Nevertheless, it is possible to reconstruct a tentative model of the Galilean campaign from the few topographical indications provided in his Gospel.

Jesus launched the second phase of his ministry by formally instructing the Apostles in their new role as *shelichim*, or delegates. He charged them to go and reconnoiter the hamlets and villages of the region, to see which ones would be receptive to his sermons. "He called the twelve and began to send them out two by two," says Mark; "He ordered them to take nothing for their journey except a staff; no bread, no bag, no money in their belts; but to wear sandals and not to put on two tunics." (Mark 6:8-9) In Matthew and Luke, Jesus' instructions are even harsher: The Apostles also have to do without sandals or a staff, and take no payment for their missionary work, for "you received without payment; give without payment." (Matthew 10:8-10)

These directives made the Apostles utterly dependent on the compassion of the people they would encounter. Whether they would have food, drink, or shelter at the end of the day was to be up to the mercy of the village or hamlet at hand. Only in this manner could the Apostles serve as a "test case" of Jesus' vision: whether Galileans would open their hearts to one another and embrace the kingdom of God. "I am sending you out like sheep into the midst of wolves," Jesus warned; "so be wise as serpents and innocent as doves." (Matthew 10:16)

To mitigate the difficult terms of this social experiment, Jesus assured them that once they found a house that welcomed them, they could "stay there until you leave the place." In other words, they wouldn't have to go around and beg at every house, which would perhaps strain the villagers' tolerance. Nor should they get into an argument with homes that refused to offer hospitality. "If

170

any place will not welcome you, and they refuse to hear you," Jesus instructed them, "as you leave, shake off the dust that is on your feet as testimony against them." (Mark 6:11) Washing one's feet after a long journey on foot was usually the first act of kindness shown by a host to his visitors; by shaking off the dust, the Apostles could silently, but pointedly, make their displeasure known and be on their way.

Jesus fully understood that this new strategy could lead to displacement anxiety among his disciples. The repeated references to "Peter's House" in the Gospels suggest that up to this point, the Capernaum house had served as Jesus' headquarters, allowing the disciples to go to their own homes at the end of the day. Now, they would have to travel without knowing where they might sleep, and whether they would have to camp out in the fields at night—not a pleasant prospect in a region filled with thieves and wild animals. "Foxes have holes, and birds in the air have their nests," Jesus warns one prospective disciple, a scribe,

The ruins of the second-century Roman spa resort of Hamat Gader in the Golan Heights feature ancient Roman baths.

PART II | THE LIFE OF JESUS

"but the Son of Man has nowhere to lay his head." (Matthew 8:20)

Inevitably, the prolonged absence would exact a heavy price from those disciples who lived with their families; but these sacrifices had to be borne for the campaign to succeed. "Whoever loves father or mother more than me is not worthy of me," Jesus says unequivocally; "and whoever loves son or daughter more than me is not worthy of me." (Matthew 10:37) Serving in Jesus' ministry was to be an effort of supreme self-denial; the stakes were too high to permit a half-hearted commitment.

And, says Matthew, "When Jesus had finished instructing his twelve disciples, he went on from there to teach and proclaim his message in their cities."

In the Country of the Gerasenes

In order to visit as many communities as possible, Jesus began to use the Sea of Galilee as the principal gateway to quickly move between the lake's ports and coastal cities. Peter and some of the other Apostles may have owned a boat, or a partial lease on a fishing boat; now, their access to such a vessel became key as Jesus tried to expand his ministry beyond the Capernaum region.

One of his stops was Bethsaida, the city that may have offered Jesus shelter in the difficult days following the arrest of John the Baptist. As soon as Jesus landed, the local townspeople brought a blind man to him. Jesus led him away, put some "saliva on his eyes and laid his hands on him," and the man could see. Jesus then ordered the man to go straight home, saying, "Do not even go into the village," perhaps in an effort to avoid the crowds of miracle-seekers that had followed him in the Capernaum area (Mark 8:22-26).

From Bethsaida, Jesus sailed to "the other side of the sea," which Mark refers to as the "country of the Gerasenes." Here too, Jesus was immediately approached for his healing powers. In this case, it involved a possessed man "with an unclean spirit" who dwelled in a graveyard, and was so strong that no shackles could restrain him. Jesus asked for his name, and the man replied, "My name is Legion; for we are many." Jesus drove out the demons that possessed him; these evil spirits then fled to a herd of swine feeding nearby. "And the unclean spirits came out and entered the swine," says Mark, "and the herd, numbering two thousand, rushed down the steep bank into the sea, and were drowned in the sea." (Mark 5:1-13)

> SUCH A VERY LARGE CROWD GATHERED AROUND HIM THAT HE GOT INTO A BOAT ON THE SEA AND SAT THERE, WHILE THE WHOLE CROWD WAS BESIDE THE SEA ON THE LAND.
>
> GOSPEL OF MARK 4:1
> *Circa 66–70 C.E.*

The Galilean Campaign

The rather bizarre ending to this exorcism has a specific meaning: It shows that Jesus has power over Satan and his acolytes, the demons, regardless of their number. That demoniacs such as the Gerasene man are controlled by Satan is proven by the fact that only *they* recognize Jesus for what he is: the "Son of the Most High God"—a concept that at this point is still beyond the comprehension of the Apostles (Mark 5:7).

But where was this "country of the Gerasenes"? After he was healed, Mark tells us, the demoniac "began to proclaim in the Decapolis how much Jesus had done for him." (Mark 5:20) The Decapolis (literally, Ten Cities) League was a region of ten major urban areas that stretched across most of today's Kingdom of Jordan and southern Syria. The Decapolis was not so much a cohesive political unit than a commercial federation of Hellenistic cities, which served as the principal commercial, cultural, and religious centers of their individual regions. While most were located to the east of the Jordan River and the Sea of Galilee, at

The remains of dwellings in the ancient city of Bethsaida were excavated from 1987 onward by a group of universities from the United States, Germany, and Poland.

Italian artist Duccio di Buoninsegna (ca 1260–1318) painted this panel of "Jesus Healing the Blind Man" (opposite) around 1311.

PART II | THE LIFE OF JESUS

The richly cultivated eastern shore of the Sea of Galilee is referred to as the "country of the Gerasenes" in the Gospels.

British Romantic artist George Percy Jacomb-Hood (1857–1929) painted this impression of "Jesus and Jairus' Daughter" (opposite).

the eastern frontier between the Roman Empire and the Arabian peninsula, one city—Scythopolis, formerly known as Beth She'an—was located west of the Jordan, on the border between Galilee and Judea, close to the Jezreel Valley.

The reference to the Decapolis in Mark's story suggests that "the country of the Gerasenes" refers to the territory dominated by Gerasa, today's Jerash. Gerasa was one of the leading cities of the Decapolis, since it served as a major nexus in the caravan trade of spices, frankincense, and other luxuries from the East, having traveled from the Syrian city of Damascus in the north or the Nabatean capital of Petra in the south.

During the eight decades since the Roman conquest of the East, both Gerasa and Petra had enjoyed explosive growth, given Rome's policy to try to steer much of Rome's eastern trade through the Arabian peninsula rather than the Silk Route, which ran through the hostile territory of the Parthians. Located some 25 miles north of Amman, Gerasa is today one of the best preserved Greco-Roman cities in the world, inclusive of a unique, oval forum surrounded by a colonnade, though much of what we see today was built during the reign of Emperor Hadrian in the early second century C.E.

This doesn't mean that Jesus actually visited Gerasa; he merely limited himself to the coastal region, which like many such satellite regions was considered "the country" of Gerasa in a commercial and political sense. Indeed, the profoundly Gentile nature of this region is corroborated by the presence of a large herd of swine, which Judaism considers impure.

Some ancient versions of Mark's Gospel, however, refer to the "country of Gadarenes" rather than "Gerasenes," which also appears in Matthew's version of the event (Matthew 8:28). This would point to the city of Gadara, today's Umm Qays, also located in Jordan. Gadara, which likewise formed part of the Decapolis, was located closer to the Sea of Galilee. Though only a few ruins have been excavated, including a theater and part of a Roman colonnade, Gadara may have once rivaled its larger neighbor Gerasa in splendor.

The Daughter of Jairus

Then, says Mark, "Jesus crossed again in the boat to the other side," presumably the western shore of the Sea of Galilee, though he does not name the port.

The Galilean Campaign

Here Jesus was once again met by a large crowd. Among them was a man named Jairus, "one of the leaders of the synagogue." He fell at Jesus' feet and begged him, "My daughter is at the point of death. Come and lay your hands on her, so that she may be made well, and live." (Mark 5:21-24) Before Jesus could move, however, the crowd pressed in on him, no doubt clamoring for him to heal them as well. Among these petitioners was a woman who had suffered from continuous hemorrhage for 12 years. Knowing that she could never make herself heard above the cries of the crowd, she "came up behind him and touched his cloak, for she thought, "If I but touch his clothes, I will be made well." And she was made well; but Jesus was "aware that power had gone forth from him." He confronted the woman, who fell on her knees and trembled with fear. Jesus comforted her, saying "Your faith has made you well." (Mark 5:27-34)

This incident, however, had delayed Jesus, and soon some people arrived with the dreadful news that Jairus's daughter had died. "Why trouble the teacher any further?" they said. Nevertheless, Jesus set out for Jairus's house, accompanied only by "Peter, James and John, the brother of James"—the original core of the Baptist's disciples. When they arrived, the house was full of people weeping and

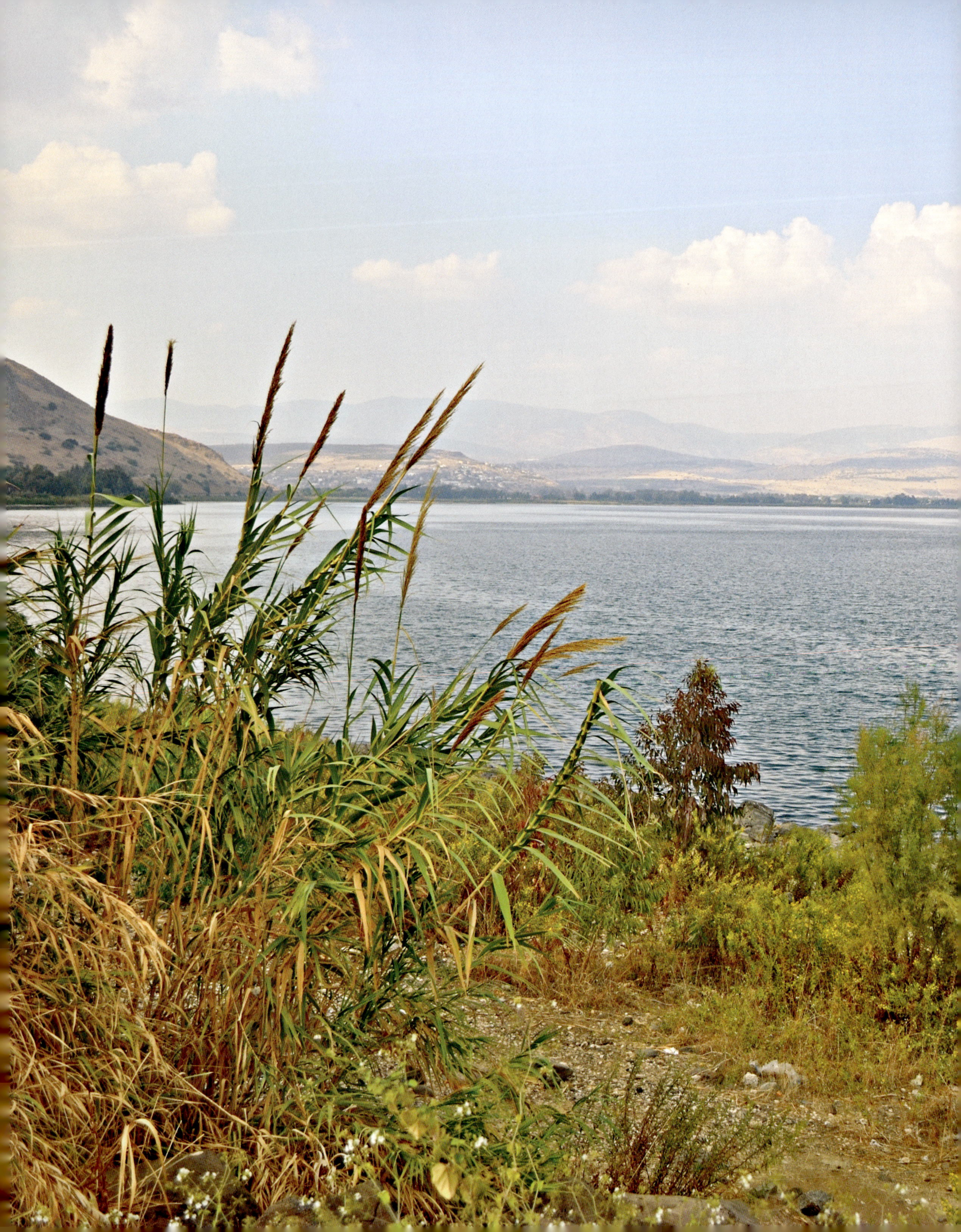

The Galilean Campaign

wailing loudly—a possible reference to professional wailers, who were often hired to attend funerals in well-to-do homes. But Jesus said, "Why do you make a commotion and weep? The child is not dead, but sleeping." He ordered everyone out of the house, and asked the child's father and mother to take him to the dead girl's room. And, says Mark, "He took her by the hand and said to her, "Talitha cum," which means, "Little girl, get up!" And immediately the girl got up and began to walk about." Here as elsewhere, Mark cites Jesus in his own words, in Aramaic.

Mary of Magdala

Next, Jesus may have traveled to the town that Matthew refers to as Magadan, which could mean Magdala (in fact, certain Greek manuscripts actually use the word "Magdala"). Magdala, located on the western shore of the lake, was a major processing center of the Galilean fishing industry. Among others, it was renowned throughout the region for its fish sauce, a popular condiment in Antiquity. The Talmud refers to the city by its Aramaic name, *Magdala Nunayya* (Magdala of the Fishes), while in Greek it was called *Tarichaea* (Fish Salters).

One of Jesus' followers actually came from Magdala. Her name was Mary, "the Magdalene," but the Gospels give us very little information about her background. Unlike other women named Mary in the Gospels, who were related to either Jesus or to his Apostles, Mary Magdalene appeared to be unattached, which was unusual. As K. C. Hanson and Douglas Oakman have argued, Palestine in the time of Jesus was an overwhelmingly patriarchal society. A woman was loved and respected, but her movements were subject to the consent of the senior man in the family, i.e., her father before marriage, and her husband thereafter. Unwed women were not supposed to leave their home without a relative as an escort; but apparently, Mary ignored such restrictions, and freely went wherever the Teacher went.

The answer to this puzzle may be that Mary Magdalene hailed from an affluent family, and thus enjoyed a greater level of independence. Luke suggests as much when he says that she belonged to a group of women who "provided for them out of their own resources." (Luke 8:2-3) There is no question, however, that by the end of Jesus' ministry, Mary had become one of the Rabbi's most prominent followers. It is she who, together with another small group of women, stood fearlessly at

This depiction of Mary Magdalene in the cave was painted by French classicist artist Jules Joseph Lefebvre (1836–1912) around 1876.

Reeds and shrub cover the western shore of the Sea of Galilee near the remains of the ancient town of Magdala, with the modern town of Migdal in the distance (opposite).

> AFTER SENDING AWAY THE CROWDS, HE GOT INTO THE BOAT AND WENT TO THE REGION OF MAGADAN.
>
> Gospel of Matthew 15:39
> *Circa 75–90 c.e.*

PART II | THE LIFE OF JESUS

Jesus' cross after all the Apostles had gone in hiding, lest they be arrested and condemned as well (Mark 15:40-41).

The relationship between Mary Magdalene and Jesus has been sensationalized in fictional thrillers like *The Da Vinci Code*. The sober truth, however, is that scholars have known about the so-called revelations in *The Da Vinci Code* for a long time, particularly since the discovery of the Nag Hammadi codices in Egypt in 1945. This collection includes a number of "Gospel"-type documents written for Gnostic Christian communities. The Gospel of Philip, for example, states that "the companion *(koinōnos)* of the [Savior is] Mary Magdalene." This does not necessarily imply a romantic relationship; the choice of the word "companion" merely suggests that Jesus respected Mary as much as he respected the 12 male Apostles. Indeed, when in the same Gospel the disciples confront Jesus about Mary Magdalene, saying, "Why do you love her more than all of us?", his reply is, "Why do I not love you as [I love] her?"—meaning, he loved all of them equally. The early second-century Gospel of Mary ascribes her exalted status to her exemplary behavior and her clear grasp of Jesus' vision. According to this Gnostic Gospel, it is Peter who asks Mary to "tell us the words of the Savior which you remember— which you know (but) we do not."

Elaine Pagels, one of the leading scholars of Gnostic texts, believes that Mary Magdalene came to exemplify the tensions between the early Church and Gnostic Christians. In many Gnostic groups, women worked as teachers, healers, and even priests—roles they did not always enjoy in the early Church. Eventually, some Church traditions began to cast the Magdalene in a disparaging light, referring to her as "the penitent woman."

There is no evidence anywhere in the Gospels that Mary Magdalene lived a sinful or promiscuous life, but by the third century she had become fully assimilated with the unnamed woman in Luke, "a sinner," who bathes Jesus' feet with her tears, and dries them with her hair (Luke 7:38). By the sixth century, Pope Gregory I declared Mary Magdalene to be a "fallen woman" guilty of "forbidden acts"—attributes of a prostitute, which would burden her through the centuries right through to the motion picture *The Passion of the Christ*. Not until 1969 did Pope Paul VI explicitly separate the figure of Mary Magdalene from the "sinful woman" character.

From Magdala to Gennesaret

In the Gospels themselves, however, she is none of these things. Luke merely tells us that as Jesus "went on through cities and villages," some women joined him "who had been cured of evil spirits and infirmities." Mary may therefore have come into contact with Jesus because of his healing powers. "Seven demons had gone out of her," says Luke without referring to an actual exorcism,

---

FISH SPECIES IN JESUS' TIME

Israeli scientists have established that there are some 27 species of fish in the Sea of Galilee, many of which are also described in ancient sources. The Apostles, like all the fishermen of their day, would have been keen to capture one of three edible types of Galilean fish. The first type were common sardines, which may be the "few small fish" that "a small boy" brought to the feeding of the 4,000 in the Gospel of Mark (Mark 8:7). The second species is a carplike fish known as "Barbels," so called because of the barbs at the corners of their mouths. The third and most popular type, however, is today called the Galilee tilapia *(amnun* in Hebrew), more popularly known as St. Peter's Fish. This fish has a long, comb-shaped dorsal fin and can grow from one to one and a half feet in length and 3.3 pounds in weight. Since the St. Peter's Fish feeds on seaweed, it is quite essential to the ecosystem of the lake, for it controls growth that could change the sea's chemical balance.

which may suggest that Mary suffered from a disease like epilepsy; in Antiquity, epileptics were often thought to be possessed by spirits (Luke 8:2).

Some scholars believe that the Magdalene may be the same woman as Mary, the sister of Martha and Lazarus, but there is no evidence to support this claim. Mary, or Miriam, was simply a very common name in first-century Palestine. Given the critical role that the Magdalene was destined to play in the aftermath of the Passion, there is no reason not to recognize her as an important follower and disciple in her own right.

Today, the ruins of ancient Magdala lie in close proximity to the Sea of Galilee resort of Migdal Beach. In 2009, Israeli archaeologist Dina Avshalom-Gorni discovered the remains of an ancient synagogue, which includes a carved stone representing the seven-branched candelabra known as a menorah. Like the synagogue of Capernaum, it featured stone benches along its walls, which were decorated with colorful frescoes. Avshalom-Gorni believes that the synagogue dates from the Early Roman Period, which would have placed it in the time of Jesus; perhaps it suffered damage or destruction during the Jewish War of 66–70 C.E. Josephus tells us that the citizens of Magdala put up a fierce defense against the troops led by Vespasian, which led to the slaughter of 6,500 inhabitants once the Romans emerged victorious.

Mary Magdalene may have walked these hills near the putative location of ancient Magdala, a city renowned for its fishing industry.

This fresh catch (opposite) from the Sea of Galilee suggests the variety of species caught in the lake.

PART II | THE LIFE OF JESUS

The excavations of Tel Kinrot, believed to be the place referred to as Gennesaret in the Gospels, have so far uncovered impressive remains from the Iron Age.

"The prophet Elisha heals the Syrian Captain Naema" (opposite) was painted around 1520 by Dutch artist Cornelis Engebrechtsz (1468–1533).

The next village Jesus may have visited is Gennesaret. "And when they had crossed over," Mark tells us, "they came to land at Gennesaret and moored the boat." (Mark 6:53) Gennesaret, known as Kinnereth in the Book of Joshua, was located just north of Magdala, on a prominent hill overlooking the Via Maris, the principal trade route in the region. Gennesaret was a major city in the Iron Age as attested by its stout walls, as well as fragments of pottery and goods that hailed from Egypt, Syria, and Phoenicia. The site, known as Tel Kinrot, is currently being excavated by an international team of German, Finnish, and Swiss archaeologists.

"When they got out of the boat," Mark continues, "people at once recognized him, and rushed about that whole region." (Mark 6:54-55)

Jesus' Miracles

Miracle stories are impossible to separate from Jesus' ministry in Galilee. At times it seems that the purpose of Jesus' mission, to propagate his social and

The Galilean Campaign

theological ideas, is in danger of being overshadowed by his fame as a "doer of miraculous works *(paradoxa),*" in Josephus's words. Indeed, most visits by Jesus to the towns and villages of Galilee result in crowds eager to witness a miracle with their own eyes, or be healed of an illness themselves. Is there a conflict between Jesus the Teacher and Jesus the Healer, or do both conform to the same message?

For the evangelists, the answer is clear: The Teacher and Healer are one and the same, for the miracles serve as visible evidence of God's power on earth, thus anticipating the kingdom of God. Some scholars, however, have suggested that the miracle accounts, like many other events in the Gospels, are modeled on parallel episodes in Scripture—in particular, those featuring Elijah and Elisha, who often serve as prophetic models for the evangelists. So, for example, could the miraculous multiplication of loaves and fishes near Tabgha be compared to Elijah's multiplication of meal and oil of the

> PEOPLE RUSHED ABOUT THAT WHOLE REGION AND BEGAN TO BRING THE SICK ON MATS TO WHEREVER THEY HEARD HE WAS.
>
> GOSPEL OF MARK 6:54-55
> *Circa 66–70 C.E.*

THE MINISTRY OF JESUS IN LOWER GALILEE

MAP KEY

- ←— Transfer of ministry to Capernaum
- ←→ Ministries to Lower Galilee
- ←— Journey to Tyre and Sidon
- ←— Travels through the Decapolis via Tyre
- ←— Ministry to Caesarea Philippi
- • Historic city
- • Present-day city
- ○ Location uncertain
- • City of the Decapolis

0 — 4 — 8 kilometers
0 — 4 — 8 miles

Present-day country boundaries are represented. Modern names appear in parentheses.

Jesus chose Capernaum, presumably Simon Peter's hometown, as the base for his Galilean ministry and travels.

Chorazin was another important town along the northern shores of the Sea of Galilee, though it was denounced by Jesus for its lack of faith (Luke 10:13).

The transfiguration of Jesus, presumably on Mt. Tabor, prompted the building of several churches on the site, the remains of which still abut the current basilica.

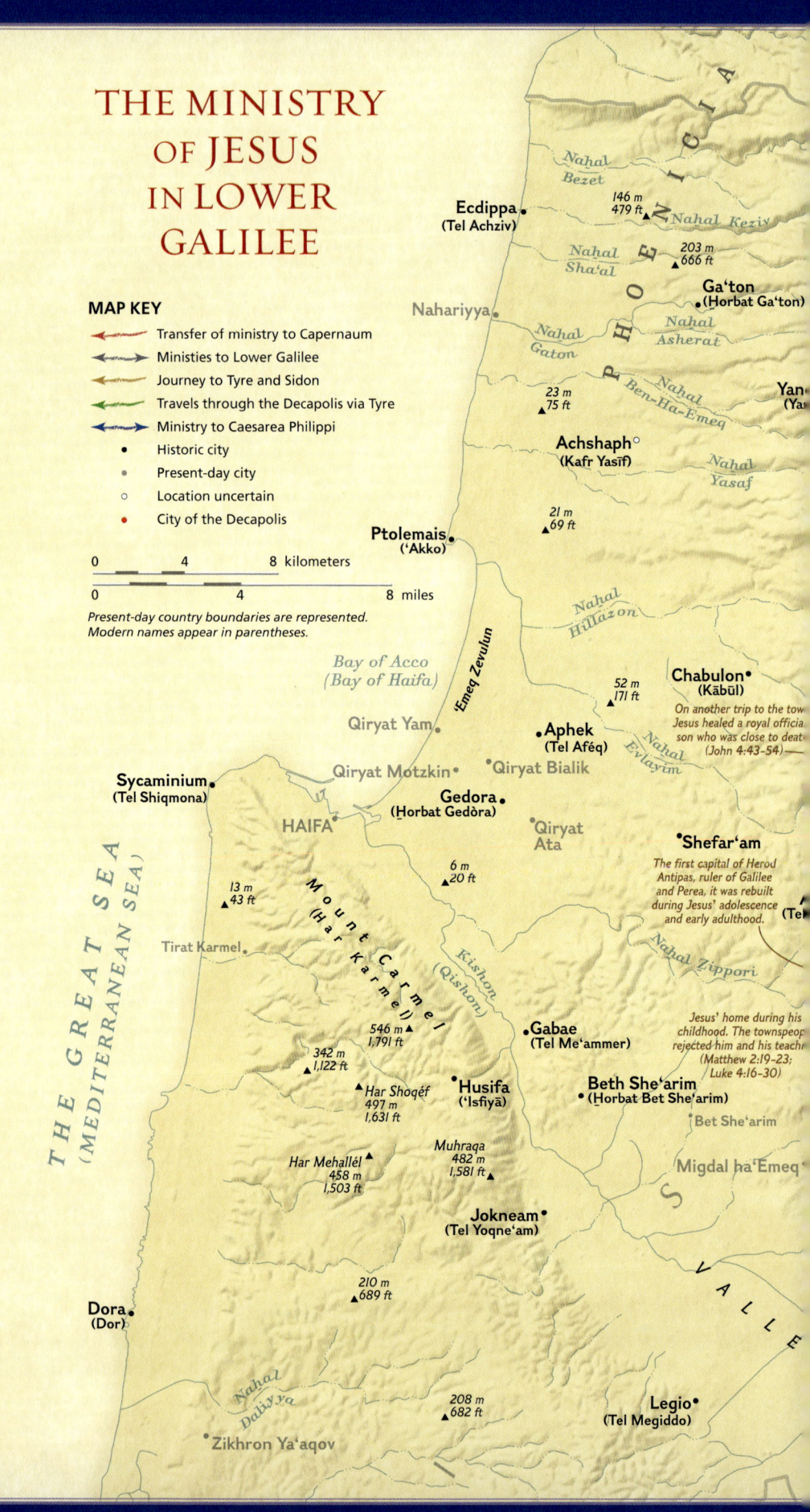

Labels on map

- Ecdippa (Tel Achziv)
- Nahariyya
- Ga'ton (Horbat Ga'ton)
- PHOENICIA
- Nahal Bezet — 146 m / 479 ft
- Nahal Keziv — 203 m / 666 ft
- Nahal Sha'al
- Nahal Gaton
- Nahal Asherat
- Nahal Ben-Ha-Emeq
- Yan (Ya)
- Achshaph (Kafr Yasīf) — 23 m / 75 ft
- Nahal Yasaf — 21 m / 69 ft
- Ptolemais ('Akko)
- Nahal Hillazon
- Chabulon (Kābūl) — 52 m / 171 ft

  On another trip to the town Jesus healed a royal official's son who was close to death (John 4:43-54)

- Aphek (Tel Aféq)
- Nahal Evlayim
- Bay of Acco (Bay of Haifa)
- Emeq Zevulun
- Qiryat Yam
- Sycaminium (Tel Shiqmona)
- Qiryat Motzkin
- Qiryat Bialik
- Gedora (Horbat Gedòra)
- HAIFA
- Qiryat Ata — 6 m / 20 ft
- Shefar'am

  The first capital of Herod Antipas, ruler of Galilee and Perea, it was rebuilt during Jesus' adolescence and early adulthood.

- THE GREAT SEA (MEDITERRANEAN SEA)
- 13 m / 43 ft
- Tirat Karmel
- Mount Carmel (Har Karmel) — 546 m / 1,791 ft
- Kishon (Qishon)
- 342 m / 1,122 ft
- Gabae (Tel Me'ammer)
- Nahal Zippori

  Jesus' home during his childhood. The townspeople rejected him and his teaching (Matthew 2:19-23; Luke 4:16-30)

- Har Shoqéf — 497 m / 1,631 ft
- Husifa ('Isfiyā)
- Beth She'arim (Horbat Bet She'arim)
- Bet She'arim
- Har Mehallél — 458 m / 1,503 ft
- Muhraqa — 482 m / 1,581 ft
- Migdal ha'Emeq
- Jokneam (Tel Yoqne'am)
- 210 m / 689 ft
- Dora (Dor)
- VALLE[Y]
- Nahal Dabiyya
- 208 m / 682 ft
- Legio (Tel Megiddo)
- Zikhron Ya'aqov

LEBANON
Cadasa (Tel Qedesh)
To Tyre and Sidon
To Caesarea Philippi and returning to Capernaum
Lake Hula
From Tyre and Caesarea Philippi
Har Avital 1,204 m 3,950 ft
540 m 1,772 ft
82 m 269 ft
504 m 1,654 ft
Har Yosifon 981 m 3,219 ft
Nahal Dishon
160 m 525 ft
Nahal Gilbon
372 m 1,221 ft
GAULANITIS
Har Addir 1,006 m 3,301 ft
885 m 2,904 ft
Gischala (Jīsh)
Har Ben Zimra
Asor (Tel Hazor)
Nahal Hazor
Nahal Keziv
Har Merom 1,208 m 3,963 ft
After his resurrection, Jesus met the disciples in Galilee and commissioned them to "go make disciples of all nations." (Matthew 28:16-20)
CAPERNAUM
Called, "his own town," Jesus based his ministries from this city and performed many of his miracles there. A frontier town between the lands of Antipas and Philip, the city was astride an important trade route that would have helped spread his message throughout the region. (Matthew 9:1)
taught his "good news of kingdom" and healed es, large crowds from the ding regions followed him om place to place. Matthew 4:23-25)
Merom
Zefat
Jordan
Har Ha'ari 1,047 m 3,435 ft
Har Hillel 1,071 m 3,514 ft
Nahal 'Ammud
Jesus denounced the cities most of his miracles had been performed in because of their lack of repentance. He also included Bethsaida and Capernaum in his judgment. (Matthew 11:20-24)
Nahal Meshushim
435 m 1,427 ft
Bersabe (Horbat Be'er Sheva')
Bet Kerem
One possible location where the feeding of the multitude could have taken place. (Matthew 14:13-21; 15:32-39) Jesus healed many when he and the disciples visited. (Mark 6:53-56)
Har Kena'an 486 m 1,595 ft
A likely location where the feeding of multitude and the multiplication of the loaves and fishes took place. (Matthew 14:13-21; 15:32-39)
Hanania (Zomet Hananya)
armi'el
Chorazin (Korazim)
Gamala (Gamla)
Har Kammon 598 m 1,962 ft
Har Hazon 584 m 1,916 ft
Tradition places the Sermon on the Mount here.
Bethsaida (Zomet Bet Zayda)
Nahal Daliyyot
Mary Magdalene was from here. She was one of several women who had been healed or cleansed, and who provided support for Jesus and the disciples. (Luke 8:2-3)
Capernaum (Kefar Nahum)
Bethsaida was the hometown of disciples Peter, Andrew, and Philip. (Luke 1:44)
Jesus healed a blind man by spitting on his eyes and laying his hands on him. (Mark 8:22-26)
Jesus performed his first miracle here, turning water into wine at a wedding. (John 2:1-11)
Nahal Zalmon
Heptupegon ('En Sheva')
Nahal Kanaf
Gennesaret (Ginnosar)
After sending the disciples on ahead by boat, Jesus walked on the water out to them during the night. (Matthew 14:22-33)
Har Netofa 526 m 1,726 ft
Magdala / Taricheae (Migdal)
Sea of Kinnereth, Lake Tiberias (Sea of Galilee)
Nahal Samakh
Cana (Horbat Qana)
Bet Netofa
151 m 495 ft
Horns of Hattin (Qarne Hittim) 326 m 1,070 ft
Gergesa (Kursi)
A possible site where Jesus cast out demons that entered swine, which then rushed down the slope to drown in the water. Another possible place is near the city of Gadara south of the Yarmuk River. (Luke 8:26-39)
Arbela (Horbat Arbel)
261 m 856 ft
Haré Tir'an
548 m 1,798 ft
Tiberias (Teverya)
Aphek (Afiq)
Nahal Yiftahel
Bethmaus (Horbat Bet Ma'on)
Hammath (Hammat)
Hippos (Horbat Susita)
Nahal Raqqad
Taking his ministry to the towns of the region, Jesus cleansed a leper, and his fame spread throughout Galilee. (Mark 1:38-45)
Biq'at Yavne'el
Shaken by a sudden storm, the disciples despaired until Jesus awoke and "rebuked the wind and the waves," quieting the maelstrom. (Matthew 8:23-27)
Garis (Kefr Kanna)
The second capital of Herod Antipas, whom Jesus called "that fox." He ruled Galilee and Perea in Jesus' time. (Luke 13:32)
Yarmuk
Har Yona
532 m 1,745 ft
144 m 472 ft
Philoteria (Tel Bet Yerah)
Sennabris
368 m 1,207 ft
Nazerat 'Illit
A possible site of the Transfiguration. Jesus also healed an epileptic boy in the area. (Matthew 17:1-13; 17:14-22)
Nazareth (Nazerat)
Exaloth (Iksāl)
Mt. Tabor 588 m 1,929 ft
Har Yavne'el
368 m 1,207 ft
DECAPOLIS
Emmatha (Hammat Gader)
Yarmuk
Jordan
Biq'at Kesullot
Gadara (Umm Qays)
565 m 1,854 ft
Endor ('En Dor)
335 m 1,099 ft
Jesus brought the dead son of a widow back to life before the whole funeral procession. (Luke 7:11-17)
Nain (Nein)
Giv'at Hamore 515 m 1,690 ft
Wādī 'Arab
Nahal Tavor
147 m 482 ft
Shunem (Sūlam)
Ramot Yissakhar
Kamon (Qam)
JEZREEL
Jesus healed a deaf and mute man in the Decapolis. (Mark 7:31-37)
Esdradela (Yizre'el)
377 m 1,237 ft
GALILEE
JORDAN
SYRIA

PART II | THE LIFE OF JESUS

The Galilee Boat was discovered along the shore of the Sea of Galilee in 1986 and has since been dated to the early first century C.E.

A Greek plate (opposite) is equipped with a central depression for fish sauce, a highly popular condiment in Antiquity.

widow at Zarephath (1 Kings 17:14), while the raising of Jairus's daughter could have been inspired by Elijah's breathing life into the widow's son, who had died (I Kings 17:22).

Similarly, the multiple accounts of Jesus healing a leper (Mark 1:41) are comparable to the story of Elisha curing Naaman, a leprous commander of the Syrian army (II Kings 5:14), just as Elisha's conversion of Jericho's toxic wells into fresh water (II Kings 2:21) may have served as the model for Jesus' conversion of water into wine in Cana (John 2:9).

What is clear, however, is that the miracle accounts appear in the oldest strata about Jesus—the earliest traditions that circulated before they were collected and edited by the evangelists. In other words, from the earliest of times the memory of Jesus was closely associated with accounts of his miraculous works. We should also remember that Jesus lived in a society that, unlike ours, believed in magic and miraculous phenomena as vivid proof of the supernatural powers that controlled their lives. As we have seen, exceptional men and women, possessed by the Spirit of God, were expected to be able to do extraordinary things. It validated their claim of prophecy and their ability to speak on God's behalf, and to do his will. In the Book of Exodus, for example, Moses engages in a contest with Pharaoh's magicians to see who can accomplish miraculous feats. Similarly, the Babylonian Talmud describes numerous rabbis who had the gift of producing either rain or drought through prayer.

Scholars such as John Meier have sought to address the question by distinguishing between (1) healing miracles, (2) exorcisms, or (3) nature miracles. A close analysis shows that the healing stories follow a predictable format and vocabulary, whereas the nature miracles have a less recognizable pattern. This may suggest that the healing stories reflect historical events observed by eyewitnesses, whereas the nature miracles may carry a more symbolic message. One example of such a nature miracle appears in Mark's Gospel, just before Jesus' journey to the country of the Gerasenes. As Jesus and the Apostles embarked in their boat after night had fallen, "a great windstorm rose, and the waves beat into the boat, so that the boat was already swamped." Jesus, however, was sleeping peacefully in the boat's stern—an image that reminds us of Jonah, who was also found sleeping in the hold of a ship in the midst of a storm (Jonah

1:5). His disciples panicked and woke him up. Jesus rose "and rebuked the wind, and said to the sea, 'Peace! Be still!' Then the wind ceased, and there was a dead calm." (Mark 4:35-39)

The parallel source for this miracle could be one of several passages in Hebrew Scripture in which God and his prophets are able to command the waters. The story of Moses separating the Red Sea in Exodus is one obvious example, but other instances may be found in the Psalms. "O Lord God of hosts, who is as mighty as you?" says Psalm 89. "You rule the raging of the sea; when its waves rise, you still them." (Psalms 89:8-9) "He made the storm be still," sings another Psalm, "and the waves of the sea were hushed." (Psalms 107:29)

When it comes to the healing stories, however, a different narrative style prevails. Often, Mark is able to provide a level of detail about the location or the illness in question that is lacking in other miracle accounts. What's more, many healing stories are reported across all four Gospels, even that of John, whereas most nature miracles only appear incidentally. There also seems to be a consistent pattern to Jesus' diagnostic approach. He observes the patient, then touches him, saying, "Your sins are forgiven." (Mark 2:5) To our ears, accustomed to countless hospital dramas, this seems like a very strange way to initiate a medical intervention. But in Jesus' day, birth defects and chronic diseases were often regarded as God's punishment for sins—either by the patient or by his parents. A child who was born deaf, blind, or malformed was assumed to have been conceived in sin; the child thus bore the penalty for the immoral actions of his parents. When, in the Gospel of John, the disciples encounter a man who has been blind from birth, they ask Jesus, "Rabbi, who sinned, this man or his parents, that he was born blind?" (John 9:1-2)

Jesus resolutely rejected such perceptions of the ill. "Neither this man nor his parents sinned," Jesus states emphatically in the Gospel of John. "He was *born* blind so that God's works might be revealed in him." (John 9:3)

The first and crucial component of his healing technique, therefore, was to eliminate the belief that the ill suffered *because they deserved to*. This is the meaning of the words "your sins are forgiven," which was as much directed to the patient as to the villagers standing around him. The prospect of being welcomed back into the village, freed of sin, must have been a powerful tonic, perhaps infusing the patient with the psychological motive to see, hear, or walk again.

The second part of Jesus' healing formula involved the question of faith. "Do you have faith?" he invariably asks the sufferer. Faith in God's power to do

THE GALILEE BOAT

Scholars have often wondered whether the fishermen of Galilee had access to boats large enough to accommodate as many disciples as the Gospels suggest. These doubts were put to rest by a major discovery in 1986, after a severe drought brought water levels in the Sea of Galilee to historic lows. The sinking waters revealed an ancient boat preserved in the mud, some five miles from Migdal Beach. Led by Israeli archaeologist Shelley Wachsmann, experts conducted a number of tests using the carbon-14 dating technique. This showed that the vessel was built sometime between 50 B.C.E. and 50 C.E.—precisely the period straddling Jesus' ministry. The "Galilee Boat" is 26 feet long and 7.5 feet wide—large enough to comfortably accommodate ten people including pieces of equipment, such as nets and baskets. The planks were bonded together with "mortise-and-tenon" joints, fastened with wooden pegs—the construction method favored by shipbuilders in Antiquity.

PART II | THE LIFE OF JESUS

An anonymous Frankish artist created this miniature of St. John the Evangelist in the ninth century.

THE CHRONOLOGY OF JOHN'S GOSPEL

In the Gospel of John, Jesus travels more widely, which conforms to this Gospel's theme of developing the original traditions about Jesus into sophisticated theological discourse. Whereas the Synoptic Gospels suggest a Galilean ministry of one year or 18 months, with one visit to Jerusalem during Passover, John's Gospel places Jesus primarily in Jerusalem and surrounding regions, with visits to the Temple during the three Jewish festivals of Passover (*Pesach*), Weeks or Pentecost (*Shavuot*), and Booths (*Sukkot*). Perhaps John's purpose was to expand his literary canvas so as to fully explore the full range of his theological ideas, in direct or indirect relationship to Scripture. In fact, John's chronology imagines a ministry that would have lasted at least three years, since the annual Passover festival appears three times in his narrative: first at the beginning of Jesus' ministry (John 2:13), then while feeding the crowds in Galilee just before Passover in the second year (John 6:4), and again in the third year, when Jesus returns to Jerusalem to begin his Passion (John 12:1).

The Galilean Campaign

magnificent things is, of course, central to Jesus' teachings. Time and again, he tells his Apostles, "If you have faith and do not doubt;" "If you have faith as little as that of a mustard seed;" "O ye of little faith." (Matthew 21:21; 17:20; 6:30)

But faith also means faith in oneself. Modern research has revealed the incredible power of the mind in restoring our health and wellness—an adage long acknowledged by Asian mind-body medicine, before it was upstaged by our excessive reliance on prescription drugs and surgical intervention. Without faith, Jesus appears to say, one cannot heal. Indeed, Jesus' closing statement is almost always the same. As he tells the woman healed from her blood flow, "Daughter, your faith has made you well." (Mark 5:34)

None of these factors may suffice to "explain" Jesus' healing miracles, which to an extent can never be corroborated by purely scientific means. Indeed, many modern scholars still debate how to interpret these reports of miraculous healings. For the evangelists, however, the miracle stories have one overarching objective: to illustrate the power of Jesus' teachings. By feeding the 5,000, Jesus illustrates the aphorism "Blessed are those who hunger." Curing the sick is vivid proof of the mercy that awaits the faithful in the reign of God. For the Gospels, in short, the healing miracles are Jesus' Beatitudes made into flesh; they are the living proof that the kingdom of God is at hand.

This aerial view of Mount Tabor shows the rear view of the neo-Byzantine basilica completed in 1923, as well as remnants of older churches built on the site.

THE TRANSFIGURATION

The journeys of Jesus and his Apostles in Lower Galilee culminate in a mysterious event, known as the Transfiguration. Together with his most trusted disciples—Peter, James, and John—Jesus ascended a hill, "a high mountain apart," where "he was transfigured before them, and his clothes became dazzling white." At the same time, Jesus was joined by two heavenly figures. One was the now familiar figure of Elijah; the other was Moses. "Then a cloud overshadowed them," says Mark, "and from the cloud came a voice, 'This is my Son, the beloved; listen to him!'" (Mark 9:3-7)

While for us the purpose of this event may be puzzling, for Mark's audience the symbolic meaning would have been readily apparent. Moses and Elijah represent the Law *(Torah)* and the Prophets *(Nevi'im)*, the two principal divisions of Hebrew Scripture in Jesus' day. The appearance of these two figures thus illustrates one of the principal theological ideas of the Gospels, that Jesus is the true fulfillment of God's promise of redemption in the Hebrew Bible.

PART II | THE LIFE OF JESUS

"The Transfiguration" by Raphael (1483–1520), completed by his pupil Giulio Romano after the artist's death in 1520, is considered one of the greatest paintings of the High Renaissance.

The purpose of God's voice coming from a cloud is to reiterate Jesus' spiritual anointing in the waters of the Jordan. In Christian terms, therefore, the scene confirms Jesus as the Messiah who seals God's covenant—a new *testament* fulfilling the old.

The story of the Transfiguration is unique in the Gospel literature. Its imagery is described in almost apocalyptic terms, which is unusual for Mark; what's more, this is the only miracle event that transforms Jesus himself.

Christian tradition has long placed the Transfiguration on Mount Tabor, in the heart of the Jezreel Valley. Seen from afar, this hill certainly appears as a "high mountain apart," given that it is surrounded by flat rolling fields and orchards on all sides. As early as the second millennium B.C.E., the mount was used as a Canaanite shrine dedicated to the god Baal. Later, Tabor served as the place where Deborah and Barak rallied their forces to defeat the army of the king of Hazor, led by Sisera (Judges 4:12-16). The Seleucid king Antiochus III (223–187 B.C.E.) built a fortress on the hill to exploit its strategic position in the Jezreel Valley, a major crossroads between north and south.

The earliest identification of Tabor with the Transfiguration probably occurred in the third century, after which the first of many churches was built in the late fourth or early fifth century. The current edifice was completed by the Franciscans in 1923. Although modern, the style of the church, designed by Antonio Barluzzi, deliberately seeks a blending of Crusader and Byzantine motifs, which may explain its popularity among modern pilgrims. In one of the chapels is a mosaic believed to date to the earliest structure built in the fourth century. Nearby is the Greek Orthodox church of St. Elias, built in 1911 on the remains of a Crusader church.

Other scholars do not accept the Tabor location for this event, given that the old Hasmonean fortress on top of the hill may have been occupied by Roman forces, or their proxies, at the time of Jesus. Other possible locations include Mount Hermon, today located at a critical juncture between Israel, Lebanon, and Syria. Another possibility is Mount Nebo in today's Jordan, from where Moses surveyed the Promised Land.

The Transfiguration has a special significance in Orthodox liturgy as the intersection of humanity and God, of heaven and earth, with Jesus as the crucial bridge between the two. As such, the Transfiguration has been depicted in countless icons and mosaics and often graces the apse dome in Orthodox churches. Some theologians believe that, since the actual Resurrection event is neither observed nor reported in Mark's Gospel (or in any other Gospels for that matter), the Transfiguration fills this critical gap; it enables the faithful to imagine what the Resurrection would have looked like.

> SIX DAYS LATER, JESUS TOOK WITH HIM PETER AND JAMES AND JOHN, AND LED THEM UP A HIGH MOUNTAIN APART, BY THEMSELVES.
>
> GOSPEL OF MARK 9:2
> *Circa 66–70 C.E.*

The Galilean Campaign

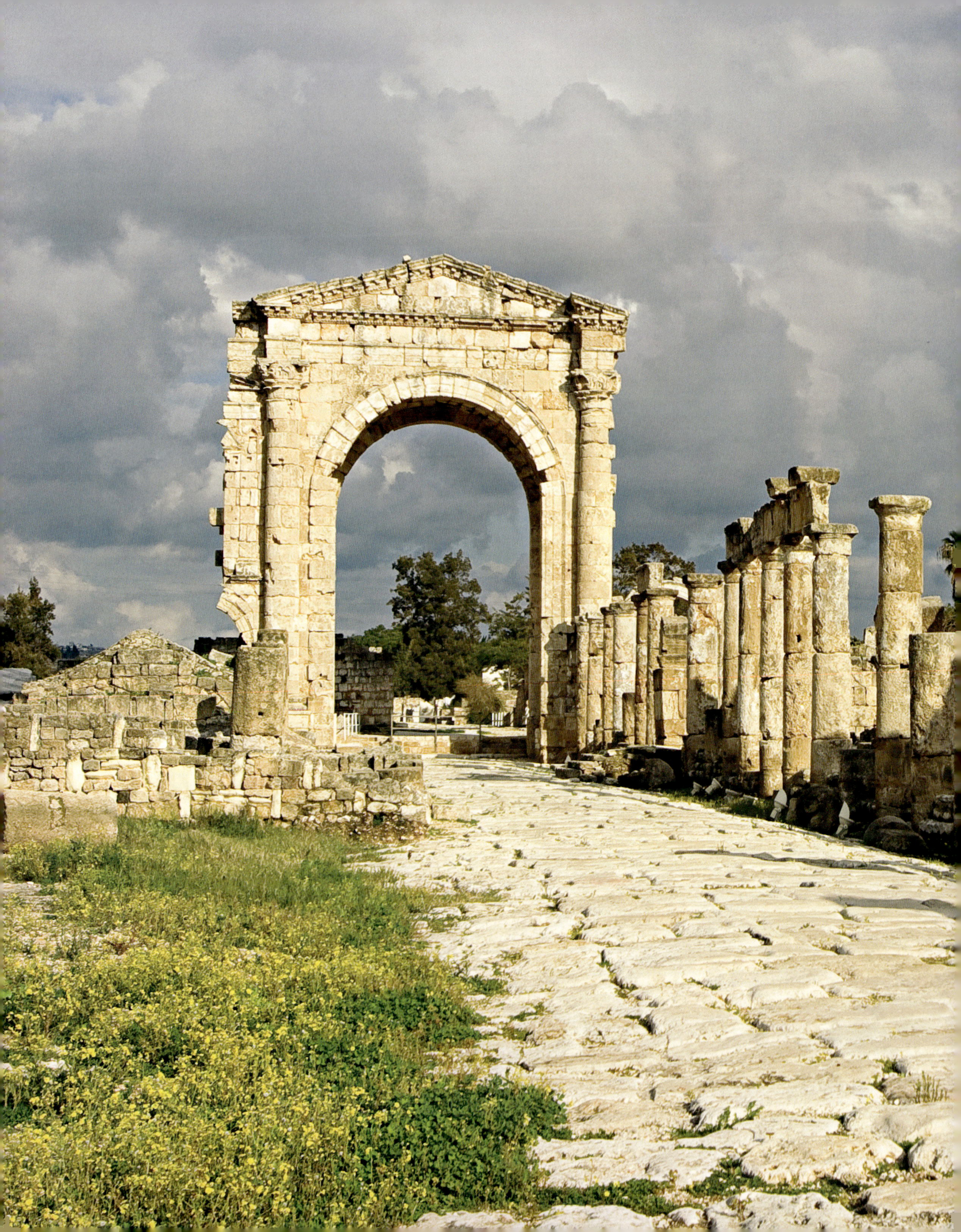

| CHAPTER |
9

JOURNEYS
Beyond
GALILEE

THEN JESUS LEFT
THAT PLACE AND WENT AWAY,
TO THE DISTRICT OF
TYRE AND SIDON.

GOSPEL OF MATTHEW 15:21
Circa 75-90 C.E.

This Roman triumphal arch once stood at the center of the ancient city of Tyre in today's Lebanon.

PART II | THE LIFE OF JESUS

After his journeys to the principal regions surrounding the Sea of Galilee, Jesus began to cast his net wider, beyond the borders of his native Galilee. "From there he set out and went to the region of Tyre," Mark tells us (Mark 7:24). Tyre lay to the north of Galilee, in Phoenicia, which was a Hellenized and predominantly Gentile region. Tyre was one of the oldest cities in the Near East; it had been continuously inhabited since the third millennium B.C.E.

In Ezekiel's sixth-century oracles, the prophet condemns Tyre as one of the foreign nations that secretly welcomed the Neo-Babylonian invasion of Judah. "Your heart was proud because of your beauty," says Ezekiel, grudgingly acknowledging Tyre's fame as one of the loveliest cities of Phoenicia; "You corrupted your wisdom for the sake of your splendor." (Ezekiel 28:17)

Much of that splendor was the result of Tyre's position as the principal harbor and depot of much of the trade in the Near East. Further proof of Tyre's economic prominence is provided by the Romans, who after their conquest of the region hurried to restore Tyre as an independent city, lest its pivotal role in sustaining the region's prosperity was affected in any way.

Jesus' motive for traveling to this city is therefore a bit of a mystery. From the beginning of his ministry, Jesus had made plain that his teachings were intended for "the lost sheep of Israel" only. "Go nowhere among the Gentiles," he instructed his Apostles (Matthew 10:5-6). It is true that Jesus agreed to heal the servant of a centurion (*ekatóntarchos*, literally commander of a hundred) who was possibly a Gentile officer of Antipas's militia, but this encounter took place in Jesus' base of Capernaum, not in Gentile territory (Matthew 8:5). One possible reason for Jesus' journey to Tyre and another Phoenician city called Sidon was, as Mark noted at the beginning of Jesus' ministry, that crowds "from Judea, Jerusalem, Idumea, beyond the Jordan, and the region around Tyre and Sidon" had come to Capernaum to see him. Perhaps Jesus was intrigued by the idea that Gentiles from the sophisticated urban centers of Phoenicia would travel so far to hear a Galilean Rabbi speak. Mark's Gospel, however, does not say that Jesus actually visited the city itself, but traveled in "the region of Tyre," which could also mean the vast swath of land along the Phoenician coast, just north of the border with Galilee.

Having arrived in this foreign territory, Jesus "entered a house and did not want anyone to know he was there," says Mark. "But a woman whose little

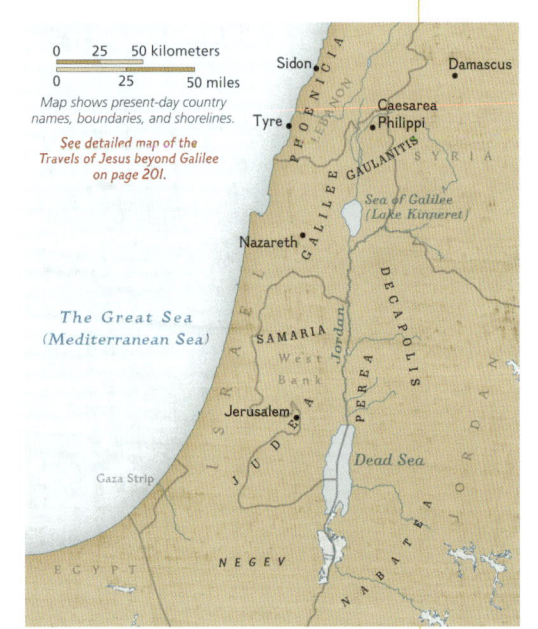

Map shows present-day country names, boundaries, and shorelines.

See detailed map of the Travels of Jesus beyond Galilee on page 201.

daughter had an unclean spirit immediately heard about him, and she came and bowed down at his feet," even though, Mark adds, she "was a Gentile, of Syrophoenician origin." (Mark 7:24-26) Jesus was reluctant to attend to her daughter. "Let the children be fed first," he replied, "for it is not fair to take the children's food and throw it to the dogs." This was a not-so-subtle rebuke, reminding the woman that his healing grace was reserved for "the children" of Israel, not for pagan Gentiles, whom Jesus disparagingly referred to as "dogs." But the woman was ready with a quick riposte. "Sir," she said, "even the dogs under the table eat the children's crumbs," implying that even those who were *not* chosen by God as his people, might still yearn for his grace.

Jesus was clearly impressed with her answer. "For saying that, you may go," he replied, and added, "the demon has left your daughter." And indeed, when the woman arrived back home she found her daughter up in bed, "and the demon gone." (Mark 7:27-30)

Palestinian women carry in the harvest in the time-honored manner of gathering the husks in a sheaf and tying them.

PART II | THE LIFE OF JESUS

Jesus may have walked through these fields north of Hazor on his way to the Phoenician coastal city of Tyre.

This inscription found on a 2,000-year-old limestone vessel (opposite) excavated in 2009 is believed to refer to the purity of fluids contained in stone jars.

The enigmatic episode in Tyre reveals several things about Jesus' career at this stage. On the one hand it may show a man who is trying to determine how far he can carry his message, and if indeed the interest from people from "Judea, Idumea, beyond the Jordan and Tyre" indicate that his kingdom of God teachings could be carried *outside* his native Galilee. Most prophets in Israel's history had operated in a specific geographical area; in a time bereft of mass media, a prophet only had his voice to spread his message. But the idea that his kingdom of God theology, shaped and nurtured in Galilee for Galileans, could have a far-reaching, international appeal must have intrigued Jesus. Indeed, following his visit to Tyre he continued on to Sidon, another Phoenician coastal city some 35 miles north of Tyre, before curving south for a visit to the Decapolis, the Gentile territory east of the Jordan (Mark 7:31). He had briefly set foot in the "country of the Gerasenes" earlier, during one of his excursions on the Sea of Galilee by boat,

Journeys Beyond Galilee

but this time he traveled over land. It is possible that during this return journey Jesus visited Caesarea Philippi, as reported by Mark and Matthew, because this city was located in the far north, at the base of Mount Hermon near one of the sources of the Jordan River.

The second impression from the visit to Tyre is that Jesus is concerned about keeping his whereabouts secret, and to curb the news of his healings. In Tyre, he "did not want anyone to know he was there." After curing Jairus's daughter, "he strictly ordered them that no one should know about this." (Mark 5:43) And when upon his return from Tyre and Sidon, he was introduced to a deaf man, he restored his hearing and his speech but ordered all witnesses "to tell no one." (Mark 7:36) Why would Jesus want to keep his actions secret, just as he was trying to spread the good news of the kingdom?

Throughout the 20th century, this question has given rise to various theories trying to explain the "Messianic Secret." One early version, advanced by William Wrede, suggests that Mark deliberately sought to downplay Jesus' role as the Messiah, given that this concept was the source of considerable tension between Jews and Jewish Christians, as we will see. Another answer is that Jesus did not want to be overrun by the sick, nor by crowds eager for the thrill of witnessing a miracle. Time and again, the Gospels tell us that wherever Jesus went, "into villages or cities or farms, they laid the sick in the marketplaces, and begged him that they might touch even the fringe of his cloak." (Mark 6:56) Such reticence is understandable if, as the Gospels suggest, Jesus' healing powers required an intense physical effort. Mark says that as soon as the woman who suffered from hemorrhages touched his cloak, Jesus was "immediately aware that power had gone forth from him." (Mark 5:30)

Yet another explanation, however, is that Jesus was aware of a growing opposition against his ministry. In fact, this is one of the key themes of Mark's Gospel: the idea

> AND JESUS ASKED THE LAWYERS AND THE PHARISEES, "IS IT LAWFUL TO CURE PEOPLE ON THE SABBATH OR NOT?" BUT THEY WERE SILENT.
>
> GOSPEL OF LUKE 14:3
> *Circa 75–90 C.E.*

PART II | THE LIFE OF JESUS

Paolo Veronese (1528–1588) painted this depiction of Jesus and Levi the tax collector from a large canvas entitled "The Feast in the House of Levi" in 1573.

that Jesus' arrest and execution was the result of a carefully laid conspiracy, which unfolded over many months prior to the fateful Passover events. The core of this opposition, the evangelists tell us, were the Pharisees (Mark 3:6; Matthew 12:14).

JESUS AND THE PHARISEES

The Pharisees first make their appearance in Capernaum. "As [Jesus] was walking along," Mark says, "he saw Levi son of Alphaeus sitting at the tax booth." (Mark 2:14) Such tax booths were common in town, given that Capernaum sat on one of the principal trade routes in the region. Taxes were levied whenever goods crossed from one jurisdiction into another—in this case, from Philip's Tetrarchy of the Gaulanitis into Antipas's territory of Galilee. In the next scene, we see Jesus sitting at dinner in Levi's house, "accompanied by many tax collectors and sinners." The general antipathy against these publicans ran deep, since they not only collected tolls but also taxes on property, harvest, fishing, and the sale of salt. In many cases they were also the people from whom one would borrow money, so as to pay for those very same taxes, and usually at exorbitant rates. The fact that publicans collaborated closely with the Herodian regime of Antipas, or with the Roman occupying authorities in Judea, did little to improve their reputation.

A group of scribes of the Pharisees took issue with Jesus' apparent willingness to socialize with these "sinners." As we saw, scribes were not priests, but educated laymen who practiced a professional trade that combined dictation and legal drafts with our modern concept of a notary public. "Why does he eat with tax collectors and sinners?" they asked (Mark 2:16), directly challenging Jesus for breaking bread with these individuals. The antipathy against tax collectors would continue well into the third century. "When (tax) collectors enter into a house, the house (is considered) unclean," says the *Tosefta,* a supplementary collection to the Mishnah.

> NOW WHEN THE PHARISEES AND SOME OF THE SCRIBES WHO HAD COME FROM JERUSALEM GATHERED AROUND HIM, THEY NOTICED THAT SOME OF HIS DISCIPLES WERE EATING WITH DEFILED HANDS, THAT IS, WITHOUT WASHING THEM.
>
> GOSPEL OF MARK 7:1-2
> *Circa 66–70 C.E.*

In Mark's Gospel, this confrontation between Jesus and the Pharisees then leads to five conflict situations, in which the Pharisees repeatedly question Jesus' observance of Jewish customs and the Law. Immediately after the episode in Levi's house, Jesus is asked, "Why do John's disciples and the disciples of the Pharisees fast, but your disciples do not fast?" (Mark 2:18) Fasting was not generally prescribed in the Law, though Jews did fast at times, notably at Yom Kippur—the Day of Atonement (Leviticus 16:29). Some factions, such as the Qumran community and John the Baptist, also fasted, but they were motivated by a quest for ascetic abstention. The purpose of this dispute about fasting is therefore not entirely clear, except as an occasion for Jesus to declare that "The wedding guests cannot fast while the bridegroom is with them, now can they?" (Mark 2:19)

Journeys Beyond Galilee

PART II | THE LIFE OF JESUS

The Neo-Byzantine Church of the Multiplication in Tabgha is shown against the dramatic backdrop of the Jordanian Hills on the eastern shore of the Sea of Galilee.

THE QUESTION OF SABBATH OBSERVANCE

This is followed by a third challenge, since the disciples were observed plucking heads of grain in a field, even though it was the Sabbath. Contrary to the first two disputes, Sabbath observance was an issue that the Pharisees vigorously debated among themselves. The Torah clearly specified that the seventh day was "a Sabbath to the Lord your God" during which "you shall not do any work." (Exodus 20:10) As such, the accusation in Mark may have involved two transgressions: one, the harvesting of grain, which was prohibited by the Law, and two, taking a long walk through the fields, which was prohibited on the Sabbath by custom. The Qumran community, which advocated an even stricter adherence to Torah than the Pharisees, held that "No man shall walk in a field to do services for himself on the Sabbath."

But what if it involved an essential need, such as satisfying one's hunger? What was allowed, and what wasn't? These were the questions that, in the Mishnah, elicited heated debates between two schools: the House of Hillel and the House of Shammai. One such dispute addressed the type of effort one was permitted to undertake if, for example, one's house was burning. On the Sabbath, a Jew was forbidden to try to put out the fire, but he was allowed to take out just enough food for his family to last through the Sabbath. He could allow a Gentile to try to extinguish the fire, but he couldn't go and ask him to do so. And so forth.

RITUAL PURITY

One source of contention between Jesus and the Pharisees was the Pharisaic approach to ritual purity. Traditionally, the purity system as defined in the Law was a matter for the priests, to be used within the Temple. After the Pharisees lost their dominant role in religious governance to the Sadducees, the Pharisees sought to transfer the purity cult to their own homes and lifestyles. This was meant to bring the sacred to every town and village. In the process, the Pharisees formulated detailed rules governing food preparation, ritual bathing, tithing, and Sabbath observance. For example, the Pharisees insisted that one should wash before the Sabbath and before meals. In Mark's Gospel, they castigate the Apostles for "eating with defiled hands, that is, without washing them." (Mark 7:1) Jesus responds that "It is what comes *out* of a person that defiles." (7:20-22) In his opinion, Pharisaic concern with the minutiae of the Law, how they "tithe mint, dill, and cumin," has led them to neglect "the weightier matters of the law: justice and mercy and faith." (Matthew 23:23) Mark's Gospel translates the Jewish concepts of purity into theological terms. Whereas the Holy Spirit is the force of God that will propel the Kingdom of God, the force of Satan is the "unclean spirit" that possesses man in the form of demons, and only Jesus can exorcize them.

This mikveh, or ritual bathing pool, was excavated just outside the walls of Temple Mount in Jerusalem.

In the Babylonian Talmud, the second-century Rabbi Judah ben El'ai is cited as saying that "[on the Sabbath] one may pluck (grain) by hand and eat, but only if one plucks without a utensil; and one may rub [a husk] and eat, but only if one does not rub a lot in a utensil"—i.e., without the intervention of a tool. This would suggest that there were some who were in sympathy with Jesus' approach to plucking grain on the Sabbath, particularly if one avoided implements, such as a utensil, that could have qualified the activity as "work."

The fourth challenge posed by the Pharisees also relates to Sabbath observance. Jesus "entered a synagogue, and a man was there who had a withered hand. They watched him to see whether he would cure him on the Sabbath, so that they might accuse him," says Mark (Mark 3:1-2). Jesus was aware that his every move was being scrutinized, for he turned and said, "Is it lawful to do good or to do harm on the Sabbath, to save life or to kill?" This issue went to the very heart of the Sabbath debates among the Pharisees. What if Sabbath observance was used as an excuse for not intervening in a potentially life-threatening event? Once again, the Mishnah contains a number of discussions on the topic. Matters of life and death—such as the birth of a baby—were generally considered a valid reason to "break" or "push aside" (i.e., postpone) Sabbath observance, but a twisted ankle or a dislocated hand was not. Consequently, a "withered hand" may not have been considered a life-threatening injury that permitted violation of the Sabbath. Jesus, however, was "grieved at their hardness of heart and said to the man, 'Stretch out your hand.'" And, says Mark, "the hand was restored." (Mark 3:5)

Mark is careful to emphasize that Jesus did not touch the man, which was usually part of his healing formula. Nor did he make any other gesture that could conceivably be called "work." He merely said "Stretch out your hand," and as soon as the man did so, the hand was cured. While the healing was undoubtedly occasioned by Jesus' healing powers, technically it did not involve any act that would have violated the rules of the Sabbath. Jesus summarized his view on Sabbath observance in one pithy sentence: "The Sabbath was made for humankind, and not humankind for the Sabbath." (Mark 2:27) The same point would later be made in the Talmud.

The Pharisees: Foes or Allies?

In the Gospels, the Pharisees are often portrayed as, in Bruce Chilton's words, the "straw men" of the story. They chase Jesus up and down Galilee, into fields, villages, and synagogues, in a determined effort to "entrap" him. They accuse him of not observing the laws of purification when eating or preparing meals, or of violating the Sabbath by healing the sick. Jesus counters that "there is nothing outside a person that by going in can defile, but the things that come out are what defile." (Mark 7:15)

Mark's Gospel is the only one that directly implicates the Pharisees in the grand conspiracy to destroy Jesus' ministry. After the healing of the man with the withered hand, Mark says, "the Pharisees went out and immediately conspired with the Herodians against him, how to destroy him." (Mark 3:6) "Watch out," Jesus warns to the Apostles in response, "beware of the yeast of the Pharisees and the yeast of Herod." (Mark 8:15) Later in the story, when Jesus is teaching in the Temple, the chief priests "sent to him some Pharisees and Herodians to trap him in what he said." (Mark 12:13)

Scholars have questioned the idea that the Pharisees and Herod Antipas's court would somehow be in collusion to try to remove Jesus from the scene. First off, Antipas did not need a pretext, legal or otherwise, to apprehend Jesus. If the tetrarch truly believed that the crowds flocking to Jesus posed a threat to his rule, he could have done the same thing he did with John the Baptist: send his militia to arrest him and throw him in a dungeon. Galilee was Antipas's territory; to maintain law and order and to nip any form of protest in the bud was what his Roman masters expected him to do.

Indeed, the Gospels of Matthew and Luke indicate that there was considerable kinship between the Pharisees and Jesus. From the second century B.C.E. onward, it was the Pharisees who had begun to advance the idea that the Law was *not* cast in stone, but served as a set of precepts meant to guide the people in the everyday circumstances of their lives. Therefore, it was acceptable to subject the Law to interpretation and discussion; God encouraged such debate and sent his divine Spirit to guide them. In addition, the Pharisees believed in the resurrection of the dead and the immortality of the soul. All of these ideas lie at the core of Jesus' teachings as well.

A closer look reveals that the sharp debates on the Sabbath and ritual purity, which Mark portrays as a conflict between Jesus and the Pharisees, were actually the type of vigorous disputes that the Pharisees enjoyed *amongst themselves*. For them, issues such as Sabbath observance, tithing, marriage, divorce, and caring for the sick—themes that return in many of Jesus' teachings—would later form the core of the Mishnah discussions. The idea that some Pharisees would seek out Jesus for his view on these matters could therefore be considered a mark of

French artist James Jacques Joseph Tissot (1836–1902) painted this impression of "Jesus and the Man with the Withered Hand" around 1894.

THE TRAVELS OF JESUS BEYOND GALILEE

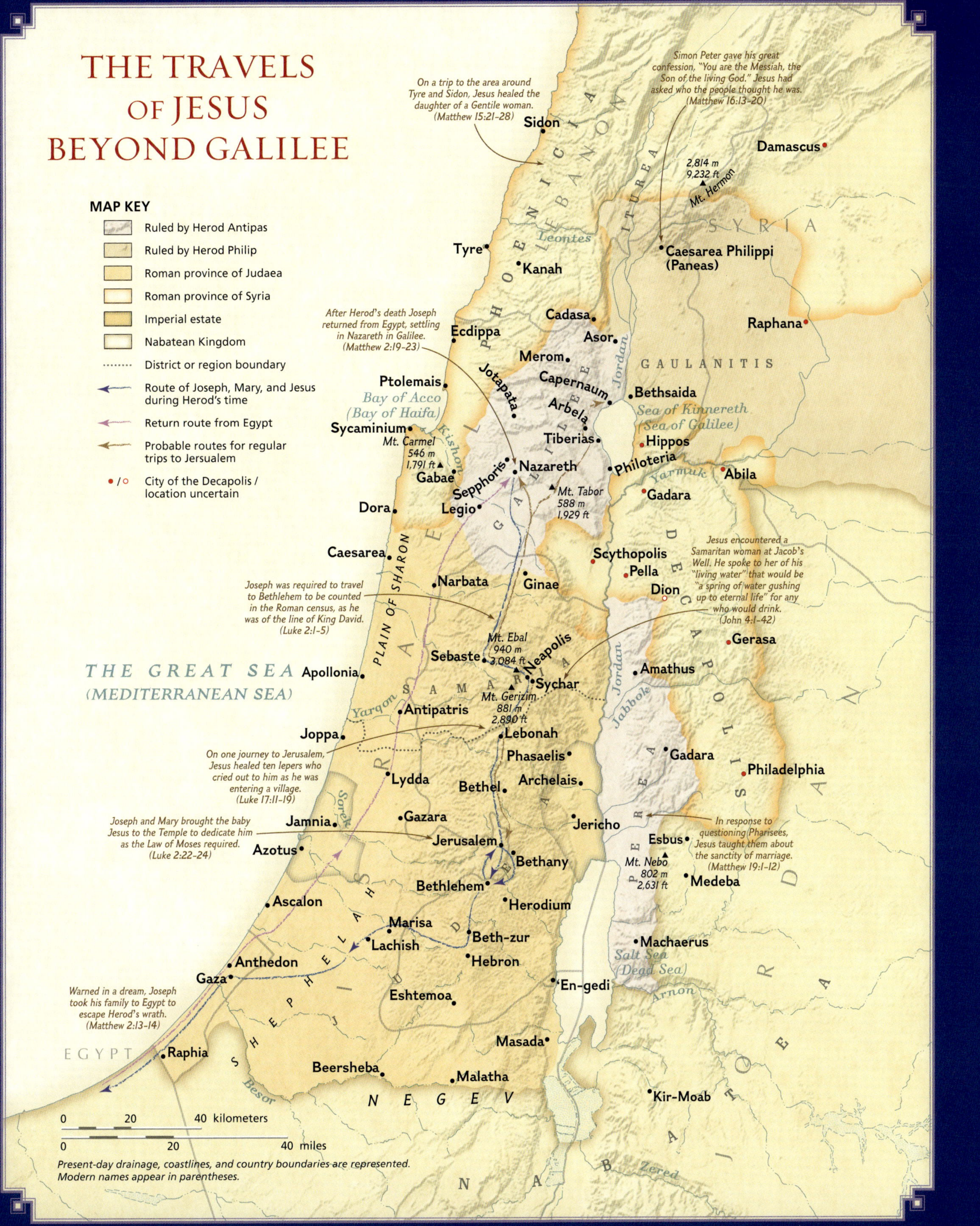

PART II | THE LIFE OF JESUS

JESUS AND SCRIPTURE

Time and again, Jesus reveals an intimate knowledge of Scripture. Does this mean that Jesus read Hebrew? It is impossible to answer this question with certainty. Previously, in the third century B.C.E., the Jewish community of Alexandria had created a translation of the Jewish Bible into Greek, known as the Septuagint. It is very likely that in Jesus' day, several translations in Aramaic, the language Jesus himself spoke, would have been available as well. One such *Targum*, an Aramaic translation of the Book of Job, is mentioned in reference to Rabbi Gamaliel I, a contemporary of Jesus. A Targum of Job was also found in one of the caves in Qumran, dating to the first century B.C.E. Another Aramaic translation of Scripture was reportedly compiled by Jonathan ben Uzziel, a disciple of the great Jewish sage Hillel (active 30–10 B.C.E.). Jesus' familiarity with such Targumim is suggested by the Gospels, who quote him crying out a verse from Psalm 22, in Aramaic, during his last moments on the cross: *Eloi, Eloi, lema sabachthani?* ("My God, my God, why have you forsaken me?") The Dead Sea Scrolls, furthermore, suggest that our version of the Hebrew Bible is fairly close to the version that Jesus was familiar with.

In Jesus' time, Torah scrolls such as this one (opposite top) were sometimes written in Aramaic, the language most commonly used in ancient Palestine.

Ancient Caesarea-Philippi was located at the base of Mount Hermon within the Golan Heights (opposite bottom).

great respect. While many Pharisees would have taken issue with some of Jesus' precepts, the reports in the Gospels suggest that the Pharisees solicited Jesus' opinion because they believed his ideas had merit and deserved consideration. By the time these stories were incorporated in the Gospel of Mark, however, they were used as evidence of a growing opposition between Jesus and the Pharisees.

The sympathy that many Pharisees may have harbored for Jesus' ministry is attested to in other Gospel stories as well. Luke, for example, tells us that when Jesus "went through one town and village after another," he was approached by "some Pharisees." They had come to warn him that Herod Antipas was aware of his growing following. "Get away from here," these Pharisees urged, "for Herod wants to kill you." (Luke 13:31) This scene directly contradicts Mark's theory that the Pharisees and Herod were in collusion to kill Jesus. Indeed, shortly after this episode, Jesus sits down for dinner with "a leader of the Pharisees." (Luke 14:1) Much later, it is Gamaliel, a noted Pharisaic sage, who defends Peter and other Apostles during their hearing in front of the Sanhedrin (Acts 5:59).

So why would Mark choose to depict the Pharisees as the principal opponents of Jesus' ministry? Several scholars believe that this conflict is a reflection of the growing antagonism between Jews and Christian Jews in the latter part of the first century, when the Gospels were arguably written. Following the destruction of the Temple in 70 C.E., which all but destroyed the priestly community of the Sadducees, the Pharisees emerged as the new leaders of post-Temple Judaism. Now that the long tradition of Temple sacrifice had been brought to an end, the Pharisees developed an alternative form of Judaism that they themselves had followed for so many years: to interpret and debate the Law, and to transfer these insights into everyday practice. This led to the era of *Rabbinic* Judaism, in which the study of Scripture replaced worship and sacrifice at the Temple. Unfortunately, this coincided with a growing discrimination of those Jews who continued to attend synagogue meetings but insisted that Jesus was the Messiah. Many of these Jewish Christians were ostracized from their communities, which may have inspired the bias against the Pharisees in the Gospel stories.

The Opposition Grows

Mark's Gospel is notable because, as the first Gospel, it would set the stage for the narrative arc of the Gospels of Matthew and Luke, and in terms of the Passion narrative, the Gospel of John as well. According to this narrative arc, Jesus reaches the apogee of his ministry in Galilee, surrounded by throngs of eager crowds, only to enter into a spiral of conflict and opposition that will inexorably lead him to Golgotha. This sense of alienation even involves Jesus' family. In Mark's Gospel, they

Journeys Beyond Galilee

appear confounded by his activities. One day, says Mark, when Jesus "went home," he was pursued by so many crowds that "they could not even eat." Jesus' family—the individuals involved are not otherwise identified—went out to "restrain him, for people were saying, 'He has gone out of his mind.' " (Mark 3:19-21) John's Gospel says, "even his brothers did not believe in him." (John 7:5)

A few verses later, Jesus was surrounded by crowds when "his mother and his brothers came; and standing outside, they sent for him and called him." When Jesus did not respond, some people in the crowd said, with evident surprise, "Your mother and your brothers and sisters are outside, asking for you." Jesus replied, "Who are my mother and my brothers?" And looking at those who sat around him, he said, "Here are my mother and my brothers! Whoever does the will of God is my brother and sister and mother." (Mark 3:32-35)

Clearly, any mother would have been deeply wounded upon hearing these words. It is very unlikely that this was Jesus' intention; Mary, his mother, remained devoted to him and was reportedly with him at the

PART II | THE LIFE OF JESUS

Artist Palma il Giovane (1548–1628) depicted Mark the Evangelist, revered as the patron saint of Venice, against the backdrop of Venice's San Marco Basilica.

> **POINTING TO HIS DISCIPLES, HE SAID, "HERE ARE MY MOTHER AND MY BROTHERS! FOR WHOEVER DOES THE WILL OF MY FATHER IN HEAVEN IS MY BROTHER AND SISTER AND MOTHER."**
>
> GOSPEL OF MATTHEW 12:49-50
> *Circa 75–90 C.E.*

very end. Elsewhere in the Gospels, as attested by the story of Mary and Martha, Jesus is capable of showing great warmth and affection. The purpose of this story may be simply to buttress Mark's principal theme: that Jesus was increasingly abandoned by those around him—not only his family and his disciples, but even by the crowds, who soon will be baying for his Crucifixion—before his ultimate glorification.

The Apostles, too, are not always depicted in favorable terms. They seem confused by Jesus' often veiled references to the kingdom of God, and they struggle to understand what it means. "Do you not yet understand?" an exasperated Jesus tells them (Mark 8:21) before launching into another parable. "The Kingdom of God," he explained, "is like a mustard seed, the smallest of all the seeds on earth, that, when sown, becomes the greatest of all shrubs." (Matthew 13:31) Or: "The Kingdom of God is like a seed that sprouts while the farmer is asleep; it grows into a stalk, the head, and finally the grain, which the farmer cuts with his sickle." (Mark 4:26-29) "Do you not understand this parable?" Jesus asked at length. "Then how will you understand all the parables?" (Mark 4:13)

But why speak in parables at all? Why did Jesus not explain, in clear and lucid terms, what his vision of the kingdom of God entailed? Indeed, many of Jesus' parables are so shrouded in mystery that it is sometimes difficult to understand their purpose. The answer, said Jesus, is that "for those outside" his immediate circle of followers, "everything comes in parables in order that they may indeed look, but not perceive, and may indeed listen, but not understand." (Mark 4:11-12)

Some authors explain Jesus' reticence in view of the fact that any talk of a *kingdom* would inevitably have been interpreted by the Romans in political terms—as indeed was the case in the end. Unlike some other protest movements of his era, Jesus tried to avoid any conflict with the Romans. According to Luke, he was once asked, "Is it lawful for us to pay taxes to the emperor, or not?" As we saw, this was a sensitive issue, which had elicited a major revolt in 6 C.E.—when Jesus would have been about ten years old. Jesus asked for a coin, a denarius, and replied, "Give to the emperor the things that are the emperor's, and to God the things that are God's." (Luke 20:22-24)

While scholars continue to debate the framework of Jesus' kingdom, most reject the idea that it has any political dimension. Many believe that by contrast, it is the *social* dimension that typifies Jesus' kingdom theology, with its concern for bridging the gap between landowner and tenant, between toll collector and fisherman, between the wealthy and the poor. This is perhaps the reason why, time and again, Jesus reaches out to the elites of the land, dining with tax collectors and

Journeys Beyond Galilee

THE SON OF MAN

While the Synoptic Gospels proclaim Jesus is the Messiah, Jesus prefers to refer to himself as the "Son of Man." (Mark 2:10-12) In the four canonical Gospels alone, the words "Son of Man" appear 81 times, though they are always spoken by Jesus himself—never by his followers. The term originates from Hebrew Scripture. In the Book of Ezekiel, for example, the prophet is addressed by God as "son of man" *(ben adam)* more than 90 times. Scholars believe that the phrase is a synonym for "a mortal human being," to express the prophet's humility before God. In the Book of Daniel, "one like a son of man" is seen "coming with the clouds of heaven" (Daniel 7:13), suggesting a herald, possibly an angel, who will announce the coming reign of God. Some scholars believe that this is how Jesus saw himself. In Luke, Jesus says, "Then they will see 'the Son of Man coming in a cloud' with power and great glory." (Luke 21:27) Others, however, argue that Jesus used "Son of Man" in the traditional sense, as a mere mortal like any other human being.

Breaking with Baroque paradigms, Dutch artist Rembrandt van Rijn (1606–1669) painted this very intimate and human portrait of Jesus around 1648–1650.

PART II | THE LIFE OF JESUS

The ancient city of Caesarea-Philippi (opposite) was a major pilgrimage destination because of the holy spring of Paneas, located in a sanctuary dedicated to the Greek god Pan.

other powerful individuals. They were the ones responsible for the growing social divides in Galilee, and were thus in a position to correct it. "Those who are well have no need of a physician, but the sick," says Jesus when asked why he chooses to sit down with "sinners and tax collectors"; "I have come to call not the righteous but the sick." (Mark 2:17)

The Son of Man

Jesus' journeys outside Lower Galilee reach a dramatic conclusion at Caesarea Philippi. The town, which a few years later would be expanded into a splendid Greco-Roman city, was a center of the cult of the Greek god Pan, who was worshipped in several of the nearby grottoes and a spring known as Paneas. In this Gentile region, on the threshold of returning to his native land, Jesus may have felt the need to reflect on the impact of his ministry to date, and to wonder whether the Galileans were indeed prepared to embrace the kingdom of God. He turned to his disciples and asked, "Who do people say that I am?" Some Apostles said, "John the Baptist." Others said, "Elijah." Still others hedged their bets and said, "One of the prophets." Then Jesus asked them, "But who do *you* say that I am?" A difficult question. Simon Peter stood up and proclaimed, "You are the Messiah." Jesus' response, says Mark, was a rebuke: "He sternly ordered them not to tell anyone about him." (Mark 8:30)

> **NOW WHEN JESUS CAME INTO THE DISTRICT OF CAESAREA PHILIPPI, HE ASKED HIS DISCIPLES, "WHO DO PEOPLE SAY THAT THE SON OF MAN IS?"**
>
> Gospel of Matthew 16:13
> *Circa 75–90 C.E.*

Matthew relates the story differently. In his Gospel, Jesus warmly commends Simon Peter, saying, "Blessed are you, Simon son of Jonah!" And Jesus adds a pun on Peter's nickname (*Petros* in Greek, or rock), "You are Peter, and on this rock I will build my Church." (Matthew 16:17-18) By the time this Gospel was written, there were indeed many flourishing Christian communities throughout the empire. Nevertheless, in Matthew's story Jesus also "sternly ordered the disciples not to tell anyone that he was the Messiah." (Matthew 16:20)

Whether this suggests that Jesus was concerned about the political liability of the title of Messiah, or whether his reticence should be explained in strictly theological terms is not clear. What we do know, based on the Gospel record, is that Jesus continued to refer to himself as the Son of Man, which may have been inspired by the eschatological visions in the Book of Daniel.

Jesus then "called the crowd with his disciples" and set out to clarify the role that God intended for him. "He began to teach them that the Son of Man must undergo great suffering, and be rejected by the elders, the chief priests, and the scribes, and be killed," Mark says, "and after three days rise again." Peter couldn't believe what Jesus was saying, and he started to argue with him. Jesus replied, "You are setting your mind not on divine things, but on human things." (Mark 8:31-33)

206

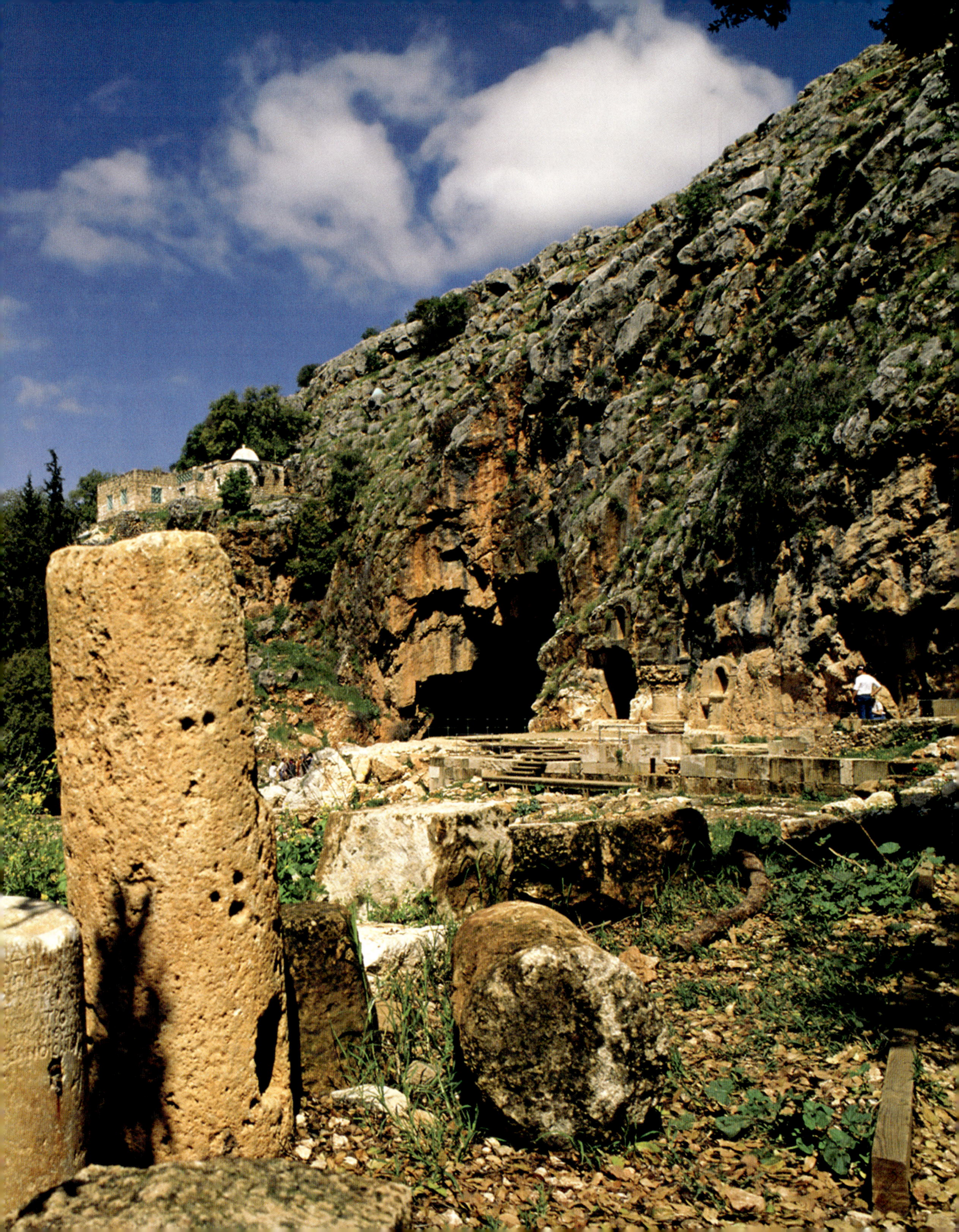

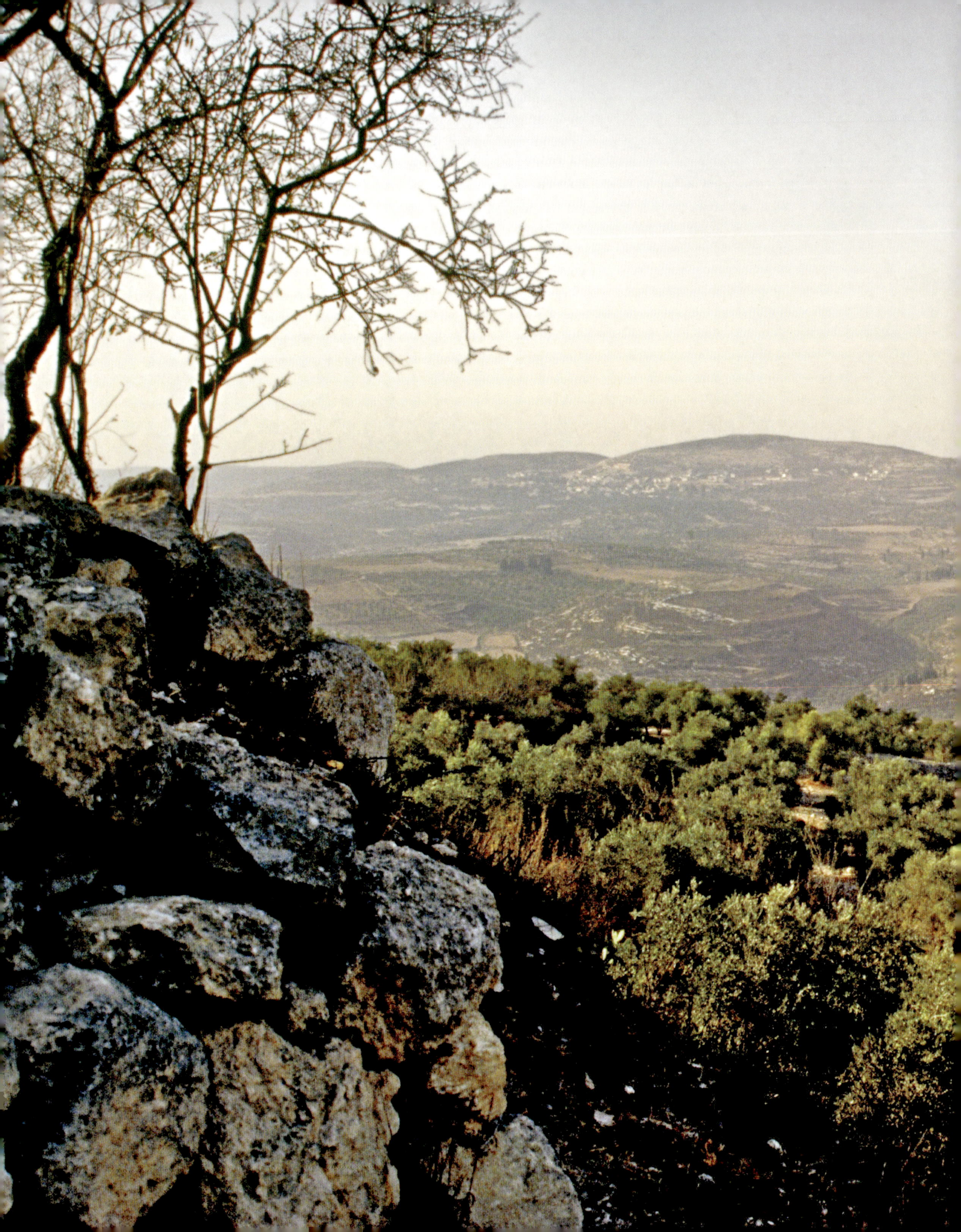

CHAPTER 10

The ROAD to JERUSALEM

SEE, WE ARE GOING
UP TO JERUSALEM,
AND THE SON OF MAN
WILL BE HANDED OVER
TO THE CHIEF PRIESTS
AND SCRIBES, AND THEY WILL
CONDEMN HIM TO DEATH.

GOSPEL OF MATTHEW 20:18
Circa 75–90 C.E.

A rocky outcropping near the old city of Samaria, renamed Sebaste by King Herod, offers a view of the valley through which ran the ancient road to Jerusalem.

PART II | THE LIFE OF JESUS

At some point following his return from Tyre and Sidon, Jesus confronted the reality that his teachings had not accomplished what he had hoped: a groundswell of support for refashioning Galilean society as a kingdom of God. Several outbursts directed at the crowds around him convey a certain sense of frustration. "You faithless and perverse generation!" Jesus says to a man who has come to plead for his epileptic son, "How much longer must I put up with you?" His anger is keenly felt by his Apostles, who previously tried to heal the boy, but were unable to do so. "Why could we not cast it out?" they ask. Jesus replies, "Because of your little faith." (Matthew 17:14-20)

But the greatest scolding is reserved for the cities that once formed the heart of Jesus' Galilean ministry. "Woe to you, Chorazin!" he cries in the Gospels of both Luke and Matthew; "Woe to you, Bethsaida! If the powerful deeds performed among you had been done in Tyre and Sidon, they would have changed their ways long ago, sitting in sackcloth and ashes!" (Matthew 11:21; Luke 10:13) For his Jewish audience, this was a harsh rebuke indeed. If the "powerful deeds" Jesus had performed could sway even the pagans of Phoenicia, then truly the hearts of the Galileans must be as hard as stone. "And you, Capernaum," Jesus continued, directing his spite at the town that once served as his home and base, "will you be exalted to heaven? No, you will be brought down to Hades." (Luke 10:15)

Perhaps it is this sense of disillusionment, combined with the growing opposition to his ministry in Galilee, that prompted Jesus to leave the region, never to return—at least not in mortal form. "He set his face to go to Jerusalem," Luke says (Luke 9:51). According to the Gospel of John, Jesus first moved into the Gaulanitis, to a place named Bethany-across-the-Jordan (John 10:40). John the Baptist had operated there not too long before. Some early Church documents suggest that Jesus had relatives living in the nearby region of Basanitis, east of the Jordan, in the town of Kochaba.

Mark, Matthew, and Luke, on the other hand, suggest that this is the moment when Jesus decided to go down south, to Jerusalem in Judea. It is possible that he was inspired by the example of the prophet Jeremiah. Jeremiah, too, had lost heart at one time, only to be exhorted by God: "Stand up! Gird your loins, and tell them everything that I command you." (Jeremiah 1:17) Jeremiah had heeded God's call and had gone to proclaim, at the very portal of the Temple, "the word of the Lord" to "all you people of Judah, all that enter these gates to worship the Lord!" (Jeremiah 7:2) The result was one of the most magnificent speeches in Hebrew Scripture: Jeremiah's Temple sermon. Jesus was certainly familiar with this sermon, for soon he would quote from it, standing on the same place, in the forecourt of what was Herod's Second Temple, some 500 years after Jeremiah had preceded him.

To preach in Jerusalem was to preach for all of Judea, indeed the whole Jewish nation, at home and abroad. The timing was auspicious, for the Jewish month of Nisan had begun. Soon, thousands of Jews from all over Palestine and the Diaspora would converge on Jerusalem for the great Feast of Passover. Standing in the Temple, Jesus' audience would be multiplied tenfold, and his message would be carried back to all corners of the empire.

The walls of today's old city of Jerusalem were built by the Ottoman Sultan Suleiman the Magnificent around 1535.

> WHEN JESUS HAD FINISHED SAYING THESE THINGS, HE LEFT GALILEE AND WENT TO THE REGION OF JUDEA BEYOND THE JORDAN.
>
> Gospel of Matthew 19:1
> *Circa 75–90 c.e.*

And so, Jesus embarked on his fateful journey to Jerusalem. "They were on the road, going up to Jerusalem," Mark says, "and Jesus was walking ahead of them; they were amazed, and those who followed were afraid." (Mark 10:32) Their fear was not without justification. It was a mere two years since the bloody suppression of protestors in Jerusalem by the prefect, Pontius Pilate. During Passover, moreover, the Roman forces in Jerusalem were known to be on even higher alert than usual, since there was a unique political undertone to the Passover Feast. It celebrated Israel's liberation from another despot, a tyrant known as Pharaoh of Egypt. No doubt security would be tight, with the Roman military carefully monitoring all that went on in the Temple, as they had ever since 28 c.e.

Sensing their apprehension, Jesus "took the twelve aside again and began to tell them what was to happen to him, saying, 'See, we are going up to Jerusalem, and the Son of Man will be handed over to the chief priests and the scribes, and they will condemn him to death.' " (Mark 10:32-33) Jesus' premonition of his Passion is a cardinal element of Mark's story, for it shows that Jesus' Crucifixion was part of God's plan. The "foretelling of the death and resurrection" is likewise included in the

Gospels of Matthew, Luke, and John. Some scholars, however, have argued that Jesus' decision to shift his ministry from Galilee to Judea during Passover was a conscious effort to rejuvenate and broaden the appeal of his teachings.

THE AMBITION OF THE APOSTLES

The Apostles may have sensed that with the move to Judea, Jesus' ministry had entered a new and perhaps decisive phase, because this is the moment when they begin to quarrel amongst themselves, maneuvering for a prominent position in what they believe is the imminent establishment of God's kingdom. "Look," Peter says reasonably, "we have left everything and followed you." (Mark 10:28) "What then will we have?" (Matthew 19:27) Jesus responds by assuring his disciples that "when the Son of Man is seated on the throne of his glory, you who have followed me will also sit on twelve thrones, judging the twelve tribes of Israel." (Matthew 19:28) This statement doesn't satisfy the disciples; in fact, it only serves to increase their anxiety about who will reap the greatest positions and rewards.

In Matthew, the mother of John and James enters the fray to lobby on behalf of her sons. "Declare that these two sons of mine will sit, one at your right hand and one at your left, in your kingdom," she boldly demands (Matthew 20:21). "You do not know what you're asking," Jesus responds; "Are you able to drink the cup that I am about to drink?"—an obvious allusion to the two crucified men on either side of him on Golgotha. They answered, "We are able." (Matthew 20:20-22)

Confronted by the growing ambition of his followers, Jesus then turns to a group of young children who are being brought to him for his blessing. The Apostles scold their parents but Jesus silences them, saying, "Let the little children come to me, and do not stop them." He lays his hands on them by way of a blessing, and says, "For it is to such as these that the kingdom of heaven belongs." (Matthew 19:13-15) In Mark, Jesus expresses himself even more succinctly: "Whoever welcomes one such child in my name welcomes me." (Mark 9:37) To enter the kingdom, Jesus seems to say, one has to have the innocence and trust of a child; without these attributes, it is impossible to make the necessary leap of faith.

THE ROAD TO JUDEA

According to John's and Matthew's Gospels, Jesus and his group traveled to Judea using the southern route along the Jordan River—perhaps the same route that Jesus used when he first came down to join the movement of John the Baptist. From Kochaba they would have followed the course of the River Yarmuk through

Dutch artist Rembrandt van Rijn (1606–1669) painted this portrait of "Jeremiah Lamenting the Destruction of Jerusalem" in 1630.

The stark hills of Jericho (opposite) stand in sharp contrast to the palm groves along the Jordan River; the groves were renowned throughout the ancient world.

PART II | THE LIFE OF JESUS

Hamat Gader, which means "the hot springs of Gadara"—close to the border of today's Israel and Jordan—was developed into a sprawling spa resort by the Romans in the second century C.E.

the rugged hills of the Transjordan plateau. After a day or so, they would have passed the sprawling gardens of Hamat Gader on their left. Known for its mineral springs, Hamat Gader would soon be transformed into a resort for the growing expatriate community of Roman officials. From there, the Yarmuk led to the Jordan just below the Gentile city of Scythopolis. Here the landscape changed: the hills and cliffs of Moab gave way to the dry landscape of the Jordan Rift Valley, dotted with copses of date palms. The temperature would be rising steadily, even in the month of Nisan (between March and April), as they further descended toward Jericho and the Dead Sea.

Luke, on the other hand, tells us that Jesus took a more direct road from Galilee to Jerusalem. "On the way to Jerusalem," his Gospel says, "Jesus was going through the region between Samaria and Galilee." (Luke 17:11) In fact, it is Luke who gives us the most detailed description of the journey. Along the way, he relates parables that are not only unique to his Gospel, but also rank as some of the most beloved allegories told by Jesus. One of these is the parable of the Good Samaritan. Most Jews in Jesus' day tried to avoid contact with Samaritans, the inhabitants of Samaria. This prejudice went back 700 years, to the time of the Assyrian king Sargon II (721–705 B.C.E.). Stung by rumors of a conspiracy hatched by King Hosea of the Northern Kingdom, Sargon invaded Israel and brutally ravished the population of Hosea's capital, Samaria. Not content with mere looting and rape, Sargon then forced-marched the survivors north, where he "placed them in Halah and in Habor by the river of Gozan, and in the cities of the Medes." (II Kings 17:6) Their homes, fields, and cattle were subsequently appropriated by so-called Babylonian settlers, many of whom came from Cuthah in Babylonia. Over time, these foreign farmers assimilated with what remained of the population in Samaria, and eventually adopted Jewish cultic practice and faith. Nevertheless, Babylonian blood still coursed through the veins of their children and grandchildren, and subsequent generations of Judeans and Galileans would never forget it. Thus the Jewish population of Samaria was scathingly referred to as "Samaritans," or worse, as "Cuthaeans," after the ancient city of Cuthah in Babylonia.

Apparently, the antipathy was mutual. Luke relates how the advance party sent by Jesus to prepare his way "entered a village of the Samaritans to make ready for him; but they did not receive him." (Luke 9:52-53) The indignant Apostles clamored for Jesus to punish the village by raining down fire from heaven, but Jesus refused.

THE GOOD SAMARITAN

In Luke's Gospel, the parable of the Good Samaritan is immediately preceded by Jesus' forceful denunciation of Chorazin, Bethsaida, and Capernaum, which perhaps served to seal his Galilean campaign. This is followed by a paragraph in

---

JESUS' PRAYER

The idea of the kingdom of God as a compact with God and one's fellow man resonates in the prayer that Jesus taught his disciples. Scholars including John Meier have tried to trace the *Our Father* back to its original Aramaic form, using the putative sayings document of "Q" as a source. One possible reconstruction is as follows:

*Our Father,
hallowed be your name.
Your kingdom come.
Tomorrow's bread give us today.
And forgive us our debts/sins,
as we forgive our debtors.
And do not lead us to the test.*

The structure of this prayer, says John Meier (who includes this version in the second volume of his book *A Marginal Jew*), "is tight and laconic, perfectly suitable for memorization." Other scholars have pointed to the appellation "our Father" (Hebrew: *avinu*), which suggests that Jesus wanted his followers to also embrace God as their *Abba*, their Father in heaven. Referring to God as "Father" was a familiar invocation in Jewish prayers from Antiquity to today.

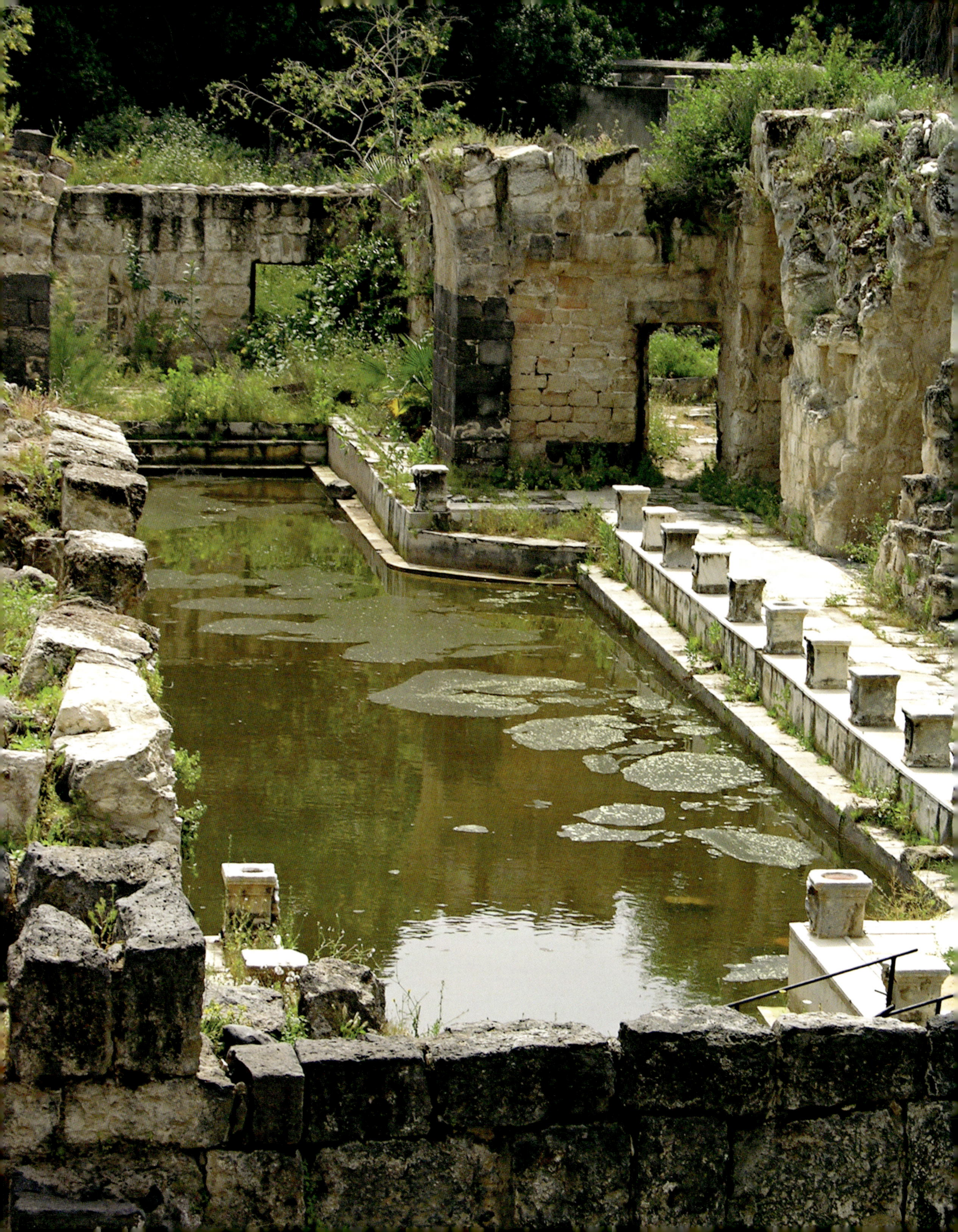

PART II | THE LIFE OF JESUS

Italian artist Francesco Bassano (1549–1592) set the scene of "The Good Samaritan" in a forest in northern Italy.

A young Samaritan woman (opposite) looks out over Nablus, the biblical Shechem, from the Mount Gerizim, which is sacred to Samaritans.

which Jesus describes his relationship to the Father. "All things have been handed over to me by my Father," Jesus explained, "and no one knows who the Son is except the Father, or who the Father is except the Son and anyone to whom the Son chooses to reveal to him." (Luke 10:22) The statement may serve to answer the question that Jesus had asked his Apostles in Caesarea Philippi: "Who do people say that the Son of Man is?" As such it is a more explicit description of Jesus' relationship with the Father than any other found in the Synoptic Gospels.

Jesus was then confronted by "a lawyer," not otherwise identified, who asked, "Teacher, what must I do to inherit eternal life?" The answer, said Jesus, is the commandment in the Law to love the Lord your God, and to love your neighbor as yourself. To illustrate such compassion for one's fellow man, Jesus then told the story of a man who "was going down from Jerusalem to Jericho, and fell into the hands of robbers, who stripped him, beat him, and went away, leaving him half dead." (Luke 10:30) In post-Herodian Samaria and Judea, roaming bands of thieves and robbers were common; many of them had lost

The Road to Jerusalem

their lands, while others were former soldiers in Herod's employ, whose units had been disbanded after the Roman takeover of the country. What's more, the road from Jerusalem to Jericho was particularly hazardous, for it involved a drop in elevation from about 2,500 feet above sea level to some 800 feet below sea level while traveling through a harsh, desertlike terrain. Villages were few and far in between, and the forbidding landscape of cliffs and rocky outcroppings offered plenty of opportunity for robbers to hide. For this reason, many travelers on the roads to and from Jerusalem carried arms to defend themselves—including, apparently, the Apostles, for one of them would soon raise his sword to cut off the ear of one of the Temple slaves (Luke 22:50).

> BUT A SAMARITAN WHILE TRAVELING CAME NEAR HIM; AND WHEN HE SAW HIM, HE WAS MOVED WITH PITY.
>
> GOSPEL OF LUKE 10:33
> *Circa 75-90 C.E.*

"Now by chance," Jesus continued, "a priest was going down that road; and when he saw him, he passed by on the other side." A Levite, a Temple official from the tribe of Levi, likewise came upon the victim and pretended not to have seen him. But then a Samaritan approached, "and when he saw him, he was moved with pity. He went to him and bandaged his

THE ROAD TO JERUSALEM

MAP KEY
- Ruled by Herod Antipas
- Ruled by Herod Philip
- Roman province of Judaea
- Roman province of Syria
- Imperial estate
- Nabatean Kingdom
- ······ District or region boundary
- ← Route of Jesus to Jerusalem
- • / ○ City of the Decapolis / location uncertain

Jesus entered the city to the praising cries of "Hosanna," meaning "save us" in Hebrew. He would later be turned over to authorities, crucified, then buried, and resurrected in the city. (Matthew 21:9)

Zacchaeus, a chief tax collector, was converted. (Luke 19:1–10)

Blind Bartimaeus is given sight by Jesus. (Mark 10:46–52)

Jesus raised Lazarus from the dead after four days in the tomb. (John 11:1–44)

Jesus was anointed in the house of Simon the Leper. (Matthew 26:6–13; Mark 14:3–9; John 12:1–8)

THE GREAT SEA (MEDITERRANEAN SEA)

Mt. Hermon 2,814 m 9,232 ft
Mt. Carmel 546 m 1,791 ft
Mt. Tabor 588 m 1,929 ft
Mt. Ebal 940 m 3,084 ft
Mt. Gerizim 881 m 2,890 ft
Mt. Nebo 802 m 2,631 ft

Bay of Acco (Bay of Haifa)
Sea of Kinnereth (Sea of Galilee)
Salt Sea (Dead Sea)

PHOENICIA · LEBANON · ITUREA · SYRIA · GAULANITIS · GALILEE · DECAPOLIS · SAMARIA · PLAIN OF SHARON · PEREA · SHEPHELAH · JUDEA · MOAB · NEGEV · NABATEA · EGYPT

Sidon, Damascus, Tyre, Kanah, Ecdippa, Cadasa, Asor, Caesarea Philippi (Paneas), Raphana, Merom, Ptolemais, Jotapata, Capernaum, Bethsaida, Sycaminium, Arbela, Hippos, Gabae, Tiberias, Philoteria, Abila, Sepphoris, Nazareth, Dora, Legio, Gadara, Caesarea, Scythopolis, Pella, Narbata, Ginae, Dion, Sebaste, Neapolis, Sychar, Gerasa, Apollonia, Amathus, Antipatris, Lebonah, Joppa, Phasaelis, Gadara, Philadelphia, Lydda, Bethel, Archelais, Jamnia, Gazara, Jericho, Azotus, Jerusalem, Bethany (Al 'Ayzarīyah), Esbus, Ascalon, Bethlehem, Herodium, Medeba, Marisa, Beth-zur, Antheodon, Lachish, Hebron, Machaerus, Gaza, Eshtemoa, 'En-gedi, Raphia, Masada, Beersheba, Malatha, Kir-Moab

0 20 40 kilometers
0 20 40 miles

Present-day drainage, coastlines, and country boundaries are represented. Modern names appear in parentheses.

wounds, having poured oil and wine on them." The Samaritan then loaded the wounded man on his donkey and took him to an inn, where he gave the innkeeper two denarii for the victim's care, promising him that "When I come back, I will repay you whatever more you spend."

Jesus then asked, "Which of these three, do you think, was a neighbor to the man who fell into the hands of the robbers?" The answer was, "The one who showed him mercy." Jesus nodded and said, "Go and do likewise." (Luke 10:30-37)

The parable of the Good Samaritan has deservedly entered our popular lore, for it is a powerful story of how human compassion can overcome deeply ingrained ethnic prejudice and social indifference. But some scholars believe that the story also highlights Jesus' criticism of the prevailing attitude toward purity, and the prioritization of ritual practice over social responsibility. The story deliberately uses a "priest" and a "Levite," both officials employed at the Temple, as characters who might be more concerned about contracting impurity from a man who was bloodied and on the verge of death, than about the moral obligation to help a human being in need.

The Greatest Commandment

For Jesus, these were not novel ideas, but values that lay at the very core of what it meant to be a Jew. It is interesting that Jesus told the story of the Good Samaritan in response to a lawyer, who questioned Jesus about what it takes "to inherit eternal life." Luke presents this as a test, but as we have seen, such questions were routinely debated among rabbis as part of the accumulation of Oral Law. Jesus parried the question by asking the lawyer, "What is written in the law? What do you read there?" The man answered by reciting the first verse of the *V'ahavta*, a profession of faith taken from Deuteronomy: "You shall love the Lord your God with all your heart, and with all your soul, and with all your strength, and with all your mind." (Deuteronomy 6:5) The lawyer then added a citation from Levitus: " . . . and your neighbor as yourself." (Levitus 19:18; Luke 10:27-28) Treating a fellow human being "as one's neighbor," in Jesus' words, was a core tenet of Jewish thought, shared by many Pharisees of his time.

In Mark's Gospel, Jesus reiterates the link between love of God and "love of your neighbor as yourself" by citing both the *Shema* and Leviticus, adding that "there is no other commandment greater than these." (Mark 12:28-31) In doing so, Jesus may have paraphrased similar rabbinical statements in the Mishnah and the Talmud. One example is Jesus' contemporary, the great Jewish sage Hillel, who at one point was also asked to summarize the Law. His response was, "What

> HEROD ALSO BUILT A CITY IN THE VALLEY OF JERICHO, WHEREBY HE RENDERED THE NEIGHBORING COUNTRY MORE FRUITFUL BY THE CULTIVATION ITS INHABITANTS HAD INTRODUCED.
>
> JOSEPHUS, *ANTIQUITIES OF THE JEWS*
> Circa 95 C.E.

PART II | THE LIFE OF JESUS

This circular structure once formed part of Herod's Palace in Jericho, built after an earthquake in 31 B.C.E. It was still standing when Jesus passed through the city.

Jan Vermeer (1632–1675), a renowned painter of the Dutch School, painted this intimate scene of "Christ in the House of Martha and Mary" (opposite) around 1654.

is hateful to you, do not do to your neighbor: this is the whole Law; the rest is the explanation; go and learn."

Jesus Arrives in Jericho

John's putative route along the eastern bank of the Jordan and Luke's route through Samaria both converged in the city of Jericho, located some 18 miles from Jerusalem. Even in Jesus' time, Jericho was one of Israel's oldest cities, and far grander than the somewhat dilapidated town of 20,000 people we see today. Herod, who originally leased the city and its lavish palm groves from Cleopatra, received full control of the region as a gift from Augustus in 30 B.C.E. The king thereupon enlarged the city and built a palace for himself as well as a hippodrome—a stadium for chariot races—and an aqueduct, which was partly restored in the Muslim era. The Roman geographer Strabo praised its "cultivated and fruitful trees of all kinds," watered "everywhere with streams."

Because of its strategic location, Jericho sat on the crossroads of caravan traffic between Arabia, Jerusalem, and the Mediterranean, a position it exploited with numerous toll stations. One chief tax collector in the city, says Luke, was a man named Zaccheus, who "was rich." Jesus soon attracted a crowd, but since Zaccheus was short in stature, he ran ahead and climbed into a sycamore tree, hoping to see Jesus as he passed by. Jesus looked up and said, "Zaccheus, hurry and come down; for I must stay at your house today." (Luke 19:1-5)

Surprisingly, Zaccheus proved to be a willing convert. "Look, half of my possessions, Lord, I will give to the poor," the tax collector exclaimed, "and if I have defrauded anyone of anything, I will pay back four times as much." (Luke 19:1-8) Zaccheus's dramatic embrace of "the kingdom" must have been a shot in the arm for Jesus and the disciples after the disappointments suffered in Galilee. It was a hopeful sign, and perhaps an indication that Judea would be far more receptive to Jesus' teachings than his native region. "They supposed that the kingdom of God was to appear immediately," Luke adds (Luke 19:11).

Jesus and his disciples then rejoined the crowd of pilgrims streaming through Jericho on the way to Jerusalem for the Passover festival. A blind beggar named Bartimaeus, son of Timaeus was sitting by the roadside. When he heard that Jesus was among the crowd, he called out, "Jesus, Son of David, have mercy on me"—an allusion to the Messiah, who was expected to descend from King David. Jesus summoned him, and asked, "What do you want me to do for you?" "My teacher," the blind man responded, "let me see again." "Go," Jesus replied in Mark's Gospel, "your faith has made you well." (Mark 10:46-52)

Mary and Martha of Bethany

On they went, climbing the steep winding road from Jericho to Jerusalem. Just before the road rose to the top of the Mount of Olives, they stopped in the village of Bethany. Here lived a family with whom Jesus was closely befriended. The Gospels don't specify the nature of the friendship, but it is possible that Martha, Mary, and Lazarus were in some way related to Mary, the mother of Jesus. In first-century Palestine, friendship—certainly friendship with people in other towns or regions—was usually defined in terms of blood relations. Their house would serve as the setting for two important events that are recorded in the Gospels of Luke and John, respectively.

Luke tells us that once Jesus entered the house, he sat down and started teaching, as was his wont. Mary "sat at the Lord's feet and listened to what he was saying."

> NOW AS THEY WENT ON THEIR WAY, HE ENTERED A CERTAIN VILLAGE, WHERE A WOMAN NAMED MARTHA WELCOMED HIM IN TO HER HOME.
>
> GOSPEL OF LUKE 10:38
> *Circa 75–90 C.E.*

PART II | THE LIFE OF JESUS

This depiction of "The Raising of Lazarus" from 1631 was painted by Rembrandt's pupil Jan Lievens the Elder (1607–1674).

This is another example of the courtesy that Jesus showed to women. Unfortunately, Mary's rapt attention to Jesus' words meant that her sister Martha had to work twice as hard to get everything ready for Jesus' stay. Then as now, the paramount duty of hospitality ran deep in the people of the Near East. Martha soon felt compelled to complain to Jesus about her sister's obvious neglect of her duties. "Lord, do you not care that my sister has left me to do all the work by myself?" she asked. "Tell her then to help me." But Jesus corrected her, saying, "Martha, Martha, you are worried and distracted by many things; there is need of only one thing." (Luke 10:40-42) Jesus meant the overriding priority of spiritual renewal, but he also implicitly endorsed the idea that women could be taught as well as men.

The Raising of Lazarus

The Gospel of John gives us another story involving Martha and Mary's family. While Jesus was still "across the Jordan," Lazarus fell ill, and his sisters

LAZARUS'S TOMB

The Gospels tell us that before Jesus and his disciples reached Jerusalem, they stopped in the village of Bethany. Here lived a family with whom Jesus was closely befriended: Lazarus and his two sisters, Martha and Mary. The root of the name Bethany has alternatively been interpreted as *beth anya*, "house of figs," or *beth 'ani*, "house of the poor." The biblical site is traditionally associated with a small Arab town in today's West Bank, called Al 'Ayzarīyah. Lazarus is called *Eleazar* ("God is my help") in Hebrew, and El-Azar in Arabic. Located under the slopes of the Mount of Olives, the village of El-Azariya faces east, toward the Jordan valley. In the fourth century, a small chapel was built near the spot believed to mark Lazarus's tomb, which happened to be located at the village cemetery. In the 11th century, a mosque was built on the site. After the arrival of the Crusaders, however, the tomb was covered by a church, which after the Muslim reconquest was converted into a mosque once again. In 1953, when East Jerusalem and the West Bank were ruled by the Kingdom of Jordan, the Franciscans received permission to erect a new church near the remains of the Crusader church, which still stands today. Excavators have also discovered many ossuaries in the region, with names that suggest that ancient Bethany once had a fairly large population with Galilean roots. This may further buttress the theory that Martha, Mary, and Lazarus could have been related to Jesus' family.

Some believe this tomb in today's Al 'Ayzarīyah is the place where Jesus raised Lazarus from the dead.

feared for his life. They sent a message to Jesus, saying, "Lord, he whom you love is ill." (John 11:3)

Uncharacteristically, Jesus did not decide to rush to Bethany right away. He tarried on the East Bank of the Jordan for "two days longer" before finally moving to Judea. Some theologians have argued that Jesus deliberately waited for Lazarus to die, so as to demonstrate his power to raise a man from the dead, in anticipation of his own resurrection. "Our friend Lazarus has fallen asleep, but I am going there to awaken him," Jesus explained to his disciples (John 11:11). Other commentators believe that by the time the message arrived, Lazarus was already dead, so that the delay of two days ensured that Jesus arrived on the third day, just as he himself would rise on the third day. This elapse of "three days" carried a special significance in ancient Judaism. During this time period, the relatives of the deceased were expected to visit the tomb and inspect the corpse, to insure he or she was not just in a deep coma. An ancient *Midrash* or Jewish Bible commentary suggests that "for three days [after death] the soul hovers over the body, intending to re-enter it, but as soon as it sees its appearance change, it departs, as it is written." The *Semachot* tractate of the Talmud cites two cases in which a man was found to be alive in his tomb, and subsequently lived to old age. This may be what

> WHEN HE HAD COME NEAR BETHPAGE AND BETHANY, AT THE PLACE CALLED THE MOUNT OF OLIVES, HE SENT TWO OF THE DISCIPLES AHEAD.
>
> GOSPEL OF LUKE 19:29
> *Circa 75–90 C.E.*

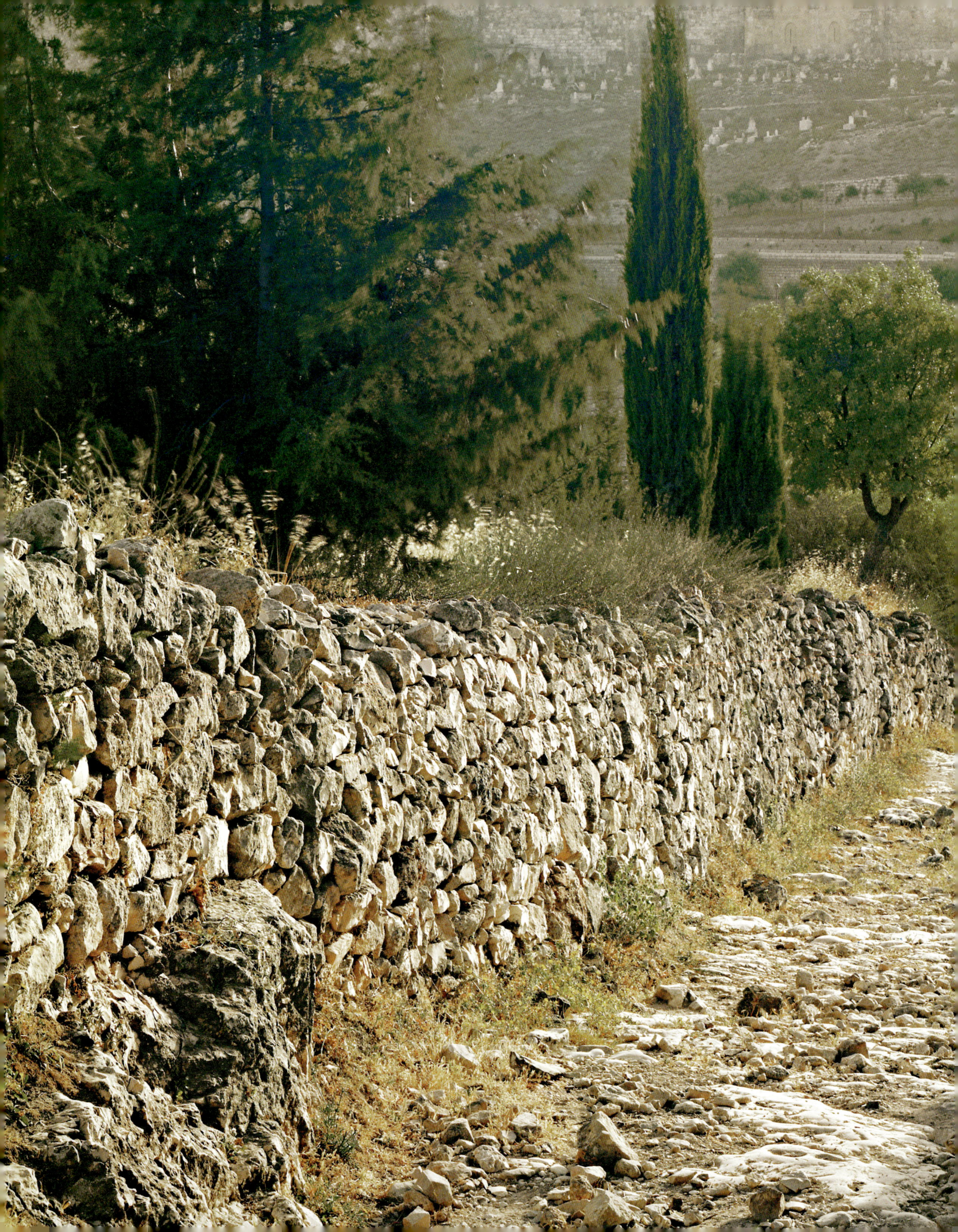

The Road to Jerusalem

Jesus had in mind when he told his followers, "Lazarus is dead. For your sake I am glad I was not there, so that you may believe." (John 11:11-16)

And so, when Jesus finally arrived in Bethany, "he found that Lazarus had already been in the tomb for four days," when the body was formally acknowledged to be deceased. Martha chided him, saying, "Lord, if you had been here, my brother would not have died." Jesus replied, "Your brother will rise again." Then Mary arrived and began to weep so bitterly that Jesus "was greatly disturbed in spirit and deeply moved"—an unusual description of Jesus' emotional state, which is rare in the Gospels, and particularly in John (John 11:17-33).

Jesus walked to the tomb and asked that the round stone, which covered the opening, be rolled away, ignoring Martha's warning that the body would probably reek of decomposition. Then he cried out in a loud voice, "Lazarus, come out!" And "the dead man came out, his hands and feet bound with strips of cloth, and his face wrapped in a cloth." And, says John, many Jews believed in him—though for "the Pharisees" this act was apparently the last straw. They met with the "chief priests" and called "a meeting of the council," arguably the Jewish Sanhedrin, to plot Jesus' arrest and execution (John 11:39-47).

The Entry in Jerusalem

The entry of Jesus in Jerusalem is described in all four Gospels, which strongly supports its authenticity. Once again, it is Mark who provides the core of the story, which was then expanded by Matthew, Luke, and John. Having spent the night in Bethany, Jesus and the disciples set out for Jerusalem early in the afternoon, joining the ever-growing throngs of worshippers who were streaming toward the holy city from all over Palestine and the Diaspora. It was only a two hour's walk from Bethany to the Mount of Olives, but no doubt the road would have been filled with men, women, and children, singing hymns and waving fronds from Jericho's palm trees. As they neared the city, they saw the crest of the Temple emerging from the afternoon dust, its gold cornices sparkling in the light of the setting sun.

At long last, Jesus turned to two of his disciples and said, "Go into the village ahead of you, and immediately as you enter it, you will find tied there a colt that has never been ridden; untie it and bring it." One of the disciples may have opened his mouth, wondering how they were supposed to pay for this luxury in peak season, at Passover, when the price of animals usually doubled, for Jesus immediately added, "If anyone says to you, 'Why are you doing this?' just say this,

When Jesus arrived in Jerusalem, he may have seen the city in this southwest view as painted by the modern Hungarian-born artist Balage Balogh.

This ancient road (opposite) down the Mount of Olives led from Bethany to the walls of Jerusalem.

PART II | THE LIFE OF JESUS

An anonymous artist painted this miniature of "Jesus entering Jerusalem" in the tenth-century illuminated manuscript The Benedictional of St. Aethelwold.

JOSEPHUS ON JESUS

Josephus's book *Antiquities of the Jews* contains a brief but controversial reference to Jesus. Many experts believe the paragraph was "expanded" by monks who copied the work. In the following, the text thought to have been added later (known as *interpolations*) is shown in brackets:

Now there was about this time Jesus, a wise man [*if indeed one might call him a man;*] for he was a doer of wonderful works, a teacher of such men as receive the truth with pleasure. He drew over to him both many of the Jews and many of the Gentiles. [*He was the Christ.*] And when Pilate, at the suggestion of the principal men amongst us, had condemned him to the cross, those that loved him at the first did not cease to be attached to him [*for he appeared to them alive again the third day as the divine prophets had foretold these and ten thousand other wonderful things concerning him*]. And the tribe of Christians, so named from him, are not extinct at this day.

Josephus thus confirms that (1) Jesus was a wise man; (2) that he was considered a teacher who did many wonderful works; (3) that he was crucified during the term of Pilate as prefect of Judaea; and (4) that his leadership produced a following that continued all through the first century C.E.

'The Lord needs it and he will send it back here immediately.'" (Mark 11:1-3) The two disciples obeyed; they went ahead and found a colt just as Jesus had described it. As soon as they untied the animal, some of the bystanders rushed over, saying, "What are you doing, untying the colt?" The disciples told them exactly what Jesus had said. The explanation sufficed, and they were allowed to lead the colt away (Mark 11:4-7).

Jesus seated himself on the colt, and thus the group continued down to Jerusalem along the winding road of the Mount of Olives, through the Kidron Valley, and up again to Jerusalem's walls. "Many people spread their cloaks on the road," says Mark, "and others spread leafy branches that they had cut in the fields." Others were shouting, "Hosanna! Blessed is he who comes in the name of the Lord! Blessed is the coming kingdom of our ancestor David!" (Mark 11:7-10)

This jubilant moment was perhaps the culmination of Jesus' ministry. Whilst the crowds in Galilee had mainly been interested in seeing signs and miracles, the throng that greeted him on the threshold of Jerusalem was very different. They greeted Jesus not as a faith healer and performer of wondrous works, but as one who had come to herald the kingdom of God. Some scholars have pointed to the analogy with the Book of Zechariah, in which the king of a restored Israel is welcomed in Jerusalem and all the city shouts with joy. "Lo, your king comes to you," the prophet says; "Triumphant and victorious is he, humble and riding on a donkey, on a colt." (Zechariah 9:9) This does not necessarily contest the veracity of the events reported by Mark, for it is possible that Jesus knew the verse and decided to enter Jerusalem just as the prophet had foretold.

Quite possibly, he passed through the Valley Gate facing the Mount of Olives, before turning right and slowly ascending the stairway that led to the Double Gate of the Temple precinct. At that time, much of the gigantic forecourt planned by Herod, as well as the large buildings surrounding the Temple including the Royal Stoa, were still under construction. Parts of the vast esplanade would have been in scaffolding. Marble and limestone dust was in the air; perhaps the disciples could taste it on their lips. Behind them, crowds of people streamed from the tunnel onto the forecourt and were soon lost in the immense stretch of this vast open space. Herod's sanctuary was, quite simply, the largest thing built by man that any of them had ever seen.

But already it was late. The operations around the sacrificial altar were closing down; soon the crowd would dwindle, gently prodded to the exits by the Temple militia. "As it was already late," Mark says, "he went out to Bethany with the twelve." (Mark 11:11)

Jesus' visit to the Temple, and the great sermon he was planning to give in the forecourt, would have to wait until the morning.

The Road to Jerusalem

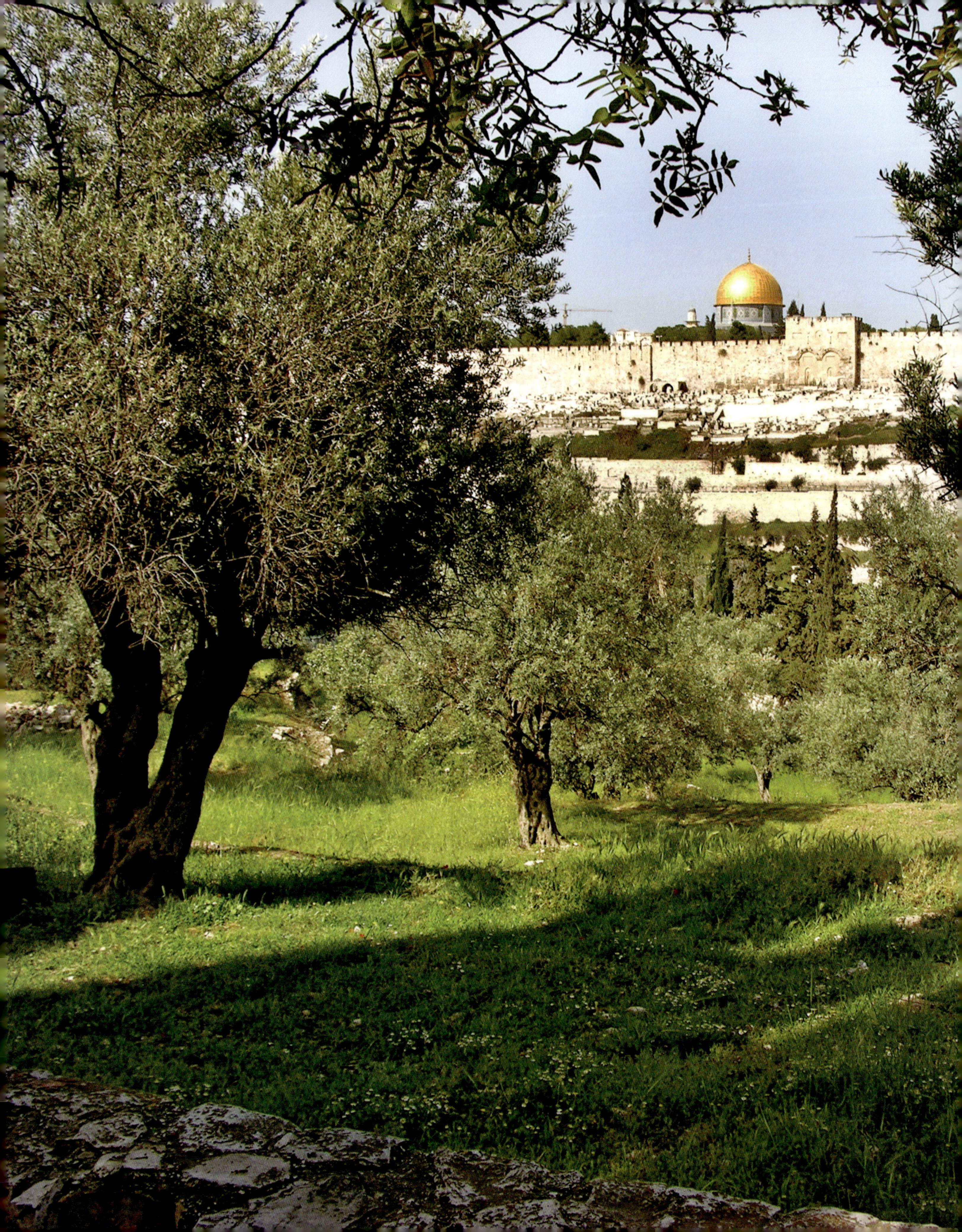

CHAPTER II

The PASSOVER EVENTS in JERUSALEM

THEN CAME THE DAY
OF UNLEAVENED BREAD,
ON WHICH
THE PASSOVER LAMB
HAD TO BE SACRIFICED.

GOSPEL OF LUKE, 22:7
Circa 75-90 C.E.

This view from the traditional location of Gethsemane on the Mount of Olives looks toward Temple Mount, where the Second Temple once stood.

PART II | THE LIFE OF JESUS

It is difficult to determine with any certainty when the events of Jesus' Passion unfolded, in part because of chronological discrepancy between the Synoptic Gospels and the Gospel of John. A further complicating factor is that Judaism reckons the start of each new day at sunset, rather than at midnight as is common in Western civilization. The Passover feast was traditionally set according to a lunar calendar, which specifies that the 14th day of the month of Nisan must coincide with the first full moon of the first month of spring (Exodus 12:2-6). Based on this information, astronomers since Newton have tried to calculate when Jesus would have been crucified. A tentative consensus has emerged around two dates: Friday, April 7, in the year 30 C.E., or Friday, April 3, if the events took place in the year 33 C.E.

Passover, or *Pesach* in Hebrew, celebrates Israel's release from bondage in Egypt, after the angel of God had slain all the Egyptian firstborn sons. To mark their homes as Israelite, rather than Egyptian, the Israelites had been instructed to sacrifice a lamb and paint the door lintel with its blood. All homes marked as such were spared, or "passed over," by the angel's wrath (Exodus 12:6-7). Then, while waiting for the signal to leave Egypt under Moses's guidance, all Israelites were told to roast a lamb and eat it with unleavened bread, since there was no time to allow the bread to rise. The Book of Exodus decreed that once the Israelites reached the Promised Land, they should observe this event every year in perpetuity, known in the Mishnah as the *Pesach Dorot,* the Passover of succeeding generations (Exodus 12:25).

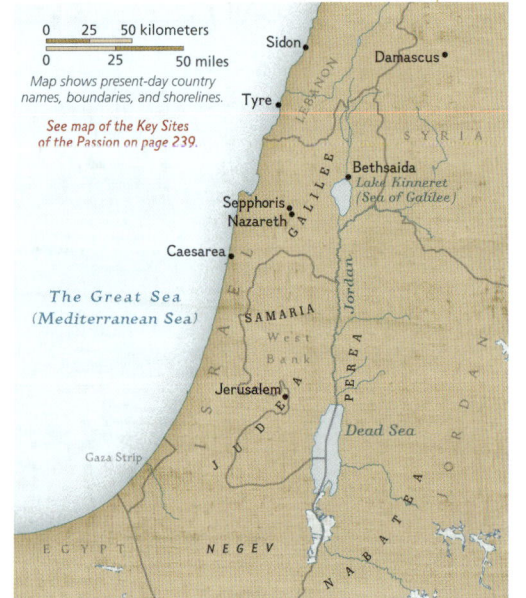

ENTERING THE JERUSALEM TEMPLE

For several days before Passover, thousands of Jews from all over Palestine and the Diaspora would make their way up to Jerusalem to do as Exodus had ordained. As soon as the great doors of the Temple precinct swung open, the pilgrims streamed into the vast open forecourt, known as the Court of the Gentiles. Passing the *soreg,* the boundary beyond which no Gentile was allowed to pass, the multitude climbed the 15 unevenly raised stairs to the gates—uneven, so that one had to ascend with care and reverence—and passed into the Court of Women. Around this court stood 13 horn-shaped depositories *(shoparoth).* Each of these chests was earmarked for a particular use. Two were set aside for the half-shekel Temple Tax. Other chests collected donations for wood and incense to be burned in the Temple, for pigeon offerings, or for voluntary gifts. In the Gospel of Luke, Jesus refers to the *shoparoth* to highlight the contrast between rich and poor. He had seen how many rich visitors placed lavish gifts into the treasury and how, by contrast, a poor widow deposited two small copper coins. "Truly I tell you," he said, "this poor widow has put in more than all of them; for the others contributed out of abundance, but she in her poverty has put in all she had to live on." (Luke 21:1-4)

The wealth of the Temple Treasury was considerable, since it contained the tithes from pious Jewish communities throughout the Roman Empire. In one legal case defended by Cicero, it was revealed that the Roman proconsul of Asia Minor, Valerius Flaccus, had tried to intercept the annual tithe collection from Jews living in Phrygia. Thus we know that one town had raised some 20 pounds of gold; another community, that of Apamea, had collected nearly 100 pounds

In the Gospel of John, Jesus healed a paralytic man by the pools of Bethesda, one of the few locations in the Gospels attested to by archaeological discovery.

PART II | THE LIFE OF JESUS

This fresco from an ancient synagogue in Dura-Europos, Syria, dated around 240 C.E., depicts the Second Temple in Jerusalem, based on extant descriptions at that time.

A silver plate (opposite) shows some key ingredients of a modern Pesach, or Passover meal.

of gold. The Temple Treasury also functioned as a central bank of sorts. It issued its own currency, the Temple shekel (struck in Tyre), and maintained the savings accounts of wealthy families. Rabbinic sources suggest that the Temple operated on a surplus, which was dispensed as the high priest saw fit.

Jewish women were not allowed to go beyond the Court of Women. They were expected to remain there, in prayer, while their husbands continued on to the Temple. Fifteen curved steps led to the magnificent brass doors of the Nicanor Gates, which opened up into the actual Temple court, known as the Court of the Israelites. There the pilgrims paused to absorb the sight of the magnificent Second Temple façade. Built on the foundations of Solomon's First Temple and subsequently destroyed by Nebuchadnezzar in 587 B.C.E., it was rebuilt in 515 B.C.E. with the assistance of the Persian treasury on orders of the Persian king Cyrus II. As part of his expansion plan, Herod the Great had dismantled the old Temple façade and replaced it with a new front elevation. In parts it was overlaid with gold leaf, while a golden vine entwined itself around the flanking columns on either side of the Temple entrance, with grape clusters said to be as tall as a man.

The Passover Events in Jerusalem

The Passover Sacrifice

Now, with the sun just rising over the Mount of Olives, its rays bathed the gold leaf in a fiery glow so that worshippers had to avert their eyes. To their left rose a huge altar on a slightly elevated platform, known as the Court of the Priests. The altar was actually a huge grill, stoked by sweating assistants on all sides, while priests threw large chunks of sacrificial meat on the fire. Some poured oil and wine on the embers, while others, standing on the steps to the sanctuary, sang hymns.

On the eve of Passover, on the afternoon of the 14th day of Nisan, all pilgrims would come to the Temple to offer a lamb as a Passover sacrifice. They would roast and eat a portion of the lamb later that night during the Passover meal and remember the night that the Israelite Exodus from Egypt began. Each family or clan would bring its own lamb or goat. These sacrificial animals had to meet strict criteria. A paschal lamb or goat had to be a one-year-old male and free of any physical blemish (Exodus 12:5). To enable pilgrims to obtain such animals, the Temple authorities organized a market where young lambs of the requisite age and condition could be had for sale.

The pilgrims were first organized in groups or *kittot* of 30 men each. Once the first group with their lambs entered the inner court, the Nicanor Gate was closed. The pilgrims were directed to an area known as the Slaughtering House, where they tied their animals to upright stakes. As a Levite choir struck up the *Hallel* Psalms (Psalms 113–118), accompanied by brass instruments, the pilgrims slaughtered their animals with a sharp cut to the throat. Priests stood by to catch the warm blood in silver vessels. According to the Jewish rite, blood was holy; it was the essence of life, and therefore belonged to God alone. The silver vessels were passed from the stakes to the altar, where priests used special whisks of silver to sprinkle the blood against the base of the altar.

Next, the lamb carcasses were hung up on special hooks and butchered. The organs destined for sacrifice—such as the neck, the liver, and the stomach—were separated from the consumable meat, which would be eaten during the Passover meal. Later that night, after sundown, it would be roasted on a spit of pomegranate wood and served during the Passover meal. High above the pilgrims, a billowing cloud of smoke rose from the altar to fill the skies over Jerusalem and, in the words of Leviticus, provide "a pleasing odor to the Lord." (Leviticus 1:13)

The Eviction of the Money Changers

It is not clear when the second visit of Jesus and the Apostles to the Temple took place. Most church authorities believe it took place on Monday, following Jesus' triumphal entry into Jerusalem on Palm Sunday, so as to

---

THE PASSOVER MEAL

In preparation for the Seder or Passover meal the lamb meat brought back from the Temple was roasted on skewers made of pomegranate wood after sundown. Since the portion allotted to each family member was usually small, the women also cooked a stew of lentils and barley, as well as cakes of unleavened bread. These dishes would then be garnished with bitter herbs prescribed for the Seder, such as parsley, mallows, chicory, and radishes. The purpose of these herbs was to remind the Jews of their bitter time in Egypt (Exodus 1:14). Rabbi Gamaliel often said that "Whoever does not make mention of the following three things on Passover has not fulfilled his obligation: namely, the Passover sacrifice, unleavened bread (matzah) and bitter herbs." Whether or not the Last Supper was a Seder as we understand it today remains a topic of intense debate. Bruce Chilton has argued that regardless of whether Jesus' last meal was at Passover or not, it is clear that many early Jewish Christians wished it so, in order to retain some Jewish character in the Easter celebrations.

PART II | THE LIFE OF JESUS

harmonize the sequence of events with the Christian celebration of Holy Week. Historically, however, the second visit could have taken place closer to Wednesday or even Thursday, the 14th of Nisan, when the paschal lambs were sacrificed in the Temple.

Upon arriving on the road from Bethany, Jesus and the Apostles would have used the wide flight of stairs to the Double Gate, which was located on the south side of the Temple precinct. Here a tunnel, lit by sputtering torches, led the worshippers underneath the Royal Stoa and into the Court of the Gentiles. What they saw is that the court had been converted into an animal market, where shopkeepers were doing a brisk trade in the sale of doves as well as unblemished paschal lambs. Nearby were the stalls of the money changers. Before they could purchase any animals, worshippers had to convert their coins into the Tyrian shekel, the only currency accepted within the Temple.

Scholars such as Bruce Chilton have argued that previously, the sale of lambs took place at some distance from the Temple precinct, in a market called *Chanut* on the Mount of Olives. Based on references by Philo as well as Josephus, they believe that all sacrificial animals, including doves, goats, and lambs, would have been kept well away from the Temple until the actual moment of sacrifice, to prevent the Temple pavement from being covered with animal waste. The high priest Caiaphas may have decided to change this custom and bring the market inside the Temple in order to exert greater control over the quality of the lambs being sold, or to prevent any animals from being injured in the crush of being taken by the pilgrims from the Mount of Olives to the Temple.

> **IN THE TEMPLE HE FOUND PEOPLE SELLING CATTLE, SHEEP, AND DOVES, AND THE MONEY CHANGERS SEATED AT THEIR TABLES.**
>
> GOSPEL OF JOHN 2:14
> *Circa 85–100 C.E.*

A Tyrian silver shekel, dated around 68 C.E. and inscribed with "Jerusalem the Holy," was the only type of currency permitted within the Temple.

"Christ Driving the Money Changers from the Temple" (opposite) was painted by the Spanish artist El Greco (born Doménikos Theotokópoulos, 1541-1614) around 1600.

What is certain, however, is that according to the Gospels, Jesus was shocked by this activity in the Temple forecourt. And, says Mark, he "began to drive out those who were selling and those who were buying in the temple, and he overturned the tables of the money changers and the seats of those who sold doves." "Is it not written," Jesus cried, quoting the book of Isaiah, "my house shall be called a house of prayer for all the nations?" And in the same breath he cited Jeremiah's Temple sermon: "But you have made it a den of robbers." (Jeremiah 7:11; Mark 11:15-17) "Making a whip of cords," says John's Gospel, "he drove all of them out of the temple, both the sheep and the cattle. He also poured out the coins of the money changers and overturned their tables." (John 2:15)

These words, "a den of robbers," may have sealed Jesus' fate. It was only two years since Pilate (and, conceivably, Caiaphas) had been accused of illegally appropriating funds from the Temple Treasury to build a Roman aqueduct. Jesus' accusation, that the Temple had been turned into a den of thieves, must have therefore struck a nerve—whether intentionally or not. Mark tells us that as soon

234

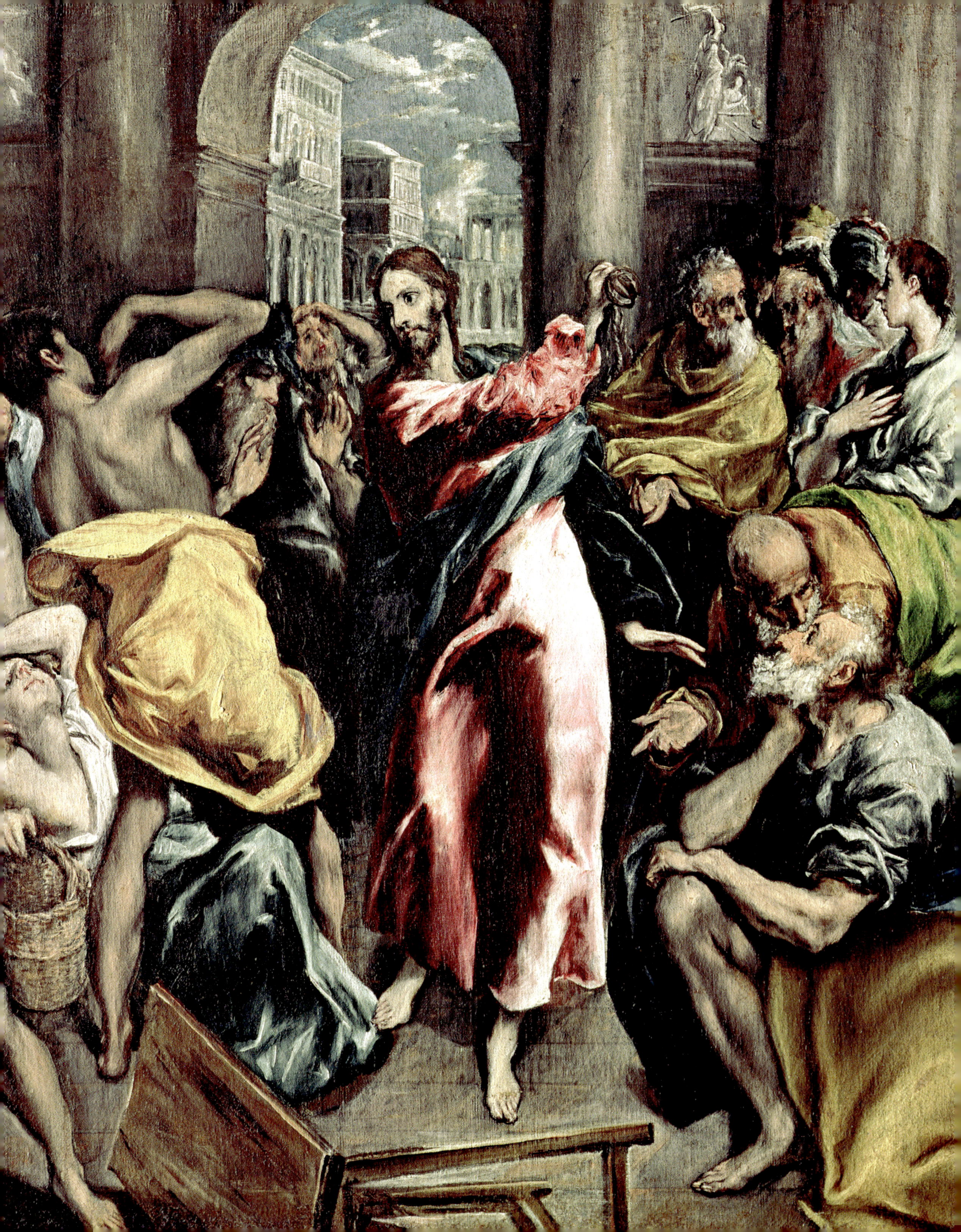

PART II | THE LIFE OF JESUS

> **ON THE FIRST DAY OF UNLEAVENED BREAD, WHEN THE PASSOVER LAMB IS SACRIFICED, THE APOSTLES ASKED HIM, "WHERE DO YOU WANT US TO GO AND MAKE THE PREPARATIONS FOR YOU TO EAT THE PASSOVER?"**
>
> GOSPEL OF MARK 14:12
> *Circa 66–70 C.E.*

as "the chief priests and the scribes heard it, they kept looking for a way to kill him." (Mark 11:18)

Roman Guards were posted along the crenellated towers of the Antonia Fortress, which abutted the Temple, in order to keep a close watch on the Temple forecourt. This large space had previously served as the flash point of mass protests, and it would do so again in the decades to come. Moreover, Passover was the most volatile time in the year; doubtless the Roman guards had been drilled to suppress the slightest sign of trouble, before the situation could get out of hand. The Gospels don't tell us if the disturbance in the marketplace prompted them to sound the alarm. If they did, Jesus and the Apostles were apparently able to slip away. Nevertheless, they were now marked men.

In Mark's Gospel, Jesus returns the next day to teach in the Temple, where "some Pharisees and some Herodians" continue to try to "trap him in what he said." (Mark 12:13) But many scholars believe that it was Jesus' attack on the money changers that prompted the call for his arrest. Neither the Romans nor the

The Passover Events in Jerusalem

Temple priests could ignore the risk that this Galilean rabbi might try to stage a violent demonstration again, if not in the Temple, then elsewhere in Jerusalem's crowded streets.

THE LAST SUPPER

On Thursday, the 14th of Nisan, Jesus and the Apostles remained in Jerusalem for the evening meal, even though most of the inns and guesthouses were overflowing with pilgrims. It has been estimated that the city, which normally numbered around 40,000 inhabitants, swelled to more than 180,000 during Passover. Jesus gave instructions for two of his disciples to go and find accommodations. They were to follow a man with a jar of water, and when he entered a house, they were told to say, "The teacher asks, where is my guest room where I may eat the Passover with my disciples?" (Mark 14:14)

The Apostles went out, says Mark, and "found everything as he had told them." (Mark 14:16) There they repeated to the owner what Jesus had said: "The teacher asks you, 'Where is the guest room, where I may eat the Passover with my disciples?'" (Luke 22:11) Some authors suggest that since Jesus refers to himself as "the teacher" rather than by name, the owner already knew Jesus. He may

Leonardo da Vinci (1452–1519) painted this famous fresco of the Last Supper between 1495 and 1498 in the monastery of Santa Maria delle Grazie in Milan, Italy.

PART II | THE LIFE OF JESUS

In the ancient world, wine was usually diluted with water prior to consumption, as attested by this first-century C.E. silver wine spoon from an affluent Roman household.

have been the disciple John Mark, who as the Book of Acts indicates, lived in a house in Jerusalem with his mother, Mary. Luke refers to a "large upper room" *(anagaion mega)*. John Mark's house certainly had a large room, for it is here that later on, according to the Book of Acts, "many had gathered and were praying." (Acts 12:12-13) Others again believe that the owner was none other than Joseph of Arimathea, who will reappear later in the Passion story. Many years later, church tradition would fasten on the belief that the hall was located above a synagogue.

As soon as the Apostles were ushered inside, says Mark, "they prepared the Passover meal"—which indicates that this meal was a Seder, the traditional Passover dinner (though the Gospel of John suggests otherwise). The fellowship of the meal was important to Jesus. Time and again, he used a shared meal to reach out to those closest to him, or those he needed to convert to his vision of the Kingdom of God. This symbolism was steeped in Scripture and Near Eastern traditions of hospitality. Abraham, for example, offers a meal to the three angels who visited him. When elsewhere in Genesis, Isaac reaches a peace pact with Abimelech, the occasion is sealed with a celebratory meal. The idea of a shared meal also lay at the core of the sacrificial rites in the Temple.

Jesus and the Apostles would most likely have dined from wooden or terracotta plates with high rims, similar to those found at Qumran, and sipped wine from clay cups, for wine was a vital component of the Seder. According to the Mishnah, even the poorest should have "no fewer than four cups of wine" on Passover night, "even if [the funds] must come from public charity."

The Judas Betrayal

Then, as they were settled, Jesus made a shocking announcement. "One of you will betray me," he said, "one who is eating with me." All began loudly to protest their innocence, including a disciple named Judas, who in Matthew's Gospel replied, "Surely not I, Rabbi?" Jesus told him, "You have said so." (Matthew 26:25)

Most scholars accept that the story of betrayal from within Jesus' inner circle is authentic, precisely because it put Jesus' followers in a bad light—something that most writers in Antiquity would have been anxious to avoid. This begs the question, *why* did Judas betray Jesus? Some authors point to Judas's full name, Judas Iskariot, which may be linked to the word *sicarius*, Latin for "daggerman." *Sicarii* were often associated with the Jewish party of the Zealots, a vocal group of dissidents who opposed the Roman occupation and, among other things, refused to pay Roman taxes. Josephus says that it was the Zealots who instigated the Jewish Revolt of 66 C.E. In the years to come—arguably around the time that Mark wrote his Gospel—many Jews and Jewish Christians would come to regard this

This garden on the Mount of Olives is traditionally associated with Gethsemane, the place where Jesus was arrested.

The Convent of the Sisters of Zion is believed to mark the location of the Antonia Fortress, where presumably Pilate sat in judgment on Jesus.

The Church of the Holy Sepulcher is traditionally identified as the location of Golgotha, where Jesus was crucified and buried.

KEY SITES OF THE PASSION

MAP KEY
- City enclosed by the time of Jesus
- Aqueduct
- Gate

Upon his triumphal entry to Jerusalem, Jesus went into the Temple and drove out the money changers. (Matthew 21:1-12)

Jesus healed a paralyzed man. (John 5:2)

Stripped, mocked, and beaten, Jesus was prepared for the Crucifixion. (Matthew 27:27-31)

Jesus faced the Roman procurator Pontius Pilate. (John 18:28-38)

The body of Jesus was placed into a new tomb near where he had been crucified. (John 19:41)

Jesus was crucified. (John 19:17)

Jesus appeared a final time before Pilate, who passed down the sentence of Crucifixion. (Luke 23:13-25)

Jesus taught in the Temple. (John 8:2)

Jesus prayed while his disciples slept. Here he was betrayed by Judas Iscariot and arrested. (Matthew 26:36-56)

The risen Jesus appeared to Mary Magdalene. (John 20:11-18)

Jesus taught his disciples while overlooking the city. (Matthew 24:3)

Alternate location for the Praetorium were Jesus faced the Roman procurator Pontius Pilate. (John 18:28-38)

Jesus was made to appear before Herod Antipas, then beaten by Roman soldiers. (Luke 23:6-11)

Jesus ascended into heaven while his disciples watched. (Acts 1:9-11)

After his arrest, Jesus was taken before Caiaphus, the chief priest. (Luke 22:54)

Jesus healed a man who had been blind from birth. (John 9:1-12)

The resurrected Jesus appeared twice to the disciples. (John 20:19-29)

Jesus ate the Passover meal with his disciples, instituting the sacrament of the Lord's Supper or Eucharist. (Mark 14:12-26)

Contour interval: 10 meters
0 .1 .2 kilometers
0 .1 .2 miles

PART II | THE LIFE OF JESUS

In this dramatic depiction of "The Taking of Christ" (ca 1602) by Michelangelo Caravaggio (1571–1610), Judas kisses Jesus as soldiers rush in to arrest him and the disciple John cries out for help.

revolt as a catastrophe. Other scholars believe that Iskariot simply means that Judas was a man (*Ish*) from Kerioth, a town in southern Judea, which would make Judas one of the few non-Galileans in Jesus' circle.

A different motive for the betrayal is presented by the so-called "Gospel of Judas," a third- or fourth-century Coptic translation of a now-lost second-century Greek manuscript, which states that Jesus *asked* Judas to betray him. This document was very likely written by an author of a Gnostic Christian community, a dissident group who believed that Jesus had always been a divine being, and merely *appeared* to be human. From a Gnostic perspective, therefore, the "betrayal" was an act of mercy that released Jesus from his corporeal bonds and restored him to his divine status. But others believe that Judas's purpose was the oldest motive in the world: money. The Gospel of John reminds us that Judas was in charge of the moneybox, the group's common purse. (John 12:6) Matthew says that the chief priests paid Judas 30 pieces of silver (shekels, most likely) for his betrayal. (Matthew 26:15) The lure of that reward may have been irresistible.

The Blessing of Bread and Wine

As soon as their meal was served, Jesus took a piece of matzah bread, blessed it, and said, "Take; this is my body." He then took a cup and, after giving thanks once more, he gave it to them, and all of them drank from it. And he said to them, "This is my blood of the covenant, which is poured out for many." (Mark 14:23-24) These words continue to be repeated in the Christian Eucharist (from the Greek word *eucharistia,* meaning thanksgiving) to this day. But so is the Jewish blessing that Jesus would have spoken at the meal. The verse "Blessed are you, Lord God of all creation, through your goodness we have this wine to offer, fruit of the vine and work of human hands," which priests read at the consecration during Mass, is taken from the traditional Jewish blessing, the Kiddush: "Blessed are you, O Lord our God, King of the universe, who creates the fruit of the vine."

Today, many Christian visitors go to see a room on Mount Zion known as the Hall of the Last Supper. As it happens, it is located right above a room that is traditionally held to be the resting place of King David, though archaeologists believe that the king would have been buried in the Davidic palace precinct on Mount Ophel. Apparently, the Hall itself was repeatedly destroyed, after which the Franciscans rebuilt it in its entirety in 1342. This explains its rather incongruous

THE WEEK OF UNLEAVENED BREAD

Mark's mention of "the first day of Unleavened Bread" refers to the start of the Feast of Unleavened Bread, which coincides with Passover. During this holy week, bread could not be baked using leavened dough. What the Bible refers to as "leaven" is actually yeast, which allows the bread to rise in the oven. In Jesus' time, yeast was made of the spoiled remains of dough made two or more days before. Women made leavened dough by kneading flour in a bowl with water and olive oil, before adding the yeast. Jesus referred to this practice in one of his parables, when he compared the Kingdom of Heaven to "yeast that a woman took and mixed in with three measures of flour, until all of it was leavened" (Matthew 13:33). The Books of Exodus and Deuteronomy decree that during the festival of Passover, Israelites should eat the flat bread made from unleavened dough, called matzah (Deuteronomy 16:3). Eating this bread would remind Jews of the day when their forefathers hastily prepared to flee from Egypt, with no time to wait for the dough to rise (Exodus 12:8). Before the Week of Unleavened Bread began, every Jewish head of a household went through his house to gather any remaining crumbs of spoiled or leavened bread, known as *chametz.* Not a single morsel of leaven could remain to despoil the house during the Passover feast.

Even today, unleavened matzah bread is used during Passover.

PART II | THE LIFE OF JESUS

A stone olive oil press in a cave near Isfiya, Israel, evokes an impression of the cave of Gethsemane in Jesus' time.

Gothic style. During the 16th century, Suleiman the Magnificent converted it into a mosque; the *qibla,* or prayer niche indicating the direction of Mecca, is still visible today. Then, during the war of 1948, a Jordanian shell destroyed part of the building's supporting wall. The subsequent excavations, led by archaeologist Jacob Pinkerfeld, uncovered sections of a stone wall in the Herodian style, built with neatly hewn stones. This could indicate the presence of a first-century ceremonial building, possibly a synagogue, as church tradition has maintained all along.

The Vigil on the Mount of Olives

Night had fallen, and Jesus decided to lead his disciples out of the city. To return to Bethany at this hour might have been too dangerous, which is perhaps why Jesus chose to go to the Mount of Olives. Nearby was a spot used for pressing oil, known as *gat-shemanim* (press of oils), the origin of the name Gethsemane. Sensing that his arrest might not be far off, Jesus asked his disciples, "Sit here while I pray." (Mark 14:32)

Unlike the traditional association of Gethsemane with a garden, the Gospels don't describe it as such. It is more likely that the location was a cave, since the relatively constant temperature inside a cave facilitated the oil-pressing process. According to the diaries of the pilgrim Egeria, exactly such a cave was revered as the location of Gethsemane as early as the fourth century. Today, a cave measuring 36 by 60 feet supported by four rock-cut pillars can still be visited on the lower slopes of the Mount of Olives.

As they sat down in Gethsemane, the Apostles were silent, filled with a sense of foreboding. Perhaps sensing this, Jesus said, "You will all become deserters; for it is written, 'I will strike the shepherd, and the sheep will be scattered.'" Peter indignantly jumped to his defense. "Even though all become deserters," he said hotly, "I will not." Jesus looked at him and replied, "Truly I tell you, this day, this very night, before the cock crows twice, you will deny me three times." (Mark 14:27-30)

Jesus then moved away and threw himself to the ground, praying, "My Father, if it is possible, let this cup pass from me; yet not what I want but what you want." (Matthew 26:39) Having finished his prayer, he went looking for his disciples, but found that all had fallen asleep.

Traditional art depicts Jesus in this supreme moment of vulnerability amid the pastoral tranquility of the Mount of Olives. But on Passover night, the Mount would have been teeming with pilgrims who were unable to afford the cost of inns and private rooms in the city. Hundreds of families would have been camping out under the stars, huddled under blankets or sitting around fires to ward

The Passover Events in Jerusalem

This fragment from the Gospel of Thomas formed part of the Nag Hammadi collection of Gnostic texts discovered near Nag Hammadi, Egypt, in 1945.

THE GNOSTIC GOSPELS

In 1945, a pair of Egyptian shepherds went digging near the town of Nag Hammadi. They were delighted to discover an ancient earthenware jar, hoping it would contain gold. From a scholarly perspective, it did, for the jar contained 13 separate codices of early Christian texts, copied from Greek into Coptic, one of Egypt's languages in the first and second centuries C.E. Among these are a great number of "Gospel" documents that do not appear in the canon of the New Testament, but instead are attributed to authors working on behalf of so-called Gnostic communities. They believed that Jesus propagated a form of total spiritual surrender, which ultimately led to a secret knowledge (*Gnosis* in Greek) of the divinity within oneself. Among the most famous of these Gnostic Gospels is the so-called Gospel of Thomas. It is, however, not a "Gospel" in the traditional sense, for it merely provides a listing of specific sayings by Jesus, without any attempt to interpret these in a theological context. "Sayings documents" of this type were common in Antiquity to disseminate the teachings of a particular sage. As such, it bears some resemblance to the sayings document known as Q, which, though never found, is believed to have been a similar collection of sayings, used by Matthew and Luke in their Gospels.

PART II | THE LIFE OF JESUS

Ancient olive trees near the site traditionally associated with Gethsemane may be more than 1,000 years old.

off the evening chill. This is exactly the reason why the Temple guards, tipped off by Judas, insisted that Judas come along, in order to identify the Galilean rabbi among the multitudes. And Judas complied; he found Jesus and gave the agreed-upon signal, by kissing the Master on his cheek (Matthew 26:49). According to Luke, one of the disciples sprang to action. He took his sword and cut off the ear of "the slave of the high priest." "No more of this," Jesus ordered sternly, and restored the ear to the man's head. (Luke 22:51)

Jesus' Arrest

With that, Jesus was placed under arrest, bound, and taken away. Where did they take him? The most obvious place would have been the Temple stockade. In the Book of Acts, after the Apostles Peter and John were arrested, they were held overnight in Temple custody before being arraigned before "Annas the [former] high priest, [and] Caiaphas." (Acts 4:15) After a passionate defense delivered by Peter, they were released.

Shortly thereafter, Peter was preaching and healing the sick near Solomon's Portico in the Temple, when according to Acts, "[the high priest] and all who were with him (that is, the sect of the Sadducees), being filled with jealousy, arrested the apostles and put them in the public prison." (Acts 5:17-18) The legal process was repeated: Peter and his companions were interrogated by the Sanhedrin and ultimately released.

Why this lenient treatment? One answer is that the full Council of the Sanhedrin was deeply divided between the Sadducee majority, "being filled with jealousy," and a highly vocal minority of Pharisees. And while many Pharisees may have taken issue with some of Jesus' teachings, they respected him as a learned rabbi, and had no motive whatsoever for seeing him executed. Indeed, during the second hearing of the Sanhedrin against Peter, it was a Pharisee, the highly respected Rabbi Gamaliel, who defended the Apostles, arguing that if their works "are not of human origin, but of God's, you will not be able to overthrow them!" (Acts 5:59) As a result of his intervention, the Apostles were flogged but thereafter promptly released.

Jesus could therefore expect that he, too, would spend the night in the Temple stockade, there to await the next available convocation of the Sanhedrin—which was unlikely to take place until after the Passover festival. And Jesus, too, would have had every reason to expect a sympathetic hearing, from the Council's Pharisaic wing.

But the guards didn't take Jesus to the Temple stockade at all. Instead, he was spirited under the cloak of darkness to the private residence of the most powerful prelate in Judea—the high priest Caiaphas.

> THEN JESUS WENT WITH THEM TO A PLACE CALLED GETHSEMANE; AND HE SAID TO HIS DISCIPLES, "SIT HERE WHILE I GO OVER THERE AND PRAY."
>
> GOSPEL OF MATTHEW 26:36
> *Circa 75-90 C.E.*

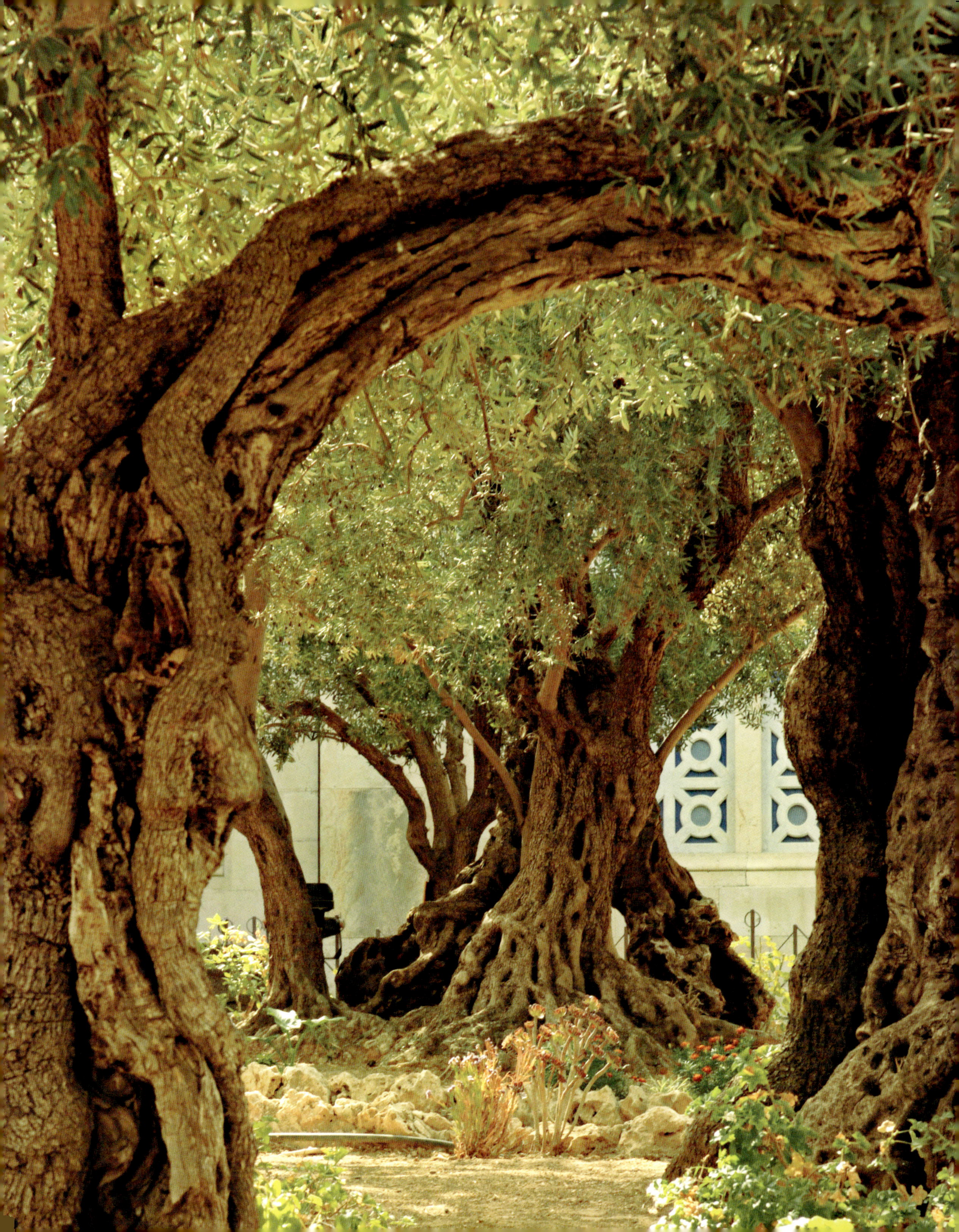

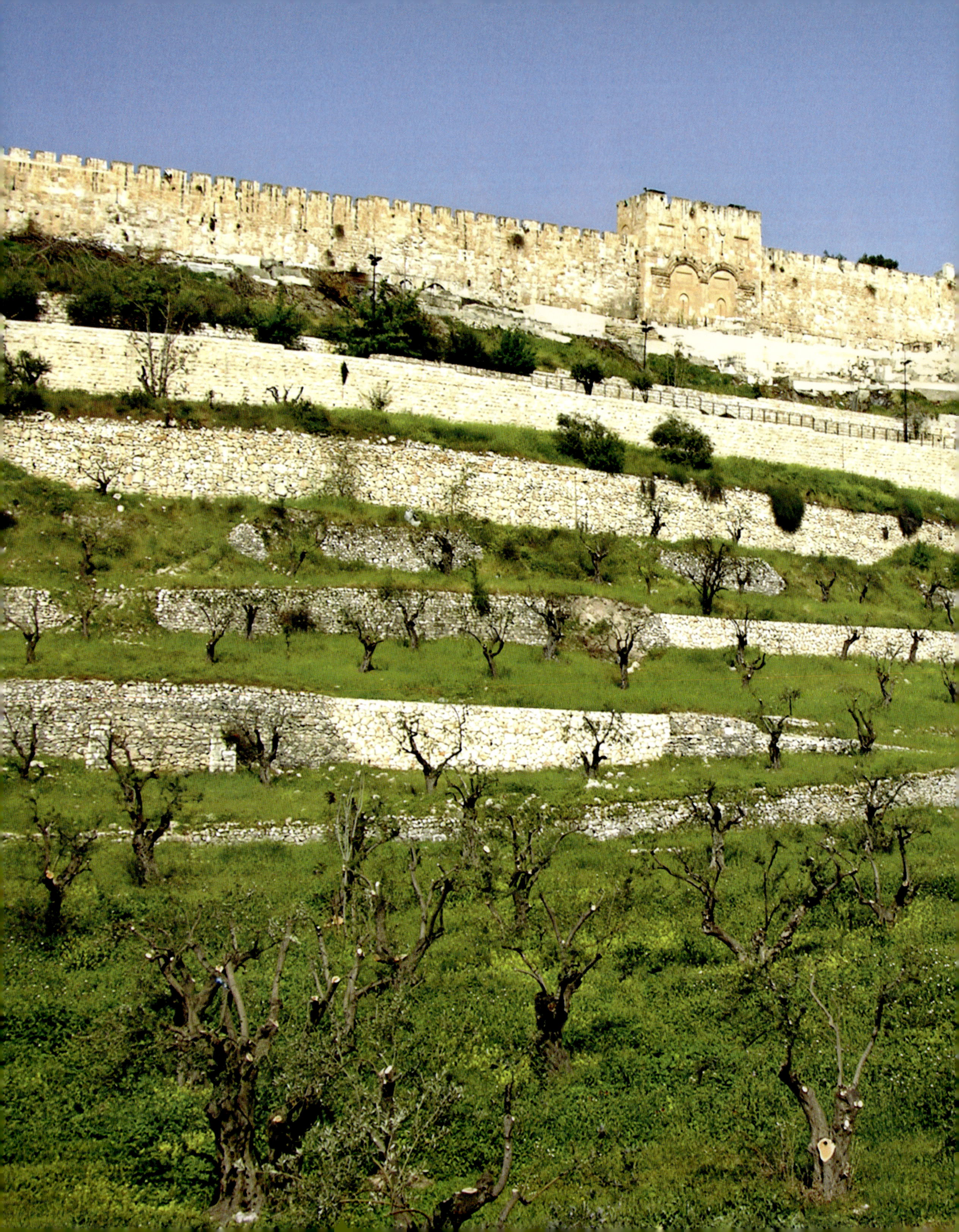

CHAPTER 12

The TRIAL and CRUCIFIXION

THEN THEY SEIZED HIM
AND LED HIM AWAY,
BRINGING HIM INTO
THE HIGH PRIEST'S HOUSE.

GOSPEL OF LUKE 22:54
Circa 75–90 C.E.

The walls of the Old City of Jerusalem, with the closed Golden Gate at its center, rise high above the terraced slopes of the Kidron Valley.

PART II | THE LIFE OF JESUS

The house of Caiaphas would have been located in the neighborhood of the Upper City, where most of the priestly aristocracy maintained their Jerusalem residences. Many of these homes were destroyed a mere 40 years after Jesus' trial, in the upheaval of the Jewish Revolt. Their remains lay submerged under successive layers of construction until the late 1960s, when after the Six Day War, Israeli archaeologists began to excavate.

In the process, Nahman Avigad found a 2,000-square-foot residence that he called the Priestly House. The home appears to closely match the Caiaphas residence as described in the Gospel of Mark: a lavish home with a large reception room, preceded by an inner courtyard with a hearth. Mark tells us that it was in exactly such a courtyard that Peter stood warming his hands by the fire, while Jesus was arraigned inside. During the month of Nisan, roughly equivalent to a March-April timeframe, nights in Jerusalem could still be quite frigid. One of the high priest's servant girls spotted him there and said, "You also were with Jesus, the man from Nazareth." Peter, deathly afraid that he might be arrested as well, denied it, not once but three times—just as Jesus had foretold (Mark 14:66-72).

The largest room in Avigad's Priestly House measured 33 by 21 feet and was located close to the entrance, which would indicate that it was a reception hall of some kind. Quite possibly, it was in such a chamber that Jesus' indictment took place. By the same token, it would have been impossible to accommodate "the whole council" in a room such as this, as Mark suggests, for such would have involved up to 71 members as well as assorted scribes and assistants (Mark 14:55). This is why formal meetings of the Sanhedrin usually took place in a special hall known as the *Lishkat La-Gazit*, or the Chamber of Hewn Stones, located in the Stoa section of the Temple. What's more, it would have been near impossible to gather all members on such short notice, and on the eve of Passover, when all council members would have been celebrating the holy feast at home with their families. According to the Mishnah, no trial by the Sanhedrin could take place at night or during a festival. Then again, we have few contemporary records that describe the actual operations of the Sanhedrin; much of what is debated today about the Sanhedrin in Jesus' time is inferred from later Talmudic sources.

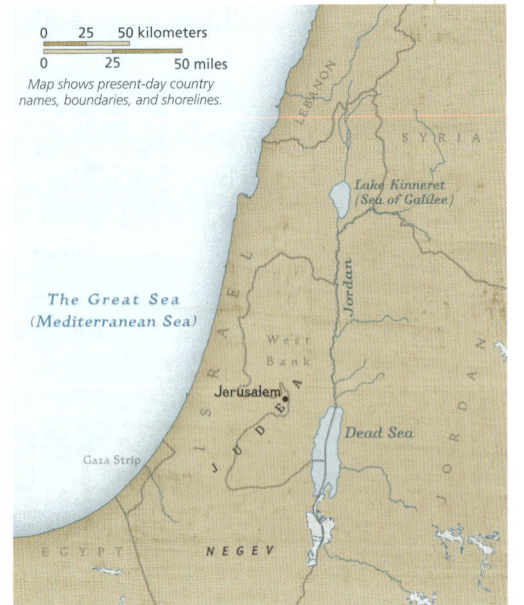

The Indictment by Caiaphas

One theory suggests that Caiaphas deliberately sought to indict Jesus in a private session to avoid having certain Council members—notably, the Pharisees—rise to

Jesus' defense. If that is true, then Caiaphas's next challenge was to come up with a charge that would justify a sentence of death. Some scholars have argued that without the full backing of the Sanhedrin, the high priest did not have the power to order a man's death. In that case, there was only one other solution, and that was to refer the whole matter to the local Roman government. This is a rather controversial conclusion, since during the preceding decades, the Sanhedrin had fought hard to retain its autonomy in domestic matters without any interference from the Roman authorities. The Romans, like Herod the Great before them, had acquiesced as long as such cases were domestic or religious in nature, since the applicable law in Judea was, after all, a *religious* law—the Torah. When it came to crimes that affected Roman interests, such as nonpayment of taxes or attempts to incite a rebellion, the Romans were quick to intervene.

Mark's Gospel says that the pro forma indictment in Caiaphas's house did not go smoothly, since the testimony of the various eyewitnesses did not agree. "We

This view of Jerusalem is taken from the south, looking toward Zion Gate and the Hagia Maria Sion Abbey, formerly known as Dormition Abbey and close to the location of the Hall of the Last Supper.

PART II | THE LIFE OF JESUS

The 700-square-yard Priestly House in the Upper City in Jerusalem, excavated by Nahman Avigad in the late 1960s, included a courtyard and a large reception room.

The remains of the Burnt House (opposite), destroyed by Roman forces in 70 C.E., suggest a lavish and possibly priestly home with a private mikveh, ovens, large stone jars, and plastered walls.

heard him say," said one, "I will destroy this temple that is made with hands, and in three days I will build another, not made with hands." (Mark 14:58) This was damaging evidence, to be sure, but not something that would warrant the death penalty. After all, for centuries prophets had warned that Jerusalem and its Temple would face imminent destruction as a result of God's wrath.

Caiaphas then faced Jesus and asked him, "Are you the Messiah?" According to Mark, Jesus replied, "I am," and then cited from the Book of Daniel and the Psalms: "You will see the Son of Man seated at the right hand of 'the Power,' and 'coming with the clouds of heaven.'" (Psalms 110:1; Daniel 7:13-14)

With these words, Jesus had given Caiaphas the perfect pretext to involve the Romans. Though Jesus had merely quoted from Scripture, the chief priests knew that words such as "power" and "coming with the clouds of heaven" would have a very different meaning for the Romans.

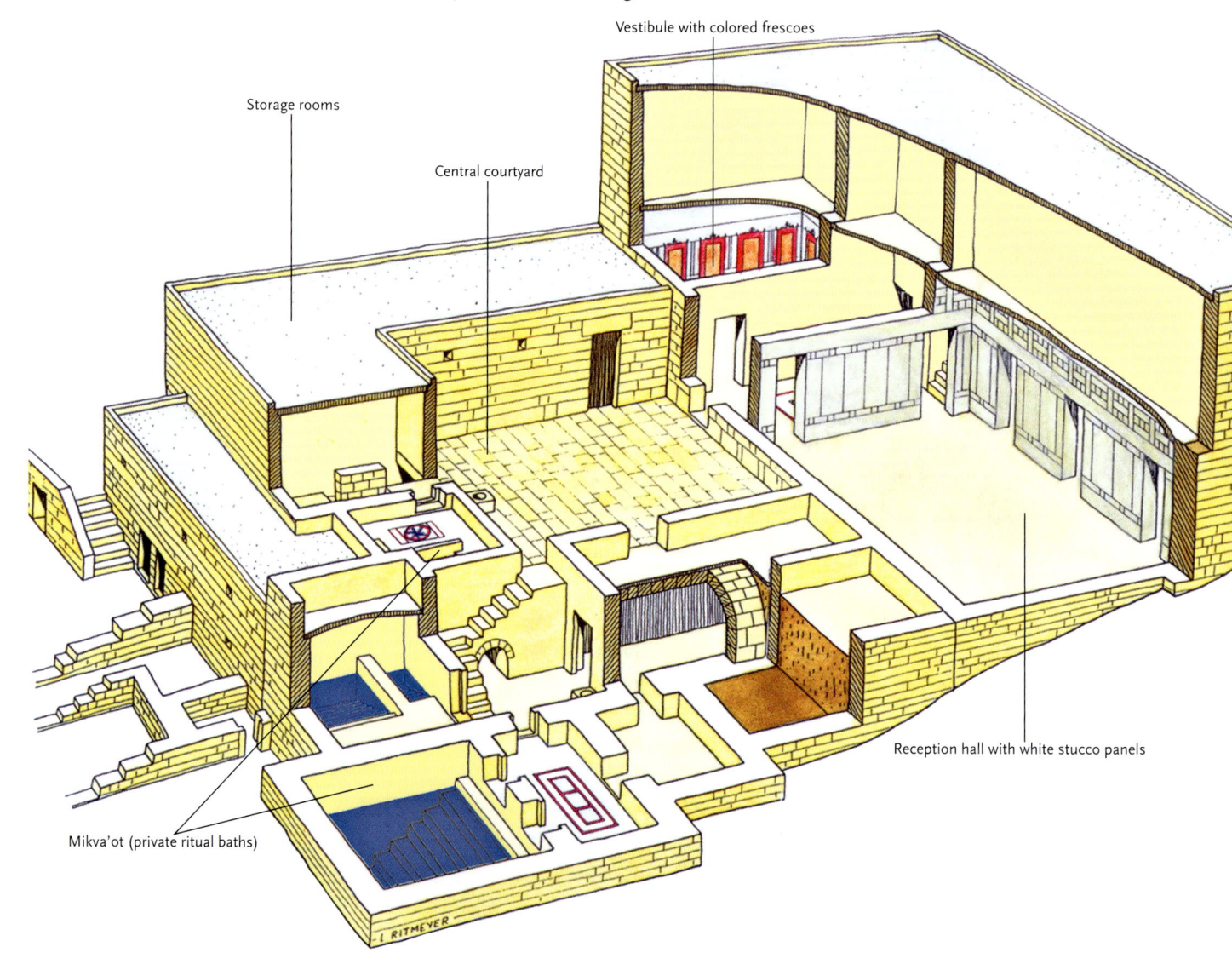

- Vestibule with colored frescoes
- Storage rooms
- Central courtyard
- Reception hall with white stucco panels
- Mikva'ot (private ritual baths)

Jesus before Pilate

It is difficult to ascertain when and where the trial before Pilate as reported in the Gospels actually took place. Ancient writers, and particularly Mark, often telescoped events into a short span of days to maintain the narrative integrity of the story. The idea of Jesus' arrest, trial, and Crucifixion all taking place in a rush of 24 hours, which some scholars have questioned, did appeal to early Christianity, for it enabled the faithful to re-create all these events in a "Holy Week." Mark's Gospel claims that "as soon as it was morning . . . they bound Jesus, led him away, and handed him over to Pilate," who thereupon initiated a hearing. This is what the Romans would have called "the first hour"—around 6 or 7 a.m., by our modern reckoning. In ten hours or so, the sun would go down and the Sabbath would begin.

The location of these proceedings is likewise uncertain. The Gospels refer to Pilate's "headquarters" or the *praetorium,* literally the seat of the *praetor* or provincial governor (Mark 15:15-6; Matthew 27:27). We know of two possible locations. One was the old palace of Herod, a sprawling complex in the southwestern part of the city, just south of today's Jaffa Gate. The other was the Antonia Fortress, the Herodian citadel adjacent to the Temple complex, where the main Roman garrison in Jerusalem was based. Scholars are divided on this issue. On the one hand, Herod's palace would have offered more comfort for the prefect from Rome. On the other hand, if there was trouble brewing, it was likely to happen in the Temple forecourt. The very purpose of Pilate's visit to Jerusalem during Passover was to suppress any form of violent protest. It would therefore seem logical that he would decide to stay at the Antonia Fortress, adjacent to the Temple. A further corroboration of this theory may be inferred from the fact that when Paul was arrested to be tried, he was taken to the "barracks" (Acts 21:37), which most scholars agree refers to the Antonia. Finally, the Gospels state that there were other "rebels" held at the *praetorium* as well. This suggests that the location contained a functioning prison, which would once again favor the Antonia.

The next question is the nature of the hearing that Pilate reportedly presided over. In the Gospels of Matthew, Luke, and John, Mark's rather sparse account is developed into a more elaborate trial proceeding that hews closely to the *Ius Civile,* Roman Law. The role of the judge, by custom the highest-ranking *praetor*

PART II | THE LIFE OF JESUS

in town, is played by the Roman prefect himself, Pontius Pilate. Accusers (or *delatores* in Roman jurisprudence) are summoned to present evidence (Luke 23:2). When such evidence is found wanting, the judge himself decides to interrogate the accused, in an attempt to ferret out the truth. Jesus disrupts the proceeding, however, by refusing to respond to Pilate's questioning (Matthew 27:14). This is a disturbing development because, according to the *Ius Civile*, the absence of a proper defense can result in a verdict being overturned or referred to a higher judicial authority. In the Gospel of John, a learned debate then ensues between Jesus and Pilate, which leads Pilate to declare that "I cannot find fault in this man." (John 18:38)

Some authors have questioned whether the trial would have unfolded in this manner, or indeed whether there was a trial at all, because Jesus was not a Roman citizen but a colonial subject. Colonials did not rate the benefit of Roman proceedings under the *Ius Civile*; instead, they were judged by a far more arbitrary set of rules, usually referred to as the *Ius Gentium*—the "law of nations." Originally, this law had been drafted for any legal issues involving foreigners on Roman soil, including subjects from the provinces. During the Imperial Period, the law was then applied as a form of "colonial law"

> AND THEN THE ASSEMBLY ROSE AS A BODY AND BROUGHT JESUS BEFORE PILATE.
>
> GOSPEL OF LUKE 23:1
> *Circa 75–90 C.E.*

According to the inscription, this elaborate ossuary contained the bones of Caiaphas (Yosef bar Caifa), quite possibly the high priest who arraigned Jesus, as well as the remains of Caiaphas's family.

| The Trial and Crucifixion |

This portrait of Annas and Caiaphas was painted by French artist James Jacques Joseph Tissot (1836–1902) around 1894.

THE OSSUARY OF CAIAPHAS

The poor buried their loved ones in the ground, but the wealthy—such as, conceivably, Joseph of Arimathea—buried their dead in a family tomb. Many of these tombs were hewn into the rocky slope of the Valley of Kidron, since this is where many Jews believed Judgment Day would begin. These tombs were essentially burial caves that were in continuous use by a given family. Inside were niches (*kokhim*) just large enough to contain a single body. These tombs, however, served two purposes: to provide a primary burial for the body while it underwent decomposition, followed by a secondary burial of the bones in small boxes known as ossuaries. In 1990, archaeologists made a sensational discovery in a small family tomb containing several ossuaries from the first century C.E. The most elaborate of the boxes bore an Aramaic inscription: *Yehoseph bar Qypa* or "Joseph Caiaphas," who may be the high priest Caiaphas who indicted Jesus. In 2002 came another major discovery: an intact ossuary believed to hold the bones of James, based on an Aramaic inscription that read as follows: "James, son of Joseph, brother of Jesus." Reportedly found in the Silwan area in the Kidron Valley, the inscription has since been uncovered as a forgery.

PART II | THE LIFE OF JESUS

Italian artist Antonio Ciseri (1821–1891) painted this view of Pilate showing the scourged Jesus to the crowds, known as "Ecce Homo," in 1880.

This coin from the reign of Tiberius (opposite) was struck around 23 C.E., some seven years before Jesus' trial and crucifixion, when the empire was increasingly ruled by Tiberius's confidant, Lucius Aelius Sejanus.

in overseas territories occupied by Rome, insofar as it pertained to matters that affected Roman interests (rather than purely domestic cases). *Praetors* who dispensed law under this legal umbrella were given wide latitude to render judgment as they saw fit, without the procedural finesse of a Roman trial. This is why upon his arrest around 63 C.E., Paul—who had inherited his Roman citizenship from his father—vehemently insisted on a proper trial in Rome, rather than being left at the mercy of a colonial court in Jerusalem or Caesarea.

It is therefore quite possible that Mark's succinct summary of the hearing before Pilate is closer to the actual events than the more dramatic and elaborate versions in the other Gospels. In Mark's portrayal, the proceeding was mercifully brief. Jesus was ushered before Pilate; the charge was read—the prisoner being accused of claiming to be the Messiah, "the King of the Jews"—and Jesus' response, "You say so," was noted for the record (Mark 15:2). Pilate then expressed his surprise that Jesus did not have anything more to say in his defense, but made no further attempt to question the prisoner. Indeed, such would have been pointless anyway. Anyone with ambitions to be crowned as king of Judea was by definition a rebel, and rebels merited only one form of punishment: crucifixion.

Pilate Offers a Choice

Before the final verdict could be read, however, a curious episode intervened. Down in the prison were various "rebels who had committed murder during the insurrection," says Mark (Mark 15:7). It is not clear which "insurrection" Mark is referring to, though it is possible that this was the massive protest, described by Josephus, that took place in Jerusalem around 28 C.E. during the Aqueduct Affair. One of these rebels was a man named Barabbas. Turning to "the crowd" that had gathered in front of the *praetorium*, Pilate offered them a choice: "Do you want me to release for you the King of the Jews?" Anticipating this, "the chief priests stirred up the crowd to have him release Barabbas for them instead." When the mob dutifully did so, Pilate was taken aback. He asked them, "Then what do you wish me to do with the man you call the King of the Jews?" They shouted back, "Crucify him!" (Mark 15:7-13)

Mark claims that this was Pilate's custom, that "at the festival he used to release a prisoner for them" (Mark 15:6), but such an amnesty is not attested in any documents of the period that specifically refer to Pilate. Some historians question the historicity of this event, arguing that Pilate was certainly not known for his merciful qualities, and that it is unlikely that Pilate would have risked releasing a convicted "rebel" like Barabbas at the beginning of so volatile a week. Others, however, point to evidence that on occasion, other Roman governors did publicly pardon malefactors, or that people were occasionally released on special holy days.

It is generally assumed that Mark wrote his Gospel in Rome for a Roman audience in a very tense time: during or immediately after the Jewish Revolt in Judea (66–70 C.E.). Most Jews living in Rome would have been careful to distance themselves from the Jewish rebellion and demonstrate their loyalty to the emperor. Moreover, this was a time when early Christianity was struggling to create a foothold in the Roman capital. To make Pilate, the highest Roman official in Judea, the villain of the story would not only have been counterproductive, but possibly dangerous as well.

This may also be the reason why Matthew, Luke, and particularly John depict these proceedings as a full-fledged Roman trial *as if* Jesus had been a Roman citizen, and why Mark shows Pilate as a man who actually comes to Jesus' *defense*. This obviously created a dilemma for the evangelists: If Pilate were not to blame, then who was responsible for Jesus' execution?

The answer may, likewise, be suggested by events then taking place in Judea. For 30 years after the Crucifixion, Jewish Christians in Palestine became increasingly isolated. As the Book of Acts attests, soon after Jesus' Crucifixion the Sanhedrin began to suppress the movement by imprisoning some of the

> NOW AT THE FESTIVAL THE GOVERNOR WAS ACCUSTOMED TO RELEASE A PRISONER FOR THE CROWD, ANYONE WHOM THEY WANTED.
>
> GOSPEL OF MATTHEW 27:15
> *Circa 75-90 C.E.*

PART II | THE LIFE OF JESUS

A Roman flagrum was a whip consisting of several thongs with sharp pieces made of metal or sheep's bone, used for scourging prisoners.

French academic artist William-Adolphe Bouguereau (1825–1905) painted "The Flagellation of Our Lord Jesus Christ" (opposite) in 1880, based on exhaustive research.

Apostles. The stoning of the disciple Stephen then resulted in a more intense persecution, which was led, among others, by Paul of Tarsus. The newly appointed King Agrippa I (r. 37–44 C.E.) joined in the suppression of Jewish Christians and ordered the execution of James, the son of Zebedee, around 44 C.E. (Acts 12:2). Josephus tells us that two decades later, the high priest Ananus condemned James, the brother of Jesus and leader of the Jerusalem church, to be stoned to death.

Seen in this context, it is not difficult to understand why Mark chose to shift the blame for Jesus' execution from the Romans to the high priest and the Council, just as John would later place the blame collectively on "the Jews" (John 19:15). To make this culpability explicit, Mark has Pilate asking the Jewish crowd whom they prefer: Jesus, or a *rebel*—this while the memory of the Jewish rebellion was still fresh. The crowd then calls for the release of the rebel. For Mark's audience, confronted by the challenges of their time, this version of the events made eminent sense. In this view, the Romans were not really responsible for Jesus' death because Pilate's hand was forced; he had to do as the Jewish crowd told him. "So Pilate, wishing to satisfy the crowd, released Barabbas for them," Mark says, "and after flogging Jesus, he handed him over to be crucified." (Mark 15:15)

The Historical Pilate

The great tragedy of these ten verses in Mark's Gospel, as well as similar passages in the other Gospels, is that they would set the stage for the persecution of Jewish communities as the "killers of Christ" from the Middle Ages right through the horrors of the 20th century. The theme of Jewish culpability is further developed in the Gospels of Matthew and John. "His blood be on us, and on our children!" the crowd cries in Matthew's account (Matthew 27:25).

The historical Pilate, however, is quite different from the sympathetic figure in the Gospels. From the beginning of his term, Pilate never shied away from deliberately provoking Jewish sensitivities, and he wasted no time in crushing anyone whom he deemed a political threat. "Pilate," says the Jewish historian Philo, writing around 41 C.E., "[used] briberies, insults, robberies, outrages, wanton injuries, and"—significantly—"constantly repeated executions without trial"; a man, in short, of "ceaseless and supremely grievous cruelty." Even Josephus, who wrote at the behest of the Roman Imperial House, felt compelled to document Pilate's misdeeds and his absolute disregard for human life. Significantly, Pilate was removed from his office in 36 C.E. for the excessive violence with which he suppressed a Samaritan religious event. Reportedly, a man claiming to be the Messiah was planning to mark the Passover festival by leading a group

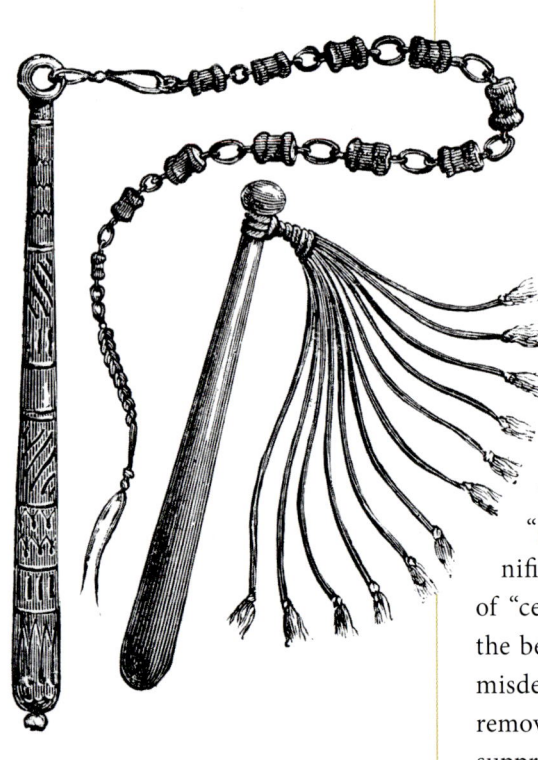

The Trial and Crucifixion

PART II | THE LIFE OF JESUS

This hill overlooking Jerusalem's main Arab bus terminal, close to the Garden Tomb, has sometimes been identified as Golgotha, given its slight resemblance to a human skull.

of followers to Mount Gerizim, a holy mountain to Samaritans, where they would find sacred vessels buried by Moses. Pilate interpreted this pilgrimage as a political demonstration, and he ambushed the worshippers. Some of the faithful were killed on the spot; others were executed later. This massacre was reported to Pilate's superior, Governor Vitellius in Antioch, Syria, who removed Pilate from office and sent him packing to Rome. Pilate did so, and subsequently faded from history—though many Christian legends about Pilate would surface later on.

THE SCOURGING

Having been condemned to death, Jesus was led away to be flogged prior to his Crucifixion. For many modern readers, this seems a rather egregious punishment. Why subject a man to rigorous flogging when he is shortly destined to die an agonizing death on the cross? Usually, flogging was a penalty inflicted on those—like Jeremiah and, later, the Apostles—who would be released in due course, but needed a reminder not to commit the same transgression again. In Jesus' case, such a punishment was obviously pointless. Why then order a scourging?

Traditionally, crucifixion was reserved for rebels or anyone else challenging Roman sovereignty—such as slaves—because it involved a torment that could stretch over many days. A case in point is the sentence that the Roman consul Crassus meted out against Spartacus and his slave rebel army in 71 B.C.E. Six thousand slaves were crucified along the Via Appia, Rome's busiest road, at ten-yard intervals; many of these men survived for two days or more. For the Romans, this was the whole purpose of nailing someone to the cross: The culprit needed to serve as an object lesson for all those harboring similar seditious thoughts.

The preemptive value of crucifixion gained particular significance during the Early Imperial Roman Period, when Roman forces were stretched so thin that their ability to quell an actual insurrection was left in doubt. This was borne out by the Jewish rebellion, which erupted in 66 C.E.; it took the Romans no less than three years and a large expeditionary force to suppress it. Since retaining a large military presence in all possible trouble spots was not feasible, the Romans chose another form of deterrence. They decided to punish would-be rebels with the cruelest and most painful form of execution yet devised by man.

The idea of a man slowly dying on a cross was, however, reprehensible to Jews, for it violated the Torah's decree that every person executed for his crimes *had to be taken down before sundown* (Deuteronomy 21:22-23). To let a man wither for days on end ran the risk of enraging the Jewish population, and thus provoke the very rebellion it was designed to preempt. How

---

THE SOURCE OF THE PASSION

The principal source of Jesus' Passion is the Gospel of Mark. Neither the Gospel of Thomas nor the Q source provides any information about the Passover events. Therefore, scholars surmise that the Passion story in Matthew, Luke, and John is largely based on Mark's account, though enhanced with various embellishments. Some authors have argued that the Passion material in Mark is drawn from an older document, now lost, which may have survived in another Christian text, the so-called Gospel of Peter, discovered in Egypt in 1886. Apparently, church fathers, including a second-century bishop called Serapion, suspected the Gospel of Peter of Gnostic or *docetic* tendencies—denying the humanity of Christ in the belief that he had always been divine—and thus branded the text as heretical. Nevertheless, there is evidence that the Gospel of Peter enjoyed wide popularity in the first and second century C.E. Of the 30 Gospel manuscripts uncovered since the 1880s, there is only one version of Mark, but fragments of three separate copies of the Gospel of Peter.

to insure, then, that a condemned man died on the cross before sundown? The answer was to substantially weaken a man *before* he was taken to his place of execution, and the obvious way to do so was to cause significant loss of blood.

This may be the reason why Jesus was condemned to be flogged.

To scourge a man, the Roman army used an instrument known as a *flagrum,* which consisted of three or more thongs, each studded with sharp stones or chunks of sheep bone. When wielded by an expert executioner, the whip could systematically strip the skin off a man's back without inflicting too much damage on the muscles underneath.

According to Mark's Gospel, Jesus was then taken to Golgotha, the place of execution, on the same day. Some scholars have questioned whether Pilate would have risked inciting a popular outcry by executing Jewish prisoners during the Passover festival. On the other hand, Pilate may well have been keen to see Jesus executed immediately, lest his imprisonment would give his presumed followers time to stage new protests in the densely packed city. Crucifixion was a

> **THEN THE SOLDIERS LED HIM INTO THE COURTYARD OF THE PALACE AND THEY CALLED TOGETHER THE WHOLE COHORT.**
>
> GOSPEL OF MARK 15:16
> *Circa 66–70 C.E.*

PART II | THE LIFE OF JESUS

The so-called "Ecce Homo" arch has traditionally been associated with the location where Pilate showed Jesus to the crowd; recent research has shown that it dates from the second century C.E.

time-consuming and labor-intensive undertaking, not likely to be staged on a whim, and for just one man. It is therefore quite possible that some form of group execution had already been planned in advance to coincide with the Passover festival, and that as the Gospels state, Jesus was executed with other condemned men.

Dressed in his rough tunic, which was now encrusted with dried blood, Jesus was led out of the gates of the *praetorium* to the place of execution. He was, as Mark's Gospel tells us, compelled to carry the instrument of his execution himself. But this was probably not a full cross, as traditional depictions of Jesus' Passion suggest. Wood was sparse in Judea, and therefore expensive, while crucifixions were common. For this reason, punishments were usually carried out in a designated execution ground. Even Rome itself had such a crucifixion ground, just outside the Esquiline Gate. In Jerusalem, this killing field was called Golgotha, or "place of the skull" in Aramaic. Given that the cost of each wooden cross was substantial, it is likely that the Romans would have set up permanent upright stakes. In that case, all the prisoner was required to carry was the so-called *patibulum,* the crossbeam. This beam would still have weighed around 75 pounds, so the anecdote in Mark's Gospel in which a bystander, Simon of Cyrene, is pressed to carry Jesus' cross part of the way, still rings true.

> AND CARRYING THE CROSS BY HIMSELF, HE WENT OUT TO WHAT IS CALLED THE PLACE OF THE SKULL, WHICH IN HEBREW IS CALLED GOLGOTHA.
>
> GOSPEL OF JOHN 19:17
> *Circa 85–100 C.E.*

THE VIA DOLOROSA

The exact route that Jesus followed to Golgotha, known as the Via Dolorosa (or Road of Sorrows) is still the subject of debate. Apart from the uncertainty about the location of the *praetorium*, the Jerusalem of Jesus' day was thoroughly demolished after the Second Jewish Uprising in 132–135 C.E. In an act of vengeance, which he hoped would extinguish the spirit of Jewish rebellion forever, Emperor Hadrian decreed that Jerusalem should cease to exist. A new Roman city, Aelia Capitolina, was to rise from its ashes. The basic outline of this Roman city, with two parallel roads—Cardines Maximi—and a Decumanus Maximus at right angles, is still visible in today's Old City of Jerusalem. But Hadrian's order, which was executed with typical Roman efficiency, makes it extremely difficult to establish which route Jesus would have taken to reach Golgotha.

Most scholars, however, accept that the Church of the Holy Sepulcher, today located in the western part of Jerusalem's Old City just north of the Roman Decumanus, is indeed the place of Jesus' Crucifixion and burial. Moreover, tradition has firmly fastened itself on the belief that Jesus' journey began at the Antonia Fortress. For a long time, the remains of a monumental arch and Roman-style pavement inside the Church of the Sisters of Zion were believed

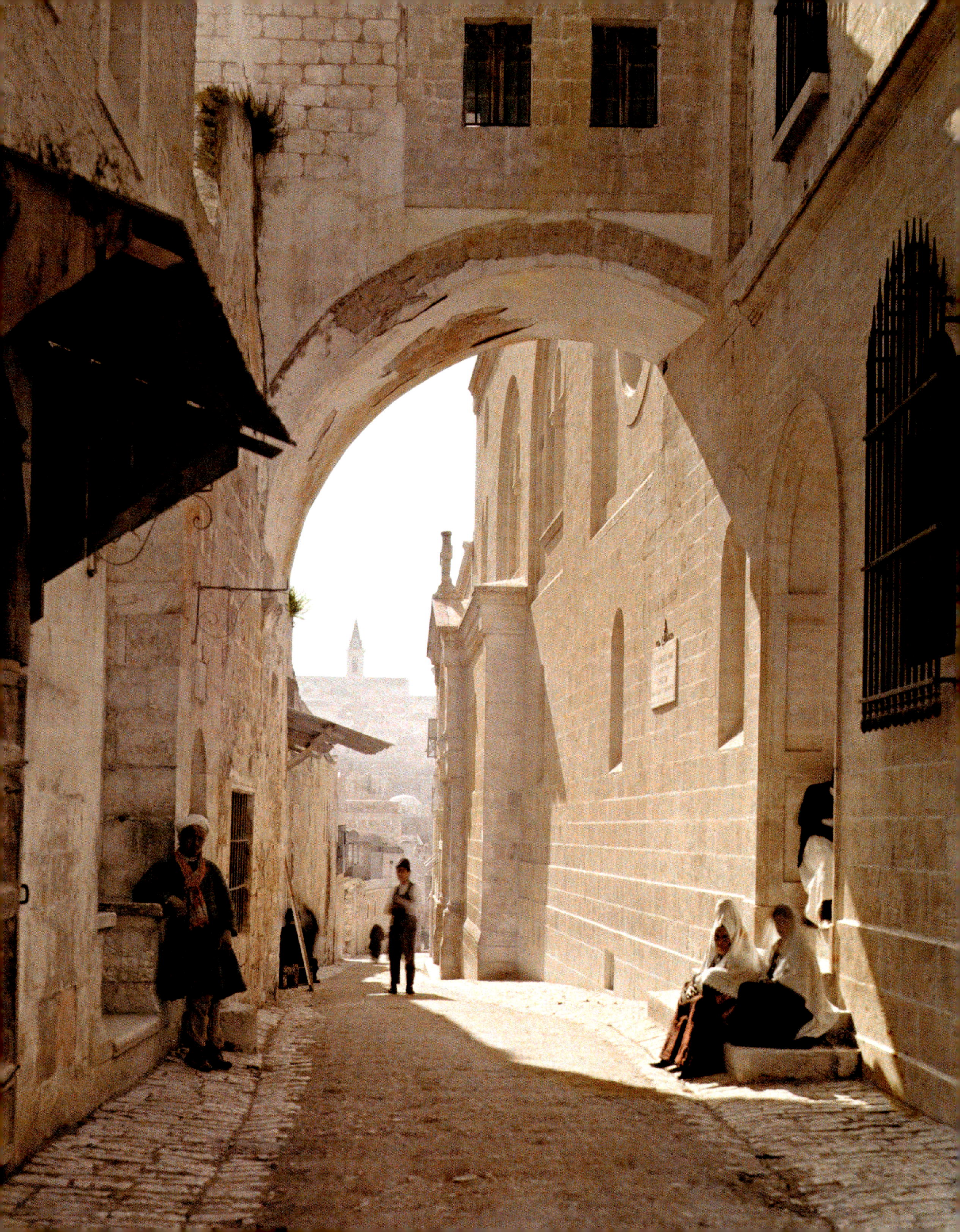

This chapel in the Church of the Holy Sepulcher is believed to mark the location of Golgotha hill.

This Roman game board (opposite), associated with the Basilinda game, was thought to have been carved in the Antonia Fortress pavement, though recent research suggests it dates from the second century C.E.

to be part of the Antonia. The soaring arch was held to be the place where, according to the Gospel of John, Pilate showed Jesus to the crowd after his flogging with the words *Ecce Homo*—"Behold the Man" (John 19:5). One section of the pavement even features a Roman game board scratched in the stone, which some believe was used by the soldiers to play *Basilinda,* the King's Game, while mocking Jesus.

Recent research by scholars such as Jodi Magness, however, has convincingly shown that these Roman remains actually formed part of a triple gate of Hadrian's city Aelia Capitolina, built a century after the Crucifixion. Moreover, the official route of the Via Dolorosa and its 14 "Stations of the Cross" changed repeatedly over the centuries as various Christian communities built a growing number of chapels or hospices in the city, all of which clamored to be recognized in the route. While in the Byzantine era, the pilgrimage began on the Mount of the Olives, by the Middle Ages the Via Dolorosa had shifted to a number of competing routes that all reflected the interest of one European

The Trial and Crucifixion

community or another. The situation became so chaotic that around 1350, Pope Clement VI issued a bull that placed all holy sites, real or presumed, under the custody of one body, namely the Franciscan Order. This tradition has continued in modern times; today, the Franciscans not only maintain a vast number of shrines and archaeological sites throughout the Holy Land, but also own apartment complexes in Jerusalem that are made available to needy families at low rents.

With their mandate, the Franciscans then sought to establish the exact route of the Via Dolorosa. This became the subject of such intense negotiation that a final route was not agreed upon until the 18th century. Consequently, while today's Via Dolorosa has great devotional value, its historical accuracy is difficult to determine.

Jesus Is Crucified

Mark's Gospel says that the procession of Jesus and the other condemned men reached Golgotha "on the third hour," roughly around nine o'clock in the morning. Here, an execution detail of Roman *immunes,* or army specialists, trained in crucifixion procedures, took over. They took Jesus' clothes, forced him down on the ground, and stretched his arms along the length of the crossbeam. Several strong soldiers held Jesus while two others bound his arms firmly to the beam with henna rope, which cut deep into his skin. With Jesus' arms and hands fully immobilized, the senior *immunis* took a heavy mallet and several six-inch-long nails, and sat down to choose his entry point. Contrary to traditional depictions of the Crucifixion, the nail was not driven through the palm, since the tissue of the human hand is too soft to bear the weight of an adult man. Instead, the soldier probed for a spot just below the wrist, between the radius and ulna bones of the upper forearm. Having found it, he raised his arm and brought the mallet down on the nail with all his strength, driving it through the skin and the median nerve, which caused an intense pain known as causalgia. The process was then repeated on the other arm.

With Jesus now nailed to the *patibulum,* two soldiers on either side lifted the crossbar, raised it high over their heads, and slammed it into the open notch of the nearest stake, suspending Jesus above the ground. But one last task still remained. The Roman *immunis*, assisted by other soldiers, squeezed the ankles of Jesus sideways into a small wooden block, shaped in the form of a U. Taking another nail, this block was affixed to the bottom of the upright stake in such

> **AND WHEN THEY HAD CRUCIFIED HIM, THEY DIVIDED HIS CLOTHES AMONG THEMSELVES BY CASTING LOTS.**
>
> Gospel of Matthew, 27:35
> *Circa 75–90 c.e.*

PART II | THE LIFE OF JESUS

JEWISH BURIAL CUSTOMS

According to Jewish custom, a body was prepared for burial with a cleansing and anointing, after which it was wrapped in linen—usually strips of cotton that could be easily wrapped around a corpse. Alternatively, the body of Jesus could have been wrapped in a large linen shroud. In 2002, archaeologist Shimon Gibson discovered a tomb with a body wrapped in a shroud, blackened with age. The shroud was later carbon dated to the first 50 years of the first century. This exciting discovery revealed that one-piece burial shrouds were in use in the time of Jesus, perhaps bolstering the claim of the famous Shroud of Turin, which contains the imprint of a bloody, crucified corpse in negative. Its injuries appear to include a large wound in the wrist area, puncture wounds in the feet, and lacerations on the torso and legs that could have been caused by scourging. In 1988, the Vatican consented to a number of tests using the radiocarbon dating process, conducted by three separate laboratories. All three institutions found that the cloth was created at some time between 1260 and 1390 C.E. In 1997, however, a botanist from the Hebrew University of Jerusalem recognized certain flower fragments on the shroud as those belonging to various species found near Jerusalem. This was followed in the 2000s with a report suggesting that the 1988 carbon dating tests used fragments from medieval repair patches, not from the original cloth itself. Consequently, for many the origins of the Shroud of Turin remain a mystery.

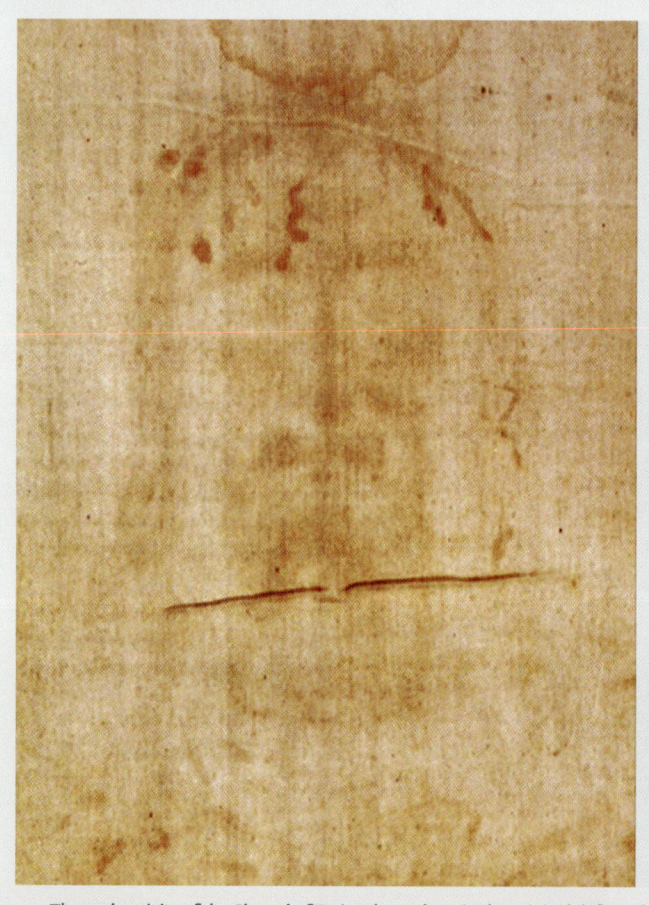

The authenticity of the Shroud of Turin, shown here in the original (left) and in negative, remains a subject of controversy and intense scientific debate.

The Trial and Crucifixion

a manner that the nail impaled both Jesus' heels and the block to the wooden post. The action also pressed the legs together and bent them, so that Jesus seemed to be kneeling sideways. This last step completed the truly horrific purpose of crucifixion. In this posture, suspended by one's arms, it becomes very difficult to breathe. In order to breathe, the condemned must lift himself up; by lifting himself up, he puts more strain on his nailed arms and feet, bringing fresh waves of pain.

The details of the Roman crucifixion procedure in Judea came to light in 1986, when the skeleton of another first-century Jewish victim was uncovered in a Jerusalem cemetery. The calcaneus, or right heel bone of the man, whose name was Yehohanan, was transfixed by a bent Roman nail about four and a half inches long. Fragments of wood were present on either side of the heel. In addition, Yehohanan's radii were chafed, showing that he had been suspended from nails driven into his forearms.

Last, says Mark, the Romans affixed a sign on Jesus' cross, which listed the charge against him. It read, mockingly, "The King of the Jews." Two other men, condemned as "bandits," were crucified and set up on his right and left (Mark 15:26-27).

Hour after hour, Jesus hung on his cross, suffering the agony of breathing at the cost of tearing his flesh against the Roman nails. "Darkness came over the whole land," says Mark. "At three o'clock, Jesus cried out with a loud voice, *'Eloi, Eloi, lema sabachthani?'*" which means, "My God, my God, why have you forsaken me?" (Mark 15:33-34) Jesus' cry is a quote from the Book of Psalms (Psalms 22:1), which was often invoked by Jews in moments of great despair. Some scholars believe the citation was interpolated by the evangelist, to emphasize Jesus' sense of abandonment. The disciples were nowhere in evidence; only a group of women remained as witnesses, including "Mary Magdalene and Mary the mother of James the Younger," who may or may not be Jesus' mother (Mark 15:40) Nevertheless, there is no reason to think that Jesus could not have spoken these words of distress in this supreme moment, on the threshold of death. He then "gave a loud cry and breathed his last." (Mark 15:37)

A tomb west of Jerusalem, which may have contained the remains of members of King Herod's family, is one of the few tombs from the first century C.E. that still retains its rolling stone.

The Burial of Jesus

As the cicadas began their late afternoon plainsong, the Roman soldiers got up, stretched, and prepared for their final task. No "hanged man" was permitted to remain after dusk, they had been told, for the Jewish Sabbath was about to begin.

PART II | THE LIFE OF JESUS

Spanish artist El Greco, born Doménikos Theotokópoulos (1541–1614), painted this haunting depiction (opposite) of Jesus on a tau-type cross around 1605.

Thus they proceeded to break the legs of the condemned, one by one (John 19:32). Without the use of their legs, the victims could not raise themselves to breathe, and thus slowly suffocated to death. One of the soldiers raised his hammer to also smash the legs of Jesus, but Jesus was no longer breathing. In the Gospel of John, the soldier used his lance to pierce Jesus' side and see if there was a reaction (John 19:34). There was none; Jesus had been dead for some time.

The soldiers then removed the crossbeams from the posts and roughly pulled the nails out of the corpses, which would then be deposited in a tomb reserved for the executed. After a year or so had elapsed, their relatives would be permitted to gather the bones and take them to a family tomb for reburial. The nails were much sought after, for many people in Antiquity attributed magical powers to nails used in a crucifixion. And then, a man came up to stop the soldiers. His name was Joseph of Arimathea, says Mark, "a respected member of the council, who was also himself waiting expectantly for the kingdom of God." (Mark 15:43) This may imply that Joseph, a member of the Sanhedrin and possibly a Pharisee, harbored sympathy for Jesus' "kingdom of God" teachings. Luke's Gospel states that he "had not agreed to their plan and action." (Luke 23:50)

Earlier in the afternoon, Joseph had petitioned Pilate for the release of Jesus' body, lest it be deprived of the final dignity of a private burial. "Pilate," says Mark, "summoning the centurion . . . asked him whether he had been dead for some time." (Mark 15:45) Some scholars believe that this verse was inserted at a later time to convince any skeptics, Christian or otherwise, that Jesus was truly dead prior to his resurrection, and not merely unconscious.

> **NOW THERE WAS A GOOD AND RIGHTEOUS MAN NAMED JOSEPH, WHO, THOUGH A MEMBER OF THE COUNCIL, HAD NOT AGREED TO THEIR PLAN AND ACTION.**
>
> GOSPEL OF LUKE 23:50
> *Circa 75–90 C.E.*

Joseph then took possession of the body and, perhaps with assistance of his servants, "wrapped it in the linen cloth, and laid it in a tomb that had been hewn out of the rock." (Mark 15:46) It was, however, Friday afternoon, "the day before the Sabbath" by Jewish reckoning. The Law specified that all burial formalities needed to be concluded before the start of Sabbath at sundown. This may be the reason why according to Mark, Jesus was hastily buried in the nearest available tomb, before the women were able to anoint the body.

Another possible reason why Mark omits the habitual anointing is that while Jesus was still in Bethany a woman had come with an alabaster jar "of a very costly ointment," which she proceeded to pour over Jesus' head. Some who witnessed this scolded her, saying, "Why was this ointment wasted in this way?" But Jesus responded, "She has anointed my body beforehand for its burial." (Mark 14:3-8)

And then the sun sank beneath the horizon, and the Sabbath began. Ushering the tearful women out of the burial place, Joseph "rolled a stone against the door of the tomb," and went on his way (Mark 15:46).

The Trial and Crucifixion

PART III

CIRCA 30 C.E. TO 380 C.E.

Reports of Jesus' resurrection and the divine inspiration of his Apostles during Pentecost prompt an apostolic mission to spread Jesus' teachings throughout Judea. The advent of Paul and other missionaries results in a vigorous evangelizing effort among Jewish and Gentile communities in Syria, Asia Minor, and Greece. Despite persecutions and dissent, the church grows and ultimately becomes the only legitimate religion of the Roman Empire.

THE LEGACY OF JESUS

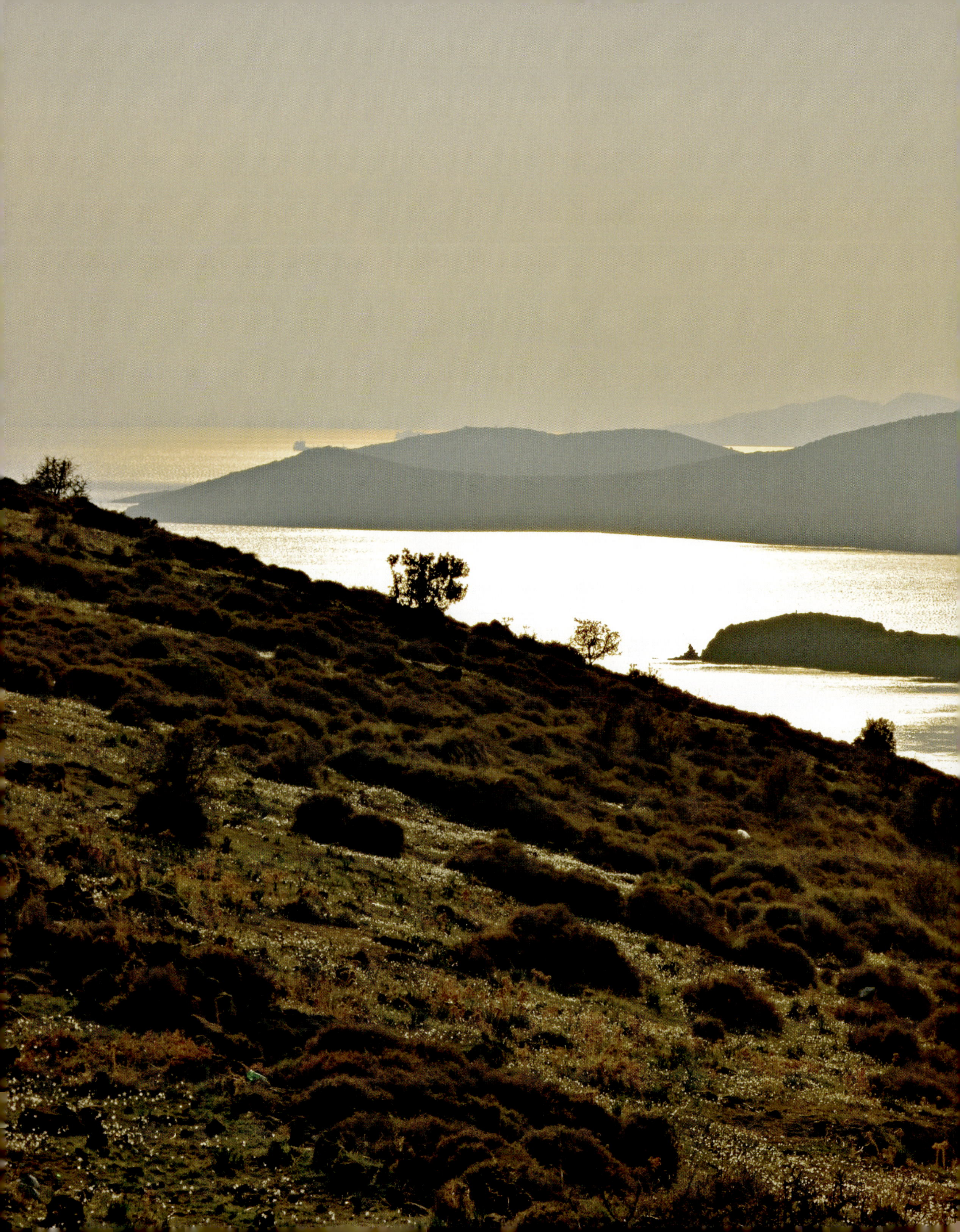

[CHAPTER] 13

The
FIRST
CHRISTIANS

AND VERY EARLY
ON THE FIRST DAY
OF THE WEEK,
WHEN THE SUN HAD RISEN,
THEY WENT TO THE TOMB.

GOSPEL OF MARK 16:2
Circa 66–70 C.E.

The Ionian Coast of Turkey, or Asia Minor as it was called in Antiquity, has changed little from the days when Paul sailed these waters.

PART III | THE LEGACY OF JESUS

A Jewish Midrash states that "for three days [after death] the soul hovers over the body, intending to re-enter it, but as soon as it sees its appearance change, it departs, as it is written." Now, the third day had come. Jesus had been crucified on a Friday; the Sabbath had come and ended at sundown on Saturday; and now, in the early chill of Sunday morning, Mary Magdalene as well as "Mary the mother of James," and a woman named Salome "bought spices, so that they might go and anoint him." (Mark 16:1)

Under normal circumstances, funerary fragrances such as myrrh and aloes mixed with frankincense would have been beyond the means of Jesus' family. But according to the Gospel of John, a wealthy individual named Nicodemus had come to their aid, "bringing a mixture of myrrh and aloes, weighing about a hundred pounds." (John 19:39)

Once again, there is no reference to any of Jesus' male disciples, which suggests that they were still in hiding. This is one reason why in Mark's Gospel, the women worried how they were going to roll away the heavy stone at the entrance to the tomb (Mark 16:3). The best they could hope for was that a friendly passerby, or a gardener perhaps, might assist them. But then they arrived at the tomb and were stupefied by what they saw: "The stone, which was very large, had already been rolled back." They went inside and found a young man, dressed in a white robe, who said, "Do not be alarmed; you are looking for Jesus of Nazareth, who was crucified. He has been raised; he is not here." (Mark 16:6) Mary Magdalene and the other women were seized with "terror and amazement," but the man calmly continued, "Tell his disciples and Peter that he is going ahead of you to Galilee; there you will see him, just as he told you. And so the women fled from the tomb, and they said nothing to anyone, for they were afraid." (Mark 16:6-8)

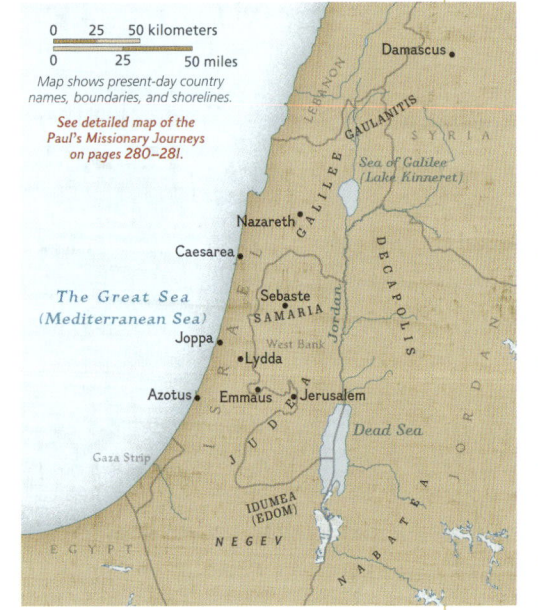

JESUS APPEARS TO HIS APOSTLES

This is where the oldest version of the Gospel of Mark ends, but the other Gospels carry the story further. Various sightings of the risen Jesus are reported throughout Judea and Galilee, though the manner of these appearances differs. At times, Jesus appears as a man of flesh and blood; at other times he is an ephemeral being. In one story told by Luke, two followers are traveling on the road to Emmaus when they meet a stranger who has not heard about the tragic Passover events. The companions are perplexed and tell him "about

Jesus of Nazareth, who was a prophet mighty in deed and word," adding mournfully that "we trusted that it was he who would have redeemed Israel." It is only later that evening, when the stranger breaks bread and blesses it, that their eyes are opened and they recognize Jesus; he then vanishes from their eyes (Luke 24:13-31).

In the Gospel of John, Jesus reveals himself to Mary Magdalene but then warns her "not to hold on to me, because I have not yet ascended to the Father." (John 20:17) Later, he appears as a transcendent being able to move in and out of rooms without passing through a door. But then, this apparition too becomes a man of flesh and blood when he invites a disbelieving Thomas to touch his wounds (John 20:26-27). Some authors believe that these discrepancies point to multiple oral traditions about the empty tomb and its aftermath.

The question of the resurrection is beyond the grasp of human science; it cannot be corroborated by historical or archaeological evidence. Belief in the

Though no longer believed to be a possible location for Jesus' burial, the Garden Tomb outside Jerusalem is a good example of a Jewish burial chamber from the Second Temple Period.

PART III | THE LEGACY OF JESUS

resurrection of Jesus is, quite simply, an act of faith. The Apostles certainly believed that Jesus had risen. Paul would later say that if Christ (or *Christos*, the Greek translation of Messiah, or Anointed One) had not been raised, then all faith would be in vain (I Corinthians 15:12-19). And indeed, the Book of Acts of the Apostles states that the spirit, the divine *ousia* that had inspired Jesus at his baptism in the Jordan, was now spreading among the disciples themselves. Even after Jesus had ascended into heaven (Acts 1:2-11), they distinctly felt his presence and listened to the words that Jesus breathed into their hearts.

The Apostolic Mission

In Acts, this divine inspiration is represented as tongues of flame descending upon Jesus' followers (Acts 2:2-4) during Pentecost. The feast of Shavuot or Pentecost, a Greek word meaning "fiftieth," took place 50 days after Passover. Shavuot once again brought many Jewish pilgrims from all over the Roman world to Jerusalem. The Apostles made good use of this opportunity by addressing the crowds "in other languages, as the Spirit gave them ability." (Acts 2:4)

Nevertheless, now that the group was bereft of its charismatic leader, many questions remained. Where should they go? How should they organize? Should they remain in Jerusalem, or disperse across their native Galilee? As Acts suggests, the decision was taken to remain in Jerusalem and to continue the mission in Judea as Jesus himself had hoped to do. Soon, Simon Peter and James, the brother of Jesus, emerged as the de facto leaders of this apostolic mission, though at this early stage the movement did not yet distinguish itself from Judaism. On the contrary. These early followers continued to follow the precepts of the Torah, observe the Sabbath, and preach in the Temple (Acts 2:45, 15:5). Peter is even credited with miracles in the Temple, such as healing the lame man at the "Beautiful Gate," which may be the Nicanor Gate that separated the Court of Women from the Temple precinct proper. Following the miracle, Peter preached in Solomon's Portico, the large colonnade to the east of the esplanade, and gained new converts whom he baptized as disciples of Jesus.

At the same time, the followers began to meet in private homes to talk about Jesus' teachings and share meals in fellowship. This idea of private assembly is the root meaning of the Greek word *ekklesia,* or gathering, which later would be translated as "church."

Soon, however, this nascent group began to experience a growing opposition, both from the Temple authorities as well as factions within its own community. Peter and John were arrested, thrown in prison, and interrogated by Caiaphas and his Sadducee associates—which some scholars believe may be a deliberate parallel to Jesus' Passion. But there were internal tensions as well.

The 1515 canvas by Tiziano Vecellio, or Titian (1490–1576), entitled "Noli Me Tangere," refers to the Latin version in the Gospel of John, in which Jesus tells Mary Magdalene, "Do not hold on to me." (John 20:17)

WITNESS TO THE RESURRECTION

According to the Gospel of Mark, the empty tomb was first witnessed by "Mary Magdalene, Mary the mother of James, and Salome," who had returned to Jesus' tomb to complete the anointing process (Mark 16:1-2). The Gospel of John claims that Mary Magdalene was the *only* person who first saw that Jesus had risen (John 20:1). This may not sound very remarkable today, but in ancient Palestine, the word of a female eyewitness had little or no credibility in a Jewish court. So why base the most important event in Christianity, Jesus' resurrection, on the testimony of a woman? The simple answer may be that this is what actually happened since all the Apostles were in hiding or had fled the city. In John's Gospel, Mary is also the first disciple to whom the resurrected Jesus revealed himself. Beside herself with joy, Mary wanted to embrace Jesus but he restrained her, saying, "Do not hold on to me, because I have not yet ascended to the Father." (John 20:17) This moment, known by its Latin translation as *Noli me tangere,* would later become a popular motif of Renaissance artists, including Titian.

PART III | THE LEGACY OF JESUS

This gold amulet with pendants, possibly crafted in Greece, attests to the wealth of many urban centers of Asia Minor.

The Nicanor Gate in the Temple (opposite), seen here in a reconstruction, may be the "Beautiful Gate" described in Acts of the Apostles as the location of one of Peter's healings (Acts 3:2).

The Martyrdom of Stephen

Among the many new disciples the Apostles had welcomed into the fold was a group of Jews whom Acts designates as "Hellenists." These were most likely Jews from Egypt and other Diaspora locations in the empire. Their native tongue was Greek, whereas the original followers (whom Acts refers to as "Hebrews") spoke Aramaic. Tensions between these factions rose to the surface with the accusation that widows among the Greek faction did not receive their fair share of food (Acts 6:1). Certain Greek followers, led by a man named Stephen, then adopted an increasingly radical and uncompromising stance toward Temple worship and sacrifice. Disenchantment with the Sadducees was not new, but Stephen went a step further and, according to Acts, began to denounce Temple worship altogether. Their agitation threatened to drive a wedge in the apostolic community, for many other followers, not only the Apostles but also a group of Freedman from North Africa and another group from Asia Minor (today's Turkey), remained faithful to Temple worship (Acts 6:9).

Eventually, Stephen was denounced to the Sanhedrin for "speaking blasphemous words against Moses and God." The Temple authorities, which had been observing the growth of Jesus' followers with alarm, seized this opportunity to suppress the movement. According to Acts, the high priest and the Council interrogated Stephen, who countered his accusers with a lengthy speech, ending with the assertion that "the Most High does not dwell in houses made with human hands." Enraged by his words, a mob dragged him off and stoned him (Acts 7:58).

The absence of the Roman prefect in the story has led some scholars to date this event to 36 C.E., during the temporary power vacuum between Pilate's departure around 35 C.E. and the arrival of the new Roman prefect, Marcellus, in 37 C.E.

Stephen's execution marked a turning point. It dramatically escalated the tensions between the priesthood and the apostolic movement and initiated a period of persecution against the followers of Jesus in Jerusalem and beyond. In response, many of the Greek disciples fled Jerusalem for Cyprus, Phoenicia, and Syria, particularly the city of Antioch on the Orontes.

A Man Named Saul of Tarsus

Notwithstanding these challenges, the Book of Acts describes these early years as a time of steady growth and expansion. Some scholars claim that the book does not always acknowledge some of the grave challenges faced by the apostolic movement. The first of these was the difficulty of propagating Jesus' teachings when the Apostles themselves had often struggled to grasp the meaning of Jesus' Kingdom of God theology. What type of liturgy, practice, and lifestyle should a follower of Jesus adopt beyond the observance of the Law?

The First Christians

The second problem was that unlike Moses (as tradition has it)—or indeed, unlike Muhammad during the gestation of Islam—Jesus had not left a corpus of scripture that could guide and inspire his followers after his death. His ministry had simply been too short. This meant that very early on, a number of oral traditions began to circulate with different emphases on Jesus' teachings, his miracles, his death and resurrection, and his relationship to God, yet all claiming equal authority.

The third challenge was even more daunting: How could they convince fellow Jews that Jesus was the Messiah, even though he had been crucified as a rebel? Given that Jesus was no longer among the living, and therefore unable to offer messianic leadership, what was the purpose of acknowledging him as the Messiah? And if Jesus had truly been a divinely guided prophet, why had God allowed him to be killed in so shameful a manner?

> NOW THOSE WHO WERE SCATTERED WENT FROM PLACE TO PLACE, PROCLAIMING THE WORD.
>
> ACTS OF THE APOSTLES 8:4
> *Circa 75–90 C.E.*

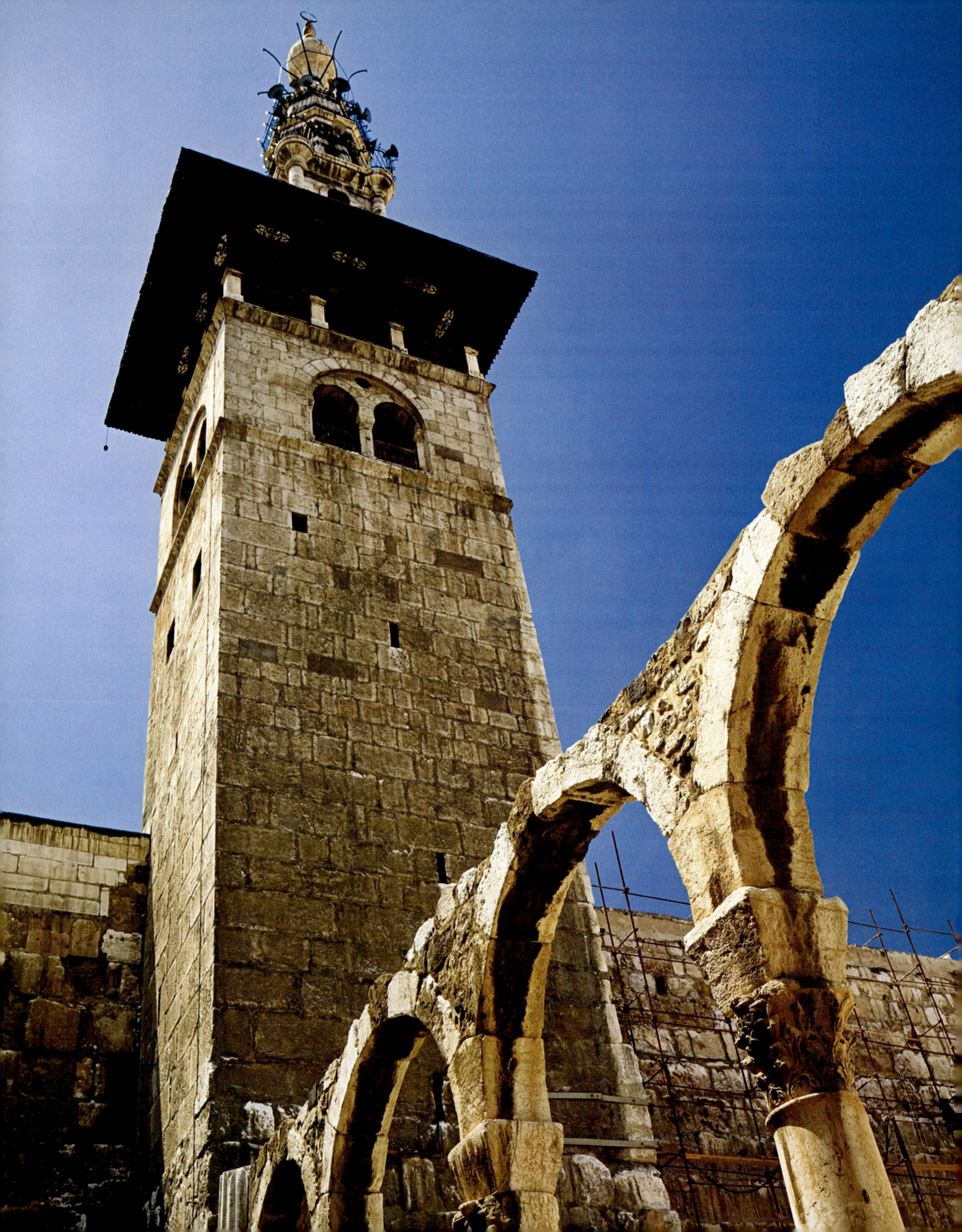

These were very real issues that the Apostles struggled with. Many of them were fishermen, after all; brave and dedicated men, to be sure, but not equipped to extrapolate a comprehensive theological program from what Jesus had talked about. Nor would they have been able to implement such a program in the face of growing hostility throughout Palestine. This, then, would become the inestimable contribution of Paul, who joined the apostolic movement just when it was most in need of such leadership.

Paul, or Saul as he was originally called, was not an instant convert, however. Born in Tarsus, the capital of Cilicia (today's southern Turkey) as the son of Jewish parents, his intellect was sharpened by Greek rhetoric and oratory that permeated the city. "The inhabitants of Tarsus have become so enthusiastic for philosophy and the area of education," wrote the first-century Roman geographer Strabo, "that they have surpassed Athens, Alexandria, and any other place." Paul claimed to hail from the tribe of Benjamin and to have been a Pharisee (Philippians 3:5). According to Acts, he was taught in Jerusalem by the distinguished rabbi Gamaliel, a leading Pharisaic sage, and possibly the same Gamaliel who had intervened on Peter's behalf during his hearing in front of the Sanhedrin. He received a thorough education in Scripture, from which he would often quote in his future epistles (from the Greek *epistolè*, or letter) to Christian communities.

Paul, whose family may have made a living as tent makers or leather workers (the record is not clear), became involved with the persecution of Jesus' disciples (Philippians 3:5). Acts suggests that he was present at Stephen's stoning and was already considered a prominent personage, since the witnesses to the execution "laid their coats at the feet of a young man named Saul." (Acts 7:58) In his letter to the Galatians, Paul confessed that he had advanced "beyond many among my people of the same age, for I was more zealous for the traditions of my ancestors." (Galatians 1:14) He continued the persecutions with vigor, "ravaging the church by entering house after house; dragging off both men and women." (Acts 8:3)

The Preaching of Philip

In response, the Jerusalem disciples dispersed. One of these was a man called Philip (not to be confused with the Apostle Philip), who was one of seven deacons charged with distributing food among the community of disciples (Acts 6:5); his name may indicate that he was a member of the Greek-speaking group of Jewish Christians. Philip, says Acts, then "went down to the city of Samaria," which may be either Herod's city of Sebaste or Shechem. Here, his preaching was so well received that "unclean spirits, crying out with loud shrieks, came out of many who were possessed, and many others who were

This minaret of the Umayyad Mosque in Damascus stands next to the remains of the Temple of Jupiter, which was under construction when Paul stayed in the city.

> **THEN BARNABAS WENT TO TARSUS TO LOOK FOR SAUL, AND WHEN HE HAD FOUND HIM, HE BROUGHT HIM TO ANTIOCH.**
>
> ACTS OF THE APOSTLES 11:25
> *Circa 75–90 C.E.*

In Paphos, Cyprus, Paul met with early success and was able to convert the local governor, Sergius Paulus (Acts 13:12).

Paul probably used this Cardo Maximus to walk from the harbor of Ephesus to the center of town, which would remain his principal base for two years.

On his way to Rome, Paul was shipwrecked along with the crew and other prisoners, and eventually landed in Syracuse, where today remains of a Roman amphitheater can still be seen.

Paul preached in Rome for two years, welcoming all who would come into his rented home. (Acts 28:30-31)

Paul wrote the epistles of Ephesians, Colossians, II Timothy, Philemon, and most likely Philippians in Rome.

Paul preached in the synagogue, some Jews stirred up a mob, wh[o] rioted. Paul and Silas left for Be[rea] (Acts 17:1-9)

Paul wrote the epistles of II Corinthians and I Timothy in Macedonia.

Buffeted by a storm, Paul was shipwrecked along with the crew and other prisoners. (Acts 27:27-44)

Paul wrote the epist[les] Romans and I an[d II] Thessalonians in Co[rinth]

PAUL'S MISSIONARY JOURNEYS

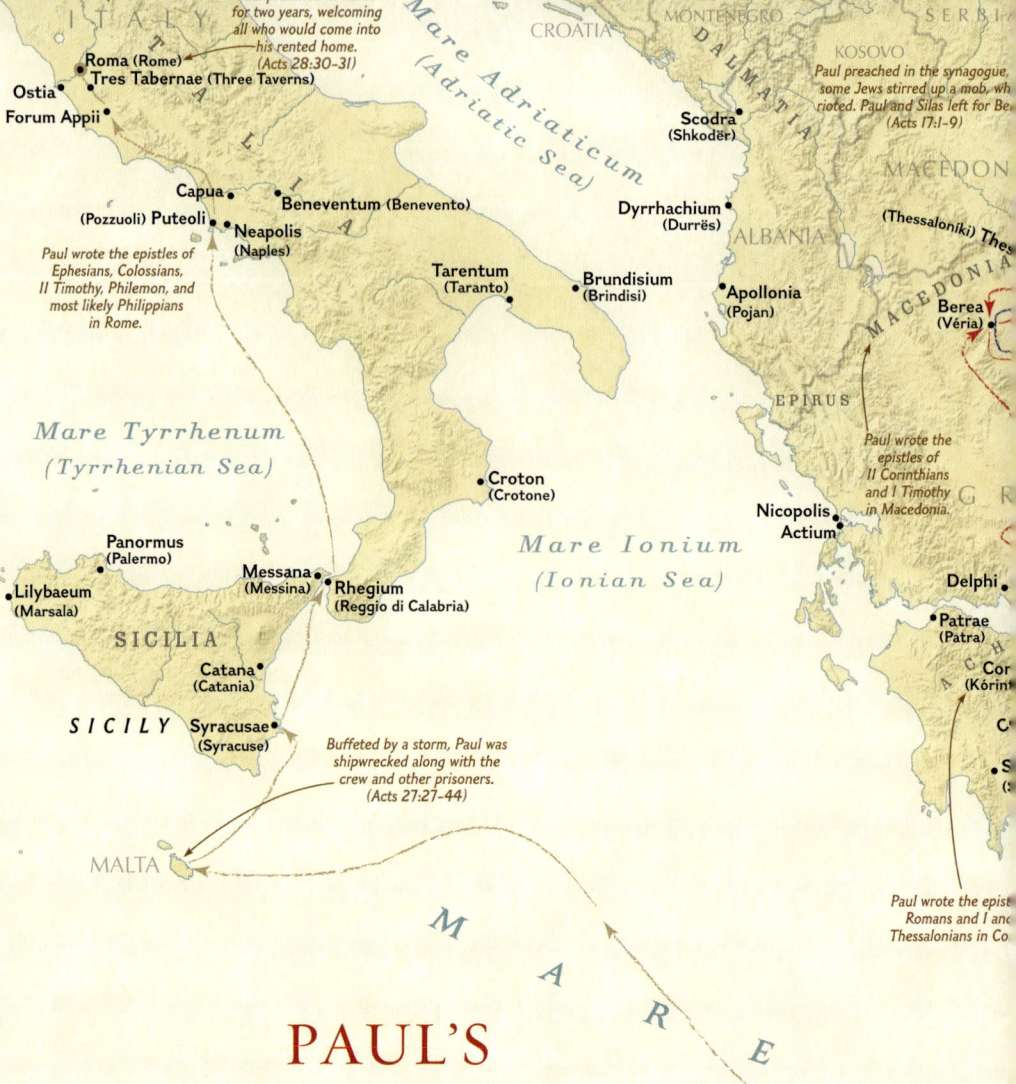

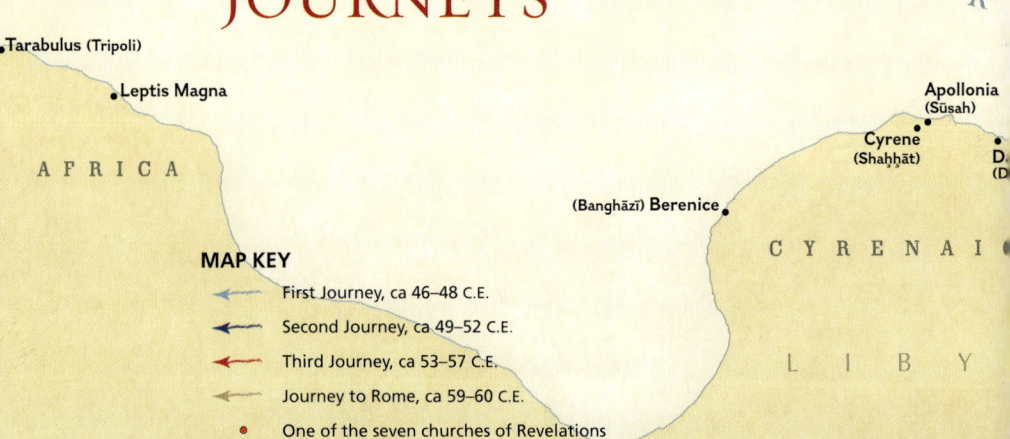

MAP KEY

- First Journey, ca 46–48 C.E.
- Second Journey, ca 49–52 C.E.
- Third Journey, ca 53–57 C.E.
- Journey to Rome, ca 59–60 C.E.
- • One of the seven churches of Revelations

0   50   100   150   200   250 kilometers
0   50   100   150   200   250 miles

Present-day drainage, coastlines, and country boundaries are represented. Modern names appear in parentheses.

Map: Paul's Missionary Journeys

Bodies of water and regions:
- PONTUS EUXINUS (BLACK SEA)
- Mare Aegaeum (Aegean Sea)
- Mare Creticum (Sea of Crete)
- Mare Internum (Mediterranean Sea)
- Lacus Tiberias (Sea of Galilee)
- Lacus Asphaltitis (Dead Sea)
- Hellespont (Dardanelles)
- Bosporus
- Nilus (Nile)
- Sangarius, Halys, Maeander, Hermus, Euphrates (rivers)

Regions: BULGARIA, THRACIA, TURKEY, ANATOLIA (ASIA MINOR), BITHYNIA, PONTUS, PHRYGIA, GALATIA, CAPPADOCIA, COMMAGENE, PISIDIA, LYCAONIA, PAMPHYLIA, LYCIA, CILICIA, ASIA, SYRIA, PHOENICIA, ABILENE, LEBANON, ISRAEL, JUDAEA, JORDAN, NABATAEA, SAUDI ARABIA, SINAI, EGYPT (AEGYPTUS), CYPRUS, CRETA, Cyclades

Cities (with modern names in parentheses):
- Philippopolis (Plovdiv)
- Neapolis (Kavála)
- Abdera
- Amphipolis (Anfípoli)
- Philippi
- Thásos, Samothrace, Imbros, Lemnos
- Byzantium (İstanbul)
- Perinthus (Marmaraereğlisi)
- Chalcedon (Kadıköy)
- Nicomedia (Kocaeli)
- Heraclea Pontica (Ereğli)
- Amastris (Amasra)
- Sinope (Sinop)
- Amisus (Samsun)
- Amaseia (Amasya)
- Cyzicus
- Lampsacus (Lâpseki)
- Alexandria Troas
- Assos
- Adramyttium (Edremit)
- Lesbos, (Mitilíni) Mytilene
- Pergamum (Bergama)
- Thyatira (Akhisar)
- Sardis
- Philadelphia (Alaşehir)
- Smyrna (İzmir)
- Ephesus
- Chios (Híos)
- Ándros
- Sámos
- Miletus
- Laodicea (Denizli)
- Colossae (Honaz)
- Apamea (Dinar)
- Pisidian Antioch (Yalvaç)
- Iconium (Konya)
- Tyana
- Archelais (Aksaray)
- Ancyra (Ankara)
- Gordium (Gordion)
- Caesarea Cappadociae (Kayseri)
- Melitene (Malatya)
- Samosata (Samsat)
- Edessa (Şanlıurfa)
- Zeugma
- Aleppo (Halab)
- Lystra, Derbe
- Portae Ciliciae (Cilician Gates)
- Tarsus
- Issus
- Alexandria ad Issum (İskenderun)
- Antiochia (Antioch)
- Seleucia Pieria (Samandağ)
- Seleucia Tracheotis (Silifke)
- Attaleia (Antalya)
- Perga, Side
- Halicarnassus (Bodrum)
- Cos, Cnidus, Rhodes
- Patara, Myra (Kale)
- Santorini, Náxos
- Cnossus (Knosós), Gortyn, Lasea, Fair Havens
- Cape Salmone (Akrotírio Pláka)
- Paphos (Kouklia), Salamis
- Tripolis (Tripoli), Byblos (Jbail)
- Sidon (Saïda), Tyre (Soûr), Ptolemais ('Akko)
- Damascus
- Caesarea, Antipatris
- Neapolis (Nablus)
- Jerusalem, Gaza
- Bostra (Buṣra ash Shām)
- Petra, Aelana (Al 'Aqabah)
- Alexandria (El Iskandarîya)
- Paraetonium (Maṭrûḥ)
- Daphnae (Kôm Dafana)
- Terenuthis, Heliopolis, Memphis, Pelusium

Annotations:

Philippopolis: Paul and Silas were thrown into prison after they cast an evil spirit out of a slave girl, costing her owners her abilities. They were miraculously freed by an earthquake. (Acts 16:16–40)

Alexandria Troas: After a night vision of a man from Macedonia begging him for help, Paul left for the region to preach there. (Acts 16:9–10)

Ephesus: Paul wrote the epistles of 1 Corinthians and possibly Titus in Ephesus.

Ephesus: Home of a great temple to Artemis (Diana), a riot ensued when Paul preached against idols. (Acts 19:23–41)

Lystra: The son of a Jewish woman and a Greek man, Timothy joined Paul on his second journey. (Acts 16:1–3)

Lystra area: After preaching and healing, Paul was stoned by a crowd stirred up by hostile Jews and left for dead outside the city. He returned to continue the ministry. (Acts 14:8–20)

Tarsus: Paul's (Saul) home city. He was a Pharisee who persecuted the church before he was converted. (Acts 9:11, Philippians 3:5–6)

Antioch: A strong bastion of early Christianity, Antioch sponsored all three of Paul's journeys. (Acts 13:3, 15:40, 18:22–23)

Antioch: Disciples of Jesus Christ were first called "Christians" in Antioch. (Acts 11:26)

Damascus: On his way to imprison Christians in Damascus, Saul (renamed Paul) was converted after a miraculous encounter with Christ. (Acts 9:1–19)

Paphos: Paul rebuked a false prophet named Bar-jesus before the Roman proconsul. The pretender was struck with blindness, and the proconsul was converted. (Acts 13:6–12)

Jerusalem: Peter, Paul, and Barnabus met with other Christian leaders to repudiate a sect who said that new Gentile converts needed to obey the Law of Moses. In unity, they agreed that salvation was by faith in Christ alone, no works of the Law were required. (Acts 15:1–21)

Athens area: Reasoning with the philosophers... Areopagus... were converted. (Acts 17:20–34)

OFF TO ROME: After returning to Jerusalem on completion of his third mission, Paul was imprisoned after the Jews accused him of inciting riots. Tried before the Roman authorities and King Agrippa, he appealed his case to Caesar as was the right of any Roman citizen. (Acts 21–26)

PART III | THE LEGACY OF JESUS

paralyzed or lame were cured." As a result, says Acts, "there was great joy in that city." (Acts 8:7-8) The success of his work in Samaria was received with great joy, and it prompted a visit by Peter and John.

Next, Philip turned southwestward toward the Mediterranean coast, traveling from Jerusalem through the Shephelah hills in the direction of Gaza. Along the way, he made another astonishing conversion: He baptized a high official from the court of Candace, Queen of Ethiopia, who was in charge of her treasury. According to Acts, the "Spirit of the Lord" then sent him to Azotus (today's Ashdod). From there, Philip turned north, moving up the coast while passing through "all the towns until he came to Caesarea," which became his base of operations (Acts 8:40). Here, he nurtured a growing Christian community while raising four daughters, each of whom "had the gift of prophecy." (Acts 21:9)

Peter, meanwhile, went south from Samaria to Lydda, which was located close to today's Lod, some nine miles from the coast. Here, he healed a man named Aeneas, who had been paralyzed for eight years (Acts 8:34). According to Josephus, the town of Lydda would be razed to the ground some 30 years later, after the outbreak of the Jewish rebellion. Not far from Lydda was Joppa, today's Jaffa. Joppa was one of the oldest cities in Palestine, whose harbor had been in almost continuous use since the second millennium B.C.E. Here lived a woman named Tabitha, a disciple, who fell ill and died. Since the local community had heard of Peter's presence in Lydda, two disciples went over there to bring him back to Joppa. Peter agreed, and he brought Tabitha back to life, in a close parallel to Jesus' miraculous resuscitation of Jairus's daughter (Acts 9:40). Peter then decided to stay in Joppa for a period of time, enjoying the hospitality of a man named Simon, who was a tanner. Joppa, too, would suffer heavily in the coming Jewish War; Josephus tells us that some 8,400 inhabitants were killed in the Roman reprisals led by the Roman governor, Cestius Gallus.

On the Road to Damascus

In the meantime, Paul (or Saul as Acts calls him at this point in the story) had requested permission to extend his persecution activities to Damascus. According to Acts, Saul was "still breathing threats and murder against the disciples" and was keen to find "any who belonged to the Way, men or women," and bring them bound to Jerusalem (Acts 9:2). Damascus had long formed part of the Decapolis, as part of Roman Syria, but in 37 C.E. (around the putative date of Saul's journey to the city) the Roman emperor Caligula transferred control of the city to Nabatea, the kingdom ruled by Rome's faithful vassal King Aretas IV. This was quite possibly the same king whose daughter had been married to Herod Antipas, tetrarch of Galilee. Acts indicates that there were several synagogues in the city.

Saul's wish was granted, but as he set out on his voyage, something extraordinary happened. Riding on the road to Damascus, "a light from heaven flashed

The First Christians

around him." He fell to the ground and heard a voice saying, "Saul, why do you persecute me?" (Acts 9:4) Saul got up and, unable to see, was led to Damascus, where a disciple named Ananias had been told in a vision to go and look after him. As soon as Ananias laid his hands on Saul, "something like scales fell from his eyes." (Acts 9:18) Saul, now renamed Paul, was baptized, and "immediately began to proclaim Jesus in the synagogues." Those who knew Saul's original purpose for coming to Damascus were stunned. The man who had vowed to destroy the followers of Jesus was now proclaiming that "Jesus was the Messiah." Paul was placed under constant surveillance lest he escape the gates of Damascus by night, and a plot was hatched to kill him. But, says Acts, his disciples "let him down through an opening in the wall, lowering him in a basket." (Acts 9:25)

A similar reception awaited Paul in Jerusalem. Acts asserts that when he was introduced to the Apostles, many followers remained deeply suspicious, for fear that Paul's conversion was really an infiltration attempt. The Hellenists even attempted to kill him (Acts 9:26-29). Paul had no choice but to leave Jerusalem and return to his hometown of Tarsus. The tension between him and the Apostles would cast a long shadow over the growth of early Christianity.

Paul and Barnabas

In his letter to the Galatians, Paul offers a different chronology of these events. As soon as God called him, he claims, "I did not confer with any human being, nor did I go up to Jerusalem to those who were already Apostles before me." Instead, he "went away at once into Arabia," perhaps to collect his thoughts—an episode that may serve as a parallel of Jesus' 40 days in the desert, prior to launching his ministry (Galatians 1:17). "Arabia" probably refers to the Nabatean kingdom, to whose sovereignty Damascus had recently been transferred, which lay at the very rim of the Arabian Desert. Paul says it was only after this sojourn, an interval of "three years," that he finally decided to go to Jerusalem, where he visited Cephas—Peter—and stayed with him for 15 days. Paul also claims that he saw no other Apostle "except James the Lord's brother," who was the head of the Jerusalem group. He then returned to his native city of Tarsus in Cilicia.

Michelangelo Caravaggio (1571–1610) painted this canvas of "The Conversion on the Way to Damascus" in 1601.

This head of the emperor Gaius (opposite), nicknamed Caligula, was found in Asia Minor and probably dates from 40 C.E.

PART III | THE LEGACY OF JESUS

Perga on the Pamphylian coast, which Paul visited on his first journey to Asia Minor, still has impressive remains of a vast Roman bath complex.

During his first missionary journey, Paul visited Paphos on Cyprus (opposite), the native region of his companion Barnabas.

In the meantime, a number of the Hellenists who had scattered after Stephen's death had settled in Antioch, the capital of Roman Syria and residence of the Roman governor. Among the city's cosmopolitan population, which included a sizeable Jewish community, the refugees from Jerusalem were delighted to find many like-minded spirits. In due course, says, Acts, "a great number became believers and turned to the Lord." (Acts 11:21)

News of this exciting development soon reached Jerusalem. It was decided that one of the disciples should go and investigate. The choice fell on a Jewish man from Cyprus named Joseph, who had sold all his goods and donated the proceeds to the Jerusalem church. The disciples had welcomed him in their midst and renamed him Barnabas (an Aramaic name that means "son of the prophet"). Barnabas duly traveled to Antioch and found that the reports were true; "a great many people were brought to the Lord." (Acts 11:24) According to Acts, it was the people of Antioch who first coined the term "Christians" to identify the disciples of Jesus (Acts 11:26).

Apparently, Barnabas was so overwhelmed by interest in the movement that he reached out for help. Jerusalem was obviously very far away, but Tarsus in Cilicia, Paul's hometown, was much closer. What's more, Barnabas knew Paul; according to Acts, it was Barnabas who had introduced Paul to the Apostles during his brief visit to Jerusalem. Barnabas thereupon decided to travel to Tarsus and ask Paul to join him in Antioch. Paul agreed, and together they returned to Antioch. Thus began Paul's long and pivotal campaign to convert the people around the Aegean Sea to the church of Christ.

The Conversion of Gentiles

Paul and Barnabas stayed in Antioch for a year, and in the process forged a partnership that would soon lead to the first of their missionary journeys. They also made an interesting discovery: There were many Gentiles who were interested in becoming disciples as well.

The idea of accepting a Gentile, while extraordinary, was not entirely without precedent. The Book of Acts is careful to point out that it was Peter, not Paul, who baptized the first Gentile—a centurion named Cornelius, who commanded a Roman cohort in Caesarea. At first glance, this would seem to be an obvious conflict. Jews generally abstained from close contact with Gentiles, for they did not honor the purity laws, particularly with regard to kosher food and drink. Second, Jesus himself had always stayed far from Gentile cities, focusing his ministry on "the lost sheep of Israel." Acts, however, solved the question by reporting a strange vision. While still in Joppa, staying in the house of Simon the Tanner, Peter had fallen into a trance. He saw a large sheet

The First Christians

being lowered with various unclean animals, while a voice said, "What God has made clean, you must not call profane." (Acts 10:10-15) Peter then understood that there was no longer a prohibition against the conversion of Gentiles. At that moment, several men arrived with a request for Peter to visit Cornelius in Caesarea. Peter accepted and traveled back with them.

Upon entering the centurion's house, Peter said, "You yourselves know that it is unlawful for a Jew to associate with or to visit a Gentile; but God has shown me that I should not call anyone profane or unclean." (Acts 10:28) Cornelius and those with him were subsequently baptized. Nevertheless, the practical consequences of inviting large numbers of Gentiles to join the early Christian movement were not yet properly understood.

> SO, BEING SENT OUT BY THE HOLY SPIRIT, THEY WENT DOWN TO SELEUCIA; AND FROM THERE THEY SAILED TO CYPRUS.
>
> ACTS OF THE APOSTLES 11:25
> *Circa 75-90 C.E.*

Paul's First Missionary Journey

During the next 14 years, Paul would embark on three major campaigns to bring the Gospel to communities throughout the eastern empire. His first journey,

Upon his arrival in Athens, Paul preached on a hill known as the Areopagus (foreground), from where his listeners had an impressive view of the ancient Acropolis.

These tempera panels (opposite), painted by the Italian artist Bicci di Lorenzo (1375–1452), depict the Apostles Peter and Paul.

accompanied by Barnabas and the disciple John Mark, took him to Cyprus, Barnabas's native region, where he preached in synagogues from Salamis to the capital of Paphos. This first mission met with success; Paul was even able to convert the Roman proconsul, Sergius Paulus (Acts 13:12). Paul and Barnabas then continued to Asia Minor, landing in Perga on the Pamphylian coast, while John Mark returned to Jerusalem. From there, Paul and Barnabas traveled to another city, also called Antioch, though located in Pisidia. Here they met with fierce opposition from the local Jewish community. In response, they diverted to Iconium in Roman Lycaonia, only to be rebuffed once more. Rumors of a plot to kill them propelled the travelers to Lystra, where Paul healed a lame person. In response, the crowd shouted, "The gods have come down to us in human form!" (Acts 14:10-11) The local Jewish community rose in anger and tried to stone Paul. The travelers then moved on to Derbe, a town that proved to be more receptive to their preaching. At last, having recovered from their travails, Paul and Barnabas retraced their steps to Perga, where they embarked for their home base in Antioch on the Orontes in Syria.

The First Christians

In the process, Paul developed a comprehensive theological foundation that sought to explain what it meant to be a disciple of Jesus, and how followers should apply their faith to the questions and practices of everyday life. He had never known Jesus in the flesh, but as a Pharisee, schooled in debating the issues of the Law, he was uniquely qualified for the task. What's more, he felt guided by Jesus' spirit; as he later wrote, "We have the mind of Christ." (I Corinthians 2:16)

During his journeys, Paul found that many Gentiles were attracted to the simple nobility of a religion that recognized but one God; a truly *merciful* God, moreover, who cared for his people, unlike the gods of Roman mythology. Throughout the empire there were thousands of men and women, both freedman and slaves, who yearned for an end to the senseless divisions and injustice of the Roman world. They were attracted to the joyous teachings of a man who preached that the righteous would find ultimate salvation in heaven—and performed miracles to prove it. The Roman world was ripe for a new form of spirituality, a *true* spirituality, rather than the Roman imperial cult that anointed each emperor a god upon his death.

Paul, however, also recognized that there was a significant deterrent for many Gentiles, and that was the practice of the Law. If a Gentile was to be baptized, was he also expected to behave as a Jew? Should he abide by the Jewish Law? Should his food be kosher—an important question, particularly since table fellowship, the early Eucharist, was such a key feature of the early church? And last, was he expected to be circumcised as well?

The original Apostles, who remained practicing Jews, responded yes. For them, faith in Jesus was inseparable from Jesus' own example as a rabbi. But Paul felt otherwise. He believed that the Jewish rite of circumcision had now been replaced by baptism and faith in Christ. "Real circumcision is a matter of the heart," he wrote; "it is spiritual, not literal." (Romans 2:29) Consequently, "a person is justified not by the works of the Law but through faith in Jesus Christ." (Galatians 2:16) In the process, Paul unmoored the early apostolic movement from its Jewish roots, making it more open to the influx of Gentiles—thus laying the foundation for Christianity as we know it.

Though he never met Jesus himself, Paul argued that his "gospel" was nevertheless inspired by Christ himself; "[it] is not of human origin," he told the Galatians, for "I received it through a revelation of Jesus Christ." (Galatians 1:12)

The Jerusalem Conference

Eventually, news of Paul's activity filtered back to Jerusalem and was met with alarm. While the Apostles had no objection in principle against evangelizing

PART III | THE LEGACY OF JESUS

among the Gentiles, they felt strongly that "unless you are circumcised according to the custom of Moses, you cannot be saved." (Acts 15:1) Paul and Barnabas were asked to explain themselves. The opportunity for such a visit came about after a terrible famine in Judea, which is also described in the books by Josephus. According to Acts, Paul was asked to bring desperately needed relief from Antioch (Acts 11:27-30). In his letters, however, Paul says that the purpose of the visit was to defend his work among the Gentiles (Galatians 2:1-10). Scholars believe that this momentous conference took place sometime between 45 and 48 C.E.

Paul presented his case, knowing full well that the Jerusalem church was foundering under the relentless pressure of persecution, whereas Paul's Christian communities in Asia Minor were experiencing rapid growth. It came down to a simple question: Could a Gentile be baptized if his faith in Jesus was true, regardless of the need to observe the Law and Jewish customs such as circumcision? Paul's answer was yes. As he wrote in his letter to the Romans, "Is [God] not the God of Gentiles also?" (Romans 3:29)

James and the Apostles were not so easily persuaded. Even Peter, who previously "used to eat with the Gentiles," had a change of heart—"for fear of the circumcision faction," Paul says bitterly (Galatians 2:12). And so, the Jerusalem Conference ended in a compromise. Paul could minister to the Jews and Gentiles of Syria and Asia Minor, but James and his followers would preach among the circumcised. The only condition that James placed on Gentile converts was that they abstain from idolatry and illicit sexual activity, and pledged not to eat any meat of an animal that has been strangled or still contained any blood (Acts 15:20). These were the same regulations that Leviticus had imposed on foreigners living on Israel's soil (Leviticus 17:10). Therefore, this compromise retained some observance of the Law while releasing Gentiles from the need to become practicing Jews as part of their baptism.

Though heavily destroyed, Corinth was rebuilt by Julius Caesar and prospered as one of Greece's leading cities while Paul stayed here during his second missionary journey.

"St. Paul Writing His Epistle" (opposite) was painted by French artist Valentin de Boulogne (1591–1632) in 1620.

Paul's Second Missionary Journey

Encouraged by the outcome of the Jerusalem Conference, Paul soon left on a second, even more ambitious journey. This time, he was accompanied by the disciple Silas. Barnabas and Paul had argued over the question whether John Mark should go with them. Paul said no, after which Barnabas took John Mark to Cyprus, while Paul and Silas left for the long journey overland to Derbe, Lystra, and Antioch-in-Pisidia. The initial purpose of this second visit was to strengthen the Christian communities that Paul and Barnabas had founded on their first journey—including certain communities that Paul would later address in his "letter to the Galatians." In Lystra he was joined by a disciple named Timothy, who would become one of his most devoted assistants (Timothy 1:1-8).

Paul's original plan was to proceed to the western part of Asia Minor (today's western Turkey), but a vision took him from Troas across the Aegean Sea to the port of Neapolis in Macedonia. This is where the narrative in the Book of Acts changes from the third to the first person ("we immediately tried to cross over to Macedonia"), which some scholars believe may suggest that Luke, the presumed author of the Book of Acts as well as the Gospel of Luke, joined Paul at this point in the journey (Acts 16:10).

Paul and his companions then continued along the Via Egnatia, one of the main military highways built by Rome throughout the empire. Traveling across the Greek mainland, he made his first convert in Philippi—a woman called

PART III | THE LEGACY OF JESUS

In 130 C.E., Tiberius Iulius Aquila built this "Library of Celsus" in Ephesus to honor his deceased father, given that building tombs within the city was prohibited.

Lydia—and eventually reached Thessalonica. Here, his preaching appeared to be successful, until a mob forced him to flee to the city of Beroea. Here, too, he began to gather converts until he was once again denounced by Jewish protestors, many of whom had hurried down from Thessalonica (Acts 17:5-10). Despite these setbacks, Paul was able to establish several Christian communities, whom he charged with the task of carrying the Gospel farther inland (I Thessalonians 1:8).

Paul then continued on to Athens, where he engaged Epicurean and Stoic philosophers in a debate on the Agora, the central marketplace—the same place where Socrates and Plato had once taught. He also preached to Athenians on a hill known as the Areopagus. Here, he referred to an altar that he had found in the city, dedicated "to an unknown God." "What therefore you worship as unknown," Paul said, "this I proclaim to you now." (Acts 17:23) Some of the listeners scoffed, while others "joined him and became believers." (Acts 17:34)

> AND WHEN CAESAR WAS INFORMED THAT AGRIPPA WAS DEAD, HE WAS SORRY FOR THE NEWS. ACCORDINGLY HE SENT CUSPIUS FADUS TO BE PROCURATOR OF JUDEA.
>
> JOSEPHUS, *ANTIQUITIES OF THE JEWS*
> Circa 95 C.E.

From Athens Paul traveled on to Corinth, where he remained for 18 months—an exceptionally long time, which may reflect Paul's belief that Corinth could become a major Christian center. At the time, Corinth was the capital of Roman-occupied Greece, known as Achaia, which included the Peleponnese, Central Greece, and a part of Thessaly. As such it had become a leading commercial and administrative center of the Roman Empire. Based on his later letters to the Corinthians (I and II), written from about 54 C.E. onward, the Christian congregation in Corinth was mostly Gentile and featured people from across the city's social stratum.

According to Acts, a group of Jews then brought Paul before a tribunal, accusing him of "persuading people to worship God in ways that are contrary to the law." The presiding judge named Gallio, "proconsul of Achaia," dismissed the charge, given that it was not pertinent to Roman law (Acts 18:12-17). As Bart Ehrman has argued, Rome was a polytheistic culture and tolerant of a wide variety of cults, provided these did not negate the Roman religion proper; it therefore expected its subject peoples to tolerate other faith traditions as well. The mention of proconsul Gallio in Acts is very fortunate, for archaeologists found an inscription in the Greek city of Delphi with a reference to a governor named "L. Iunius Gallio" from 52 C.E., which has helped scholars to date Paul's journeys.

OTHER CHRISTIAN MOVEMENTS

Paul eventually made his way back to Asia Minor, landing at Ephesus. All along the way, he established new communities dedicated to *Christos*. Some of these were Jewish; others were Gentile. While on the road, Paul sought to provide these congregations with ongoing guidance in the form of pastoral letters. These Epistles, which are the oldest Christian texts still extant today, reminded the early Christians how

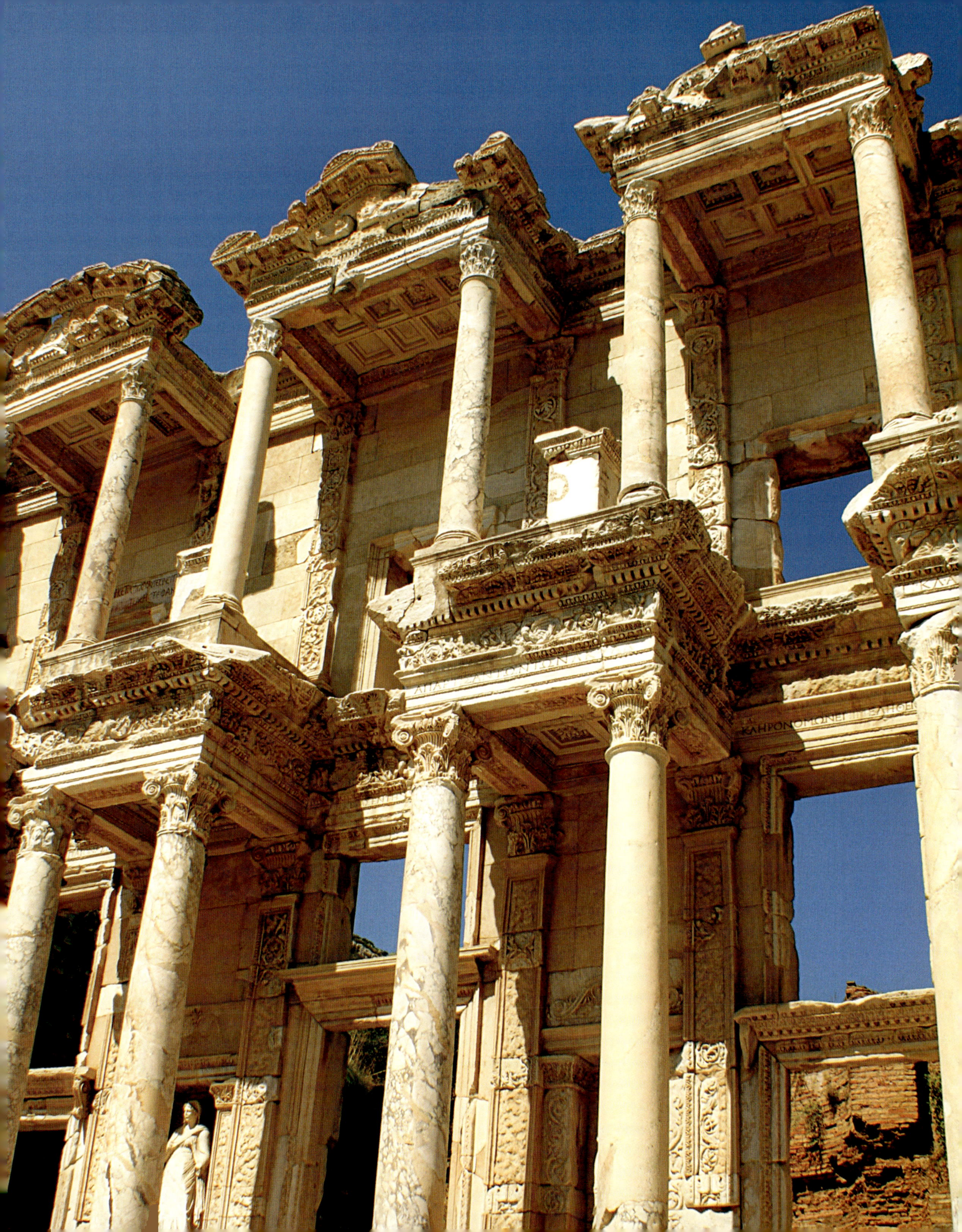

PART III | THE LEGACY OF JESUS

THE PERSECUTIONS IN ROME

After the Great Fire of Rome devastated the city in 64, Nero decided to blame the Christians. As the Roman historian Tacitus writes, "Nero fastened the guilt . . . on a class hated for their abominations, called Christians [Chrestians] by the populace." The historian then describes, in gruesome detail, the grotesque methods of execution. "Some, dressed in the skin of wild animals, were torn to pieces by dogs," Tacitus writes; "others were crucified, or made into torches that were ignited after dark so as to function as lanterns. Nero provided his Gardens for the spectacle, and staged displays in the Circus." Nero's Gardens were probably located on the Palatine Hill, where the emperor later built his famous Domus Aurea or Golden House. The property had once been owned by Maecenas, whose wealth was legendary. Traditionally, the Circus was thought to refer to the Coliseum (properly known as the Flavian amphitheater), but this arena wasn't built until some ten years after the fire—not by Nero but by Emperor Vespasian. Tacitus probably meant the Circus Maximus, one of Rome's largest entertainment venues. Built before the time of Julius Caesar, in the days of the Republic, it boasted a track of some 550 yards often used for chariot racing. Indeed, shortly after the fire, Nero extended the racetrack by about 100 yards.

The interior of the Colosseum in Rome, originally called the Flavian Amphitheater, was commissioned by Emperor Vespasian in 72 C.E. to accommodate up to 50,000 spectators.

men and women should live in the imitation of Christ, and what practical deeds were required to ensure that they would enter the Kingdom of God. Many times, Paul would find that the initial enthusiasm of a particular community had waned, or that they had fallen victim to other Christian influences. This is why Paul's letters sometimes carry a strident tone, reproaching one community for its lack of faith or submission to "false prophets." "Keep an eye on those who cause dissensions and offenses, in opposition to the teaching that you have learned," Paul urged the Roman community; "avoid them." (Romans 16:17) To the Galatians, he wrote, "There are some who are confusing you and want to pervert the gospel of Christ." (Galatians 1:7) Likewise, the Epistle of II Peter, probably written in the late first century C.E., warned its readers that "there were also false prophets among the people, just as there will be false teachers among you." (II Peter 2:1)

These references appear to acknowledge that a number of other Christianities were emerging within the Roman Empire, outside of the control of either the Jerusalem church or Paul's communities in Greece and Asia Minor. Apparently, the various oral traditions that were circulating about Jesus had prompted Christian movements with a different interpretation of his ministry, many of which continued well into the second century C.E. As we saw earlier, some of these communities rejected Paul's acceptance of Gentiles and remained steadfast in their Jewish practice, whereas others were so-called Gnostic Christians. Recent research has shown that even within these Gnostic movements there were a number of divergent ideologies. Some, such as the Docetists, believed that Jesus' physical presence had been an illusion and that, by contrast, he had always been a divine being; others, such as the Ebionites, held that Jesus had always been a mere mortal. Some sought to reconcile the Pauline duality of matter and spirit with Plato's teachings. Others did not subscribe to the resurrection theology and believed that Jesus should be remembered for his teachings, rather than his death on the cross. A later movement known as Marcionism, initiated by a wealthy individual named Marcion (ca 85–160 C.E.) from Sinope (today's Sinop in Turkey), rejected both Jewish Scripture and Jewish practice. Meanwhile, the Ebionites—who may have been an offshoot of the Jerusalem church and eventually wound up in the Transjordan—remained fervently true to their Jewish roots.

As the rivalry between these groups increased, some began to produce their own Gospel documents, often attributed to a noted Apostle so as to bolster their authenticity. Thus we know of a Gospel of Philip, and the aforementioned Gospels of Thomas, Peter, and Mary. Many of these Gospels do not refer to the Crucifixion and resurrection, preferring to focus on the light of divine spirituality that Jesus urged his followers to discern within themselves. A Gnostic sage named Tatian "the Assyrian" (ca 120–180 C.E.) went as far as to create a single Gospel, known as the *Diatessaron,* which claimed to "harmonize" Mark, Matthew, Luke, and John into one narrative.

The Roman emperor Claudius, who ruled from 41 to 54 C.E., turned Judea back into a Roman province upon the death of King Agrippa in 44 C.E.

PART III | **THE LEGACY OF JESUS**

The French classicist artist Hubert Robert (1733–1808) painted this canvas of "The Great Fire of Rome."

The Ionic Stoa on the Sacred Way (opposite) was the center of Miletus when Paul arrived here on his third missionary journey.

In later years, as the church slowly emerged as the dominant form of Christianity (possibly due to its strict hierarchical discipline, as Elaine Pagels has argued), all the followers of these other Christian sects would be branded as heretics. Even then, these Christian movements continued to vex the Mother Church, for the Greek mind could not resist debating the paradox of the corporeal and spiritual, of the mortal and the divine duality of Jesus.

THE REIGNS OF CALIGULA AND CLAUDIUS

In the meantime, Judea had undergone some major political changes. Emperor Gaius (nicknamed Caligula), Tiberius's successor who ruled from 37 to 41 C.E., favored a policy of ruling the empire through vassal kings, rather than Roman governors. He installed a friend of his, a grandson of Herod the Great named Herod Agrippa, as ruler over Philip's former territory of the Gaulanitis. After Caligula deposed Herod Antipas, ruler of Galilee, in 39 C.E., his territory of Galilee and Perea were added to Agrippa's domain. Caligula then became quite insane, possibly as a result of a severe illness. He declared himself a living god and insisted that a statue of himself be installed in the Second Temple in Jerusalem.

The First Christians

Agrippa sought to dissuade Caligula of this decree, warning that such an act was sure to incite a rebellion. Caligula's assassination in 41 C.E. ended the crisis and brought a more rational emperor to the throne, named Claudius (10 B.C.E.–54 C.E.). Claudius extended Agrippa's territory by adding Judea, Samaria, and Idumea. Hence, for a brief time, Herod Agrippa ruled over a territory that was roughly the size of the kingdom of his illustrious grandfather. According to Acts, it was King Agrippa who ordered one of the Jerusalem Apostles, James the son of Zebedee, to be put to the sword—apparently, in order to curry favor with the local population (Acts 12:1-3).

Agrippa died shortly thereafter in Caesarea in 44 C.E. Since his son and heir, Marcus Julius Agrippa II, was only 17 years old, Claudius decided to turn Judea back into a Roman province governed by a Roman procurator, beginning with Cuspius Fadus (r. 44–46 C.E.). Eventually, Agrippa II was given control over a number of smaller territories, including Philip's old tetrarchy, which was later expanded with Antipas's former realm of Galilee and Perea.

Elsewhere, however, Claudius's policies toward Judaism were ambivalent. On the other hand, he reaffirmed the special rights and privileges accorded to Jews throughout the empire by Augustus—such as dispensation from the need to sacrifice to the statue of the ruling emperor. But as a devout believer in Rome's ancient religion, he worried about the growing popularity of "eastern mysteries" in the city of Rome proper. When, as the Roman historian Suetonius wrote, it was determined that "the Jews were constantly causing *disturbances* at the instigation of Christ" (Chrestus), Claudius decided to evict all Jews living in Rome—regardless of whether they were Christian or not. This edict, issued in 49 C.E., had little effect, for soon thereafter many Jewish families began to drift back. Among these families were early Christians who apparently had embraced Jesus as the Messiah long before Paul landed on their shores.

Paul's Third Missionary Journey

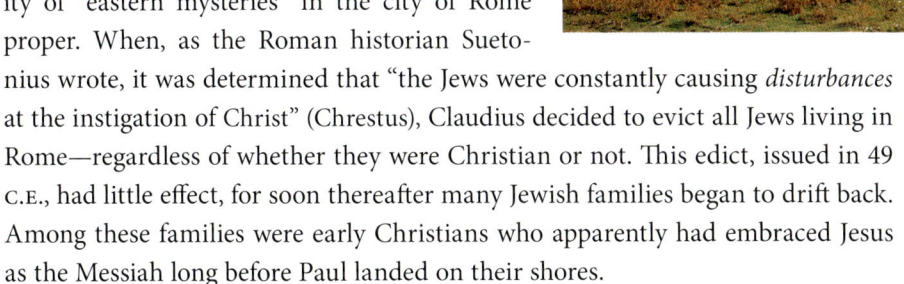

Paul, meanwhile, had embarked on a third journey, probably around 54 C.E. He stayed in Ephesus, before returning to Corinth for a sojourn that may have lasted until 56 C.E. In his letter to the Romans, written in Corinth, Paul refers to "Erastus, the city treasurer" who may be the same official who is listed on a first-century limestone fragment, found in Corinth in 1929 (Romans 16:23). He then

PART III | **THE LEGACY OF JESUS**

Michelangelo Caravaggio (1571–1610) painted this canvas of "The Crucifixion of St. Peter" in 1601.

traveled to Jerusalem, where he was arrested for allegedly taking a Gentile past the *soreg*, the sacred enclosure surrounding the Temple precinct (Acts 21:26-30). Paul was remanded in Caesarea, but the chief priests in Jerusalem insisted that he stand trial before the Sanhedrin. As a Roman citizen, however, Paul insisted on a hearing in front of the "emperor's tribunal" in Rome. The case gained such notoriety that even Agrippa II felt compelled to interrogate him (Acts 25:22). Finally, around 60 C.E., Paul and other prisoners embarked on a ship for Rome. After many misadventures, including being shipwrecked, he made it to the Roman capital where he was placed under house arrest. He then "lived there two whole years at his own expense," but the details of what happened after that are uncertain (Acts 28:30).

Back in Judea, the Roman procurator Cuspius Fadus remained in office for only two years, and none of his successors lasted long either. Porcius Festus, the fourth governor since Fadus, died suddenly in 62 C.E. Judea thus experienced a temporary power vacuum, which is when the high priest Ananus chose to strike a blow against the Jerusalem church. Josephus tells us that Ananus won the Sanhedrin's backing to indict "James, the brother of Jesus known as Christ," leaving us an important attestation of the early apostolic mission in Jerusalem. James was thrown off the Temple parapet and stoned to death. The early Christian movement in Palestine was now without a leader. Within a decade, it would all but cease to exist.

> NERO FASTENED THE GUILT AND INFLICTED THE MOST EXQUISITE TORTURES ON A CLASS HATED FOR THEIR ABOMINATIONS, CALLED CHRISTIANS.
>
> TACITUS,
> THE ANNALS OF IMPERIAL ROME
> *Circa 116 C.E.*

THE PERSECUTIONS IN ROME

Two years later, a great fire swept through Rome. Some Romans suspected that Emperor Nero (r. 54–68 C.E.) had set the fire deliberately so as to realize a new design for the city of Rome. According to the Roman historian Tacitus (ca 56–117 C.E.), Nero decided to place the blame on Rome's Christian communities. Scores of Christians were arrested and executed in the most hideous fashion imaginable. A late first-century letter by Clement I, a Christian prelate in Rome, claims that Peter was swept up in the persecution. According to church legend, Peter was condemned to be crucified, but he insisted that he be crucified upside down, lest he die in the same position as Jesus. Peter was buried in a rural spot on the right bank of the Tiber River, called the Ager Vaticanus.

The Christian theologian Tertullian of Carthage (ca 160–220 C.E.) wrote that Paul was also put to death at this time. According to church tradition, other Apostles likewise died a martyr's death, with the exception of John, son of Zebedee. If that is true, then by 65 C.E., just one year before the outbreak of war in Palestine, all the principal leaders of the early Christian church had been killed. Thus the church—and many other Christian factions as well—were left to face the coming upheaval without the leadership that had sustained them up to this time.

The First Christians

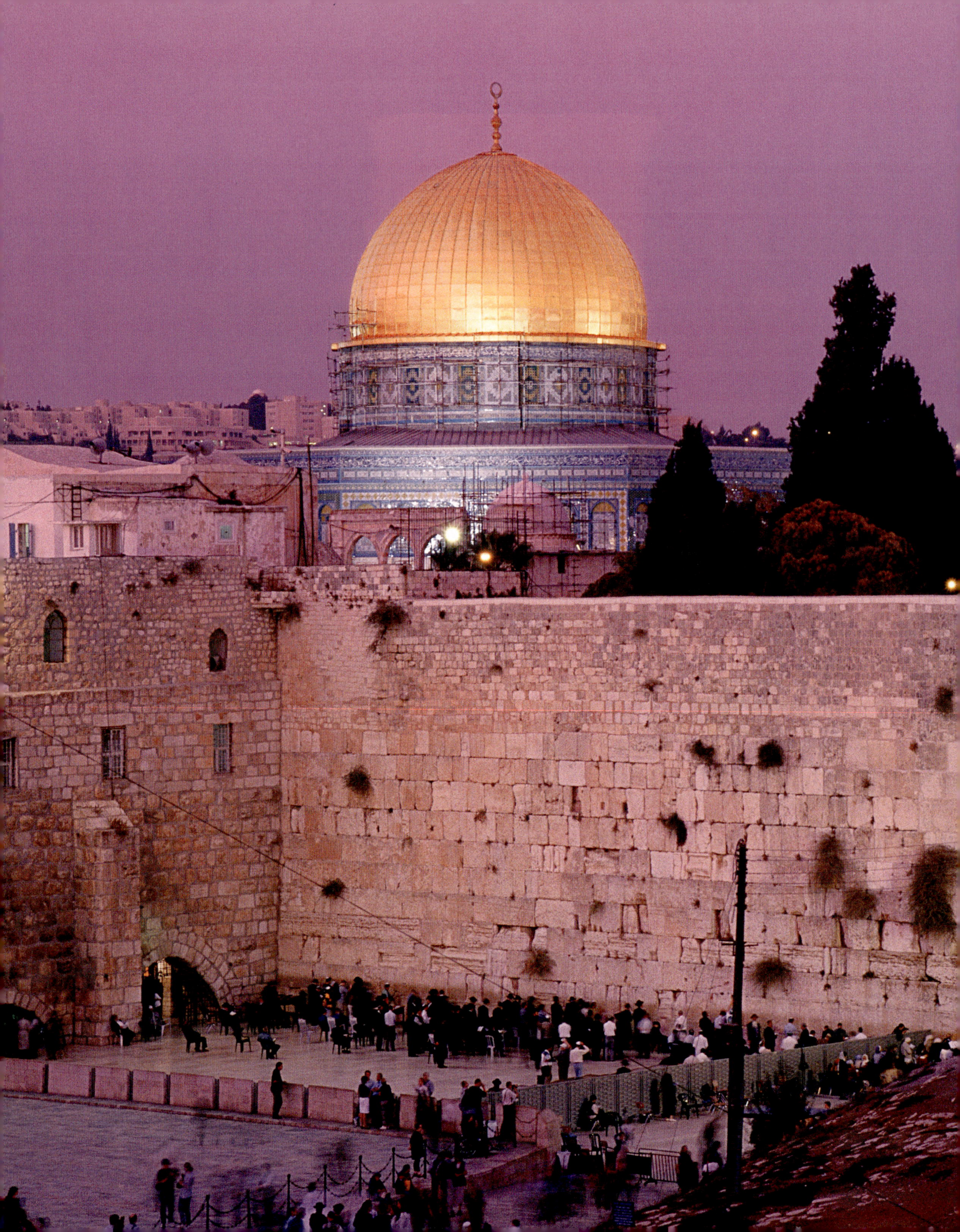

CHAPTER 14

The GROWTH of the CHURCH

[TITUS] CAESAR ORDERED
THE ENTIRE CITY AND
THE TEMPLE SMASHED
TO THE GROUND,
LEAVING ONLY THE TALLEST
OF THE TOWERS STANDING,
AND PART OF
THE WESTERN WALL
TO SHOW TO POSTERITY.

JOSEPHUS, *THE JEWISH WAR*
Circa 95 C.E.

The Dome of the Rock looms over the Western Wall, a Herodian retaining wall that once supported the vast Second Temple complex and is today the holiest site in Judaism.

PART III | **THE LEGACY OF JESUS**

The long-simmering tensions between Romans and Jews finally erupted in 66 C.E., leading to an all-out war of rebellion against the Roman occupation of Palestine. The fuse was lit, according to Josephus, when a Greek was seen sacrificing birds on the doorstep of a synagogue in Caesarea. A scuffle ensued, which led to riots across town as well as in other cities. Eventually, a Jewish delegation petitioned the serving procurator, Gessius Florus, who had been appointed by Emperor Nero. But rather than coming to their aid, Florus threw them in prison. It also transpired that Florus had helped himself to 17 talents from the Temple treasury. This led to massive protests in Jerusalem, which Florus suppressed with his cavalry; as a result, thousands were killed. Jewish rebels then captured the city, prompting many luminaries, including Agrippa II, to flee. Florus appealed to his superior, Governor Cestius Gallus of Syria, for help. Gallus responded by leading his only available legion, the XII Fulminata, together with a force of auxiliaries, into Judea. To the dismay of Rome, however, he was ignominiously defeated in the Beth Horon pass, close to today's West Bank village of Beit Ur al-Fauqa.

The rebels, led by the Zealots, established a "revolutionary government" while mobs tore into the palatial mansions of the high priest Ananias and other chief priests, venting their wrath on these perceived collaborators. Elsewhere, crowds set fire to the archives, which held records of all debts incurred under the Herodian and Roman tax regimes. In the weeks and months that followed, the revolt steadily spread through all of Judea and Palestine.

THE ROMAN REPRISALS

Eventually, Nero was prevailed upon to act. The emperor ordered the dispatch of a large expeditionary force, consisting of the X Fretensis and V Macedonia under the command of General Vespasian, which landed in Ptolemais, today's Acre, in April of 67. There he was joined by his son Titus, who led the 15th Legion, Apollinaris, as well as various other auxiliary forces, thus boosting Vespasian's strength to some 60,000 men. As this vast army moved down to pacify Galilee, fierce debates erupted among the rebels. Some believed the time had come for peace negotiations, while others, led by the Zealots, insisted on continuing the fight to the bitter end. That end came in 70 C.E., after Vespasian had left for Rome to be crowned emperor, and Titus was able to capture the city of Jerusalem following a brutal and protracted siege. The Second Temple complex, which had only been completed a decade earlier, was burned to the ground; the sacred menorah, the seven-armed lamp stand from the Temple interior, was carried away in triumph—a scene captured in one of the inner panels of the Arch of Titus in Rome. Writing a decade or more later, Matthew also refers to the Temple's destruction, suggesting that Jesus had prophesied these events. While his disciples stood and admired the Temple buildings, Jesus had said, "Truly I tell you, not one stone will be left here upon another; all will be thrown down." (Matthew 24:1-2)

The Tenth Legion then moved into the Judean desert to root out remaining pockets of Zealot resistance. The fortresses of Herodion and Machaerus were quickly overrun, but at Masada, ensconced in Herod's impregnable palace, the Zealots were able to hold out until 73 C.E. Along the way, the Romans destroyed the settlement of Qumran, but not before the Qumranites hid their precious rolls

After the outbreak of the Jewish War, many members of Jerusalem's Christian community found refuge in Pella, located near today's village of Tabaqat Fahl, Jordan.

PART III | THE LEGACY OF JESUS

of Hebrew Scripture and other documents in nearby caves. There they would remain for nearly 2,000 years, until they were brought to light in 1947 as the Dead Sea Scrolls.

Now that the Second Temple in Jerusalem was gone, and with it the flow of pilgrims for the three great annual festivals, the Sadducee priesthood had lost its *raison d'être*. The entire priestly apparatus ceased to exist as a cohesive community and became a genealogical relic. So did the rites of Temple worship and animal sacrifice, which had been a key feature of Judaism since the earliest days of Israel.

Rabbinic Judaism

A group of Jewish sages led by Yohanan ben Zakkai (ca 30–90 c.e.), a pupil of Hillel, set out to redefine Judaism in a way that would secure its survival in Palestine and beyond. It is widely assumed that Yohanan's circle was largely composed of Pharisees, since Pharisees had for decades debated the Law, independent of the sacrificial cult. Like many other rabbinical thinkers of their time—including Jesus—they had long pondered the question of what it meant to be an observant Jew in daily life beyond the obligatory Temple rites in Jerusalem. In a sense, they had unwittingly prepared themselves for the day that the Temple would no longer exist. What's more, the Romans knew that Yohanan had opposed the rebellion and had

> **IF YOU HAVE LEARNED MUCH OF THE TORAH, DO NOT TAKE CREDIT FOR IT; FOR THIS WAS THE PURPOSE OF YOUR CREATION.**
>
> Yohanan ben Zakkai
> *Circa 70–90 c.e.*

This relief inside the Arch of Titus on the Roman Forum depicts the Menorah from the Second Temple being carried by soldiers during the triumphal procession in Rome.

THE FALL OF JERUSALEM

When after a long and bloody siege, Jerusalem fell at last in 70 C.E., Titus exacted a terrible revenge. Men, women, and children were cut down and left to die in the fire that swept through the city. This massacre was vividly illustrated by a discovery in the late 1960s, when Nahman Avigad excavated the charred debris of the first-century Kathros Mansion in old Jerusalem. There, under a chunk of blackened masonry, were the skeletal remains of a young woman in the position in which she had died: clutching at the steps of the house, most likely having suffocated in the smoke that had engulfed her house. The discovery confirmed Josephus's eyewitness account: "They set fire to the houses in which the Jews had fled, and burned every soul in them, and laid waste a great many of the rest . . . the whole city ran with blood." Back in Rome, the victory was celebrated with relief. Titus himself succeeded his father Vespasian as emperor in 79 C.E.; after his death two years later, the Senate ordered a monument to be built in honor of his triumph. The Arch of Titus still stands in the Roman Forum. Two bas-relief panels in the passageway depict Titus riding at the head of his army, and the menorah, the seven-armed candelabra from the Temple, being carried off by soldiers as a piece of loot.

British artist David Roberts (1796–1864) depicted the fall of Jerusalem in this painting from 1850, entitled "The Siege and Destruction of Jerusalem by the Romans Under the Command of Titus, A.D. 70."

This Roman colonnade of the Cardo Maximus, or main boulevard, excavated in the late 1960s, formed part of Aelia Capitolina, the Roman city built on the ruins of ancient Jerusalem (after 135 C.E.).

This stylized group sculpture of Diocletian's Tetrarchy (opposite), which was removed from Constantinople in 1204 and placed at the southwest corner of St. Mark's Basilica in Venice, betrays a Roman art in decline.

strenuously pleaded for the rebels to seek peace. Hence, when Yohanan sought to establish a rabbinic center in Jamnia (Yavneh), some 12 miles south of present-day Tel Aviv, the Romans acquiesced.

Through its focus on scriptural commentary, the Yavneh School became the foundation of Jewish spiritual recovery. Yohanan often reminded his circle of what the prophet Hosea had said: "For I desire mercy and not sacrifice, and the knowledge of God rather than burnt offerings." (Hosea 6:6) By studying the Torah and debating its precepts, rabbinic scholars *(Tannaim)* would be able to build a new Temple, a *spiritual* Temple.

As it happened, there were flourishing Jewish communities all over the Roman Empire, from Spain to North Africa. Here, Jews had maintained their identity by using the synagogue as a center of prayer, study, and community gatherings. Unable to travel to the Jerusalem Temple, these Jews had celebrated the great pilgrimage feasts—Passover, Shavuot, and Booths—among their families at home. The lesson was not lost on the surviving Jews in Palestine. For the next five

The Growth of the Church

centuries, countless towns in Judea and Galilee erected synagogue buildings in their midst, as the focal point of Jewish community life. Thus ended the period of Second Temple Judaism; a new era, that of Rabbinic Judaism, had begun.

The Canonical Gospels

The turmoil of the Jewish Rebellion was equally traumatic for the early Christian communities, many of which had continued to observe the Jewish Law while professing loyalty to the Roman state. It is perhaps not surprising that the first attempt to collect the sayings of Jesus into a theological treatise—a *Gospel*—was undertaken in this period of grave uncertainty. Just as Judaism sought succor in the reassuring certainty of Scripture, so too did early Christianity. Arguably, the first of these efforts took place in Rome, where the early Christian communities had strong Jewish roots and may thus have felt the brunt of Roman hostility while Roman sons were fighting the rebels in Palestine. Most scholars believe that the oldest Gospel, that of Mark, was written in Rome some time between 66 and 70 C.E. Another majority of scholars assumes that both Matthew and Luke then used Mark's Gospel as a major source. It is believed that Matthew composed his Gospel in Antioch between 75 and 85 C.E., whereas Luke may have written his between 80 and 90 C.E., although the exact dating continues to be a matter of debate, and the location of Luke is uncertain.

Emperor Vespasian (r. 69–79 C.E.) never revoked the status of Judaism as an officially permitted religion, even at the peak of the Jewish War. But the same thing could not be said for the growing Christian communities in Asia Minor, Greece, and even the Italian peninsula itself; here, Christianity remained an outlaw. Fortunately, Vespasian was too busy restoring the empire's solvency after Nero's disastrous regime to concern himself with religious persecution. Neither did his son Titus who, according to Tacitus, even contemplated marrying Berenice, the sister of Agrippa II.

But Titus's brother Domitian was of a different quality altogether. A vain and obstinate man, Domitian reportedly insisted on being addressed as *dominus et deus* (Lord and God), and rigorously persecuted anyone suspected of disloyalty. Fiercely devoted to the cult of the chief Roman god Jupiter and that of Minerva, goddess of wisdom and commerce, the emperor tolerated other faiths only insofar as they did neither deny nor threaten the official Roman religion.

As monotheistic religions that rejected pagan polytheism, Judaism and Christianity became inherently suspect. Bishop Eusebius of Caesarea (263–339 C.E.), an early historian of the church, wrote that Domitian initiated severe persecutions of Jews and Christians, though this is not attested in any Roman documents of

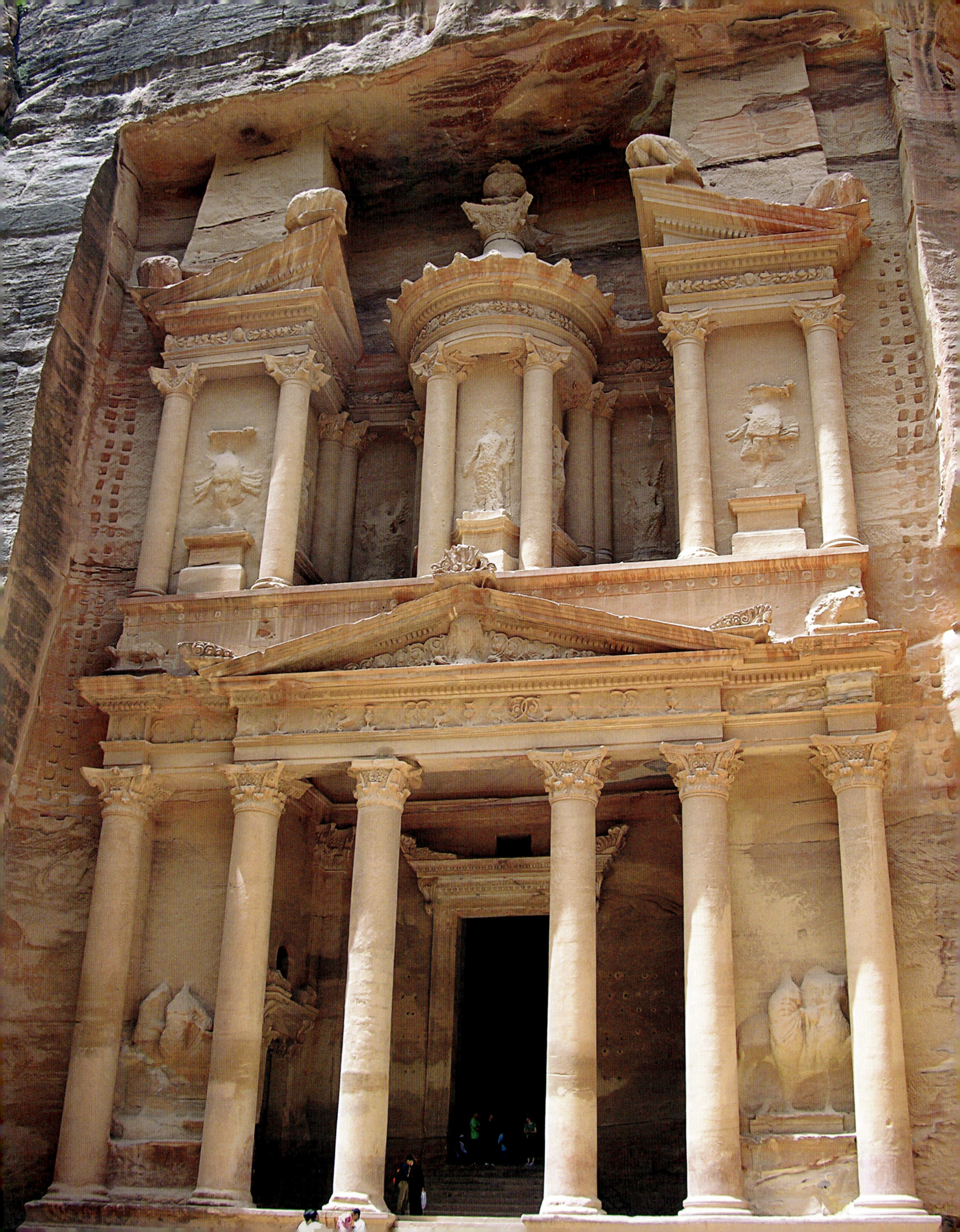

The Growth of the Church

the period. Modern research suggests that some of the hostility was the result of tensions between Jewish and Christian communities themselves. It is possible that the Book of Revelation, dedicated to seven churches in Asia Minor, was prompted by these persecutions (though some scholars believe that the book was inspired by Nero's oppression instead). The numeric code of the "beast" in Revelation, 666 (Revelation 13:18), is widely believed to refer to Nero Caesar, just as the book's references to "Babylon" are meant to allude to Rome. An alternate interpretation is that Revelation, traditionally attributed to John of Patmos, may have been composed during many decades, from the sixties to the nineties.

This imposing tomb in Petra, known as Al Khazneh, or the Treasury (based on the legend that a treasure was hidden in the urn on top of the monument), was built sometime between 100 B.C.E. and 200 C.E.

The Ebb and Flow of Roman Persecutions

After Domitian was assassinated by court officials in 96, his successor Nerva introduced a practice that would become the norm by the third century: He appointed a vice-emperor with the title of Caesar who would automatically become emperor upon his death. Its purpose was to protect Rome from the vicious infighting and rivalry that usually attended the death of an emperor, and to insure a smooth succession. As it happened, Nerva's heir apparent, Trajan (r. 98–117), proved to be a talented administrator with more than a touch of military genius. In 114 C.E., Trajan attempted to do what no emperor had accomplished before: to stem the ongoing expansion of the Parthian Empire in Persia. He captured Armenia on the Black Sea and marched south, following the ancient trade routes along the Euphrates and the Tigris, advancing as far as the Persian Gulf. But the empire lacked the military resources to enforce its rule over this vast expanse. Save for another attempt by Septimus Severus in 198 C.E., control over the region soon passed back to the Parthians—with grave consequences for the future.

> THE OFTENER WE ARE MOWN DOWN BY YOU, THE MORE IN NUMBER WE GROW; THE BLOOD OF CHRISTIANS IS SEED.
>
> Tertullian of Carthage, *Apologeticus*
> *Circa 197 C.E.*

Nevertheless, Trajan took firm control of *Arabia Petraea*, the Nabatean Kingdom (roughly today's Jordan) that was the nexus of Roman trade routes to the East, and annexed its crown jewel, the city of Petra, in 108. Just northwest of another Nabatean city, Philadelphia (today's Amman) was the town of Pella. According to Eusebius, this is where the Christian community of Jerusalem found refuge after the murder of James and the outbreak of the Jewish War. Fortunately, Trajan was not very interested in persecution. When one of his governors, the younger Pliny (61–ca 112 C.E.), proudly boasted of his pursuit of suspected Christians in Bithynia, Trajan counseled moderation, scolding the use of anonymous denunciations as "unworthy of our times."

Emperor Hadrian (r. 117–138) likewise adopted a policy of temperance, reserving his animus for the Jews of Palestine, who once again rose in revolt in late 131 under the leadership of Simon bar Kokhba ("son of a star"). This time, it took

PART III | THE LEGACY OF JESUS

This magnificent mosaic of a zodiac was discovered in the remains of the ancient synagogue of Hamat Tiberias, built between 286 and 337 C.E. when the Sanhedrin was based in Tiberias.

This late fourth-century sarcophagus of Jesus and the Twelve Apostles (opposite) is one of the early examples of the Good Shepherd motif in Christian art.

three years of hard fighting to suppress the Jewish rebellion, which ended with the complete demolition of Jewish Jerusalem and the construction of a Roman city, *Aelia Capitolina*, in its place. All Jews were evicted, permitted to return only once a year to mourn the destruction of the Temple.

Just three years after the uprising, in 138 C.E., Emperor Antoninus Pius (138–161 C.E.) reinstated Judaism as a permitted religion, though Jews were still forbidden from entering Jerusalem. By then, the center of rabbinic Judaism founded by Yohanan had moved from Yavneh to Sepphoris, ultimately settling in Tiberias, on the Sea of Galilee. Simeon ben Gamaliel (135–175 C.E.), the grandson (or great-grandson) of the rabbi Gamaliel who had once taught Paul, formed a new Sanhedrin, headed by a patriarch. Evidently, the Romans reckoned that the Sanhedrin, if granted a certain autonomy, could act as a moderating force, which proved to be the case. The rabbinate continued its legislative exegesis of the Law, which by the early third century produced the first major redaction of these oral traditions: the Mishnah, edited by Rabbi Yehuda HaNasi ("the Prince").

The Growth of Christianity

Despite the fact that it was still officially banned, Christianity benefitted from the respite of Roman oppression to grow throughout the Empire, from Rome to Pontus, from Antioch to Ephesus, and from Cappadocia to Carthage. Many Christian chapels were seeded by unknown missionaries beyond the control of Peter or Paul. Quite possibly, these were converted sailors, soldiers, officials, and traders who used the rapidly modernizing land and sea routes to bring the Gospel to the far corners of the Roman Empire. Archaeological evidence has shown, for example, that there were Christian families in Pompeii and Herculaneum before the eruption of Vesuvius in 79 C.E., Ignatius, the bishop of Antioch in Syria, is known to have sent letters to Christian communities in Philadelphia (today's Amman) and Smyrna (today's Izmir) in the early second century, places never visited by Paul. Around the same time, Pliny the Younger complained that there were so many Christians in Bithynia and Pontus (the Black Sea coastal region of today's Turkey) that pagan demand for sacrificial animals had dropped precipitously. It has been estimated that by the end of the first century, there were nearly 300,000 Christians in Asia Minor alone.

The Growth of the Church

At the same time, Christianity was introduced into Egypt via Alexandria, and from there spread rapidly among both Greek and Coptic-speaking communities; one of these would later bury the collection of Gnostic texts found at Nag Hammadi. A number of these Egyptian Christians decided to move to the desert, to seek God in the solitude of the wilderness. Eventually, these hermits formed communities, so as to share their common needs for sustenance and worship. Thus, the monastic movement was born, which soon spread to Spain, France, Britain, and Ireland, as well as the Arabian peninsula.

Elsewhere in North Africa, Carthage became a major center of Christianity; the author and theologian Tertullian was one of its most prominent converts. The faith then spread across the trade routes of Mesopotamia, straddling the Tigris and Euphrates rivers. By the middle of the second century, Edessa (located in northern Mesopotamia) had become an important center of Christian activity, based in part on the availability of the Gospels in Old Syriac, the predominant language in the region. The *Diatesseron*, a harmonization of the Four Gospels produced by Tatian in 170 C.E., was likewise written in Syriac. These efforts paid off; even the local ruler, Abgar IX (177–212), converted to Christianity, thus making the kingdom of Edessa quite possibly the first Christian state in history.

Church legend tells us that the Apostle Thomas then brought the Gospel to India, although scholars believe that it was actually Syriac missionaries who revered Thomas as their patron saint. These evangelizers created several Christian centers along the Persian Gulf, right up to the Indus River. By the time the

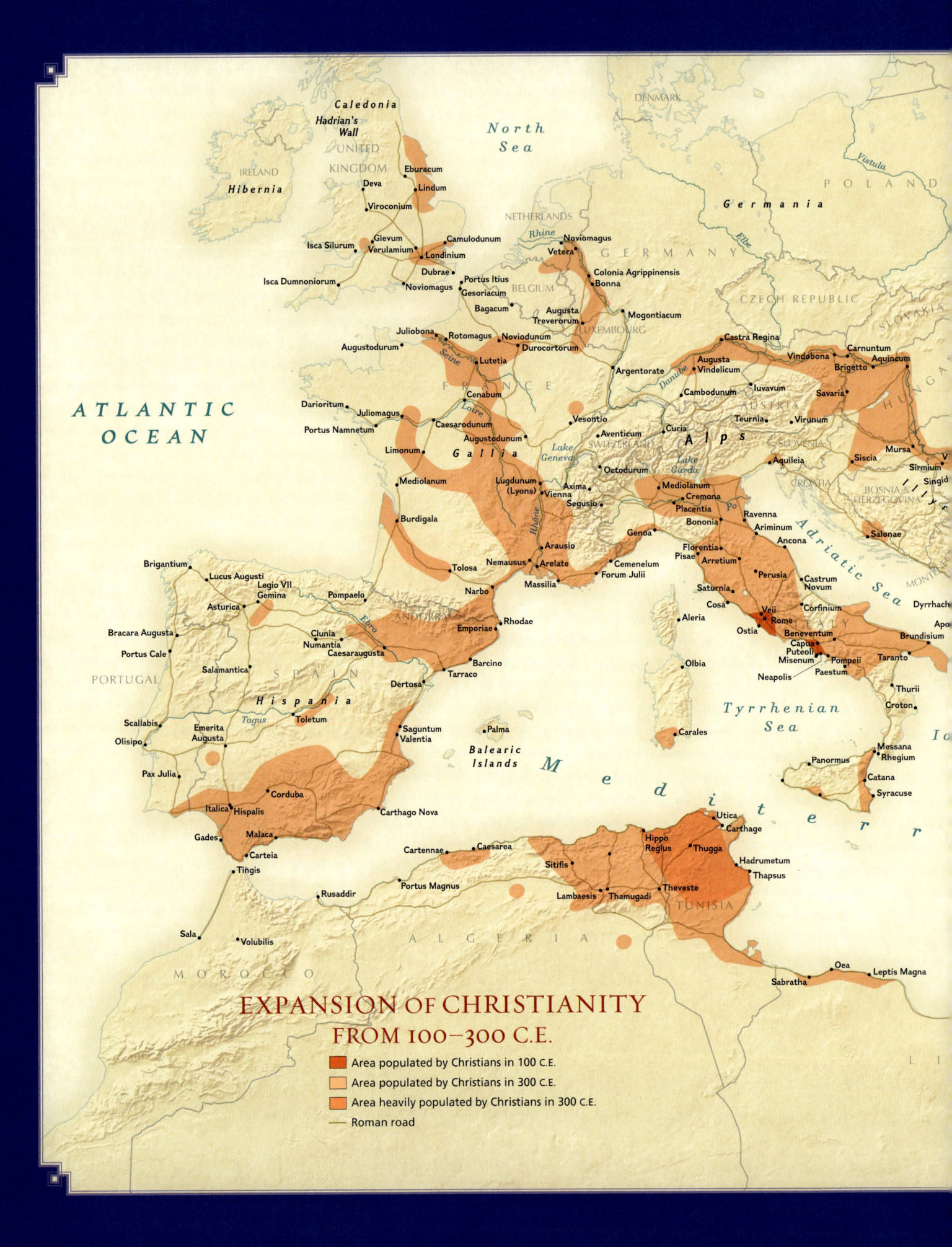

EXPANSION OF CHRISTIANITY
FROM 100–300 C.E.

- Area populated by Christians in 100 C.E.
- Area populated by Christians in 300 C.E.
- Area heavily populated by Christians in 300 C.E.
- Roman road

RUSSIA
Scythia
Volga
Don
Dnieper
Dniester
UKRAINE
Sarmatia
KAZAKHSTAN
Caspian Sea
TURKMENISTAN
Caucasus Mts.
GEORGIA
AZERBAIJAN
ARMENIA
Azerb.
Lake Sevan
Lake Van
Lake Urmia
IRAN
Parthia
Olbia
Panticapaeum
Chersonesus
Pityus
Black Sea
MANIA
ulum
Troesmis
rmizegetusa
egia
Tomis
Durostorum
Tropaeum Traiani
Danube
Oescus
Novae
BULGARIA
Serdica
Philippopolis
Nicopolis
Trapezus
Sinope
Amisus
Pompeiopolis
Amastris
Satala
Heraclea Pontica
Gangra
Zela
Megalopolis
Tigranocerta
Hadrianopolis (Adrianople)
Byzantium (Constantinople)
Perinthus
Nicomedia
Nicaea
Ancyra
TURKEY
Amida
Melitene
Caesarea
Cyzicus
Prusa
Dorylaeum
Asia Minor
Edessa
Samosata
Tigris
Thessalonica
Pergamum
Antiochia
Iconium
Cyrrhus
Tarsus
Antiochia
Dura Europos
Euphrates
Ctesiphon
Aegean Sea
Smyrna
Aphrodisias
Seleucia
SYRIA
Ephesus
Laodicea
Palmyra
IRAQ
Miletus
Attalia
Raphaneae
Emesa
racia
Delphi
Athens
Corinth
Sparta
Cnidus
Rhodus
Myra
Salamis
CYPRUS
Paphos
Tripolis
LEBANON
Heliopolis
Damascus
KUWAIT
Persian Gulf
Tyrus
Bostra
Caparcotna
Caesarea
ISRAEL
West Bank
Jerusalem
Dead Sea
Gaza
Gaza Strip
JORDAN
SAUDI ARABIA
Gortyn
Mediterranean Sea
Petra
Pelusium
Nicopolis
Alexandria
olemais
Cyrene
Memphis
Oxyrhynchus
Hermopolis
Nile
Ptolemais
Coptus
Thebae
EGYPT
Red Sea
0 50 100 150 200 250 kilometers
0 50 100 150 200 250 miles
Present-day drainage and coastlines are represented.
Modern names appear in parentheses.

PART III | THE LEGACY OF JESUS

French artist Jean-Léon Gérôme (1824-1904) painted this canvas entitled "The Christian Martyrs' Last Prayer" in 1883.

This large relief (opposite), hewn from solid rock around 260–72 C.E. near Shiraz, Iran, depicts the Victory of Shapur I over the Roman emperor Valerian.

church theologian Pantaenus of Alexandria traveled to India around 180, he found an already flourishing Christian community.

CHRISTIAN MARTYRDOM

And yet it is difficult to determine to what extent Christians were persecuted by Roman officialdom during the second century, precisely because so much of Christian martyrdom is shrouded in legend. Bishop Ignatius, who was arrested and condemned to the arena around 110 C.E., eagerly welcomed his death, writing how he longed to be "ground by the teeth of the wild beasts, [so] that I may be found to be the pure bread of Christ." Many other Christians also looked forward to martyrdom as an opportunity to suffer as Christ had suffered, and to receive the salvation that awaited them in the heavenly Kingdom of God.

Tertullian, for example, relates the story of a group of faithful who appeared before Arrius Antoninus, the Roman governor of Asia. They declared themselves to be Christians and insisted that the governor put them to death forthwith. Surprised, Antoninus agreed to have a few executed, but then declined to prosecute the rest, telling them to "jump off a cliff" if they so fervently desired death. Martyrdom also became a weapon in the ongoing strife between different Christian

312

The Growth of the Church

sects. In his *Scorpiace,* or "Antidote to Scorpion's Bite," Tertullian accused those who didn't follow the church—particularly Gnostic Christians—of lacking the requisite faith and courage to become martyrs. According to one codex found in the Nag Hammadi collection, the Gnostics fired back that it was rather absurd to think that the God of Jesus Christ would want such pointless human sacrifice.

From what little we can glean from contemporary records, it appears that in the second century, violence against Christians was often instigated by local communities who harbored deep suspicions about Christian worship and its practice of eating "Christ's body" and drinking "Christ's blood." Many of these pagan citizens also took umbrage at the refusal of most Christians to sacrifice to the statue of the reigning emperor, which they considered unpatriotic and disloyal to the sovereign state. For some Romans, this was evidence that Christianity was a foreign form of superstition, drenched in magic. The Roman historian Tacitus referred to it as a "deadly superstition," whereas Pliny the Younger called it "a superstition taken to extravagant lengths." The fact that martyrdom was eagerly sought in some Christian circles did little to change Roman public opinion on the matter.

> **THEY BOUND [QUINTA'S] FEET AND DRAGGED HER THROUGH THE ENTIRE CITY OVER THE STONE-PAVED STREETS, AND SCOURGED HER; THEN THEY STONED HER TO DEATH.**
>
> Eusebius, *The Persecutions under Decius [Church History]*
> *Circa 323 c.e.*

During the reign of Emperor Marcus Aurelius (ca 161–180), for example, the local magistrate of Lyons had little trouble inciting a mob to assault, stone, or rob local Christians, as a way of releasing tensions. In many quarters of the empire, Christian communities became isolated and ostracized, therefore serving as convenient scapegoats in future times of trouble.

A number of Christian intellectuals sought to address Roman prejudice, arguing that by contrast, Christianity was a law-abiding religion founded on love, compassion, and devotion. Quadratus of Athens (writing around 125 c.e.), Justin Martyr (103–165 c.e.), Ignatius, and Tertullian all wrote such *apologiae* in defense of their faith, though many of these works have been lost. They emphasized Christian charitable works, such as caring for the sick, the poor, or the unemployed, or those languishing in prison. Some even tried to harmonize blended Christology with

PART III | THE LEGACY OF JESUS

A detail of a Roman soldier with a defeated barbarian fighter forms part of the third-century Grand Ludovisi sarcophagus, discovered in 1621.

Greek philosophy. The theologian Origen (185–254), for example, compared the creative word of God *(Logos)* with the quintessential Platonic *Reason* that permeates all living things, just as the Jewish philosopher Philo had argued before him.

A New Wave of Persecutions

The advent of the third century introduced new challenges that very nearly succeeded in destroying Christianity as an emerging force. Rome's power went slowly into decline just as the empire became increasingly prone to barbarian invasions. At the same time, its treasury was drained by a growing trade imbalance with the East, driven by the continuing import of luxury items even as imperial revenues dropped. The productivity of agricultural estates on the Italian peninsula fell precipitously, in part because the growing cost of slaves exceeded the anticipated yields and there was no large labor force of skilled freedman to replace them.

Confronted by these threats, the Roman nation was swept by a mood of nationalistic fervor. Many rallied to the Roman gods as agents of salvation. Others turned on those suspected of unpatriotic or anti-Roman behavior, such as refusing military service—as many Christians did. According to church histories, Emperor Septimus Severus (r. 193–211) issued a law in 202 that prohibited Christianity from seeking new converts. His rule inspired a new wave of oppression, particularly in North Africa, where the father of Origen and several of his students were put to death.

But the persecution of average Christians, rather than prominent bishops and prelates, did not begin in earnest until the reign of Emperor Decius (r. 249–251). Determined to launch a religious renewal in the empire, Decius demanded that all citizens obtain a *libellus,* or certified proof of their faithful sacrifices to Roman gods. Christians who declined to do so risked torture and death. Thousands of Christian followers were rounded up; many recanted, but others refused to comply with Decius's order. They were burned or killed on the spot.

One of these victims was Pope Fabian (r. 236–250), who had previously sent a group of missionaries to Gaul (today's France) to help bolster the region's budding interest in Christianity. Among these clergymen was Trophimus, whose memory is enshrined in the magnificent 12th-century Romanesque church of St. Trophime in Arles. The Decian persecution, short-lived though it may have been, was then followed by the outbreak of plague in the empire, which in some areas, including Carthage, was blamed on the Christians.

The Reign of Gallienus

Decius's successor, Valerian (r. 253–260) maintained the law of *libellus,* but his son Gallienus had other thoughts. Gallienus ruled as Caesar at his father's

The so-called catacombs of Priscilla, located in an old quarry on the Via Salaria in Rome, were used for Christian burials as early as the second century C.E.

CHRISTIAN BURIAL

Burial, rather than the Roman custom of cremation, became an important rite for Christians, since death was merely a passage to the salvation of eternal life, and the body of the faithful would rise again on the Day of Judgment. Many Christians even devoted themselves to bury those whose family was too poor to pay for it. To do so, many Christians in urban centers such as Rome reverted to a practice that was already common among the poor, by digging subterranean burials known as *catacumbae*, or catacombs. Since for hygienic reasons, burial within the city precinct was strictly forbidden, most of these catacombs were dug in the soft volcanic rock along the main roads leading to Rome, such as the Via Appia, the Via Ostiense, and the Via Tiburtina. The dead were wrapped in linen and placed in *loculi*, or burial niches, while wealthier families commissioned large subterranean tombs, decorated with columns and friezes, and elaborate sarcophagi to hold the body of their loved one. In Rome alone, excavators have identified more than 60 catacomb networks, some equipped with galleries across multiple levels up to a depth of 60 feet. Some catacombs were lovingly decorated with frescos depicting Christian symbols, such as loaves and fishes, or scenes from the life of Christ.

THE ORGANIZATION OF THE CHURCH

Many of the early Christians, including Paul, were firmly convinced that Christ would return in their lifetime. This expectation delayed the development of a formal church organization, since Christ himself was expected to come and establish his new Kingdom. Soon, however, the question of how to administer the growing faith became urgent. Certain Christian communities began to appoint priestly leaders, or *presbyters*, on the strength of their ability and faith. These presbyters were not yet ordained priests; many of them were married. Eventually, these prelates claimed that their authority derived from the apostolate itself, and so the title of bishop emerged. These bishops created an apostolic forum or synod, so as to devise a unified defense against both dissident theologies as well as Roman persecution. During the Council of Nicaea, held in 325, the bishophric of Rome was recognized as the leading authority, closely followed by the bishops of Antioch, Alexandria, and Constantinople. The bishop of Rome adopted the Roman name for supreme priest, which was *Pontifex Maximus*, or Pope.

---

side so as to share responsibility for defending Rome's borders against the growing number of barbarian incursions. Valerian took responsibility for the eastern flank of the empire, while Gallienus fought to repel the Goths in the north. The younger Gallienus succeeded in repulsing the Alemanni, who had pushed as far as Milan, but his father suffered a crushing defeat at the hands of the Sassanid Persians. Today, a vast bas-relief carved in a mountain near Shiraz, Iran, shows Valerian as the captive prisoner of King Shapur I, ruler of the Persian Empire—a shocking humiliation unprecedented in the annals of Imperial Rome.

Gallienus, however, was now in sole control of the realm, and he made good use of the opportunity. The new emperor thoroughly reorganized the Roman military system, ending the custom of appointing senators as commanders in favor of fostering a professional corps of officers. He also encouraged a revival of Roman arts, poetry, literature, and philosophy. Among those who benefited from his patronage was a philosopher named Plotinus (204–270). Described by some scholars as "the last philosopher of Antiquity," Plotinus maintained a salon in Rome, moved in the highest circles of society, and even urged Gallienus to build a utopian city in Campania to be ruled by the principles of Plato's *Republic*, appropriately named *Platonopolis*.

Plotinus was also interested in cataloguing the diverse religious traditions in the empire, in the course of which he was introduced to Gnosticism. The result was a polemic called *Against the Gnostics*, in which Plotinus accused Gnostic Christians of distorting Plato's philosophy—an initiative that was naturally applauded by the church fathers of Catholic Christianity.

Whether Plotinus's work in religious studies had an impact on Emperor Gallienus is not certain. What we do know is that according to Eusebius, Gallienus annulled the persecution policies of his predecessor and restored confiscated property to their owners. Christians were once again permitted to use their places of worship and bury their dead in Christian cemeteries. Overjoyed, Christian communities throughout the realm initiated a vast expansion program, building churches, baptizing converts, and installing bishops in greater number than ever before. By the end of the third century, there were Christian churches deep in the western corners of the empire, including Britain, Gaul, and Spain. The Italian peninsula alone had more than a hundred bishops. In the East, Christianity had penetrated as far as Bostra and Dura-Europos in Mesopotamia, located on the Euphrates River.

The Reorganization by Diocletian

But the respite was brief. Shortly after Diocletian (284–305) acceded to the throne, the pressure of invading hordes became so great that another reorganization of the empire was necessary. In response, a tetrarchy, or *Dominate*, was formed, whereby the supreme power of emperor was divided between two rulers, each assisted by a subordinate Caesar. Serving as the senior ruler, Diocletian then divided the empire into four military prefectures, 12 "dioceses" (the term was later adopted by the Catholic Church to denote the dominion of a bishop), and 101 provinces. He also reversed the long decline of Rome's military power by raising new legions, restoring the army to a strength of 400,000 men—a larger force than Rome had held at any time since the second century. Given the poor state of the Roman treasury, however, Diocletian could pay his soldiers only partly in coin; the balance was paid in kind.

At the same time, Diocletian raised the imperial personality cult to unprecedented heights. He dressed in robes of gold, covered himself with jewelry, and presented himself as a living god who demanded to be addressed (like Domitian before him) as "Lord and God." All pretense of senatorial oversight was abandoned.

The basement of Diocletian's Palace in Split, Croatia, built around 305 C.E., suggests the immense size of the complex, which at its peak housed 9,000 people.

This sarcophagus of ca 350 C.E. displays the Chi Rho symbol (opposite)— the first two initials of Christos, the Greek translation of Messiah—above two Roman soldiers.

PART III | THE LEGACY OF JESUS

Johannes Lingelbach (1622–1674), a member of the Dutch School, painted this impression of "Constantine's Victory over Maxentius at the Battle of the Milvian Bridge" in 1696.

This head of Constantine I (306–337 C.E.) (opposite), now at the Capitoline Museum in Rome, once belonged to a colossal statue of the emperor.

The empire was in bad shape. Trade routes had been disrupted, markets had been lost to barbarian conquest, while the Roman economy was close to collapse. The middle class, deprived of land, was threatened with extinction; thousands roamed the streets, hungry and out of work. Rome needed someone to blame, and the choice fell once again on the Christians. In his polemic of 303, *Against the Christians*, the philosopher Porphyrius (or Porphyry, 232–304 C.E.) wrote that "though Christ is supposed to have been most pious, the Christians are a confused and vicious sect."

It was around this time that the *Pontifex Maximus*—the chief priest of the Roman cult—held a public augury, as was often done to discern the future of the state in times of peril. The results of the augury were unusually ominous. When it transpired that some Christians had been standing nearby, observing the ceremony, they were promptly blamed for the bad omen.

The Growth of the Church

Once again, persecutions swept the realm, though this time they were enacted with Diocletian's trademark efficiency. Churches throughout the empire were vandalized or destroyed. All Christian worship was outlawed. Scores of bishops and church leaders were arrested, tortured, and put to death. It is perhaps ironic that Diocletian, undoubtedly the ablest emperor since Hadrian, saved the empire from certain ruin and yet nearly succeeded in destroying Christianity in the process.

The Battle of the Milvian Bridge

Throughout the history of the Roman Empire, the end of an emperor's reign usually came about with his death. In 305, however, Diocletian did something unusual: He chose to retire. The emperor was in poor health and had commissioned a magnificent retirement home: a sprawling palace along the Dalmatian coast, which today is the principal tourist attraction of the Croatian city of Split. His co-emperor, Maximian (r. 286–305 C.E.) had no choice but to retire as well. This automatically elevated their caesars, or vice-regents, Galerius (r. 305–311 C.E.) in the East and Constantius I Chlorus (r. 305–306 C.E.) in the West, to the position of co-emperors.

Galerius distinguished himself by officially abrogating Diocletian's persecutions against Christians, reaffirming Gallienus's policy of tolerance—a fact largely forgotten by history, which tends to give the credit to Constantine. One year later, however, his co-emperor Constantius died suddenly in York, whereupon his troops, anxious to preserve their imperial privileges, declared his son Constantine (who was also in Britain) the new emperor.

Offended, Maxentius, the son of Maximian, rushed to declare himself emperor instead, backed by the Praetorian Guard, which prompted Maximian to come out of retirement and join his son as co-emperor. With four emperors and two Caesars now vying for power, confusion was absolute. A civil war ensued, which ultimately left two contenders standing: Constantine and Maxentius. They met in a decisive battle in 312, close to a crossing over the Tiber River known as the Milvian Bridge.

What transpired next is not altogether clear. The Christian author Lactantius (ca 240–320) tells us that on the eve of this climactic battle, Constantine had a dream in which he was told to paint the monogram of Christ on his soldiers' shields. This monogram consisted of the Greek letters chi and rho, the first two letters of the Greek word *Christos*. Eusebius, writing after Constantine's death in 337, offers a different version: Constantine had a vision of a luminescent cross in the sky just above the sun, blazing with the Greek words *en toutoi nika* ("by this [sign] conquer"). Regardless of which version is true, Constantine rode out into battle and defeated the army of Maxentius, attributing his victory to the God of the Christians.

The northern aisle of the basilica of Maxentius, later renamed after Constantine and one of the largest still standing Roman structures, features the Roman innovations of groin vaults and coffered arches, cast in cement.

> THAT WE MIGHT GRANT TO THE CHRISTIANS AND OTHERS FULL AUTHORITY TO OBSERVE THAT RELIGION WHICH EACH PREFERS.
>
> Constantine the Great,
> *The Edict of Milan*
> Circa 313 c.e.

The Edict of Milan

One year later, Constantine issued the famous Edict of Milan of 313, affirming a policy of religious toleration throughout his domain, though Constantine was at pains to specify that the edict pertained to *all* foreign cults, not just Christianity. He also made sure that Licinius, his co-emperor governing the eastern half of the empire, adopted the same policy.

But contrary to legend, Constantine did not become a Christian convert himself—at least not initially. He continued to worship pagan gods as *Pontifex Maximus,* or chief priest of the Roman cult, while also paying homage to the Mithraic sun god, perhaps in an effort to placate his troops, many of whom were fiercely devoted to the Mithras cult. Even though he actively sponsored the growth of Christianity, the emperor would not be baptized until he faced death from a long illness. Indeed, the triumphal arch that was erected in his honor—the Arch of Constantine that still stands today near the eastern end of the Roman forum—contains many pagan motifs, but no Christian symbols.

Nonetheless, Constantine recognized his debt to the Christian God, and he financed the construction of churches throughout the Roman realm, often under supervision of his mother, Empress Helena, who was a devout Christian. He also promised full restitution of all Christian property that had been confiscated in the preceding decades of official persecution. Those who had been exiled for their belief were invited back, while Christians were once again offered positions in the imperial administration.

Upon his return to Rome in 313, Constantine launched a campaign to erase all memory of Maxentius. Among others, the massive basilica that Maxentius had been building near the Roman Forum, one aisle of which still stands today, was renamed the Basilica of Constantine. All imperial appointments by Maxentius were declared invalid, and his allies were purged from the ranks. The Praetorian Guard, the elite force that had backed Maxentius's claims, was disbanded.

Taken aback by these purges, Licinius, the co-ruler in the East, suspected that Constantine was plotting to take sole control of the Roman Empire. This may be the reason why Licinius, in violation of the Edict of Milan, renewed the oppression of Christian communities in his realm. Christian properties were once again confiscated, while known Christians were sacked from the imperial administration. As it happened, barbarians chose this moment to invade Thrace (an area roughly equivalent to today's Bulgaria and European Turkey), which formed part of Licinius's jurisdiction. This gave Constantine a pretext to invade his rival's territory. In 324, Constantine defeated his co-emperor in a decisive battle at Chrysopolis (today's Üsküdar, on the Anatolian shore of the Bosporus).

Christianity was secure at last—or so it was believed.

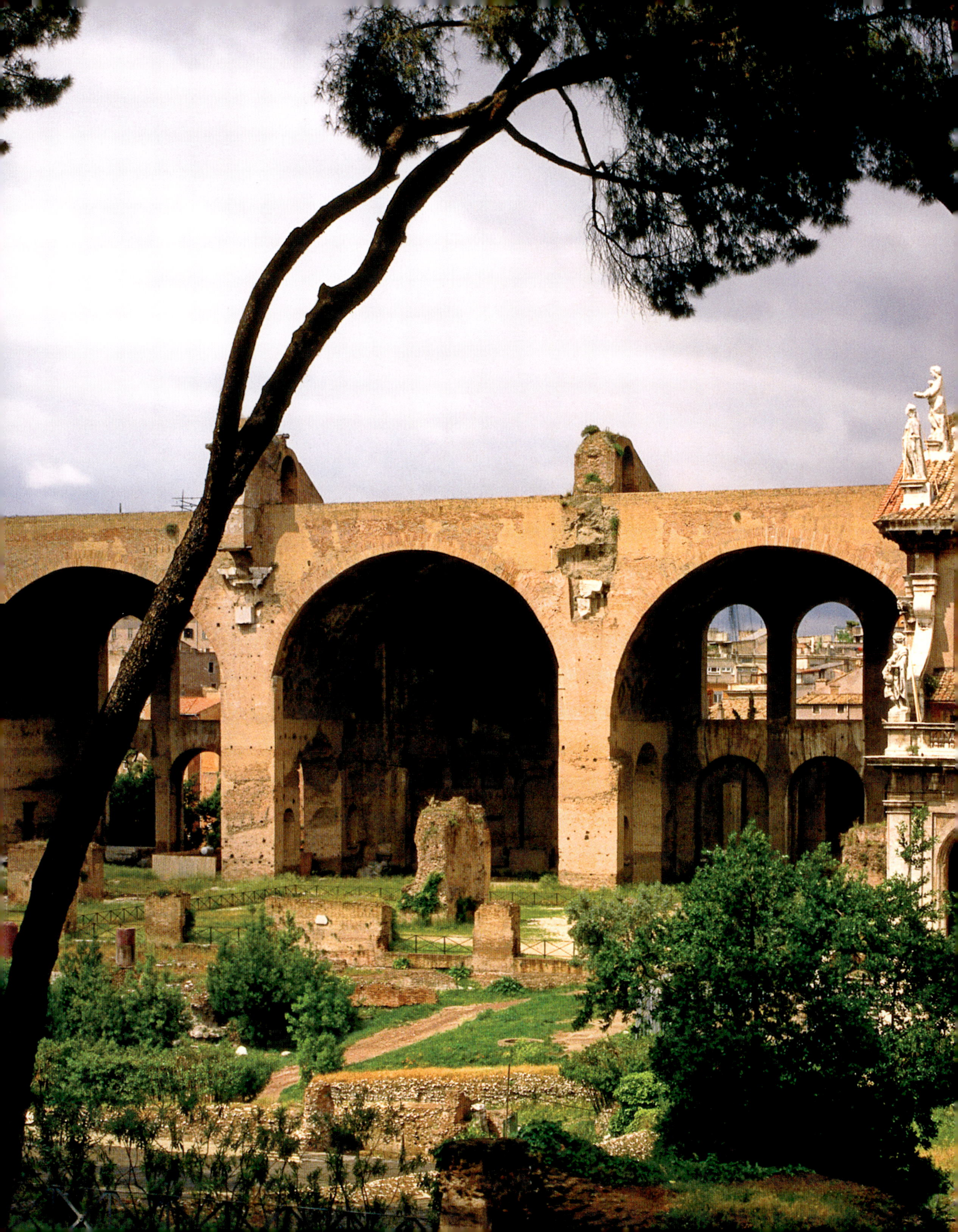

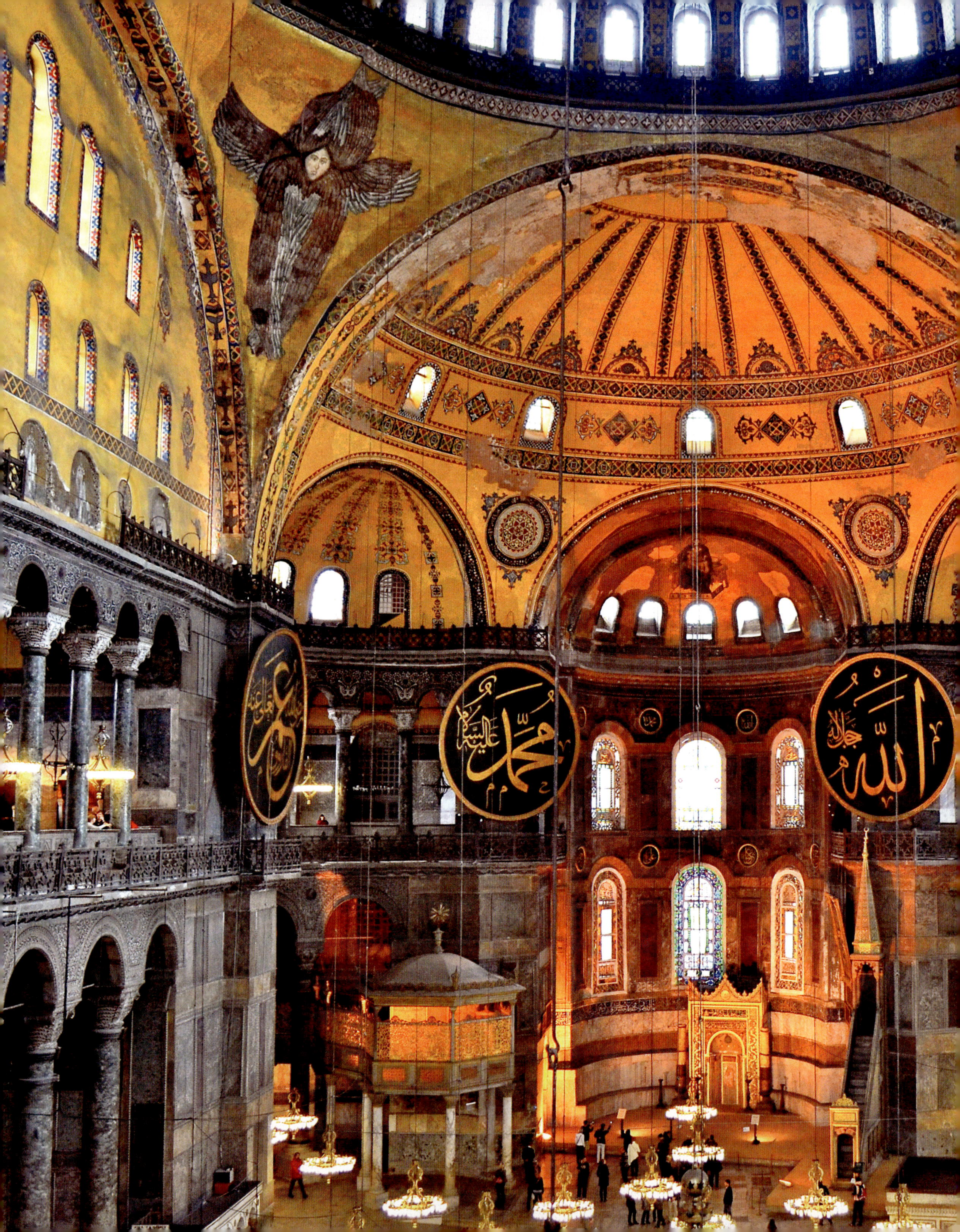
محمد عليه السلام
الله جل جلاله

[CHAPTER] 15

The CHRISTIAN TRIUMPH

NOT ONLY SHALL THIS BASILICA BE THE FINEST IN THE WORLD, BUT ITS DETAILS SHALL BE SUCH THAT ALL THE FAIREST STRUCTURES IN EVERY CITY MAY BE SURPASSED BY IT.

CONSTANTINE THE GREAT
ON THE HOLY SEPULCHER CHURCH
Circa 532 C.E.

The Hagia Sophia in Istanbul, built by Emperor Justinian I between 532–537 C.E., has been remarkably preserved despite multiple earthquakes and centuries of neglect.

PART III | **THE LEGACY OF JESUS**

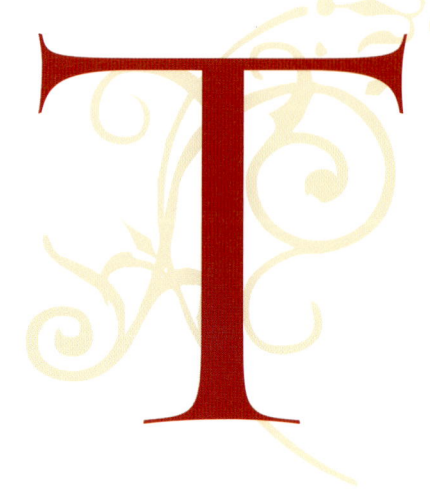

The earliest record of a pilgrimage to Palestine dates from 333 C.E., just 20 years after Constantine's Edict of Milan. Written by an anonymous pilgrim from Bordeaux, his account is of great value for historians, for it testifies to the tremendous changes that were then taking place in Palestine. Previously a mere backwater of the Roman Empire, largely administered by the Jewish Patriarchate in Tiberias, the region suddenly found itself elevated to the status of the Christian "Holy Land." Much of this change was led by Empress Helena, a pious Christian and the mother of Emperor Constantine. In 326, she had journeyed to Jerusalem to locate the site of Jesus' Crucifixion and burial and also initiated the construction of Roman-style basilicas on the Mount of Olives, in Nazareth, and in Bethlehem, as well as smaller chapels elsewhere, including the Sinai.

The return of Christianity to Palestine—as an official state religion—took the local Jewish communities by surprise. The Jewish Patriarchate watched with apprehension as their holy city, renamed Aelia Capitolina by Hadrian, reverted to "Jerusalem"—albeit in a thoroughly Christian mold. Even at this late date, more than 200 years after the Bar Kokhba Uprising, the large community of Jews still living in Palestine was prohibited from entering Jerusalem save once a year, to mourn the anniversary of the Temple's destruction.

It was in this heady atmosphere of profound change that the pilgrim from Bordeaux left Roman Gaul, using the still-functioning network of Roman roads that took him to Arles and across the Alps to Turin, Pavia, Milan, and Verona. From here, he made his way over the Julian Alps (between today's Italy and Slovenia), rode through the western Balkans and Thrace, and ultimately reached Constantinople.

Just three years before, Constantine had decided to move the capital of Rome to this very city on the Bosporus. The emperor had come to the conclusion that Rome's destiny lay closer to Asia. Constantinople (or Konstantinopolis, "City of Constantine"), formerly known as Byzantium, lay far from the invading barbaric hordes in the west. Moreover, the economy of Asia Minor was healthy and growing, in contrast to the collapse of trade and agriculture in the west.

Having paused in Rome's new capital, the pilgrim continued down along the trade routes through Asia Minor and into Syria, and from there made his way to Jerusalem via the port of Acre. He calculated that he had covered more than

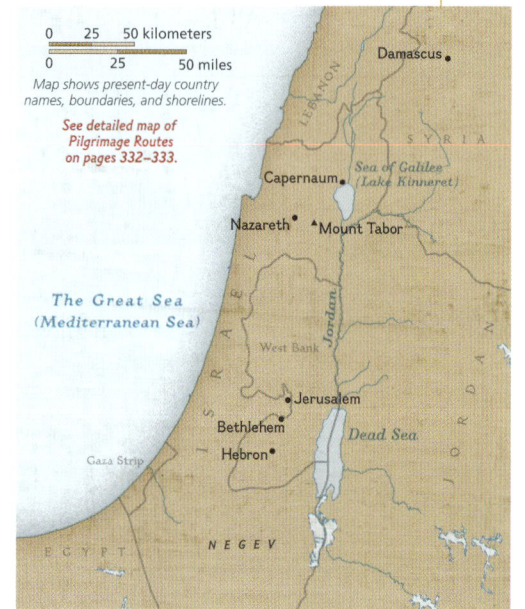

3,250 miles, using some 190 way stations and changing horses more than 360 times. Significantly, his long journey had not once passed a national frontier; at this early stage, the route of European pilgrimage to the Holy Land still fell within the borders of the Roman Empire.

Upon his arrival in Jerusalem, he rushed to the Holy Sepulcher Church, which was—then as now—the ultimate destination of every Christian pilgrim. The Temple of Venus, built by Hadrian over Golgotha, had already been torn down. Helena's architects had subsequently removed the upper portion of the hill so as to create a level surface, leaving only the presumed tomb and the place of the Crucifixion exposed. Over these, two structures were now being built: a massive, five-aisled basilica—similar to the church of St. Peter then rising on Vatican Hill in Rome—on one side, and a rotunda (known as the *Anastasis,* or "resurrection") over the spot of Christ's resurrection on the other. In between lay the rocky outcropping of Golgotha itself. The Bordeaux pilgrim called it "a church

Following Constantine's Edict of Milan in 333 C.E., thousands of churches would be built throughout Greece and Asia Minor in the centuries to come, including this Greek Orthodox church on the island of Santorini.

of wondrous beauty," but curiously, made no mention of a cross; apparently, the "True Cross" believed to have been the instrument of Jesus' Crucifixion had not yet been found.

The Council of Nicea

While Empress Helena was focused on her building activity, her son Constantine was facing quite a different challenge back home. The nature of Jesus' divinity continued to vex the learned minds of the Church. A new heresy had emerged, propagated by Arius (ca 256–336), the bishop of Alexandria, who claimed that Christ was "begotten by the Father" and was therefore *secondary* to God, rather than "of the same substance." Arianism gained so many converts that the Roman Emperor felt compelled to intervene. In 325 C.E., Constantine summoned nearly 300 bishops to a synod in Nicea, located near today's city of Iznik in Turkey. Presiding over the meeting himself, he tried hard to find a consensus on the key question: Was Christ's relationship to God one of *similar* substance *(homoiousia)* or the *same* substance *(homoousia)*. The future of the Church hung on the difference of one letter, one *iota*.

A majority of bishops agreed to a clause that still forms part of the Roman Catholic Mass to this day: "We believe . . . in Jesus Christ, the only Son of God . . . *consubstantial* with the Father" (previously phrased as "*one in Being* with the Father" before the recent revisions by Pope Benedict XVI). But a small group of bishops led by Arius rejected the so-called "Nicene Creed." They were exiled, and their books were banned. Nevertheless, Arianism continued to flourish well into the Middle Ages.

Apostasy and Restoration

Empress Helena's grand vision of a Holy Land filled with magnificent shrines and churches was suddenly cast in doubt when Constantine's successor, the son of his half-brother, Julian (r. 360–363), rejected the Christian faith upon coming to power. Perhaps under influence of Plotinus's Neo-Platonic philosophy, the new emperor favored a return to Rome's ancient pagan practices that had sustained her for centuries. Though no organized persecutions ensued, many church projects were suspended and known Christians were purged from the imperial payrolls. Some bishops who protested too loudly, such as Gemellus of Ancyra (today's Ankara), were executed. To justify his new policy, Julian personally drafted a polemic attacking Christianity under the title "Against the Galileans," of which only fragments have survived. The new emperor also restored many of the Jewish rights abrogated by Constantine. He even encouraged the Jews to think about rebuilding the Second

> JULIAN THOUGHT TO REBUILD AT AN EXTRAVAGANT EXPENSE THE PROUD TEMPLE ONCE AT JERUSALEM, AND COMMITTED THIS TASK TO ALYPIUS OF ANTIOCH.
>
> Ammianus Marcellinus,
> *History of the Roman Empire*
> Circa 391 C.E.

The Christian Triumph

Temple in Jerusalem—perhaps in the hope that Judaism could contain the growing influence of Christianity in Palestine.

But before these plans could come to fruition, Julian died in battle during an ill-fated campaign against Rome's traditional foe, the Persians, in 363. Nevertheless, the three years of Julian "the Apostate" had shocked Christians to the core. The future of Christianity, which had seemed so bright under Constantine, had been left exposed to reactionary forces stronger than anyone could have imagined. Thus, when Theodosius I (r. 379–395) rose to the throne, the new emperor was determined to eradicate any further challenges to the Christian faith. One year after his ascension he issued an imperial decree, ordering *all* his subjects to embrace Christianity and to "profess the faith which we believe has been communicated by the Apostle Peter to the Romans." Blood sacrifice to pagan gods was prohibited. Eventually, any form of pagan practice became a criminal offense. Christianity had triumphed at last; some 350 years after the Crucifixion, it had become the sole religion of the Roman Empire.

Encouraged by Bishop Ambrose of Milan, monks throughout the realm began to ransack the shuttered pagan temples, destroying thousands of statues and making off with untold treasures of silver and gold. In Alexandria, Bishop Theophilus personally supervised the wholesale destruction of every pagan structure in the city, including the legendary Mouseion complex and the still functioning Alexandrian Library. In the heat of the moment, some synagogues, such as the one in Callinicum on the Euphrates (today's Ar-Raqqah in north-central Syria), were sacked as well.

The Travels of Egeria

Just one year after Theodosius's declaration, another Christian pilgrim left a record of a voyage to the Holy Land. Various traditions have identified the author as either a nun or possibly a saint, though scholars believe that the traveler was a wealthy noblewoman from France, possibly the Rhône Valley or the

The Triumphal Arch of Constantine in Rome was built between 313 and 315 C.E. to commemorate Constantine's victory over Maxentius at the Battle of Milvian Bridge in 312.

This gold solidus *(opposite), the successor to the Roman* aureus, *depicts Emperor Julian with the inscription PP, Pater Patriae, or "father of the nation."*

PART III | THE LEGACY OF JESUS

For hundreds of years, pilgrims have climbed Mount Sinai to witness the sunrise over its summit—and to scratch their names on its weathered surface.

Saint Catherine Monastery (opposite) at the foot of Mount Sinai was originally built as a chapel by Empress Helena (ca 248–330), the mother of Constantine the Great.

Aquitaine. Nevertheless, that a fourth-century Frenchwoman would undertake such an arduous journey on her own accord is remarkable in itself. Her name was either Aetheria or Egeria (it is as Egeria that she appeared in an earlier chapter), and she recorded her impressions in a book called *Itinerarium Egeriae*, or "The Travels of Egeria." Though only a third of this manuscript has survived, one might claim that this is perhaps the first book written by a woman in the post-Roman Era.

Having sailed to Alexandria, Egeria spent some time visiting holy sites in Egypt, particularly the Sinai, as well as the early monastic settlements of local monks. Near Jebel Musa, Mountain of Moses, she was shown "the place where it rained manna and quails upon them," and the bush "out of which the Lord spake in the fire to Moses." This is the first record that denotes Jebel Musa, today known as Mount Sinai, as the place where Moses received the Ten Commandments. At the time of Egeria's visit, a chapel had been built by Empress Helena at the foot of the hill; it would later be expanded into a fortified enclosure by Emperor Justinian and become known as St. Catherine's Monastery.

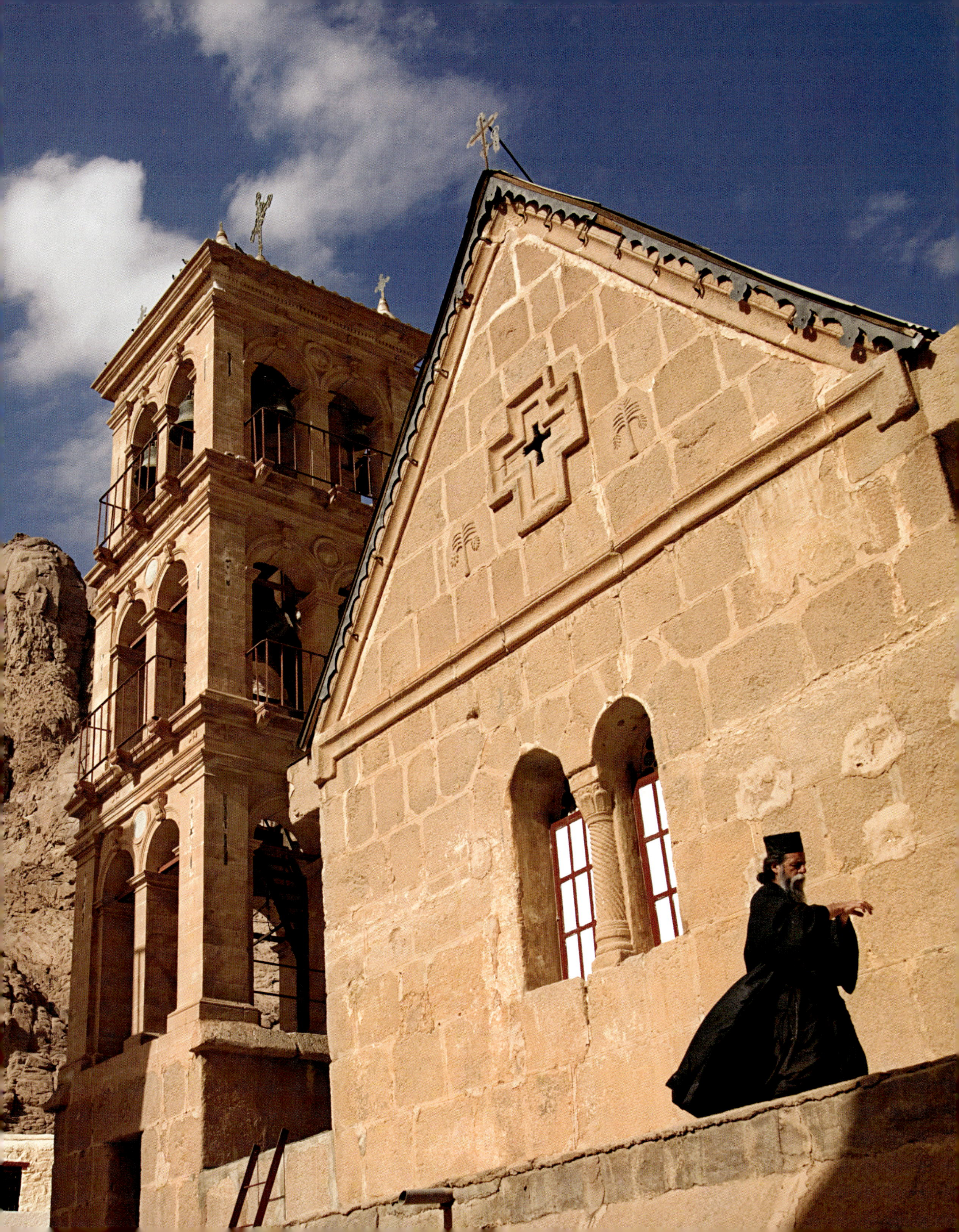

She then traveled to the Jordan Valley, where she climbed Mount Nebo, from where Moses had caught a glimpse of the Promised Land before his death. Next, she was shown the land of "the Sodomites," and was eager to see the salt pillar into which, according to the Book of Genesis, Lot's wife had been turned (Genesis 19:26). "But believe me, reverend ladies," she wrote, "the pillar itself cannot be seen, [for] it is said to have been covered by the Dead Sea, so I cannot deceive you in this."

From there she traveled to Aenon (possibly located near today's Ainun) in the upper Jordan Valley, one of the places where the baptism of Jesus by John was thought to have taken place. Still farther she went, moving north toward Antioch in Syria, where she paused before crossing the Euphrates on her way to the city of Edessa. Edessa was by now one of the great Christian centers in northern Mesopotamia, devoted to the worship of St. Thomas. "The church there is very great," she enthused, "very beautiful and of new construction." Since "there was much that I desired to see," Egeria decided to stay for a few days, much to the surprise of the local bishop, who was astonished that a woman would undertake "so great a labor in coming to these places from far-distant lands."

From Edessa she traveled farther north to Haran, where as related by Genesis, Abraham and his family had lived before his journey down to Canaan. A local prelate took her to the church built over Abraham's "house," and assured her that "it stands on the same foundations, and it is made of the same stone."

But most of her writings are devoted to Jerusalem. She describes, in great detail, the liturgical services held at the Holy Sepulcher Church, now completed, which is of great value for historians of the early Church. Her book is also the first to refer to the presence of a cross, believed to have been used in the Crucifixion of Jesus. Later known as the "True Cross," Egeria's account indicates that its discovery was not, as yet, attributed to Empress Helena. Kept in a "silver-gilt casket," the "holy wood" was only taken from its container and exhibited on Good Friday. During a solemn ceremony, all the faithful were invited to step forward and kiss the wood's surface. The event, Egeria added, was always heavily guarded, for at one point, "some one is said to have bitten off and stolen a portion of the sacred wood."

THE TRAVELS OF PAULA

The lady from France may have unwittingly crossed paths with another female pilgrim whose travels through the Holy Land were preserved for posterity,

Jesus may have walked these undulating hills in Lower Galilee between Capernaum and Tiberias.

The Christian Triumph

The Byzantine Church of Hagia Eirene (Holy Peace), the first church built in Constantinople by Constantine I and located in the grounds of the Ottoman Topkapi Palace in Istanbul, was never destroyed as it served the Sultans as an armory.

EMPRESS HELENA

The consort of Emperor Constantius and mother of Constantine the Great, Empress Helena (ca 248–330) is closely associated with the formation of the Holy Land as a pilgrimage destination for Christians in the late Roman era. Though Constantius divorced her at some time before 289 in order to marry a lady of higher birth, she was allowed to return to the imperial court by her son Constantine after his own elevation to emperor. In 325, after the Edict of Milan, Constantine charged her to identify and restore the holy sites in Palestine associated with the life of Jesus, with full support of the imperial treasury. She then traveled to Palestine in order to, as her biographer Eusebius wrote, "worship at the place whereon his feet have stood." She built churches in Bethlehem, Nazareth, and the Mount of Olives, while also supervising the construction of the first Church of the Holy Sepulcher. Church tradition credits her with the discovery of Jesus' "True Cross", an event that until recently the Roman Catholic Church observed on May 3 as the day of the "Invention [i.e., Discovery] of the Cross." But her biographer and contemporary, Eusebius, does not describe this attribution, nor do pilgrims in the fourth and fifth centuries. The legend of the cross most probably emerged later, as the swelling numbers of pilgrims to the Holy Land demanded tangible relics that could attest to Jesus' Passion.

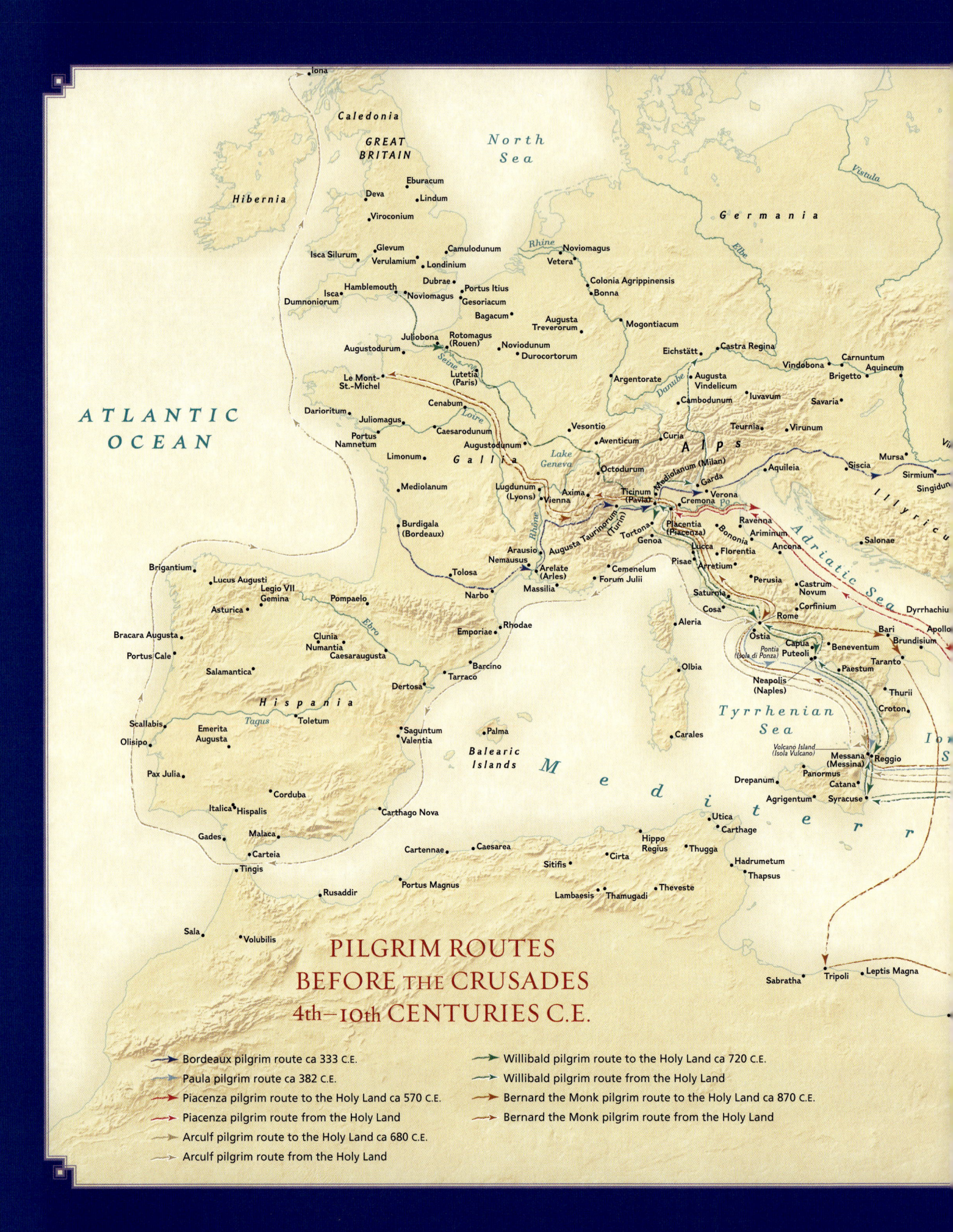

PILGRIM ROUTES BEFORE THE CRUSADES
4th–10th CENTURIES C.E.

- → Bordeaux pilgrim route ca 333 C.E.
- → Paula pilgrim route ca 382 C.E.
- → Piacenza pilgrim route to the Holy Land ca 570 C.E.
- → Piacenza pilgrim route from the Holy Land
- → Arculf pilgrim route to the Holy Land ca 680 C.E.
- → Arculf pilgrim route from the Holy Land
- → Willibald pilgrim route to the Holy Land ca 720 C.E.
- → Willibald pilgrim route from the Holy Land
- → Bernard the Monk pilgrim route to the Holy Land ca 870 C.E.
- → Bernard the Monk pilgrim route from the Holy Land

Sarmatia
Scythia
Dnieper
Dniester
Don
Volga
Caspian Sea
Caucasus Mts.
Lake Sevan
Lake Van
Lake Urmia
Parthia
Olbia
Chersonesus
Black Sea
Troesmis
Tomis
Tropaeum Traiani
Durostorum
Danube
Oescus
Novae
Thrace
Serdica
Philippopolis
Hadrianopolis (Adrianople)
Constantinople
Nicopolis
Perinthus
Nicaea
Nicomedia
Prusa
Cyzicus
Dorylaeum
Ancyra
Caesarea
Melitene
Trapezus
Sinope
Amisus
Pompeiopolis
Amastris
Heraclea Pontica
Gangra
Zela
Megalopolis
Satala
Tigranocerta
Amida
Edessa
Harran
Samosata
Cyrrhus
Asia Minor
Antiochia
Iconium
Tarsus
Antiochia
Aleppo
Chalcis
Seleucia
Thessalonica
Pergamum
Smyrna
Aegean Sea
Ephesus
Miletus
Aphrodisias
Attalia
Perga
Patara
Myra
Cnidus
Rhodus
Rhodes
Laodicea
Raphaneae
Antaradus
Emesa
Palmyra
Salamis (Constantia)
Cyprus
Paphos
Tripolis
Heliopolis
Sidon
Damascus
Bostra
AREA ENLARGED
Jerusalem
Dead Sea
Petra
Delphi
Athens
Corinth
Sparta
Cythera (Kithira)
Candia
Gortyn
Crete
Mediterranean Sea
Pelusium
Alexandria
Clymsa
Cyrene
Ptolemais
Memphis
Qubba, Babyon
Pharan
Mt Sinai 2,285 m 7,497 ft
Oxyrhynchus
Hermopolis
Nile
Ptolemais
Coptus
Thebae
0 50 100 150 200 250 kilometers
0 50 100 150 200 250 miles
Present-day drainage and coastlines are represented.
Modern names appear in parentheses.
Tyre
Leontes
Kanah
Cadasa
Ecdippa
Asor
Jordan
Merom
Ptolemais
Jotapata
Capernaum
Bethsaida
Bay of Acco (Bay of Haifa)
Arbela
Sycaminium
Tiberias
Sea of Galilee
Sepphoris
Nazareth
Mt. Tabor 588 m 1,929 ft
Dora
Legio
Gadara
Caesarea
Scythopolis
Pella
THE GREAT SEA (MEDITERRANEAN SEA)
PLAIN OF SHARON
Narbata
Ginae
Willibald took side trips to Jericho, Hebron, and Gaza.
Sebaste
Neapolis
Sychar
Amathus
Jabbok
Yarqon
Antipatris
Lebonah
Joppa
Lydda
Sorek
Bethel
Jericho
Jerusalem
Paula died in Bethlehem.
Azotus
Bethany
Bethlehem
Ascalon
SHEPHELAH
Lachish
Hebron
Salt Sea (Dead Sea)
Gaza
En-gedi
Arnon
Eshtemoa
Masada
Beersheba
Malatha
Besor
NEGEV
Elusa
0 20 40 kilometers
0 20 40 miles

PART III | THE LEGACY OF JESUS

namely a Roman aristocrat named Paula. This patrician lady had met the great Church scholar Jerome (ca 347–420), who was then serving as secretary to Pope Damasus I. Perhaps at Jerome's suggestion, Paula and her daughter chose to go on a pilgrimage to Palestine in 382. They traveled by sea, sailing on the sea link between Rome and Syria, once the principal connection between Rome and its Near East possessions. Landing in Caesarea, she visited the house of the centurion Cornelius, who had been baptized by Peter, and reported that the house had already been converted into a church. From there she went to see the house of the deacon Philip, who had reportedly lived there with his four daughters.

According to Jerome, who described her travels in *The Pilgrimage of the Holy Paula*, she then journeyed to Jerusalem to visit the Church of the Holy Sepulcher, where she prostrated herself before the cross, and "adored it as though she saw the Lord hanging upon it." Next, she visited the house where the Holy Ghost had descended on the Apostles during Pentecost. From there she continued on to Bethany to see the house of Martha and Mary, as well as Lazarus's tomb. Finally, she turned to Samaria to visit the well of Jacob, where according to the Gospel of John, Jesus had once met a Samaritan woman. Nearby was a tomb believed to be the final resting place of John the Baptist. This tomb was a major pilgrimage destination in itself, particularly for the sick, for as she reported, "people possessed with demons" were brought from all over Palestine to be cured.

Her most memorable impression, however, was her visit to the "Grotto of the Savior" in Bethlehem, where she admired "the holy inn of the Virgin and the stable." Though the Gospels do not refer to a "grotto," later Christian texts do, and so the presumed cave in which Jesus was born had become a very prominent feature of Bethlehem worship in the fourth century. At the time of Paula's visit, this "grotto" had been covered by an octagon, a favored Christian motif of Roman architects, located near the east end of a five-aisled basilica built by Empress Helena in 325 C.E.

Despite the grandeur of the Constantinian church, Paula was struck by the primitive accommodations that had been prepared for Christian pilgrims, and she was shocked by the outrageous prices charged for them. After a visit to Egypt, accompanied by Jerome (who had left Rome after the death of his patron, the Pope), she returned to Bethlehem to build a number of hospices for pilgrims, which she herself managed until her death. Jerome joined her in Bethlehem and settled in a cave adjoining the grotto. Largely supported by Paula's wealth, Jerome then devoted the rest of his life to translating the Hebrew Scriptures (the Old Testament) from Hebrew into Latin. All previous Latin translations of Hebrew Scripture had been made from the Greek version of the Septuagint, which was considered less accurate. By then, Latin had largely

WHICH PHILIP?

On July 27, 2011, the Turkish news media announced the discovery of the tomb of "St. Philip" in the ancient city of Hierapolis. The tomb was reportedly found by the Italian archaeologist Francesco D'Andria in a newly discovered church, located at some distance from a central octagon complex known as the Martyrium, previously thought to contain Philip's tomb. But which Philip is it? There are two figures in the New Testament known as Philip: One is the Apostle Philip, who like Andrew and Peter came from Bethsaida; and the other is the deacon Philip described in Acts. Neither the Gospels nor Acts tell us what happened to these men in later life, though Christian legend, Eusebius's writings, and texts such as the "Acts of Philip" try to fill in the blanks. According to the latter, "Philip the Apostle" traveled to Hierapolis with his sister Mariamne and the disciple Bartholomew, where they baptized many, including the wife of the proconsul. Enraged, the proconsul ordered the men crucified, upside down. Since Eusebius does not distinguish between Apostle and Evangelist, scholars assume that by the fourth century, the identity of the two men had been fused into one.

This Eastern Orthodox church near Nablus is traditionally believed to contain Jacob's Well, where Jesus met a Samaritan woman.

supplanted Greek as the lingua franca of early Christianity, and so Jerome's *Vulgate* translation would find wide distribution throughout the Christian world.

THE CANON OF THE NEW TESTAMENT

Around the same time, the canon of the New Testament was approaching its final form as well. As early as 180 C.E., Bishop Irenaeus of Lyons (140–ca 203 C.E.) had declared that only the gospels of Mark, Matthew, Luke, and John should be considered truly authoritative, as well as the Letters of Paul. Tertullian agreed with Irenaeus's assessment, and coined the term "New Testament" for this collection, since Jesus was believed to be the living proof of God's new covenant with mankind. Almost a century later, Eusebius completed the canon by adding the Acts of the Apostles, the Epistles of Peter, and the "Apocalypse of John," known today as Revelation, in addition to a number of other Christian texts (see the Appendix to this book). At the same time, Eusebius rejected a great many other Christian works, many of which were of Gnostic origin. Greek

PART III | THE LEGACY OF JESUS

A marble base of the obelisk at the Hippodrome of Constantinople (now Istanbul) from 390 C.E. depicts Emperor Theodosius I conferring a laurel wreath to the winner of a chariot race.

Orthodox Christianity, however, would not recognize Eusebius's canon until 692, while the Catholic Church did not formally embrace it until 1546, during the Council of Trent. Nevertheless, it is safe to say that the New Testament as we know it today was already in wide circulation by the time of Egeria's and Paula's travels in the Holy Land.

THE FALL OF THE WESTERN EMPIRE

The next century saw a steady growth in pilgrimages from Europe to the Holy Land, notwithstanding the fact that a split within the empire had become all but inevitable upon the death of Theodosius I in 395. His successors, ruling once again as co-emperors, divided their respective realms into East and West, as their predecessors had often done before. This time, however, with much of Northern Europe already captured by barbarian invasions, the rift would be permanent. The fault line ran roughly from Sirmium (today's Belgrade) straight down the Balkans and the Mediterranean to today's Surt in Libya. On paper, all territory to

The Christian Triumph

the west of this line—including southern Britannia (Britain), Gaul (France), Hispania (Spain), and Italy—still constituted a single sovereign realm, but this was an illusion. In 401 C.E., the Visigoths plunged into Italy and made their way to Rome, which was sacked nine years later. The Vandals took major parts of Spain and conquered much of North Africa, capturing Carthage in 439. Finally, the last Roman emperor in the West, Romulus Augustus, was forced to surrender to the German king Odoacer in 476, and the Western Empire ceased to exist. The Eastern Empire—now known as the Byzantine Empire—would last for another 1,000 years, until its capture by Muslim forces in 1453.

It was, however, fortunate that many of these invading tribes had previously been converted to Christianity. While this did not stop their lust for loot and land, it did prevent many massacres, particularly when the local population sought sanctuary in their churches, which were respected. Jewish communities, on the other hand, enjoyed no such protection. The Visigoths—who, despite their ferocity in combat, were pious Christians—entertained such a loathing for Jews that they forbade the practice of the religion in all the territories they controlled, including Spain.

The Growth of Holy Land Pilgrimage

This is perhaps one reason why despite the tremendous upheaval of these years, the pilgrimage traffic to the Holy Land continued. Europe was now ruled by an array of kings rather than a single emperor, but they were still Christians. Indeed, the next accounts of pilgrim journeys that have survived date from the years 440 and 530, respectively, written by Bishop Eucherius of Lyons and an anonymous author whose book became known as *The Breviary*. What distinguishes these books from preceding accounts is that they were explicitly written as "travel guides" for Christians who, likewise, might be contemplating a journey to Palestine. This suggests that Christian pilgrimage had more or less become commonplace by the sixth century.

At the same time, the nature of the pilgrimage itself had undergone some changes. While early travelers had been content with the experience of walking in the footsteps of Jesus and seeing the general locations described in the Gospels, these pilgrims searched for something more tangible, something they could touch; an experience, in short, that would make them an eyewitness to the story. Custodians of holy sites responded to that need by producing an astonishing number of sacred objects and relics, which were solemnly declared to be authentic. The author of *The Breviary*, for example, wrote that in the Church of the Holy Sepulcher, the cross so admired by Paula had now been joined by two

> LET NO MAN, REGARDLESS OF ORDER, RANK, OR QUALITY, PRESUME IN ANY PLACE, OR ANY CITY, TO OFFER SACRIFICE TO SENSELESS IMAGES, OR PAY ANY ADORATION TO HIS GENIUS OR HOUSEHOLD GODS.
>
> THEODOSIUS I,
> LAWS AGAINST PAGAN WORSHIP
> *Circa 392 C.E.*

PART III | THE LEGACY OF JESUS

other crosses, so as to complete the scene described by Mark. Elsewhere in the Sepulcher Church, the pilgrim was directed to a chamber to see "the reed, the sponge" and "the spear," which, he was assured, were the actual objects that had figured in the Passion. He was then shown "the cup which the Lord blessed and gave to His disciples."

On Mount Zion, the assumed place of the Antonia Fortress and thus the location of Jesus' scourging, *The Breviary* author visited a church that claimed to contain the column to which Jesus had been bound during the scourging. "One may still see," the pilgrim reported, "the print of His hands as He held it, marked as deep as though the stone were wax." The church exhibit also included the actual crown of thorns as well as the rod with which Jesus was scourged, "enclosed in a column of silver." Some years later, the same church was visited by the writer of another travel guide, the cleric Theodosius, who wrote *The Topography of the Holy Land*. By this time, the impressions on the scourging column had been expanded to also include Jesus' "whole countenance, His chin, nose, and eyes imprinted on it."

A number of new churches had been erected in Jerusalem as well. Across the Pool of Bethesda, where in the Gospel of John Jesus healed a man "who had been ill for thirty-eight years," a large, three-aisled basilica had risen. The structure was built with stones and columns from a nearby ruin, a second-century temple dedicated to the cult of Asclepius, the deity of health, since the pool had traditionally been credited with healing powers. Just outside the city gates, Theodosius visited a church on the spot where the disciple Stephen, the first Christian martyr, was believed to have been stoned. This church was commissioned by Aelia Eudocia, wife of Emperor Theodosius II, who had undertaken her own first pilgrimage to Jerusalem in 438. A highly educated woman who bore the emperor three children, she was accused of adultery and banished in 443, after which she settled in Jerusalem. Here, she was instrumental in restoring Jerusalem's walls and in completing St. Stephen's church, in which she would be buried upon her death. But if her hagiography is to be believed, perhaps her greatest contribution was her effort to curb the growing Byzantine antipathy toward Judaism, particularly toward Jews living in Palestine proper.

> IN [NAZARETH] THE BEAUTY OF THE HEBREW WOMEN IS SO GREAT, THAT NO MORE BEAUTIFUL WOMEN ARE FOUND AMONG THE HEBREWS.
>
> THE PIACENZA PILGRIM
> *Circa 570 C.E.*

THE OPPRESSION OF JEWS IN PALESTINE

The Byzantine oppression of Judaism was not new. It was Constantine the Great who had initiated the first of several discriminatory policies, greatly curtailing the power and autonomy of the Jewish courts. Emperor Constantius II (337–361 C.E.) followed by proscribing marriage between Jewish men and Christian women, and denying Jews the right to own slaves. Jewish communities, as

338

The Christian Triumph

well as the Samaritans, were also charged with a penalty tax that plunged many households into poverty. So odious was this tax that in 352, a revolt broke out in the Jewish quarter of Sepphoris, which quickly spread through the land. The rebellion was defeated, and countless Jews were imprisoned or sold into slavery. Sepphoris, the city built by Herod Antipas that had once served as one of the centers of the rabbinate, was burned to the ground. So was the seat of the Jewish Patriarchate in Tiberias, according to Christian sources, though this has never been confirmed by Jewish documents. The oppression was suspended during the reign of Julian the Apostate, but promptly reinstated under Emperor Theodosius. His eventual successor, Theodosius II, then purged Jews from all functions in the Byzantine administration. "No Jew shall obtain offices and dignities," his decree went; "to none shall the administration of city service be permitted."

By that time, many Jewish families in Palestine had had enough. They chose to leave the Byzantine Empire for good. Some settled along the principal caravan

These remains of a fortified Roman camp near Wadi Rum, Jordan, attest to the military power of Rome until well into the fourth century C.E.

A third-century C.E. mummy portrait of a man (opposite) shows the startling realism of Roman art in the Late Imperial Period.

PART III | THE LEGACY OF JESUS

routes in the Arabian Hejaz, or the main trade ports along the Red Sea, in Ethiopia and Yemen. In time, the links between these various Jewish settlements coalesced into a vibrant trade network, so that by the beginning of the sixth century a fair share of Mediterranean and Red Sea commerce was in Jewish hands. In 525, the king of the Himyarites in Yemen, Yusuf As'ar Yath'ar, even took the extraordinary step of converting to Judaism. His decision created the first sovereign state ruled by a Jewish king since the fall of the Hasmonean Kingdom to Pompey in 63 B.C.E.

Other Jewish families moved to Babylonia, now in the Persian Empire, where a thriving Jewish expatriate community had survived since the days of the Babylonian Captivity. Here, Jewish families were also levied with a special tax, but it was much less onerous than the Byzantine penalty tax. Many Jews accumulated extensive holdings and, like their Persian hosts, embraced polygamy—thus boosting the growth of Jewish communities. Their wealth was invested in synagogues and rabbinic centers that would eventually produce a Babylonian Talmud.

Justinian the Great

The last century of Christian Palestine opened with the reign of the greatest of Byzantine emperors, Justinian (r. 527–565). Born as Petrus Sabbatius, a man of low birth but endowed with a bright mind, he had been adopted by a consul named Justin, who seized the Byzantine throne upon the death of Emperor Anastasius in 518. The young Petrus, duly renamed Justinian in his patron's honor, then became Justin's closest advisor and succeeded him as sole emperor upon Justin's death in 527.

Anxious to hide his presumed illegitimacy, Justinian clothed his reign with the greatest pomp Byzantium had ever seen. Wherever he went, a train of magnificently attired courtiers and clergy went with him, as depicted in the shimmering mosaics of the San Vitale in Ravenna, Italy.

The glamour of Justinian's court was not without cause. The Byzantine Empire, and particularly Asia Minor, was experiencing a surprising economic renaissance. Markets rebounded as demand rose for the tantalizing luxuries from the East. To get these luxurious silks, gems, and spices, however, caravans had to traverse the treacherous routes controlled by the Sassanid Persians. In an effort to stave off any conflict, Justinian concluded a peace treaty with the Persian king, Khosrow I Anohshirvan, in 532, which was hopefully termed the "Treaty of Eternal Peace." It also cost the Byzantine treasury 11,000 pounds of gold, in keeping with Byzantium's growing custom of buying off an enemy it could not defeat. In reality, however, the cold war between the

The sixth-century Barbini Ivory is thought to portray Emperor Justinian I mounted on his horse.

The sixth-century basilica of San Vitale in Ravenna (opposite), one of the oldest Byzantine churches in Italy, contains one of the best preserved mosaics from the Justinian era.

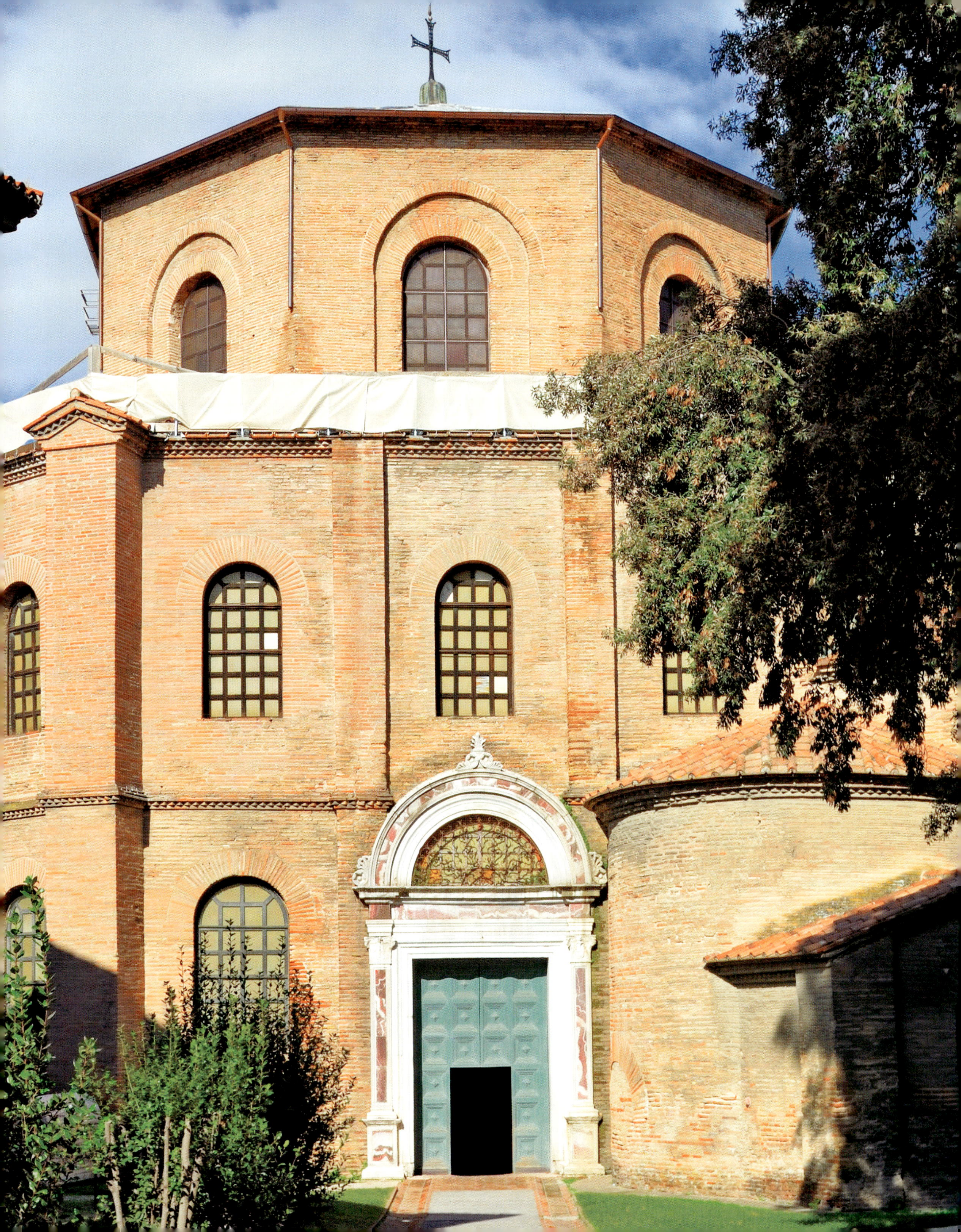

PART III | **THE LEGACY OF JESUS**

This famous mosaic in the San Vitale in Ravenna from around 548 C.E. depicts Emperor Justinian I clad in purple with a golden halo, surrounded by his courtiers.

This wall of the Bucoleon Palace (opposite) is all that remains of the Great Palace complex of the Byzantine emperors in Constantinople, now Istanbul.

Byzantine and Persian realms continued, channeled through various proxy wars in the region.

Justinian's craving for magnificence found expression in his prodigious building activity. In addition to building the great Hagia Sofia in Constantinople, he also commissioned the church of San Vitale in Ravenna, and he raised a brand-new basilica in Bethlehem, after the Church of the Nativity built by Empress Helena had been burned down by rebellious Samaritans. This basilica still stands to this day.

Prodded by the wealth of his empire, and believing that his eastern borders were now secure, Justinian embarked on a quest to reconquer Western Europe and restore the greatness of the Roman Empire. Initially, the efforts of his commanding general, Belisarius, met with stunning success. In 534, the Byzantine forces took North Africa from the Vandals. With full command of the Mediterranean Sea, Belisarius then launched an invasion of Sicily and the Italian peninsula. Rome was captured in 536. At the same time, another Byzantine general, Liberius, took control of the south of Spain.

The Christian Triumph

But these victories proved illusory. The campaigns devolved into a war of attrition when barbarian kingdoms, such as the Ostrogoths, proved too stubborn to be subdued. The coffers of the Byzantine treasury were steadily drained. Worse, with Justinian fully preoccupied in the west, the Persian king Khosrow I saw his chance for launching a surprise attack in the east. In 540, Persian forces invaded Syria and Asia Minor, capturing the city of Edessa so admired by the pilgrim Egeria, before pushing on to the Black Sea. Belisarius, rushing from the western front to the east, was able to stop the Persian king, but he could not evict him from captured territory. Another war of attrition ensued, which pushed the Byzantine state to the brink of bankruptcy. A peace treaty was finally concluded in 562, though once again at a heavy cost: an annual tribute to Persia of 500 pounds of gold.

Just five years earlier, Constantinople had been struck by an enormous earthquake; the great dome of the Hagia Sophia collapsed and had to be rebuilt completely. This disaster came on the heels of a massive outbreak of the

PART III | THE LEGACY OF JESUS

THE CHURCH OF HOLY WISDOM

In 532, a rash of disturbances known as the Nika riots led to the destruction of a Christian church in Constantinople. This church had been dedicated to God as the source of Holy Wisdom, or *Hagia Sophia*. Emperor Justinian then charged two of his finest architects, Anthenius of Tralles and Isidorus of Miletus, to build a new church to the *Hagia Sophia* that would surpass anything that had been built by Christendom to date. The result is the last great achievement of Roman architecture. Its very plan is ambiguous: Although conceived as a basilica, the emphasis rests on the central nave, shaped as an elliptical hall and anchored by four semicircular chapels. This nave is crowned by a dome, which emphasizes the illusion of a centralized church. Some 180 feet high and 100 feet wide, this huge sphere seems to float effortlessly—an impression that is reinforced by the string of windows at the very base of the dome. To accomplish this effect, Justinian's architect invented so-called pendentives, concave triangular supports that negotiate the transition from the dome to the square shape of the crossing below. That this church still stands after some 1,500 years, despite centuries of neglect, is testimony to the mastery of Roman engineering.

The 100-foot-wide dome of the Hagia Sophia in Istanbul, built by Emperor Justinian I between 532 and 537 C.E., is the last great triumph of Roman engineering.

The Christian Triumph

The central crossing of the Church of the Holy Sepulcher in Jerusalem, known as the Catholikon Dome, was originally built during the 12th-century Crusader period.

plague. The Justinian renaissance had run its course. In 565, Justinian died, leaving his successors, Justin II (565–578) and Tiberius II (574–582), with empty coffers.

The last record of a pilgrimage before 614 was written by an Italian, Antoninus, who left his native Placentia (today's Piacenza) in 570. Choosing to travel by sea, he sailed to Constantinople and from there to Cyprus, where he boarded a vessel for the Syrian coast, eventually making his way to Acre. Arriving in Nazareth, Antoninus praised the fecundity of the area, particularly its luscious grapes, oil, and honey. A true Italian at heart, he appears to have fallen under the spell of the women in the city. "Though the Hebrews have no love for Christians," he wrote, "these women are still full of charity for them." Visiting the local synagogue, he admired a book "from which our Lord had learned his ABC's." In Cana, he submitted to a temptation of countless tourists since; while reclining on the stone couch "where our Lord was present at the marriage feast," he guiltily scratched the names of his parents, "unworthy as I was."

From Galilee, Antoninus made his way to Mount Tabor, site of Jesus' Transfiguration, and described the presence of three churches. As we saw, these must have been the churches built in 422 and 553, respectively, when Tabor became the seat of its own bishopric. It is possible that these were built over three grottoes, currently contained within the modern basilica completed in 1923, which marked the three "dwellings" that Peter wanted to erect on the site

> **O SOLOMON, I HAVE SURPASSED YOU!**
>
> EMPEROR JUSTINIAN UPON ENTERING THE HAGIA SOPHIA
> *Circa 537 C.E.*

The Dome of the Rock, located on Jerusalem's Temple Mount, rises from the clutter of the Old City with the gilded onion domes of the Russian Orthodox Church of St. Mary Magdalene in the foreground.

(Matthew 17:4). Antoninus then traveled to Jerusalem, where he joined a throng of pilgrims admiring the Church of the Holy Sepulcher.

But his visit to Jesus' tomb was cause for disappointment, as it is for many visitors to this day. In the 250 years since its construction, the tomb's shrine had been burdened with "innumerable" votive ornaments, including "armlets, bracelets, chains, necklaces, coronets, waistbands, sword-belts, and crowns of emperors made of gold and precious stones." From Jerusalem, the pilgrim from Placentia traveled to Bethlehem and Hebron before retracing his steps on his way back to Italy around 573.

The Islamic Empire

The foundations of the Christian Holy Land, however, were rapidly beginning to crumble. The Byzantine armies, long without pay, revolted against Emperor Maurice (r. 582–602). The chaotic state gave the Persian king Khosrow II a pretext to invade. In 610, the year of Muhammad's first revelation on Mount Hira, the Persian armies marched into Anatolia. Antioch was invested in 611, followed by Armenia, Syria, and the Caucasus kingdom of Lazica. In 614, the Persian general Shahrbaraz entered Palestine, looting and burning his way toward Jerusalem. The Christian sites that he encountered on his march, including the churches of Nazareth, Capernaum, and Mount Tabor, were destroyed on his orders. Arriving before the gates of Jerusalem, the Persians systematically demolished every Christian structure on the hills surrounding the city, including the Mount of Olives. When Jerusalem fell at last after a siege of 21 days, the streets once again ran with blood. More than 65,000 Christians were killed. Most churches were burned to the ground, including the Church of the Holy Sepulcher. The True Cross was carried back to Persia in triumph. The Holy Land lay in ruins.

Byzantium was granted one last respite. In 627, Byzantine emperor Heraclius took his revenge by dealing King Khosrow a stinging defeat at the Battle of Nineveh. Three years later, Heraclius solemnly returned the True Cross to Jerusalem. But time had run out. A new nation was rising in Arabia under the unifying banner of Islam. Muhammad's unexpected death in 632 threatened to break up this newfound unity, as many tribal chieftains saw themselves absolved from their pledge of fealty to the Prophet. In response, Muhammad's successor, Abu Bakr, resorted to force of arms to maintain the cohesion of the new Islamic *ummah*. His military campaign soon spilled over into Arabia's borders with Persia and Byzantium, and eventually evolved into a war of conquest. In 634, just 20 years after the Persian sack of Jerusalem, Abu Bakr's successor, Caliph 'Umar ibn al-Khattab, plunged into Syria and Palestine, defeating the aging Emperor Heraclius. Three years later, 'Umar climbed down from his white camel and walked through the gates of Jerusalem.

Thus, control of the Holy Land passed to the Islamic Empire.

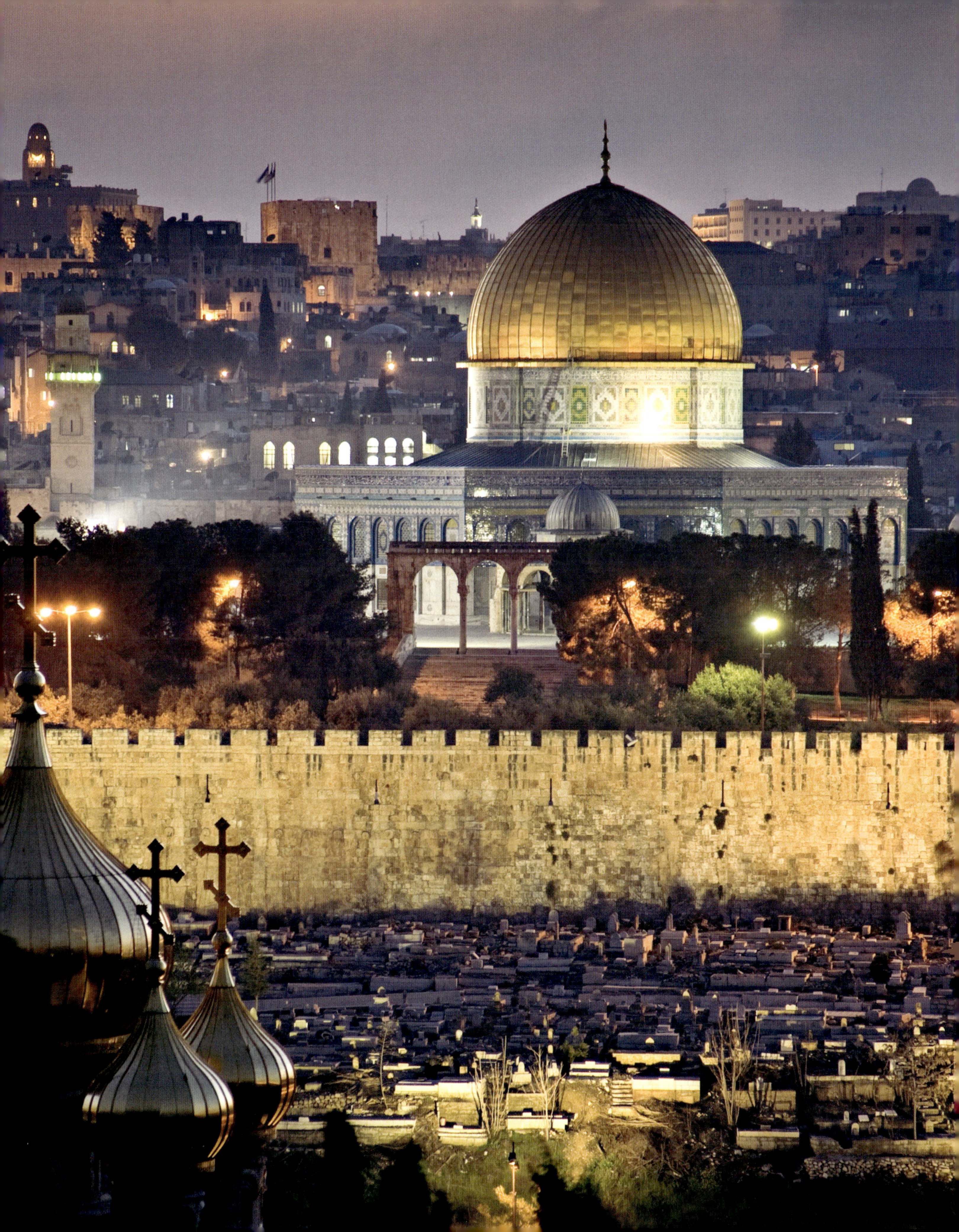

EPILOGUE
Pilgrimage after the Islamic Conquest

Remarkably, the integration of Palestine in the Islamic Empire, which save for a brief interruption during the Crusader era would continue until the early 20th century, did not stop the flow of European pilgrims to the Holy Land. This is remarkable because, as several scholars have pointed out, Christianity never ordained pilgrimage as a holy obligation, or indeed bestowed any significant redemptive status on those who braved pirate-infested seas or treacherous roads to travel to Muslim Jerusalem. For many, it seemed, these dangers made a pilgrimage even more meritorious, for it brought them closer to the fears and dangers that the Apostles and martyrs themselves had suffered on their journey. Initially, though, the new Muslim administration respected Christian worship. Countless churches and holy sites were left in peace, not in the least because Christians were considered "People of the Book," heir to revelations from the same God who had spoken to Muhammad—although in the Muslim view, the Christian interpretation of these revelations was flawed, not as pure as the Holy Qur'an. The tax on non-Muslims was raised, and no new churches could be built, but otherwise Christian communities were left to go about their business.

What's more, the Muslim caliphs recognized the commercial value of European traffic to Palestine, which otherwise was a rather unremarkable backwater. They also appreciated the spiritual importance of pilgrimage, given that the *hajj* to Mecca is one of the five pillars of Islam. Nevertheless, Christians were now considered a lesser community in Palestine.

One pilgrim who left a record of his impressions during this period was the French prelate Arculf. Arriving in Palestine sometime after 679, during Ummayad rule, Arculf visited Coptic monasteries in Egypt before moving on to Bethlehem and Jerusalem. His narrative, which was published in Bede's *Historia Ecclesiae,* generated tremendous interest and fueled a new wave of pilgrimage to

This 12th-century Crusader map, which today resides in the University Library of Uppsala, shows all key pilgrimage sites in Jerusalem.

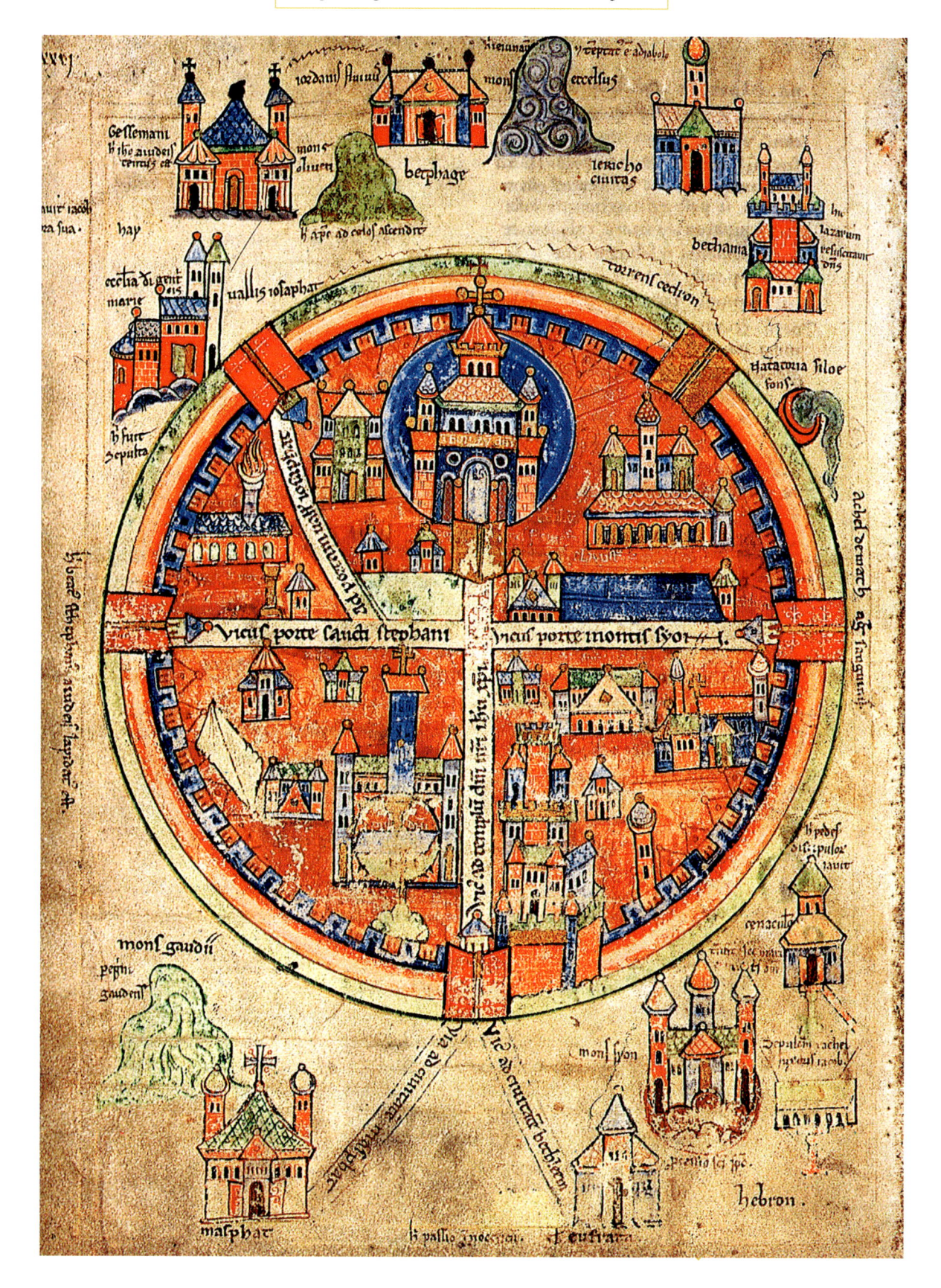

Pilgrimage after the Islamic Conquest

EPILOGUE

This sixth-century mosaic from a Byzantine church in Madaba, Jordan, provides a schematic representation of Jerusalem from that period, with the central Cardo Maximus, or main Roman boulevard, running across the city.

The Rotunda of the Church of the Holy Sepulcher (opposite), built over the traditional location of Jesus' tomb, was—and is—the ultimate destination of thousands of pilgrims to the Holy Land.

the Holy Land. That this was a time of growing tension between the Byzantine and Islamic empires did not deter these pilgrims, though many were now forced to travel by sea via Alexandria, rather than using the overland route through Asia Minor and Syria. Sometime in the late eighth century, a monk named Fidelis even claimed that he had sailed from the Nile to the Red Sea using an ancient canal once dug by Emperor Hadrian. Apparently, the Roman canal had been repaired and maintained by the local Muslim government before it was permanently blocked by Caliph Abu Giafar Almansor in 767.

Pilgrim conditions in Palestine improved considerably during the reign of the enlightened Caliph Harun-al-Rashid (786–809), who was on excellent terms with his European counterpart, Charlemagne. At Charlemagne's request, the caliph oversaw a number of improvements in pilgrim hospices throughout Jerusalem. But a hundred years later, around 870, the pendulum swung against Christian pilgrimage. One French pilgrim, a nobleman named Frotmond who undertook the voyage as an act of penance, was said to have been so savagely robbed and beaten that he was left for dead on the road, naked and bleeding.

Matters did not improve when in 969, General Gawhar al-Siqilli of the Shia dynasty of the Fatimids conquered much of the Islamic Empire, including the Holy Land. Six years later, the Byzantine emperor John I Tzimiskes (925–976) launched a war to recapture the Holy Land, pushing as far as Tiberias and Nazareth. He was, however, defeated on his way to Jerusalem and died shortly thereafter.

THE ORIGINS OF THE CRUSADES

The climate for pilgrims then moved from bad to worse when the infamous Fatimid caliph Al-Hakim (985–1021) ordered the destruction of all Christian churches as well as synagogues throughout his domain. The Church of the Holy Sepulcher, painstakingly rebuilt after the Persian sack of 617, was torn down in 1008, while other churches were converted to stables or used for other menial purposes. Both Christians and Jews were oppressed and persecuted; the few pilgrims who still made it to the Holy Land reported widespread defamations of Christian holy sites.

One of these pilgrims was a prelate named Gerbert, later to become Pope Sylvester II. Upon his return in 986, he published an open letter calling upon the Christian world to come to the aid of the beleaguered Christian communities in Palestine. The uproar created by Gerbert's letter encouraged more pilgrims to

Pilgrimage after the Islamic Conquest

make the long voyage and thus show their defiance of Al-Hakim's policies. Caliph Ma'ad al-Mustansir Billah, the grandson of Al-Hakim, tried to make amends and, prodded by Byzantine emperor Constantine IX, even authorized the reconstruction of the Holy Sepulcher Church in 1042, but the momentum for a pan-European "Holy War" against Muslim control of Palestine continued to grow. A decade later, Christianity suffered its Great Schism, splitting the church into the Eastern Orthodox and the Roman Catholic denominations. Since the Holy Land now fell under the nominal jurisdiction of the Eastern Orthodox Church in Constantinople, calls in the West for a liberation of Palestine became even more strident.

What ultimately provoked the First Crusade, however, was not Muslim oppression or Christian rivalry, but another regime change in the increasingly fractured Muslim world—this time initiated by Turkish Seljuqs led by Malik Shah (1055–1092). In 1073, the Seljuqs exploited the impact of a prolonged famine in Egypt to defeat the weakened Fatimid rule and capture Jerusalem. Fatimid Muslims as well as Jews and Christians were massacred without distinction. The population of Jerusalem revolted in response, but the rebellion was bloodily suppressed by Emir Atsiz ibd Uvaq. Pilgrims were barred from the gates of Jerusalem unless they paid a heavy tax, though many didn't even get that far, having been killed and plundered on the way. Soon thereafter, the Seljuq Empire disintegrated into various warring states, but the damage was done. During the Council of Clermont in 1095, Pope Urban II called for Holy War to deliver the Christians in the Holy Land from Muslim rule.

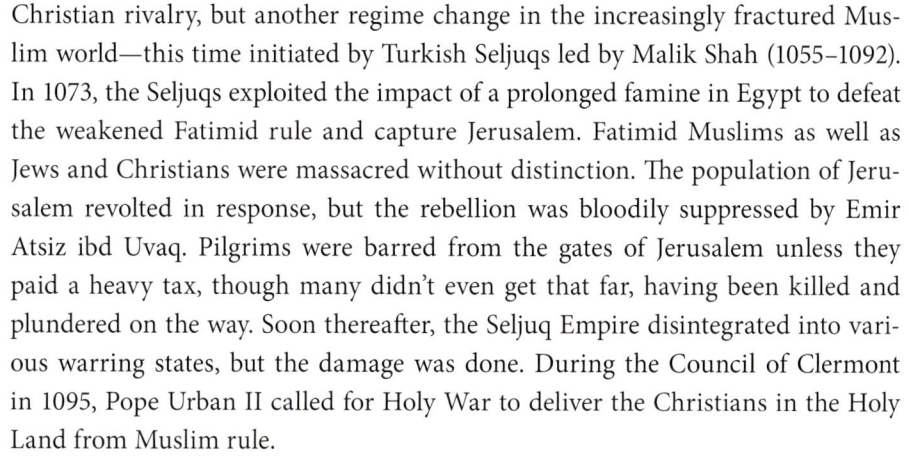

The story of the Crusades and what transpired afterward in the Holy Land falls outside the scope of this book. Suffice to say that many of Europe's knights rose to the challenge, though many were inspired by lesser motives, such as a lust for loot and pillage. In this they were considerably encouraged by a Papal pledge of "plenary indulgence." Some nine Crusades—the word *crusade* is French, meaning "taking up the cross"—were launched between 1096 and 1291. This resulted in less than a century of Crusader rule in Jerusalem, from 1099 to 1187. During this brief period, some features of the original Holy Sepulcher Church were restored while other basilicas were built afresh, including St. Anne's Church near Stephen's Gate, which today ranks as one of the finest examples of Crusader architecture in Jerusalem. The Crusaders held out in Caesarea, one of their main

EPILOGUE

British artist David Roberts (1796–1864) captured the mood of Ottoman Jerusalem, including the Holy Sepulcher Church, in this lithograph from the 1840s.

strongholds, until 1275, when they were evicted by the Mamluk Sultan Baibars. The Mamluks then remained in control of Palestine until Jerusalem fell to the Ottoman Turks in 1517, who would remain in charge for another 400 years.

Ottoman rule cast a long shadow over the Holy Land. Palestine was plunged in a prolonged period of official neglect. Churches crumbled while pilgrims fought off Barbary pirates, lice, heatstroke, thieves, and avaricious hosts, suffering appalling conditions in local hospices and inns.

Pilgrimage in Modern Times

The 19th century brought change. Growing international trade, steamships, and railways once again gave a big impetus to pilgrimage traffic. The popularity of the Holy Land was further boosted by the publication of color lithographs drawn by the Scottish painter David Roberts in the late 1840s, as well as engravings and later, photographs in popular magazines. In response, many nations began to establish societies and fraternities in the Holy Land, offering their countrymen food, shelter, and protection.

By the time British general Allenby conquered Palestine near the end of World War I, the country was a deeply impoverished region with a population of barely 700,000; Jerusalem was down to a mere 15,000 inhabitants. The proclamation of the State of Israel in 1947 and the subsequent Six Day War of 1967 transformed Palestine, and brought almost all of the principal sites related to the life of Jesus under control of the Jewish state.

Today, the lure of the Holy Land continues unabated despite the ongoing Middle East conflict. Perhaps one explanation is that for many Christians, a visit to the holy sites is a deeply spiritual experience, as it has been for thousands of pilgrims since the days of Late Antiquity. For some, the encounter with this strange and beautiful land resolves the cultural schism between European Christianity and first-century Palestine. Others see the visit as a physical manifestation of their faith, a visceral connection with the many mysteries of Christianity that escape objective reason. In Jerusalem in particular, walking the stations of the cross enables many Christians to imagine the suffering of the Passion as a real and tangible event.

That such a journey can also be a very joyful and exhilarating experience is due to the fact that today, the land of Galilee appears pristine, and possibly as it was in Jesus' day—reason why many authors refer to Galilee as the "Fifth Gospel." For this we have to thank centuries of judicious stewardship against tremendous odds by holy site custodians, including the Franciscans, as well as the great care with which both the Christian Arab population as well as successive Israeli governments have maintained Galilee's pristine condition.

That is why for many Christians, the desire to see the Holy Land is as intense as it was in the days of Paula and Egeria—and the thousands of other nameless pilgrims who have walked in the footsteps of Jesus ever since.

Pilgrimage after the Islamic Conquest

Church of the Holy Sepulchre, Jerusalem

APPENDIX

THE HEBREW SCRIPTURES (TANAKH)

THE LAW (TORAH)	THE PROPHETS (NEVI'IM)	THE WRITINGS (KETUVIM)
Genesis Exodus Leviticus Numbers Deuteronomy	*Former Prophets:* Joshua Judges Samuel (I and II) Kings (I and II) *Latter Prophets:* Isaiah Jeremiah Ezekiel *Twelve Minor Prophets:* Hosea Joel Amos Obadiah Jonah Micah Nahum Habakkuk Zephaniah Haggai Zechariah Malachi	Psalms Proverbs Job Song of Solomon Ruth Lamentations Ecclesiastes Esther Daniel Ezra-Nehemiah Chronicles (I and II)

THE BOOKS OF THE OLD TESTAMENT

Genesis Exodus Leviticus Numbers Deuteronomy Joshua Judges Ruth I Samuel II Samuel I Kings II Kings I Chronicles II Chronicles Ezra Nehemiah Esther Job Psalms Proverbs Ecclesiastes Song of Solomon	Isaiah Jeremiah Lamentations Ezekiel Daniel Hosea Joel Amos Obadiah Jonah Micah Nahum Habakkuk Zephaniah Haggai Zechariah Malachi	*Deuterocanonical/Apocryphal:* Tobit Judith Esther The Wisdom of Solomon Ecclesiasticus Baruch Letter of Jeremiah Additions to Daniel, *including:* Prayer of Azariah Song of Three Jews Susanna Bel and the Dragon I Maccabees II Maccabees I Esdras Prayer of Manasseh Psalm 151 III Maccabees II Esdras IV Maccabees

THE BOOKS OF THE NEW TESTAMENT

THE GOSPELS	TRADITIONAL ATTRIBUTION	POSSIBLE DATE
Matthew	Matthew (Levi)	75–90 C.E.
Mark	Mark, Peter's interpreter	66–70 C.E.
Luke	Luke, Paul's attendant	75–90 C.E.
John	John (disciple)	85–100 C.E.

ACTS	TRADITIONAL ATTRIBUTION	POSSIBLE DATE
Acts of the Apostles	Luke, Paul's attendant	75–90 C.E.

PAULINE EPISTLES	TRADITIONAL ATTRIBUTION	POSSIBLE DATE
Letter to the Romans	Paul	56–57 C.E.
First Letter to the Corinthians	Paul	54–55 C.E.
Second Letter to the Corinthians	Paul	55–56 C.E.
Letter to the Galatians	Paul	50–56 C.E.
Letter to the Ephesians	Paul (pseudonymous)	80–95 C.E.
Letter to the Philippians	Paul	54–55 C.E.
Letter to the Colossians	Paul	57–61 C.E.
First Letter to the Thessalonians	Paul	50–51 C.E.
Second Letter to the Thessalonians	Paul	50–51 C.E.
First Letter to Timothy	Paul (pseudonymous)	90–110 C.E.
Second Letter to Timothy	Paul (pseudonymous)	90–110 C.E.
Letter to Titus	Paul (pseudonymous)	90–110 C.E.
Letter to Philemon	Paul	54–55 C.E.
Letter to the Hebrews	Paul (pseudonymous	60–95 C.E.

GENERAL EPISTLES	TRADITIONAL ATTRIBUTION	POSSIBLE DATE
Letter to James	James, brother of Jesus	50–70 C.E.
First Letter of Peter	Peter (pseudonymous)	70–90 C.E.
Second Letter of Peter	Peter (pseudonymous)	80–90 C.E.
First Letter of John	John (disciple)	ca 100 C.E.
Second Letter of John	John (disciple)	ca 100 C.E.
Third Letter of John	John (disciple)	ca 100 C.E.
Letter of Jude	Jude, brother of Jesus	45–65 C.E.

PROPHECY	TRADITIONAL ATTRIBUTION	POSSIBLE DATE
Revelation	John (disciple)	70–100 C.E.

FURTHER READING

THE HISTORICAL JESUS

Borg, Marcus J. *Jesus: Uncovering the Life, Teachings, and Relevance of a Religious Revolutionary.* San Francisco: HarperSanFrancisco, 2006.
Charlesworth, James H. (ed.). *Jesus' Jewishness: Exploring the Place of Jesus in Early Judaism.* New York: Crossroad, 1991.
Chilton, Bruce. *Rabbi Jesus.* New York: Doubleday, 2000.
Crossan, John Dominic. *Jesus: A Revolutionary Biography.* New York: HarperCollins Publishers, 1994.
Crossan, John Dominic. *Who Killed Jesus? Exposing the Roots of Anti-Semitism in the Gospel Story of the Death of Jesus.* New York: HarperCollins, 1995.
Crossan, John Dominic, and Jonathan L. Reed. *Excavating Jesus: Beneath the Stones, Behind the Texts.* New York: HarperCollins, 2001.
Ehrman, Bart. *Jesus: Apocalyptic Prophet of the New Millennium.* New York: Oxford University Press, 1999.
Evans, Craig. *Jesus and His World: The Archaeological Evidence.* Louisville, Ky.: Westminster John Knox Press, 2012.
Fredriksen, Paula. *Jesus of Nazareth, King of the Jews.* New York: Alfred A. Knopf, 1999.
Horsley, Richard A. *Jesus and Empire: The Kingdom of God and the New World Disorder.* Minneapolis: Fortress Press, 2003.
Levine, Amy-Jill (ed.). *Historical Jesus in Context.* Princeton, N.J.: Princeton University Press, 2006.
McCane, Byron R. *Roll Back the Stone: Death and Burial in the World of Jesus.* Harrisburg, Pa.: Trinity Press International, 2003.
Meier, John P. *A Marginal Jew: Rethinking the Historical Jesus.* Vols. 1, 2, and 3. New York: Doubleday, 1994.
Porter, J. R. *Jesus Christ: The Jesus of History, the Christ of Faith.* New York: Barnes and Noble, 1999.
Reed, Jonathan L. *The HarperCollins Visual Guide to the New Testament.* New York: HarperCollins, 2007.
Sanders, E. P. *Jesus and Judaism.* Philadelphia: Fortress, 1985.
Senior, Donald. *Jesus: A Gospel Portrait.* Mahwah, N.J.: Paulist Press, 1992.
Stemberger, Günter. *Jewish Contemporaries of Jesus: Pharisees, Sadducees, Essenes.* Minneapolis: Fortress, 1995.

NEW TESTAMENT AND EARLY CHRISTIAN TEXTS, AND THE MISHNAH

Danby, Herbert. *Tractate Sanhedrin, Mishnah and Tosefta, with commentary.* New York: Macmillan, 1919.
Ehrman, Bart D. *Lost Christianities: The Battles for Scripture and the Faiths We Never Knew.* Oxford: Oxford University Press, 2003.
Fitzmyer, Joseph A., S. J. *The Gospel According to Luke I–IX.* Garden City, N.Y.: Doubleday, 1981.
Humphrey, Hugh M. *From Q to "Secret" Mark: A Composition History of the Earliest Narrative Theology.* London: T and T Clark, 2006.
Kasser, Rodolphe, Marvin Meyer, and Gregor Wurst. *The Gospel of Judas.* Washington, D.C.: National Geographic Society, 2006.
Kee, Howard Clark. *The Beginnings of Christianity: An Introduction to the New Testament.* London: T and T Clark, 2005.
Kloppenborg Verbin, John S. *Excavating Q: The History and Setting of the Sayings Gospel.* London: T and T Clark, 2000.
Mack, Burton L. *The Lost Gospel: The Book of Q and Christian Origins.* San Francisco: HarperSanFrancisco, 1993.
Moloney, Francis J. *The Gospel of John: Text and Context.* Leiden, Holland: Brill, 2005.
Mullen, J. Patrick. *Dining with Pharisees.* Collegeville, Minn.: Liturgical Press, 2004.
Neusner, Jacob. *Introduction to Rabbinic Literature.* New York: Doubleday, 1999.
Neusner, Jacob. *Judaism When Christianity Began: A Survey of Belief and Practice.* Louisville, Ky.: John Knox Press, 2002.
Neusner, Jacob. *The Mishnah: A New Translation.* New Haven, Conn.: Yale University Press, 1988.
Pagels, Elaine. *Beyond Belief: The Secret Gospel of Thomas.* New York: Random House, 2003.
Pagels, Elaine. *The Gnostic Gospels.* New York: Random House, 1979.
Porter, Stanley (ed.). *Hearing the Old Testament in the New Testament.* Grand Rapids, Mich.: Eerdmans, 2006.
Porter, Stanley (ed.). *Paul and His Theology.* Pauline Studies, Vol. 3. Leiden, Holland: Brill, 2006.
Resseguie, James L. *Narrative Criticism of the New Testament: An Introduction.* Grand Rapids, Mich.: Baker, 2005.
Robinson, J. M. (gen. ed.). *The Nag Hammadi Library.* Leiden, Holland: EJ Brill, 1977.
Sanders, E. P. *Jewish Law from Jesus to the Mishnah: Five Studies.* Philadelphia: Trinity Press International, 1990.
Schiffman, Lawrence H. *Reclaiming the Dead Sea Scrolls: The History of Judaism, the Background of Christianity, the Lost Library of Qumran.* New York: Doubleday, 1995.
Valantasis, Richard. *The New Q: A Fresh Translation with Commentary.* London: T and T Clark, 2005.
Whiston, William. *The Complete Works of Josephus.* Grand Rapids, Mich.: Kregel, 1981.

GALILEE AND GALILEAN ARCHAEOLOGY

Arnal, William E. *Jesus and the Village Scribes: Galilean Conflicts and the Setting of Q.* Minneapolis: First Fortress Press, 2001
Chancey, Mark A. *Greco-Roman Culture and the Galilee of Jesus.* Cambridge: Cambridge University Press, 2005.
Chancey, Mark A. *The Myth of a Gentile Galilee.* Cambridge: Cambridge University Press, 2002.
Goodman, Martin. *State and Society in Roman Galilee, A.D. 132–212.* Totowa, N.J.: Rowman and Allanheld, 1983.

Hezser, Catherine. *Jewish Literacy in Roman Palestine.* Tübingen, Germany: Mohr Siebeck, 2001.
Horsley, Richard A. *Bandits, Prophets, and Messiahs: Popular Movements in the Time of Jesus.* Harrisburg, Pa.: Trinity Press, 1999.
Horsley, Richard A. *Galilee: History, Politics, People.* Harrisburg, Pa.: Trinity Press, 1995.
Horsley, Richard A. *Jesus and the Spiral of Violence: Popular Jewish Resistance in Roman Palestine.* Minneapolis: First Fortress Press, 1993.
Reed, Jonathan. *Archaeology and the Galilean Jesus: A Re-Examination of the Evidence.* Harrisburg, Pa.: Trinity Press International, 2002.
Runesson, A., D. D. Binder, and B. Olsson. *The Ancient Synagogue from its Origins to 200 C.E.: A Source Book.* Leiden, Holland: Brill, 2008.

ECONOMY OF ROMAN PALESTINE

Duncan-Jones, Richard. *Money and Government in the Roman Empire.* Cambridge: Cambridge University Press, 1994.
Duncan-Jones, Richard. *Structure and Scale in the Roman Economy.* Cambridge: Cambridge University Press, 1990.
Evans, Jane DeRose. *The Coins and the Hellenistic, Roman, and Byzantine Economy of Palestine.* Boston: American Schools of Oriental Research, 2006.
Finley, M. I. *The Ancient Economy.* London: Hogarth Press, 1985.
Garnsey, Peter. *Cities, Peasants, and Food in Classical Antiquity.* Cambridge: Cambridge University Press, 1998.
Garnsey, Peter. *Social Status and Legal Privilege in the Roman Empire.* Oxford: Clarendon Press, 1970.
Hamel, Gildas. *Poverty and Charity in Roman Palestine, First Three Centuries c.e.* Berkeley: University of California Press, 1990.
Oakman, Douglas E. *Jesus and the Economic Questions of His Day.* Queenstown, Ontario: Edwin Mellen Press, 1986.
Pastor, Jack. *Land and Economy in Ancient Palestine.* New York: Routledge, 1997.
Safrai, Ze'ev. *The Economy of Roman Palestine.* London: Routledge, 1994.
Wallace, Sherman LeRoy. *Taxation in Egypt from Augustus to Diocletian.* New York: Greenwood Press, 1969.

SOCIAL CONDITIONS IN ROMAN PALESTINE

Archer, Léonie J. *Her Price Is Beyond Rubies: The Jewish Woman in Graeco-Roman Palestine.* Sheffield, England: JSOT Press, 1990.
Daniel-Rops. *Daily Life in Palestine at the Time of Christ.* London: Weidenfeld and Nicolson, 1962.
Edwards, D. *Religion and Society in Roman Palestine: Old Questions, New Answers.* New York: Routledge, 2004.
Fager, Jeffrey A. *Land Tenure and the Biblical Jubilee: Uncovering Hebrew Ethics through the Sociology of Knowledge.* Sheffield, England: Sheffield Academic Press, 1993.
Fiensy, David A. *The Social History of Palestine in the Herodian Period: The Land Is Mine.* Lewiston, N.Y.: Edwin Mellen Press, 1991.
Magnes, Jodi. *Stone and Dung, Oil and Spit. Jewish Life in the Time of Jesus.* Grand Rapids, Mich.: Eerdmans, 2011.

POLITICAL HISTORY OF ROMAN PALESTINE

Elsner, Jas. *Imperial Rome and Christian Triumph.* New York: Oxford University Press, 1998.
Grant, Robert M. *Augustus to Constantine: The Emergence of Christianity in the Roman World.* San Francisco: HarperSanFrancisco, 1970.
Ilan, Tal. *Jewish Women in Greco-Roman Palestine.* Peabody, Mass.: Hendrickson, 1996.
Jeffers, James S. *The Greco-Roman World of the New Testament Era: Exploring the Background of Early Christianity.* Downers Grove, Ill.: InterVarsity Press, 1999.
Mommsen, Theodor. *A History of Rome under the Emperors.* New York: Routledge, 1996.
Netzer, Ehud. *The Architecture of Herod the Great Builder.* Grand Rapids, Mich.: Baker, 2006.
Richardson, Peter. *Herod: King of the Jews and Friend of the Romans.* Columbia: University of South Carolina Press, 1996.
Roller, Duane W. *The Building Program of Herod the Great.* Berkeley: University of California Press, 1998.
Safrai, S., et al. (eds.). *The Jewish People in the First Century.* Vol. 2. Philadelphia: Fortress, 1976.
Sperber, Daniel. *The City in Roman Palestine.* Oxford: Oxford University Press, 1998.
Udoh, Fabian E. *To Caesar What Is Caesar's: Tribute, Taxes, and Imperial Administration in Early Roman Palestine (63 b.c.e.–70 c.e.).* Providence, R.I.: Brown Judaic Studies, 2005.

HISTORY OF HOLY LAND PILGRIMAGE

Kollek, Teddy, and Moshe Pearlman. *Pilgrims to the Holy Land.* London: Weinfeld and Nicolson, 1970.
Le Beau, Bryan, and Menachem Mor (eds.). *Pilgrims and Travelers to the Holy Land.* Omaha, Neb.: Creighton University Press, 1996.
McClure, M. L., and C. L. Feltoe (eds. and trans.). *The Pilgrimage of Etheria.* London: Society for Promoting Christian Knowledge, 1919.
Wilkinson, John. *Jerusalem Pilgrims Before the Crusades.* Warminster, England: Aris and Phillips, 1977.
Wilkinson, J. et al. (eds.). Jerusalem Pilgrimage, 1099–1185. London: The Hakluyt Society, 1988.
Wright, Thomas. Early Travels in Palestine. New York: Ktav Publishing, 1968.

ABOUT THE AUTHOR, BOARD OF ADVISERS, AND ACKNOWLEDGMENTS

ABOUT THE AUTHOR

Jean-Pierre Isbouts is a humanities scholar and graduate professor in the doctoral programs at Fielding Graduate University in Santa Barbara, California. He has published widely on the origins of Judaism, Christianity, and Islam, including the best-seller *The Biblical World: An Illustrated Atlas*, published by the National Geographic Society in 2007. His other books include *Young Jesus: Restoring the Lost Years of a Social Activist and Religious Dissident* (Sterling, 2008); *From Moses to Muhammad: The Shared Origins of Judaism, Christianity and Islam* (Pantheon, 2010); and *The Mysteries of Jesus*, published by the National Geographic Society in early 2012. An award-winning filmmaker, Dr. Isbouts has also produced a number of programs, including *Charlton Heston's Voyage Through the Bible* (GoodTimes, 1998), *The Quest for Peace* (Hallmark, 2003), and *Young Jesus* (PBS, 2008). His website is www.jpisbouts.org.

BOARD OF ADVISERS

Shaye J. D. Cohen is the Littauer Professor of Hebrew Literature and Philosophy in the Department of Near Eastern Languages and Civilizations of Harvard University. He is the author of *From the Maccabees to the Mishnah* and *The Beginnings of Jewishness*.

Craig Evans is the Payzant Distinguished Professor of New Testament at Acadia Divinity College of Acadia University in Nova Scotia, Canada. He is the author and editor of more than 60 books, including *The World of Jesus and the Early Church* and *Jesus and His World: The Archaeological Evidence*.

Amy-Jill Levine is University Professor of New Testament and Jewish Studies, E. Rhodes and Leona B. Carpenter Professor of New Testament Studies, and Professor of Jewish Studies at Vanderbilt University. She is the author of *The Misunderstood Jew: The Church and the Scandal of the Jewish Jesus* and (with Marc Brettler) the editor of the Oxford *Jewish Annotated New Testament*.

Rev. Donald Senior, C.P., is a professor of New Testament Studies and the president of Catholic Theological Union in Chicago. He is the general editor of the Oxford *Catholic Study Bible* and the author of *Jesus: A Gospel Portrait*, among other works.

ACKNOWLEDGMENTS

This book is the culmination of a 15-year quest for the Jesus of history, as well as the Jesus of faith, in my capacity as an archaeologist and art historian. First and foremost, I should thank Lisa Thomas, senior editor at National Geographic's Book Division, for developing the concept for this book in the first place, and for her unerring support throughout. Also, I wish to thank the superb editorial team at National Geographic, including editors Barbara Payne and Garrett Brown for their editorial guidance, Cinda Rose for her imaginative layouts, Rob Waymouth for his excellent photo research, Carl Mehler for his wonderful maps, and Kate Lapin for her gentle copy edit.

Special thanks are due to the panel of distinguished scholars who reviewed the manuscript, specifically Craig Evans at Divinity College of Acadia University, in Wolfville, Nova Scotia; Father Donald Senior, C.P., general editor of The Catholic Study Bible; Shaye J. D. Cohen, Littauer Professor of Hebrew Literature and Philosophy at Harvard University; and Amy-Jill Levine, E. Rhodes and Leona B. Carpenter Professor of New Testament Studies at Vanderbilt University Divinity School.

Other scholars who kindly gave their time during my research include Peter Awn, Dean of General Studies at Columbia University, New York; Elaine Pagels, Harrington Spear Paine Professor of Religion at Princeton University; Bruce Chilton, Bernard Iddings Bell Professor of Religion at Bard College, New York; Khaled Abou El Fadl, Professor of Islamic Law at UCLA; Jacob Neusner, Research Professor of Religion and Theology at Bard College in Annandale-on-Hudson, New York; Frank Peters, Professor of Religious, Middle Eastern, and Islamic Studies at New York University, New York; Professor Jean-Pierre M. Ruiz of St. John's University; and Rabbi Reuven Firestone, Professor of Medieval Jewish and Islamic Studies at USC in Los Angeles. In addition, I have profited from the research of many other scholars, notably the recent published work of Marcus Borg, Mark Chancey, John Dominic Crossan, David Fiensy, K. C. Hanson, Richard Horsley, Zvi Gal, Peter Garnsey, Martin Goodman, John P. Meier, Douglas Oakman, Fabian Udoh, and Jonathan Reed. I also wish to thank Dr. Thomas K. Tewell, formerly of the Fifth Avenue Presbyterian Church in New York, and especially my pastor, Monsignor Lloyd Torgerson of St. Monica's Church in Santa Monica, California, for his spiritual guidance. Needless to say, any errors in the narrative are mine, and mine alone.

I also owe a debt of gratitude to those who read the manuscript and offered many helpful comments, including Marian Galanis, Bianca Martino, Sophia Putnam, Philip Isbouts, and Nick Isbouts.

I would also like to thank my agent, Peter Miller, and his staff at Global Lion Management. And finally, I must express my deepest gratitude to my family for their patience and understanding, and particularly to my wife, Cathie, my muse and indefatigable companion during our many journeys through the Middle East. —*Jean-Pierre Isbouts*

ILLUSTRATIONS CREDITS

All photographs by Pantheon Studios, Inc. unless otherwise noted:

1, Olga A/Shutterstock; 4, Roman Sigaev/Shutterstock; 12, ONEN ZVULUN/Reuters/Corbis; 22, Vanni/Art Resource, NY; 28, Cleopatra, c.1887 (oil on canvas), Waterhouse, John William (1849-1917)/Private Collection/Photo © Christie's Images/The Bridgeman Art Library; 30, Christian Heeb; 33, Michael Major/Shutterstock; 35 (LO), Ms 774 (4)/1632 f.1v Historiated letter "H" depicting the author writing, from "Antiquitates Judaicae" (vellum) (detail of 94972), Netherlandish School, (12th century)/Musée Condé, Chantilly, France/Giraudon/The Bridgeman Art Library; 40-1, Michael Melford/National Geographic Stock; 44, Michael Melford/National Geographic Stock; 46, Aureu (reverse) minted by Marcus Antonius with the head of Octavian (63 B.C.–A.D. 14) (gold) Inscription: CAESAR IMP PONT III VIR R P C (for obverse see 119139), Roman, (first century B.C.)/Museo Archeologico Nazionale, Naples, Italy/The Bridgeman Art Library; 47, Duby Tal/Albatross/Alamy; 48, Jodi Cobb/National Geographic Stock; 49 (LO), Hiram Henriquez/National Geographic Stock; 50, Hanan Isachar/AWL Images/Getty Images; 51, Robert J. Teringo/National Geographic Stock; 54, Scala/Art Resource, NY; 55, Richard Nowitz/National Geographic Stock; 56, Erich Lessing/Art Resource, NY; 57, Pantheon/Deror Avi; 58, Jane Sweeney/Alamy; 59, Ms 139/1363 fol.23r The Parable of the Vineyard and the Tenants and Joshua and Caleb Carrying Grapes from the Promised Land, from "Le Miroir de l'Humaine Salvation" (vellum), Flemish School, (15th century)/Musée Condé, Chantilly, France/Giraudon/The Bridgeman Art Library; 61, Mariamne, 1887 (oil on canvas), Waterhouse, John William (1849–1917)/Private Collection/Photo © Christie's Images/The Bridgeman Art Library; 65, Erich Lessing/Art Resource, NY; 68, Photograph by Dr. Adam Bülow-Jacobsen/The Association Internationale de Papyrologues/The Cairo Museum/The Oxford Centre for the Study of Ancient Documents/The Photographic Archive of Papyri in the Cairo Museum, funded by the Andrew W. Mellon Foundation; 73, Luis Marden/National Geographic Stock; 77, Leen Ritmeyer/Ritmeyer Archaeological Design; 85, Boris Katsman/iStockphoto; 86, Isaac and Rebekah, Wedgwood, ca 1865 (porcelain), Beattie, William (fl.1865)/Indianapolis Museum of Art, USA/Bequest of Ann McClelland Ropkey/The Bridgeman Art Library; 87, JTB Photo Communications, Inc./Alamy; 88, Marriage contract (ketubah), 1617 (pen & ink, tempera, and gold paint on parchment), Dutch School, (17th century)/The Israel Museum, Jerusalem, Israel/The Stieglitz Collection and donated with contribution from Erica & Ludwig Jesselson/The Bridgeman Art Library; 89, Zev Radovan/www.BibleLandPictures.com/Alamy; 90, Noam Armonn/Shutterstock; 91, Holy Family with St. Anne and the infant St. John the Baptist, ca1550 (oil on panel) (detail of 82824), Bronzino, Agnolo (1503–72)/Louvre, Paris, France/Peter Willi/The Bridgeman Art Library; 92, CRIS BOURONCLE/AFP/Getty Images; 93, The Virgin Spring in Nazareth, 1882 (oil on canvas), Polenov, Vasilij Dmitrievich (1844–1927)/Tretyakov Gallery, Moscow, Russia/The Bridgeman Art Library; 94, Albatross/SuperStock; 96 (UP), Pair of sandals from Masada, Israel (leather), Jewish School, (first century A.D.)/Private Collection/Photo © Zev Radovan/The Bridgeman Art Library; 96 (LO), Erich Lessing/Art Resource, NY; 98, Alinari/Art Resource, NY; 101, The Annunciation (oil on panel), Weyden, Rogier van der (1399–1464)/Louvre, Paris, France/Giraudon/The Bridgeman Art Library; 102-3, Erich Lessing/Art Resource, NY; 106, The enrollment for taxation before Quirinius (mosaic), Byzantine/Kariye Camii, Istanbul, Turkey/De Agostini Picture Library/A. Dagli Orti/The Bridgeman Art Library; 106-7, Tim Kimberley/iStockphoto; 108, Scala/Art Resource, NY; 109, Cameraphoto Arte, Venice/Art Resource, NY; 110, Adoration of the Magi, ca 1305 (for detail see 67136), Giotto di Bondone (ca 1266–1337)/Scrovegni (Arena) Chapel, Padua, Italy/The Bridgeman Art Library; 111, Jerry Lodriguss/Photo Researchers/Getty Images; 112, Scala/Art Resource, NY; 114, Remi Benali/Corbis; 115, Mary breast-feeding, from the Sigmund Chapel in Mariazell, ca 1380 (painted linden wood), Austrian School, (14th century)/Germanisches Nationalmuseum, Nuremberg (Nürnberg), Germany/The Bridgeman Art Library; 116, Hanan Isachar; 117, Israelimages/Dinu Mendrea; 128, St. John the Baptist in the wilderness indicating Christ, the River Jordan beyond, 1759 (oil on panel), Favray, Antoine de (1706–91)/Private Collection/Photo © Christie's Images/The Bridgeman Art Library; 129, Kenneth Garrett/National Geographic Stock; 133, CamPot/Shutterstock; 134 (LE), Ink pot found in Qumran (terracotta), Roman/Private Collection/Photo © Zev Radovan/The Bridgeman Art Library; 134 (RT), Erich Lessing/Art Resource, NY; 137, Community Rule scroll, Qumran cave 1, ca 100 B.C.–A.D. 100 (parchment)/The Israel Museum, Jerusalem, Israel/The Bridgeman Art Library; 139, The Baptism of Christ, ca1515 (oil on panel), Patinir, Joachim (1480–1524)/Kunsthistorisches Museum, Vienna, Austria/Giraudon/The Bridgeman Art Library; 140, Herod's Birthday Feast, 1868 (oil on canvas), Armitage, Edward (1817–96)/© Guildhall Art Gallery, City of London/The Bridgeman Art Library; 142, George Steinmetz/Corbis; 143, Salome Receiving the Head of St. John the Baptist, 1637 (oil on canvas), Guercino (Giovanni Francesco Barbieri) (1591–1666)/Musée des beaux-arts, Rennes, France/Giraudon/The Bridgeman Art Library; 145, Rudolf Tepfenhart/Shutterstock; 151, St. Andrew and St. Peter Responding to the Call of Jesus, from the main nave (mosaic), Byzantine School, (sixth century)/Sant'Apollinare Nuovo, Ravenna, Italy/Giraudon/The Bridgeman Art Library; 156, Erich Lessing/Art Resource, NY; 159, The Palsied Man Let Down Through the Roof, illustration for "The Life of Christ," ca 1886–94 (gouache on paper), Tissot, James Jacques Joseph (1836–1902)/Brooklyn Museum of Art, New York, USA/The Bridgeman Art Library; 160, Jesus driving out the unclean spirit, relief, tenth century/Hessisches Landesmuseum, Darmstadt, Germany/The Bridgeman Art Library; 160-1, Hanan Isachar; 162, Sermon on the Mount, Scenes from the Life of Christ (mosaic), Byzantine School, (sixth century)/Sant'Apollinare Nuovo, Ravenna, Italy/Giraudon/The Bridgeman Art Library; 164, Ella Hanochi/Shutterstock; 167, Erich Lessing/Art Resource, NY; 168-9, Hanan Isachar; 171, Eddie Gerald/Alamy; 172, Jesus Opens the Eyes of a Man Born Blind, 1311 (tempera on panel) (detail of 188963), Duccio di Buoninsegna, (ca 1278–1318)/National Gallery, London, UK/The Bridgeman Art Library; 175, The Raising of Jairus's Daughter, 1885 (oil on canvas), Jacomb-Hood, George Percy (1857–1930)/© Guildhall Art Gallery, City of London/The Bridgeman Art Library; 177, Mary Magdalene in the Cave, 1876 (oil on canvas), Lefebvre, Jules Joseph (1836–1912)/Hermitage, St. Petersburg, Russia/The Bridgeman Art Library; 179, Hanan Isachar; 181, Erich Lessing/Art Resource, NY; 184, Zev Radovan; 186, Gianni Dagli Orti/The Art Archive at Art Resource, NY; 187, Ilan Arad/Getty Images; 189, The Transfiguration, ca 1519–20 (oil on panel) (b/w photo), Raphael (Raffaello Sanzio of Urbino) (1483–1520)/Vatican Museums and Galleries, Vatican City, Italy/De Agostini Picture Library/The Bridgeman Art Library; 190-1, Ali Kabas/Picade; 193, Esaias BAITEL/Gamma-Rapho via Getty Images; 197, Alfredo Dagli Orti/The Art Archive at Art Resource, NY; 200, The Man with the Withered Hand, illustration from "The Life of Our Lord Jesus Christ" (w/c over graphite on paper), Tissot, James Jacques Joseph (1836–1902)/Brooklyn Museum of Art, New York, USA/The Bridgeman Art Library; 203 (UP), Tetra Images/Corbis; 203 (LO), LeonP/Shutterstock; 204, St. Mark, Palma Il Giovane (Jacopo Negretti) (1548–1628)/Hatton Gallery, University of Newcastle Upon Tyne, UK/The Bridgeman Art Library; 207, Nowitz Photography/CIR, Inc.; 212, Jodi Cobb/National Geographic Stock; 213, Jeremiah mourning over the Destruction of Jerusalem, 1630 (oil on canvas), Rembrandt Harmensz. van Rijn (1606–69)/Rijksmuseum, Amsterdam, The Netherlands/The Bridgeman Art Library; 216, Erich Lessing/Art Resource, NY; 217, MENAHEM KAHANA/AFP/Getty Images; 220, Michael Melford/National Geographic Stock; 221, Christ in the House of Martha and Mary, ca 1654–56 (oil on canvas), Vermeer, Jan (1632–75)/© National Gallery of Scotland, Edinburgh, Scotland/The Bridgeman Art Library; 222, The Raising of Lazarus, 1631 (oil on canvas), Lievens, Jan the Elder (1607-74)/Royal Pavilion, Libraries & Museums, Brighton & Hove/The Bridgeman Art Library; 223, Erich Lessing/Art Resource, NY; 224, Erich Lessing/Art Resource, NY; 225, Balage Balogh/Archaeology Illustrated; 227, Erich Lessing/Art Resource, NY; 232, Art Resource, NY; 233, diligent/Shutterstock; 234, Pantheon/Classical Numismatic Group, Inc.; 235, Christ Driving the Traders from the Temple, ca 1600 (oil on canvas) (for detail see 26048), Greco, El (Domenico Theotocopuli) (1541–1614)/National Gallery, London, UK/The Bridgeman Art Library; 237, Richard T. Nowitz/Corbis; 241, Mordechai Meiri/Shutterstock; 242, Amos Gal/PhotoStock-Israel.com; 243, Kenneth Garrett/National Geographic Stock; 245, Kenneth Garrett/National Geographic Stock; 250, Leen Ritmeyer/Ritmeyer Archaeological Design; 251, Hanan Isachar/Corbis; 252, Ossuary of the High Priest Joseph Caiaphas, North Talpiot, Jerusalem (stone)/The Israel Museum, Jerusalem, Israel/Israel Antiquities Authority/The Bridgeman Art Library; 253, Annas and Caiaphas, illustration for "The Life of Christ," ca 1886–94 (w/c & gouache on paperboard), Tissot, James Jacques Joseph (1836–1902)/Brooklyn Museum of Art, New York, USA/The Bridgeman Art Library; 256, 19th era/Alamy; 259, Radius Images/Corbis; 261, Hans Hildenbrand/National Geographic Stock; 263, Richard T. Nowitz/Corbis; 265, www.BibleLandPictures.com/Alamy; 267, Christ on the Cross (oil on canvas), Greco, El (Domenico Theotocopuli) (1541–1614)/Private Collection/Photo © Christie's Images/The Bridgeman Art Library; 274, Noli me Tangere, ca 1512 (oil on canvas), Titian (Tiziano Vecellio) (ca 1488–1576)/National Gallery, London, UK/The Bridgeman Art Library; 277, Leen Ritmeyer/Ritmeyer Archaeological Design; 278, WitR/Shutterstock; 283, Scala/Art Resource, NY; 287, St. Peter and St. Paul (tempera on panel), Bicci di Lorenzo, (1375-1452)/Galleria dell' Accademia, Florence, Italy/The Bridgeman Art Library; 288, Tatiana Popova/Shutterstock; 292, Bernard Jaubert/Photodisc/Getty Images; 294, Bridgeman-Giraudon/Art Resource, NY; 297, Scala/Art Resource, NY; 298-9, Richard Nowitz/National Geographic Stock; 301, Robert Harding Picture Library Ltd/Alamy; 302, Vanni/Art Resource, NY; 303, The Destruction of Jerusalem in A.D. 70, engraved by Louis Haghe (1806-85) (litho), Roberts, David (1796–1864) (after)/Private Collection/The Stapleton Collection/The Bridgeman Art Library; 309, Sarcophagus depicting Christ and the Apostles, Roman (marble)/Louvre, Paris, France/Peter Willi/The Bridgeman Art Library; 312, The Christian Martyr's Last Prayer, 1863–83 (oil on canvas), Gerome, Jean Leon (1824–1904)/© Walters Art Museum, Baltimore, USA/The Bridgeman Art Library; 313, SEF/Art Resource, NY; 318, bpk, Berlin/Art Resource, NY; 321, Independent Picture Service/Alamy; 326, Solidus (obverse) of Julian the Apostate (361-363) draped, cuirassed, wearing a diadem. Inscription: FL CL IVLIANVS P P AVG (gold), Roman, (fourth century A.D.)/Private Collection/The Bridgeman Art Library; 328, lexan/Shutterstock; 329, Matt Moyer/National Geographic Stock; 330, John Bigelow; 335, Michael Melford/National Geographic Stock; 341, Claudio Zaccherini/Shutterstock; 342, Emperor Justinian I and his retinue of officials, guards and clergy, ca A.D. 547 (mosaic), Byzantine School, (sixth century)/San Vitale, Ravenna, Italy/Giraudon/The Bridgeman Art Library; 344, Artur Bogacki/Shutterstock; 347, Richard Nowitz/National Geographic Stock; 353, Church of the Holy Sepulchre, Jerusalem, plate 11 from Volume I of The Holy Land, engraved by Louis Haghe (1806-85) pub. 1842 (litho), Roberts, David (1796–1864) (after)/Private Collection/The Stapleton Collection/The Bridgeman Art Library.

INDEX

Boldface indicates illustrations.

A

Abgar IX (Edessa ruler) 309
Abraham 96, 238, 330
Abravanel, Isaac 108
Absalom, tomb of 26, **27**
Abu Bakr 346
Acts of the Apostles, Book of
    Christians in Antioch 284
    conversion of Gentiles 284–285
    early Christian growth and expansion 276
    Last Supper 238
    Paul's escape from Damascus 283
    resurrection 275
    Sabbath observances 157
Aelia Capitolina 260, 262, **304**, 308
Aelia Eudocia, Empress 338
Aetheria *see* Egeria (pilgrim)
Agriculture **58**
    crop yield 118
    Galilee 44, **45**, 56, 66, 67, 68, 118, **174**
    Lower Galilee **67**
    Palestine 39
    tenant farmers 67
    women's roles 69
Agrippa, King *see* Herod Agrippa, King
Agrippa II, Marcus Julius 295, 296, 300
Alexander the Great 20, **22**, 36, 66, 68
Alexandria, Egypt 38
"Altar of Augustan Peace" (*Ara Pacis Augustae*) 32, **32**
Ambrose, Bishop of Milan 327
Ananias (disciple) 283
Ananus (high priest) 256, 296, 300
Andrew (Apostle) 148, **151**, 153, 154
Annas 253
Annunciation 87, **98**, 98–100
Anthony, Mark *see* Antony, Mark
Antigonus (Hasmonean usurper-king) 46, 47
Antioch 33, 284
Antiochus III (Seleucid king) 22, 58, 188
Antiochus IV (Seleucid king) 22, 38
Antiochus XIII Asiaticus, King (Syria) 26
Antipas (ruler of Galilee and Perea)
    arrest of John the Baptist 150
    collusion with Pharisees 200, 202
    construction of Tiberias 120
    deposition 294
    father-in-law 77–78
    and John the Baptist 138–140, 142, 143–144
    machinations for crown 76, 77
    rebuilding of Sepphoris 78, 121–122
    relationship with Tiberius 120
    rule of Galilee and Perea 71, 132
Antipater (governor of Idumea) 26, 42, 43–44, 46
Antonia Fortress 236, 239, 251, 260, 262, **263**, 338
Antoninus (pilgrim) 345–346
Antoninus, Arrius (Roman governor of Asia) 312
Antoninus Pius, Emperor (Roman Empire) 308
Antony, Mark 31, 43, 46, 56
Aphrodite (goddess) 23, **23**
Apollo, Temple of 78, **79**
Apollo Barberini (statue) **76**, 77
Apostles
    ambition 213
    commissioning 166
    as delegates 170–171
    fishing 155
    Jerusalem Conference 287–288
    Jesus' appearance (post-resurrection) 272–273, 275
    on Jesus' purpose 206
    mission 275, 276–277, 279
    Mount of Olives vigil 242
    number of 153
    personal sacrifices 170–172
    purpose 153
    resurrection beliefs 275
    Sanhedrin hearing 202
Aqueducts **40–41**, 41
Ara Pacis Augustae ("Altar of Augustan Peace") 32, **32**
Aramaic language 134, 202, **203**
Arav, Rami 150
Arbel, Mount 165
Arch of Titus, Rome **21**, 301, 302, **302**, 303
Archelaus (ethnarch of Judea, Idumea, and Samaria) 71–72, 75–76, 78, 105, 112
Architecture 36–37
Arculf (pilgrim) 348, 350
Aretas IV Philopatris, King (Nabatea) 77–78, 143, 144, 282
Arianism 326
Aristobulus I, Hasmonean king 68
Aristocracy 9, 23
Arius (bishop of Alexandria) 326
Ark of the Covenant **156**
Arnal, William 118
Asia Minor
    Christian population 308
    wealth 276
Athens 7, **286**, 290
Athronges (shepherd) 77
Augustus, Emperor (Roman Empire) **31**
    architecture 36, 37
    censuses 104
    conferring Roman citizenship 34–35
    conflict with Mark Antony 31
    control of Judea 76, 78, 105–106
    Pax Romana 31–33
    regime 19
    religion 23
    Roman Civil War 43, 46
Aureus (coin) **46**, 47
Avigad, Nahman 248, 251, 303
Avshalom-Gorni, Dina 179
El-Azariya *see* Bethany

B

Babatha of Maoza 94
Babylonian Jewish community 340
Babylonian Talmud 199
Bagatti, Bellarmino 84, 93
Balaam (magician) 108
Baptism 138
Bar Kokhba Revolt 94, 307–308

Barabbas 255, 256
Barluzzi, Antonio 166, 188
Barnabas 283–284, 286, 288
Bartholomew (Apostle) 150, 153, 334
Bartimaeus (blind man) 221
Basilica of Constantine and Maxentius, Rome **21**
Basilica of the Annunciation, Nazareth *see* Church of the Annunciation, Nazareth
Basilinda game 262, **263**
Bassano, Francesco **216**
Beatitudes 163–164
    see also Sermon on the Mount
Beatitudes, Mount of 165–166
Beit Netofa Valley **85**
Belisarius (Byzantine general) 342, 343
Bethany 131–133, 221–222, 266, 334
Bethesda 231, **231**, 338
Bethlehem
    census **106**, 107
    as Jesus' birth place 111–112
    map 104
    pilgrimages 334
    role in Scripture 112–113
Bethlehem-in-Galilee 112–113
Bethsaida 149, 150, 172, **173**, 210
Bible lands, map 10–11
Binder, Donald 157
Bishops 316
Blind, healing of 172, **172**, 173, 221, 283
Bread 241, **241**
Brutus, Marcus 30–31, 43
Bucoleon Palace, Constantinople 342, **343**
Burial customs 264, **264**, 315, **315**
Burnt House **250**, 251
Byzantine churches **158**, 159
Byzantine Empire 338–339, 340, 342, 343, 346

C

Caesar, Julius
    aid from Antipater 42
    assassination 30–31, 43
    intervention in the Near East 23
    land grants to legionnaires 118
    reign 29–30
    Roman Civil War 29
Caesarea 50, **50**
    aqueduct **40–41**, 41
    Christian community 282
    monumental frieze **49**
    Roman theater **129**
    Sebastos harbor **43**, **50**, 51, **51**
Caesarea-Philippi 195, 202, **203**, 206, **207**
Caiaphas (high priest) 253
    arrest of Apostles 275
    arrest of Jesus 244
    indictment of Jesus 248–250
    ossuary 252, **252**, 253
    residence 248, **252**
    sacrificial animals 234
Caligula *see* Gaius (Caligula)
Canonical Gospels 305, 307
Capernaum **182**
    artifacts **156**

excavations 156, 158
exorcism 156, 161
Jesus' ministry 150, 153, 156, 158–159, 163, 210
location 153
Peter's house 158, **158**, 159–160
residential structures **152**, 153
synagogue 156, **157**, 158–159
tax collectors 196
Carthage 21, 309
Case, Shirley 122
Cassius, Gaius 30–31, 43–44, 46
Catacombs 315, **315**
Catholic Church *see* Roman Catholicism
Cave of Letters 94, **94**
Censuses 104–105, **106**, 107, 111, 121
Cephas *see* Peter (Apostle)
Ceramics *see* Pottery
Chancey, Mark 69, 122
Charlemagne 350
Chi Rho symbol **316**, 317, 319
Childbirth 112, **112**, 113–115
Children 213
Chilton, Bruce 112–113, 199, 233, 234
Chorazin **182**, 210
Christ *see* Jesus
Christianity
  Church organization 316
  expansion in Roman Empire 316
  Great Schism 351
  growth 298–321
  map of expansion 300, 310–311
  movements 290, 293–294
  as sole religion of Roman Empire 327
  as superstition 313
  theology 287
  tolerance of 320
  triumph 322–347
Christians 270–297
  blame for Roman decline 318
  conflicts with Jews 202
  fellowship 275
  impact of Jewish Rebellion on 301, 305
  internal tensions 276
  leadership vacuum 296
  persecution (third century) 314
  persecution by local communities 313
  persecution in Damascus 282
  persecution in Jerusalem 276, 296
  persecution in Palestine 255–256
  persecution in Rome 292, 296
  persecution under Diocletian 319
  persecution under Domitian 305, 307
  Temple worship 275, 276
Church of the Annunciation, Nazareth 84, 87, **87**, 93, 100
Church of the Beatitudes **146–147**
Church of the Holy Sepulcher, Jerusalem **239**, 262, 353
  Catholikon Dome 345, **345**
  Crusader-era restoration 351
  destruction 350
  location 260
  as location of Golgotha 239, 260, 262
  pilgrimages 325–326, 330, 334, 346

relics 337–338, 346
rotunda 351
Church of the Multiplication, Tabgha **164**, 165, **165**, 198, **199**
Church of the Nativity, Bethlehem 115, **116**
Cicero (Roman orator) 33, 129, 231
Circumcision 113–115, 287, 288
Class divisions 9, 59–60
Claudius, Emperor (Roman Empire) 293, **293**, 294–295
Clement I (Christian prelate) 296
Clement VI, Pope 263
Cleopatra, Queen (Egypt) **28**, 29, 31
Clothing 92, **116**
Coins 89, **89**, 232, 254, **255**, **327**
Colosseum, Rome 292, **292**
Constantine, Emperor (Roman Empire) 319
  basilica 320, **321**
  churches **331**
  conversion to Christianity 320
  Council of Nicea 326
  discrimination against Jews 338
  Edict of Milan 320
  establishment of holy sites in Palestine 331
  movement of capital to Constantinople 324
  religious tolerance 320
  victory over Maxentius **318**, 319
Constantinople 324
Constantius I Chlorus, Emperor (Roman Empire) 319, 331
Constantius II, Emperor (Roman Empire) 338–339
Convent of the Sisters of Zion **239**, 239
Coponius (prefect of Roman Judea) 106, 107, 118
Corbo, Virgilio 56, 142, 158
Corinth **288**, 290, 295
Cornelius (centurion) 284–285, 334
Council of Nicaea 316, 326
Crassus (Roman nobleman) 23, 29
Cross 260, 330, 331, 346
Crossan, John Dominic 151
Crucifixion 263, 265, **267**
  blame for 255
  calls for 255
  as deterrent 258
  site 239
  timing of 230, 259–260
  as violation of Jewish Law 258–259
Crusader map (Jerusalem pilgrimage sites) 349
Crusades 350–352
Cyrus II (the Great), King (Persia) 20, 66

D

"Daily bread" 116–117
Damascus 282–283
D'Andria, Francesco 334
Daniel, Book of 131
Dead Sea Scrolls **132**, 133, 135, 202, 302
Decapolis 173–174, 282
Decius, Emperor (Roman Empire) 314
Delos (island) 38, **39**
Denarius (coin) 89, **89**
Diatessaron (harmonizing Gospel) 293, 309

Diocletian, Emperor (Roman Empire) 304, **305**, 316–319, **317**
Disciples
  demands on 154–156
  departure for Galilee 149–150
  gathering of 150, 153–154
  learning of God's intentions for Jesus 206
  recognizing Jesus as Messiah 148
  renaming 148–149
Docetists 293
Dolls **95**
Dome of the Rock, Jerusalem **8**, 9, **298–299**, 347
Domitian, Emperor (Roman Empire) 305, 307
Dowry 86, 87

E

Eastern Orthodox Church 351
Ebionites 293
"Ecce Homo" arch 254, 260, **261**, 262
Edessa 309, 330
Edict of Milan 320
Education
  of boys 92–93, 95, 122
  of girls 89–90, 92
  of Jesus 122
Egeria (pilgrim) 159, 160, 166, 242, 327–328, 330
Egypt
  Christianity 309
  taxation 59
  trade 36
Ehrman, Bart 290
Elijah (prophet) 127, 155, 181, 184, 187
Elisha (prophet) 155, 181, **181**, 184
Elizabeth (Mary's relative) 99
Elkanah 99
Endogamy 86
Ephesus 280, **280**, **291**, 295
Eremos, Mount 165–166
Eschatology 128, 131
Essenes 128, 134–135, 137
Eternal life, pathway to 219–220
Eucharist 241
Eucherius, Bishop of Lyons 337
Euromos **18–19**, 19
Eusebius of Caesarea, Bishop 305, 307, 319, 331, 334, 335
Exorcisms 156, **160**, 161, 172–173, 184
Ezekiel, Book of 192

F

Fabian, Pope 314
Fadus, Cuspius (Roman procurator) 295, 296
Faith, importance in healing 175, 185, 187
Family life 94, 116, **116**, **117**, 118
Fasting 196
Feast of Unleavened Bread 241
"Feeding of the Five Thousand" miracle *see* Loaves and fishes miracle
Fidelis (monk) 350
Fish sauce 177, 184
Fish species 178, **178**

INDEX

Fishermen
  assisting Jesus 153
  boats **155, 184,** 185
  cooperatives 154–155
  fish hook **150**
  hauling in nets **153**
  Sea of Galilee 151
Fishes and loaves miracle *see* Loaves and fishes miracle
Flagrum (whip) 256, **256,** 259
Flavius Josephus *see* Josephus (Jewish historian)
Florus, Gessius (Roman procurator) 300
Frotmond (pilgrim) 350

G

Gabriel (archangel) 87, **98,** 98–100
Gadara 174
Gaius (Roman general) 78
Gaius (Caligula), Emperor (Roman Empire) 282, **282,** 283, 294–295
Gaius Octavian *see* Augustus, Emperor (Roman Empire)
Gal, Zvi 69
Galatians, Paul's letter to 283, 293
Galerius, Emperor (Roman Empire) 319
Galilean campaign 168–189
  maps 170, 182–183
Galilee
  agriculture 44, **45,** 56, 66, 67, **67,** 68, 118, **174**
  in Biblical times 65–66
  conflicts between Jews and Gentiles 68
  cultural transformation 66, 68
  estrangement from Judea 66, 68
  geography 64–65
  Hasmonean control 68
  Hellenistic influences 68, 69–70
  Jesus' scolding 210
  Jewish and Gentile influences 68–70
  map 74
  poverty 118
  religious diversity 66
  Seleucid control 22, 58, 68
  synagogues 157, **157**
  taxation 44–45, 56–60
  tenant farmers 67
  towns and cities 70
  see also Lower Galilee
Galilee, Sea of **62–63,** 97, **171,** 176
  anchorage 166, **167**
  fish species 178, **178**
  fishermen 151
  fishing vessel **155**
  Galilean Campaign 172
  northern shore **149**
  in Scripture 64
  shores near Tabgha **154**
  storms 160, **160–161**
  sunrise **168–169**
Galilee Boat **184,** 185
Gallienus, Emperor (Roman Empire) 314, 316
Gallio (proconsul) 290
Gallus, Cestius (Roman governor) 282, 300
Gamaliel (Pharisaic sage) 202, 233, 244, 279

Garden Tomb **273**
Gawhar al-Siqilli (Shia general) 350
Gemellus of Ancyra 326
Gennesaret 180
Gentiles
  conversions 284–285
  Jesus' healing of 192–193
  and Jewish Law 287
Gerasa **75,** 174
Gethsemane **228–229,** 239, **239,** 242
Gibson, Shimon 144, 264
Glassware 37, **37, 70,** 71
Gnostic Christians 293, 313, 316
Gnostic Gospels 178, 240, 243, **243**
Golgotha 239, 258, 259, **259,** 260, 263
Good Samaritan parable 214, **216,** 216–217, 219
Good Shepherd motif 308, **309**
Gospel of Mark *see* Mark, Gospel of
Gospels
  inspired by Scripture 108
  language of 13
  parallels with Scripture 13, 96, 99, 127, 143, 148, 155, 184–185
  setting 13
  symbolism in 13, 108, 148
  see also Canonical Gospels; John, Gospel of; Luke, Gospel of; Mark, Gospel of; Matthew, Gospel of
Greece
  pilgrimages 34
  religion 23, **23,** 38
  trade 36
Greek language 134
Greek Orthodox church **325,** 335–336
Gregory I, Pope 178

H

Hadrian, Emperor (Roman Empire) 36, 260, 307–308, 350
Hagar 96
Hagia Eirene, Constantinople **331**
Hagia Maria Sion Abbey, Jerusalem **249**
Hagia Sophia, Istanbul **322–323,** 343, 344, **344**
Al-Hakim (Fatimid caliph) 350–351
Halley's Comet 108–109, **110,** 111, **111**
Hamat Gader **130, 171,** 214, **215**
Hamat Tiberias 308
Hannah 99
Hanson, K. C. 177
Harun-al-Rashid, Caliph 350
Hasidim 22
Hasmonean Kingdom 26, 58, 68
Hazor, northern Galilee **97**
Healing miracles
  analysis 184, 185, 187
  blindness 172, **172,** 173, 221, 283
  commemorative basilica 338
  Gentiles 192–193
  Jairus's daughter 174–175, **175,** 177, 184
  leprosy 184
  paralytic man 231
  by Peter 275, 276, 282
  raising of Lazarus **222**

  role of faith in 175, 185, 187
  on the Sabbath 199, **200**
  servant of centurion 192
  slave's ear 244
  strength required for 175
  withered hand 199, **200**
Hebrew Scriptures *see* Scripture
Helena, Empress (Roman Empire) 331
  Church of the Annunciation 100
  establishment of Holy Land sites 324, 331
  Holy Land journey 132, 133
  Holy Sepulcher Church 325–326, 331
  Saint Catherine Monastery 328
  supervision of church-building 320, 331
Hellenists (early Christians) 276, 283, 284
Hellenization 37–38, 68, 69–70
Heraclius, Emperor (Byzantine Empire) 346
Herakleia *see* Euromos
Herculaneum **72,** 308
Heretics 294
Herod Agrippa, King of the Jews 294–295
Herod Antipas *see* Antipas (ruler of Galilee and Perea)
Herod Archelaus *see* Archelaus (ethnarch of Judea, Idumea, and Samaria)
Herod Philip I 143
Herod the Great, King (Judea) **47**
  appointment of high priest 52, 55, 72, 128
  assets 75–76
  assistance to Cassius and Brutus 31, 43–44
  assistance to Mark Antony 56
  background 42
  birthday feast **140**
  breakup of his kingdom 78
  building projects 37, **40–41,** 41, 70, 220
  control of Judea 46–47
  father 26, 42
  fortresses **48,** 48–49, **49**
  as governor of Galilee 42–45
  map of kingdom 42
  and Mariamne 46, 48, 60, **61**
  in Nativity story 104
  palace 251
  paranoia 60
  rebuilding the Temple 232
  reign 16, 60
  relationship with Rome 105
  Roman Civil War 43–45, 46
  Second Temple expansion 55–56
  source of wealth 56–59
  successor 70–71, 112
  Suspended Palace 44
  taxation 44–45, 56–57, 58–59
  tomb 56, 57, **57**
  urban projects 49–52
Herodias (Philip's wife) 143–144
Herodion (fortress) **48,** 48–49, **49,** 56, 57, **57,** 301
Herod's Palace, Jericho **220**
Hezekiah 45
High priesthood 9, 55, 72, 128
Hillel (Jewish sage) 219–220
Holy Sepulcher Church *see* Church of the Holy Sepulcher
Horsley, Richard 58–59

House of the Vestals, Rome **21**
Hum, Tell 156
  see also Capernaum
Hyrcanus II 26, 29, 42, 45, 46

I

Ignatius, Bishop of Antioch 308, 312, 313
India, Christianity in 309, 312
Ionian Coast, Turkey **270–271**
Irenaeus, Bishop of Lyons 335
Isaac 86, **86,** 96, 238
Ishmael 96
Islamic Empire 346, 348–353

J

Jacob's Well, Nablus 335, **335**
Jaffa *see* Joppa (Jaffa)
Jairus's daughter 174–175, **175,** 177, 184
James (brother of Jesus) 253, 256, 275, 288, 296
James, son of Alphaeus (Apostle) 153
James, son of Zebedee (Apostle)
  accompanying Jesus to Jairus's house 175, 177
  commitment 155
  execution 256, 295
  mother 213
  prominence 153–154
  selection by Jesus 153
  at Transfiguration 187
Jerash, Jordan *see* Gerasa
Jeremiah (prophet) 164, 210–211, **213,** 234
Jericho 51, **106–107, 212, 220,** 220–221
Jerome (Church scholar) 334–335
Jerusalem **225, 249, 350**
  apostolic mission 275
  archaeology **12**
  under Archelaus 71–72
  attacks on church 296
  ban on Jews 308, 324
  Christian church 288
  as Christian city 324
  Christian pilgrimages 324–325
  conquest by Pompey 26
  Crusader rule 351
  destruction 260, 308, 346
  fall 303, **303**
  Herod's building projects 52
  Jesus' entry in 225–226, **226**
  Jesus' road to 208–227
  map of pilgrimage sites 349
  massacres 75, 76, 141
  Ottoman control 352, **353**
  Paul in 296
  persecution of Christians 296
  rebellion 76–78
  Temple looting 22
  walls **211, 246–247**
Jerusalem Conference 287–288
Jesus
  agricultural knowledge 118
  alienation from family 202–204
  anger and frustration 210
  Apostle selection 153, 166
  Aramaic language 134

  arrest 236–237, **240,** 244
  audience reaction 161, 162
  baptism **124–125,** 126, **139,** 140–141, 143
  birth as fulfillment of Scripture 96, 112
  birth date 104, 107, 111
  birth place 111–113, 334
  burial 265–266
  in Capernaum 150, 153, 156, 158–159
  as carpenter 118, 122
  childhood in Nazareth **115,** 115–117
  circumcision 113–115
  "daily bread" prayer 117
  debates with Pharisees and scribes 9
  departure for Galilee 149–150
  disciples 148–149, 150, 153–154
  education 122
  eviction of money changers from Temple 233–234, **235,** 236–237
  exhortations to followers 92
  exorcisms 156, **160,** 161, 172–173
  fasting 148
  and fishermen 151, **151,** 153
  on frugality of women 87
  genealogy 84–85
  healing as part of ministry 163
  indictment by Caiaphas 248–250
  inspiration from Jeremiah 210–211
  as itinerant preacher 153
  in Jericho 220–221
  in Jerusalem 186, 211, 225–226, **226**
  and John the Baptist 126
  and Judaism 164–165
  in Judea 210–211, 213
  knowledge of Scripture 202
  and Levi (tax collector) 196, **197**
  map of early ministry 148
  with Martha and Mary **221**
  as Messiah 148, 188, 206, 250, 277
  ministry focus on Jewish communities 70
  Mount of Olives vigil 242, 244
  name 98–99, 114
  Nativity story 104–107, 111
  observance of Jewish Law 196
  opposition to his ministry 195–196
  on Palestine's puppet regimes 9
  and the Pharisees 196, 198–200
  post-resurrection appearance 272–273, **274,** 275
  power over Satan 173
  prayer 153, 214
  preaching 160–162, 211
  premonition of his Passion 212
  presentation in the Temple (as baby) **102–103,** 115
  prophesy 301
  raising the dead 174–175, **175,** 177, 184
  reading Isaiah scroll 160–161
  relationship to God 326
  return to Nazareth 160–163
  road to Jerusalem 208–227
  road to Judea 213–214
  role intended by God 206
  Sabbath observance 198–199
  scourging **254,** 256, **257,** 258–260, 338
  second coming 316

  secrecy 195, 206
  Sermon on the Mount 118, 147, **162,** 163–165
  as shepherd **309**
  siblings 116
  as Son of Man 205, **205,** 206, 212, 213, 216
  synagogue attendance 93
  and tax collectors 204, 206
  tomb 346
  trial 248–252, **254,** 254–256
  in Tyre 192–195
  women in his entourage 90
  see also Galilean campaign; Last Supper; Miracles; Parables; Resurrection; Transfiguration
Jewish Law
  for Gentile converts 287
  Jesus' observance of 196
  storage of liquids 69
Jewish Revolt (66 C.E.) 238, 248, 258, 300–302
Jewish War (66–70 C.E.) 179, 300
Jews
  antipathy toward Samaritans 214
  under Augustus 23
  barred from Jerusalem 308, 324
  burial customs 264, **264**
  conflicts with early Christian Jews 202
  family life 94
  independence 22, 29
  Maccabean revolt 22
  oppression in Palestine 338–340
  persecution of 256, 305, 307
  provocation by Pilate 141
  response to Hellenization 37–38
  Sabbath observance 26
  see also Judaism
John (Apostle)
  accompanying Jesus to Jairus's house 175, 177
  arrest 244, 275
  commitment 155
  death 296
  Jesus' arrest **240**
  mother 213
  prominence 153–154
  at Transfiguration 187
John, Gospel of
  chronology 186
  Jews as Christ killers 256
  as non-Synoptic Gospel 9, 148
John Hyrcanus, King (Hasmonean Empire) 42
John I Tzimiskes, Emperor (Byzantine Empire) 350
John Mark (disciple) 238, 286, 288
John of Patmos 307
John the Baptist
  arrest 143–144, 149, 150
  baptism of Jesus 126, 141
  baptism symbolism 138, 141, 143
  base of operations 131–133
  on corrupt soldiers and officials 139–140
  execution 142, **143,** 144
  followers 149–150
  and Herod Antipas 138–140
  Jordan River region 126–128
  parallels with Elijah 127
  parents 99

INDEX

preaching about coming of Messiah 131
as prophet 143
and Qumran 137–138
tomb 144
in the wilderness **128**
John the Evangelist, Saint **186**
Joppa (Jaffa) 282
Jordan Rift Valley **127**
Jordan River **73, 124–125**
    maps 126
    source streams 144, **145**
    tributaries **4,** 126
Joseph (husband of Mary)
    acceptance of Jesus as his own 114
    betrothal or marriage **82–83**
    children 116
    education 92–93, 95
    genealogy 84–85
    Jesus' circumcision 113–114
    journey to Bethlehem 111–112
    marriage contract 85–87, 89
    on Mary's premarital pregnancy 100
    omission from Gospels 161
    place of residence 111, 112
    poverty 115
    sexual relations with Mary 115
    work experience 122
Joseph of Arimathea 238, 266
Joseph of Tiberias 100
Josephus (Jewish historian) 35, **35**
    on Ananus's attacks on Jerusalem church 296
    on Antipas and Tiberius 120
    on Aretas's destruction of Galilee towns 78
    on bandits 47
    on Caesarea 50
    on Cassius's cash needs 43
    on destruction of Jerusalem 303
    on Essenes 128, 134–135, 137
    on exorcism 156
    on Galilee 64, 70
    on Halley's Comet 109
    on Hasmoneans in Galilee 68
    on Herodion 49, 56
    on Herod's espionage 60
    on Herod's taxation 45
    on Herod's tomb 56
    on hippodrome 52
    on Jerusalem rebellion 76
    on Jesus 226
    on Jewish War 179, 282, 300
    on John the Baptist 138, 140
    on John the Baptist's execution 142, 143, 144
    on Judas the Galilean 118, 121
    on Palestine's economy 56
    on Pilate 256
    on Pompey's conquest of Jerusalem 26
    on synagogues 157
    on Zealots 238
Judah
    capture by Seleucids 22
    control of 20–21
    religious autonomy 66
Judah ben El'ai (Rabbi) 199
Judaism
    and Jesus 164–165

outlaw under Visigoths 337
under Roman Empire 295, 326–327
see also Jewish Law; Jews; Rabbinic Judaism
Judas (Hezekiah's son) 76
Judas, Gospel of 240
Judas Iscariot (Apostle) 153, 238, 240–242, 244
Judas the Galilean 118, 121
Judea
    under Antipas 71
    apostolic mission 275
    assets 75–76
    census 104–105, 107
    estrangement from Galilee 66, 68
    independence 68
    internal conflict 26
    Jesus in 210–211
    Jesus' road to 213–214
    Parthian invasion 46–48
    Roman control 38, 105–106, 296
    Roman Legion 33
Julian, Emperor (Roman Empire) 326–327, **327**
Justin Martyr 313
Justinian I (the Great), Emperor (Byzantium) 340, **340, 342,** 342–343, 345–346
    building projects 115, 342, 344, **344**

K

Kazrin, North Golan **117**
Kepler, Johannes 108
Ketuvim (Writings) 12–13
Al Khazneh (tomb), Petra **306**
Khirbet Qumran *see* Qumran
Khosrow I Anohshirvan, King (Persia) 340, 343
Khosrow II, King (Persia) 346
Kiddush (Jewish blessing) 241
Kidron Valley **2–3,** 26, **27,** 226, **246–247,** 253
Kingdom of God 163, 164, 204, 214, 276
Kingdom of Heaven 163
I Kings, Book of 12
King's Highway (trade route) 30, **30**
Kinrot, Tel 180, **180**
Kokhba, Simon bar 307–308
Kraemer, Ross 94

L

Lactantius (author) 319
Lamia, Lucius Aelius (governor of Greater Syria) 141
Lamps **121**
Land ownership 8–9, 39, 59, 118
Languages
    abilities of Apostles 275
    Aramaic 134
    of early Christians 276
    of Gospels 13
Last Supper 233, **236–237,** 237–238, 241–242
Lazarus of Bethany 221–223, **222, 223,** 225
Lepers 184
Levenson, David 131
Levi, son of Alphaeus (Apostle) 155, 196, **197**
Levites 57, 217, 219
Leviticus, Book of 114–115, 288
Licinius, Emperor (Roman Empire) 320

Loaves and fishes miracle **164,** 165, 166, 181, 184
Loving one's neighbors 219–220
Lower Galilee 64, **67, 330**
    maps 64, 182–183
Luke
    on Paul's second missionary journey 289
Luke, Gospel of
    date written 305
    sources 305
    symbolism in 148
    as *Synoptic Gospel* 9
    use of Q (collection of sayings) 243
Lydia (convert) 289–290

M

Ma'ad al-Mustansir Billah (Caliph) 351
Maccabean Revolt 22, 38, 68
Maccabeus, Judas 68
Maccabeus, Simon 68
Machaerus (fortress) 49, 142, **142,** 301
Madaba Map 132
Magdala 177, 179, **179**
Magi 107–109, **109, 110,** 111
Magness, Jodi 262
Malthace (wife of Herod) 71
Maps
    Bible lands today 10–11
    Crusader map (Jerusalem pilgrimage sites) 349
    expansion of Christianity 300, 310–311
    Herod's Kingdom 42, 53
    Jesus' early ministry 148
    Jesus' early years 104
    Jesus' Galilean campaign 170, 182–183
    Jesus' travels beyond Galilee 192, 201
    Jordan River region 126
    key sites of the Passion 230, 239
    Lower Galilee 64, 74
    Nazareth 84
    Paul's journeys 272, 280–281
    pilgrim routes 324, 332–333
    road to Jerusalem 210, 218
    Roman Empire 20, 24–25
Marble 37
Marcionism 293
Marcus Aurelius, Emperor (Roman Empire) 313
Mariamne (Hasmonean princess) 46, 48, 60, **61**
Mariamne (Philip's sister) 334
Mark, Gospel of
    arrangement 170
    estrangement theme 162
    Jews as Christ killers 256
    narrative arc 202–204, 251
    symbolism in 13
    as *Synoptic Gospel* 9
    time written 305
Mark Antony *see* Antony, Mark
Mark the Evangelist **204**
Marriage
    age of men 95
    age of women 90
    contracts 85–87, **88,** 89
    divorce and remarriage 94
    wedding ceremonies 95

364

Martha of Bethany **221**, 221–223, 225
Martyrdom **312**, 312–314
Mary (mother of James the Younger) 265, 272, 275
Mary (mother of Jesus)
    Annunciation 87, **98**, 98–100
    betrothal or marriage **82–83**
    breast-feeding **115**
    children 115–116
    at crucifixion 265
    education 90
    journey to Bethlehem 111–112
    marriage contract 85–87, 89
    paternal house in Nazareth 84
    perpetual virginity 116
    poverty 115
    pregnancy 95–96, 98–100, 112–113
    presence in Gospels 161
    presentation of Jesus in Temple 115
    purification after Jesus' birth 113–115
    sexual relations with Joseph 115
    support for Jesus 203–204
Mary, Gospel of 178
Mary Magdalene
    background 177–178
    in cave **177**
    at crucifixion 265
    healing of 178–179
    in Jesus' entourage 90
    Jesus' resurrection 272, 273, **274**, 275
Mary of Bethany **221**, 221–223
Masada **44**, 48–49, 301
Matthew (Apostle) 153, 206, 238
Matthew, Gospel of
    date written 305
    parallels with Scripture 155
    sources 305
    symbolism in 108, 148
    use of Q (collection of sayings) 243
Matzah 241, **241**
Maxentius, Emperor (Roman Empire) **318**, 319, 320, **321**
Maximian, Emperor (Roman Empire) 319
Meier, John 184, 214
Messiah
    Chi Rho symbol **316**, 317, 319
    identity 131
    Jesus as 148, 188, 206, 250, 277
"Messianic Secret" 195
Meyers, Eric 69, 122
Micah (prophet) 112
Miletus **295**
Milvian Bridge, Battle of the 317, **318**, 319
Miracles 180–181, 184–185, 187
    calming wind 184–185
    exorcisms 156, **160**, 161, 172–173, 184
    illustrating power of Jesus' teachings 187
    multiplication of loaves and fishes **164**, 165, 166, 181, 184
    nature miracles 184
    parallels with Scripture 181, 184–185
    by Peter 275
    as proof of supernatural powers 184
    on the Sabbath 199, **200**
    Transfiguration 153–154, **182**, 188, **189**

water into wine 184
    see also Healing miracles
Miriam see Mary (mother of Jesus)
Mishnah 89, 198, 199, 308
Molten Sea vessel 12
Monastic movement 309
Money changers, eviction from Temple 233–234, **235**, 236–237
Moses, at Transfiguration 187
Mother Church 294
Mussolini, Benito 166
Mustard seed parable 204
Muzio, Giovanni 100

N

Nablus **217**, 335, **335**
Nag Hammadi codices 178, 243, **243**, 313
Nahum's Village see Capernaum
Nathanael 149–150
Nativity story 104–108, **113**
Nature miracles 184–185
Nazareth
    Jesus' return 160–163
    location 84
    village well **93**
Nero, Emperor (Roman Empire) 292, 296, 300, 307
Nerva, Emperor (Roman Empire) 307
Netzer, Ehud 56
Nevi'im (Prophets) 12–13, 38
New Testament 9, 12
    canon 335–336, 355
    language of 13
    works cited 9, 12
Nicodemus 272
Nimrud artifacts **66**

O

Oakman, Douglas 86, 118, 177
Octagonal churches **158**, 159, 166
Octavian see Augustus, Emperor (Roman Empire)
Oil and oil presses 37, **37**, 97, 118, **242**
Old Testament see Scripture
Olive trees 64, **90**, **105**, **119**, 244, **245**
Olives, Mount of **224**, 226, 242, 244
Olsson, Birger 157
Origen (theologian) 314
Ottoman Turks 352
Our Father (prayer) 214

P

Pagels, Elaine 178, 294
Palestine
    agriculture 39
    as Christian "Holy Land" 324
    Christianity as state religion 324
    definition 14
    Holy Land sites 331
    Jewish revolt (352 C.E.) 339
    oppression of Jews 338–340
    puppet regimes 9
Pantaenus of Alexandria 312

Paphos, Cyprus 280, **280**, 284, **285**
Parables
    Good Samaritan 214, **216**, 216–217, 219
    leavened dough 241
    mustard seed 204
    Pharisee and the Publican **54**
    rich-poor divide 59–60
    servants who were beaten 67
    sower 67
    three servants 44
    vineyard and orchard metaphors 69
    "Vineyard and Tenants" **59**
    wicked tenants 60
Parthians 46–48, 307
Passion 212, 230, 239, 258
Passover 212, 228–245, **233**
    see also Seder (Passover meal)
Paul (Apostle) **287**
    arrest 35, 251, 254, 296
    background 279
    and Barnabas 283–284
    conversion 282–283, **283**
    conversion of Gentiles 284
    in Ephesus 280
    execution 296
    Jerusalem Conference 287–288
    as leader 279
    letters 12, 283, **289**, 290, 293
    map of his journeys 272
    missionary journeys 285–290, **288**, 294, **295**, 295–296
    persecution of Christians 256, 279, 282
    resurrection beliefs 275
    road to Damascus 282–283
    Roman citizenship 35, 254
    Sabbath observances 157
    as Saul of Tarsus 276–277, 279
    shipwreck 280
    in Syracuse 280
    tensions with other Apostles 283
    theology 287
    travel to Antioch 284
    visit to Paphos, Cyprus 284
    visit to Perga 284
Paul VI, Pope 100, 178
Paula (pilgrim) 330, 334–335
Pax Romana 31–34
Peasant class 9, 39, 118, 151
Pella **301**
Pentecost 275
Perea (Transjordan) 49, 71, 132, 144
Perga 284, **284**
Persian Empire
    attack on Byzantine Empire 343, 346
    metalwork **108**
    see also Sassanid Persians
Persian Guard of the Immortals 14, **15**
Pesach see Passover
Peter (Apostle) **287**
    accent 134
    accompanying Jesus to Jairus's house 175, 177
    ambition 213
    apostolic mission 275, 282
    arrest 244, 275
    conversion of Gentiles 284–285, 288

INDEX

crucifixion 296, **297**
denying Jesus 242, 248
fishing 151, **151**
healing miracles 275, 276, 282
hearing in front of the Sanhedrin 202
house in Capernaum 158, **158,** 159–160
Jesus as Messiah 206
Jesus' promise to 153
mother-in-law 163
Paul's visit to 283
prominence 153–154
renaming 148
ties to Capernaum 150
at Transfiguration 187
Peter, Gospel of 258
II Peter, Epistle of 293
Petra **306,** 307
Pharisees
    administrative positions 9
    collusion with Antipas 200, 202
    on Council of the Sanhedrin 244
    differences from Sadducees 54, 128
    internal debates 199, 200–201
    and Jesus 9, 196, 198–200
    Paul as 279
    and Qumran community 134
    rabbinic Judaism 302
    ritual purity 198
    Sabbath observance 198
    as villains 199–200, 202
Phasael 42, 46
Philip (Apostle) 149, 153, 154, 334
Philip (deacon) 279, 282, 334
Philip (Tetrarch of the Gaulanitis) 71, 78, 143
Philip, Gospel of 178
Philippi, Paul's missionary journey to 289–290
Philo (Jewish historian) 135, 256, 314
Pilate, Pontius 129
    Greek language 134
    in history 256, 258
    Jesus' crucifixion 259
    Jesus' trial 239, 251–252, **254,** 254–256
    provocation of Jews 141
Pilgrimages
    after Islamic conquest 348–353
    Christian 324–328, 330
    Greco-Roman Empire 34
    Holy Land 337–338
    maps 324, 332–333
    modern times 352
    Passover 230, 233, 242, 244
    Shavuot (Pentecost) 275
Pinkerfeld, Jacob 242
Pliny the Younger 307, 308, 313
Plotinus (philosopher) 316
Pompeius Magnus (Pompey the Great) 23, 26, 29, 42
Popes 316
Porphyrius (philosopher) 318
Pottery **71, 131**
Poverty 118
Prayer 214
Presbyters 316
Priesthood 9, 52, 55, 57, 302
    see also High priesthood

Prophets *see* Nevi'im
Ptolemaic dynasty 21, 22, 68
Ptolemy II Philadelphus, King (Egypt) **29,** 38, **38**
Ptolemy III Euergetes, King **38**
Ptolemy V, King (Egypt) 22, 58
Ptolemy XIII, King (Egypt) 29

Q

Q (collection of sayings) 243
Quadratus of Athens 313
Quirinius, Gaius Publius Sulpicius **106,** 106–107, 111, 118
Qumran **135, 136**
    caves **132,** 133
    community 133–134
    community identity 134–135, 137
    Community Rule scroll 135, 137, **137**
    grave artifacts **131**
    ink pots 134, **134,** 135
    Jewish War 301–302
    and John the Baptist 137–138
    Sabbath observance 198

R

Rabbinic Judaism 202, 302, 304–305
Rebekah **86**
Reed, Jonathan 69
Relics 337–338
Resurrection 188, 272, 275
Revelation, Book of 12, 307
Rhyton (drinking cup) **108**
Ritual purity 198, **198,** 219
Road of Sorrows *see* Via Dolorosa
Roman Catholicism 317, 326, 336, 351
Roman Empire
    architecture 36–37
    censuses 104–105, 121
    Christianity as sole religion 327
    citizenship 34–36, 252, 254
    city planning 36–37, 50
    Civil War 29–31, 43–45, 46, 319
    coins **46,** 47, 48, 89, **89**
    cultural unification 34–37
    decline blamed on Christians 318
    division 336–337
    expansion under Augustus 20
    fall of Western Empire 336–337
    growth 22–23
    intervention in the Near East 23, 26, 29
    maps 20, 24–25
    Pax Romana 31–34
    religious pilgrimages 34
    reorganization under Diocletian 316–319
    roads 32, **33,** 33–34
    standing army 33
    succession 307
    trade 34, 35, **35,** 36, **36**
    Triumvirate 23, 29, **46,** 47
Roman Forum **21**
Roman gods 23, **23,** 38, 305, 314, 318, 320
Roman Legion 300, 301, **339**
Roman Republic 21, 22

Rome (city)
    Great Fire 292, **294,** 296
    origins 20
    persecution of Christians 292, 296
    Temple of Apollo 78, **79**
Runesson, Anders 157

S

Sabbath 26, 57, 157, 160, 198–199
Sabinus (Roman legate) 75–76, 76–77
Sadducees
    arrest of Apostles 275
    control of Temple cult 52, 128
    on Council of the Sanhedrin 244
    differences from Pharisees 54, 128
    and Qumran community 134
    as relic 302
    road to salvation 128
Safrai, Ze'ev 116, 118
Saint Catherine Monastery 328, **329**
Salome (daughter of Herod) 76, 78, 105
Salome (daughter of Herodias) 71, 144
Salome (resurrection witness) 272, 275
Salome (sister of Herod) 60, 71
Samaria
    administrative unit 58
    antipathy toward Jews 214
    early Christian successes 279, 282
    Good Samaritan parable 214, **216,** 216–217, 219
    history 214
    pilgrimages 334
    Roman Legion 33
    sacred mountain 216, **217**
Samuel (prophet) 99
San Vitale, Ravenna, Italy 340, **341,** 342
Sandals 92, **97**
Sanders, E. P. 59, 161
Sanhedrin 120, 244, 248–249, 255–256, 296, 308
Sarah 96
Sargon II (Assyrian king) 214
Sassanid Persians **313,** 316, 340, 342
Satan, Jesus' power over 173
Saul of Tarsus *see* Paul (Apostle)
Scribes 9, 156
Scripture 12–13, 354
    Bethlehem in 112–113
    date written 133
    inspiring Gospels 108
    Jesus' knowledge of 202
    language of 13
    parallel with Beatitudes 163
    parallel with Gospel 13, 99, 127, 143, 148, 155
    parallel with miracles 181, 184–185
    translations 202, 334–335
Second Jewish Revolt, refuge from 133
Second Temple 52, 55, **232**
    destruction 301, **302**
    expansion 55–56
    Jesus in 211
    model **55**
    rebuilding 232, 326–327
    sanctuary platform **77**
Second Temple Period tombs **273**

Seder (Passover meal) 233, **233**, 238
Sejanus, Lucius Aelius 129, 254
Seleucid Empire 21, 22, 23, 26, 58, 68
Seljuq Empire 351
Sepphoris **65,** 78, **105, 121,** 121–122, **123,** 339
Septimus Severus, Emperor (Roman Empire) 307, 314
Septuagint 38, 202
Sermon on the Mount 118, 147, **162, 163,** 163–166
　see also Beatitudes
Shahrbaraz (Persian general) 346
Shapur I, Emperor (Persian Empire) **313,** 316
Shared meals 238
Shavuot 275
Shekels 89, 232, 234, **234**
Shimon bar Yochai (rabbi) 120
Shroud of Turin 264, **264**
Sidon 194
Silas (disciple) 288
Simeon ben Gamaliel 308
Simeon ben Shetach 93
Simon (former slave) 77
Simon bar Kokhba 131
Simon Peter see Peter (Apostle)
Simon the Cananaean (Apostle) 153
Sinai, Mount 328, **328**
Sirach, Book of the Wisdom of 85–86
Slavery 8
Social classes 9, 59–60
Soldiers **138,** 139–140
Son of Man 205, 206, 212, 213, 216
Soranus (Greek physician) 112
Sphinx **29**
Spice trade 34, 35, **35**
Star of Bethlehem 108–109
Stations of the Cross 262
Stephen (Apostle) 256, 276, 279, 338
Stone vessels 69, 133, 194, **195**
Strabo (Roman geographer) 26, 220, 279
Suetonius (Roman historian) 31, 295
Susa 12, **13,** 14, **15**
Suspended Palace **44**
Swine, evil spirits in 172
Sylvester II, Pope 350–351
Symbolism
　baptism symbolism 138, 141, 143
　Chi Rho symbol **316,** 317, 319
　in Gospels 13, 108, 148
　in nature miracles 184–185
Synagogues 93, 156, 157, **157,** 158–159, 304–305
Synoptic Gospels 9, 148, 153
Syracuse 280, **280**
Syria, control of Judea 106

T

Tabor, Mount **182, 187,** 188, 345–346
Tacitus (Roman historian) 292, 296, 313
Talent (currency) 43–44
Talmud 199, 223
Targumim 202
Tarsus 35, 279
Tatian "the Assyrian" 293, 309
Tax collectors 8–9, 59, 60, 104, 196, **197**

Tax revolt 45, 118, 121
Taxation
　Galilee 44–45, 56–57, 58–59
　Islamic Empire 348
　Jesus on 204
　of Jews 338–339, 340
Temple
　apostolic mission 275
　Court of Gentiles 230, 234
　Court of the Priests 233
　Court of Women 230, 232
　entering 230–233
　eviction of money changers 233–234, **235,** 236–237
　expansion of Temple complex 55–56
　inscriptions **56,** 57
　looting to pay Roman indemnities 22
　Nicanor Gate 232, 275, **277**
　Passover 230–233
　Peter's healing miracles 275, 276
　presentation of Jesus (as baby) 115
　priests 9
　Roman burning of 76
　shekels 89, 232
　stockade 244
　taxes 56–57
　Treasury 52, 230–232
　voluntary gifts 231
　see also Second Temple
Temple Mount, Jerusalem **2–3**
　see also Dome of the Rock, Jerusalem
Temple of Jupiter, Damascus **278,** 279
Tertullian of Carthage (theologian) 296, 309, 312, 313, 335
Tetrarchy 304, **305**
Thaddaus (Apostle) 153
Theodosius (cleric) 338
Theodosius I, Emperor (Roman Empire) 327, **336,** 339
Theodosius II, Emperor 338, 339
Theophilus, Bishop of Alexandria 327
Thessalonica 290
Thomas (Apostle) 153, 273, 309
Thomas, Gospel of 243, **243**
Tiberias (ancient city) 120, **120,** 339
Tiberias (modern city) **97**
Tiberius, Emperor (Roman Empire) 120, 129, 254
Timothy (disciple) 289
Titus, Emperor (Roman Empire) 300–301, 303, 305
Tomb of Absalom, Kidron Valley 26, **27**
Torah (Law) 12–13, 202, **203**
Trajan, Emperor (Roman Empire) 36, **89,** 307
Transfiguration 153–154, **182, 188, 189,** 345–346
Triumphal Arch of Constantine, Rome 327, **327**
Trophimus (clergyman) 314
True Cross see Cross
Tyre **190–191,** 192–195
Tyrian shekels 234, **234**

U

'Umar ibn al-Khattab (Caliph) 346
Umayyad Mosque, Damascus **278,** 279
Upper Galilee 64

V

Valerian, Emperor (Roman Empire) **313,** 314, 316
Valerius Flaccus 231
Varus, Quinctilius 75, 76, 77
Vaux, Roland de 134, 135
Verres, Gaius 129
Vespasian, Emperor (Roman Empire) 23, 35, 36, 179, 300, 305
Via Dolorosa (Road of Sorrows) 260, 262–263
Virgin Mary see Mary (mother of Jesus)
Visigoths 337
Votive statuettes **141**

W

Wachsmann, Shelley 185
Waheeb, Mohammad 132–133
Water into wine miracle 184
Weaving 90, 92, **92**
Weddings 95
　see also Marriage
Weights **66**
Western Wall 55, **298–299**
Wine spoon **238**
Wise men see Magi
Women
　age at marriage 90
　education 89–90, 92
　frugality 87
　hauling water **93**
　in Jesus' entourage 90, 177–178
　roles 69, 94, 116–117, **193**
　see also Childbirth; Marriage
Wrede, William 195

Y

Yadin, Yigael 94
Yehuda HaNasi ("the Prince"), Rabbi 308
Yemen 340
Yohanan ben Zakkai 302, 304
Yusuf As'ar Yath'ar, King (Yemen) 340

Z

Zaccheus (tax collector) 221
Zaddok (Pharisee) 121
Zealots 121, 128, 142, 238, 300, 301
Zebedee 153, 155
Zechariah (priest) 99
Zenon (official) 68
Zenon Papyri 68, **68,** 69
Zeus temple, Euromos **18–19,** 19
Zodiac mosaic **308**

IN THE FOOTSTEPS OF JESUS

Jean-Pierre Isbouts

Published by the National Geographic Society

John M. Fahey, *Chairman of the Board and Chief Executive Officer*

Timothy T. Kelly, *President*

Declan Moore, *Executive Vice President; President, Publishing and Digital Media*

Melina Gerosa Bellows, *Executive Vice President; Chief Creative Officer, Books, Kids, and Family*

Prepared by the Book Division

Hector Sierra, *Senior Vice President and General Manager*

Anne Alexander, *Senior Vice President and Editorial Director*

Jonathan Halling, *Design Director, Books and Children's Publishing*

Marianne R. Koszorus, *Design Director, Books*

Lisa Thomas, *Senior Editor*

R. Gary Colbert, *Production Director*

Jennifer A. Thornton, *Director of Managing Editorial*

Susan S. Blair, *Director of Photography*

Meredith C. Wilcox, *Director, Administration and Rights Clearance*

Staff for This Book

Barbara Payne, *Editor*

Garrett Brown, *Text Editor*

Cinda Rose, *Art Director*

Rob Waymouth, *Illustrations Editor*

Sanaa Akkach, *Design Consultant*

Linda Makarov, *Contributing Designer*

Carl Mehler, *Director of Maps*

Matthew W. Chwastyk, *Cartographer*

Marshall Kiker, *Associate Managing Editor*

Judith Klein, *Production Editor*

Lisa A. Walker, *Production Manager*

Galen Young, *Rights Clearance Specialist*

Katie Olsen, *Production Design Assistant*

Manufacturing and Quality Management

Phillip L. Schlosser, *Senior Vice President*

Chris Brown, *Vice President, NG Book Manufacturing*

George Bounelis, *Vice President, Production Services*

Nicole Elliott, *Manager*

Rachel Faulise, *Manager*

Robert L. Barr, *Manager*

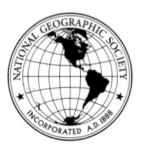

The National Geographic Society is one of the world's largest nonprofit scientific and educational organizations. Founded in 1888 to "increase and diffuse geographic knowledge," the Society works to inspire people to care about the planet. National Geographic reflects the world through its magazines, television programs, films, music and radio, books, DVDs, maps, exhibitions, live events, school publishing programs, interactive media and merchandise. *National Geographic* magazine, the Society's official journal, published in English and 33 local-language editions, is read by more than 60 million people each month. The National Geographic Channel reaches 435 million households in 37 languages in 173 countries. National Geographic Digital Media receives more than 19 million visitors a month. National Geographic has funded more than 10,000 scientific research, conservation and exploration projects and supports an education program promoting geography literacy. For more information, visit www.national geographic.com.

For more information, please call 1-800-NGS LINE (647-5463) or write to the following address:

National Geographic Society
1145 17th Street N.W.
Washington, D.C. 20036-4688 U.S.A.

For information about special discounts for bulk purchases, please contact National Geographic Books Special Sales: ngspecsales@ngs.org

For rights or permissions inquiries, please contact National Geographic Books Subsidiary Rights: ngbookrights@ngs.org

Copyright © 2012 National Geographic Society.
All rights reserved. Reproduction of the whole or any part of the contents without written permission from the publisher is prohibited.

ISBN: 978-1-4262-0987-1
ISBN: 978-1-4262-0993-2 (deluxe)

Printed in the United States of America

13/RRDW-LPH/2